URBAN LIFE IN THE DISTANT PAST

In this book, Michael E. Smith offers a comparative and interdisciplinary examination of ancient settlements and cities. Early cities varied considerably in their political and economic organization and dynamics. Smith introduces a coherent approach to urbanism that is transdisciplinary in scope, scientific in epistemology, and anchored in the urban literature of the social sciences. His new insight is "energized crowding," a concept that captures the consequences of social interactions within the built environment resulting from increases in population size and density within settlements. Smith explores the implications of features such as empires, states, markets, households, and neighborhoods for urban life and society through case studies from around the world. Direct influences on urban life – as mediated by energized crowding – are organized into institutional (top-down forces) and generative (bottom-up processes). Smith's volume analyzes their similarities and differences with contemporary cities and highlights the relevance of ancient cities for understanding urbanism and its challenges today.

Michael E. Smith is a Professor in the School of Human Evolution and Social Change at Arizona State University. An archaeologist who has directed excavations at Aztec sites, he has forged a new approach to the scientific and comparative analysis of early cities based on transdisciplinary research projects that link ancient and contemporary urbanism. He has published fifteen books and more than 150 articles.

URBAN ARCHAEOLOGICAL PASTS

The book series *Urban Archaeological Pasts* presents new studies and syntheses in the archaeology and ancient history of urban societies across the world. The past few decades have seen an explosion of urban excavations, in which new methods and approaches are greatly advancing the detail and scope of knowledge of the urban past. *Urban Archaeological Pasts* presents this exciting new research to the wider scholarly community. Each book is written by a leading specialist in a clear and concise format. The books include theoretical statements proposing new conceptual agendas, regional syntheses exploring new perspectives, and comparative accounts. The series is published in collaboration with the Centre for Urban Network Evolutions (UrbNet) at Aarhus University, and the initial books are based on the annual *UrbNet Lectures* presented by residential scholars, held since 2016.

Series Editors

Rubina Raja is Professor of Classical Archaeology at Aarhus University, Denmark, and Centre Director of the Danish National Research Foundation's Centre of Excellence for Urban Network Evolutions. She specializes in Mediterranean and Near Eastern Archaeology in a diachronic perspective, often with a focus on urban societies.

Søren M. Sindbæk is Professor of Medieval Archaeology at Aarhus University, Denmark, and Co-Director of the Centre of Urban Network Evolutions. He specializes in Viking and early medieval Europe, with a focus on urbanism and social networks.

Michael E. Smith is Professor of Archaeology at Arizona State University and Director of the ASU Teotihuacan Research Laboratory in Mexico. He specializes in Aztec provincial archaeology and comparative urbanism.

URBAN LIFE IN THE DISTANT PAST

THE PREHISTORY OF ENERGIZED CROWDING

MICHAEL E. SMITH

Arizona State University

CAMBRIDGE
UNIVERSITY PRESS

CAMBRIDGE
UNIVERSITY PRESS

Shaftesbury Road, Cambridge CB2 8EA, United Kingdom

One Liberty Plaza, 20th Floor, New York, NY 10006, USA

477 Williamstown Road, Port Melbourne, VIC 3207, Australia

314–321, 3rd Floor, Plot 3, Splendor Forum, Jasola District Centre, New Delhi – 110025, India

103 Penang Road, #05–06/07, Visioncrest Commercial, Singapore 238467

Cambridge University Press is part of Cambridge University Press & Assessment, a department of the University of Cambridge.

We share the University's mission to contribute to society through the pursuit of education, learning and research at the highest international levels of excellence.

www.cambridge.org
Information on this title: www.cambridge.org/9781009249003

DOI: 10.1017/9781009249027

First published 2023
First paperback edition 2024

A catalogue record for this publication is available from the British Library

ISBN   978-1-009-24904-1   Hardback
ISBN   978-1-009-24900-3   Paperback

The Urban Archaeological Pasts series is published in collaboration with the Centre for Urban Network Evolutions (UrbNet) at Aarhus University. This volume is based on the annual *UrbNet Lectures* by residential scholars, and is supported by the Danish National Research Foundation under the grant DNRF119.

I dedicate this book to the memory of George Cowgill, who got me started in ancient urbanism as an undergraduate at Brandeis University.

CONTENTS

FIGURES

TABLES

CASE STUDIES

PREFACE

This book is the culmination of a career of comparative research on early cities. My professional trajectory has taken me from excavations of Aztec cities, towns, and villages in Mexico, to comparative studies of early urbanism in Mesoamerica and around the world, including a series of transdisciplinary urban projects that have tried to link early cities with urbanism today. As my work has proceeded, I have become increasingly convinced of two things. First, early cities have much to teach us about cities, settlements, and societies today; and, second, archaeological information about early cities has yet to be systematized, compared, or analyzed adequately. Yes, there are countless excellent studies about cities and urban systems in many regions. But the most important questions have not been answered. What are the general patterns of city growth, layout, and operation, and how are they manifested in the many unique cases? What are the overall trends through time? Most important for this book, what was life like in the cities of the distant past? How were cities shaped by their overall society, and how did cities, in turn, influence broader social phenomena?

These questions were on my mind in 2017 when I received an invitation to spend several months writing a book at the Centre for Urban Network Evolutions at Aarhus University in Denmark ("UrbNet"). The present volume is my attempt to answer these and other questions about cities before the modern era. The book serves several needs. It synthesizes a large amount of information on early cities around the world. It promotes a view of cities and societies that emphasizes the importance of population and social context. My key concept is "energized crowding," which is the creative and generative process that results when people are concentrated together in cities. Energized crowding is important because it led to change and expansion in cities and settlements, and it helps explain many of the salient factors of cities, from social interactions and economic growth to crime and poverty.

This book is timely for several reasons. First, archaeologists now have much more data on early urbanism than ever before, resulting from both expanded fieldwork and new analytical techniques. Second, urbanism has become a dominant process in the world today, and the achievement of urban sustainability is a high priority for our species and the planet. Scholars and practitioners working on cities today need all the help they can get, and I believe that the record of early cities can contribute useful knowledge. This will only be possible, however, if archaeological (and historical) data are analyzed in an interdisciplinary fashion, following a scientific epistemology and taking advantage of a wide range of social scientific findings. Many of my archaeologist colleagues are content with particularistic local studies, interpreted from a nonscientific perspective. That is fine for some purposes, but if archaeology is going to take its place as a historical social science, we need analysis, synthesis, comparison, and quantification.

There are not many new archaeological finds reported in this book. Nevertheless, many well-known sites, buildings, and artifacts are given a new twist by putting them into an explicitly comparative framework. I include twenty-nine case studies, examples of sites chosen to illustrate particular points in the text. I take a broad view of urbanism, and archaeologists will find new material on ancient social, economic, political, and demographic patterns and how they relate to cities and settlements. I include longer discussions than one might expect in an urban book on topics like commercial economies, autocratic regimes, social inequality, collective action, and generative processes.

Scholars and students of urbanism who are not archaeologists will find data and descriptions of early cities that are intended to be accessible to social and natural scientists and humanities scholars. Readers who want to know about spectacular finds may be disappointed. I do mention the "Death pits" of Ur, the pyramids of Egypt and Mesoamerica, and the colossal architecture of capital cities from Persepolis to Teotihuacan. But, for me, such features are only interesting for the information they provide about ancient kings, urban planning, economic organization, and class structure.

This book began with my four-month stay in 2018 as a visiting researcher at UrbNet at Aarhus University in Aarhus, Denmark. I gave a series of lectures that formed the basis for the book, and I wrote three chapters during my stay. I wrote an additional chapter at UrbNet in 2019. UrbNet provided me with two able research assistants, Line Egelund and Nikoline Petersen, and a stimulating place to think and write. I thank the director and deputy director of UrbNet, Rubina Raja and Søren Sindbaek, for giving me the opportunity and support to get this book started. I also thank the community of faculty, postdocs, and students at UrbNet for good discussions and feedback as I presented my ideas. Hard questions from Johan S. Larsen and Felix Riede were especially appreciated. Christina Levisen, the UrbNet administrator, helped in many ways. My stay at UrbNet was supported by the Danish National Research Foundation under grant DNRF119 – Centre of Excellence for Urban Network Evolutions (UrbNet).

My experience working on transdisciplinary research projects has contributed to the development of the ideas in this book. As part of Late Lessons in

Early History, overseen by Sander van der Leeuw, a project on neighborhoods and open spaces developed into a grant-supported project on access to urban services. I thank the members of those projects – colleagues Christopher Boone, George Cowgill, Sharon Harlan, Barbara Stark, and Abigail York, and students and postdocs Wen-Ching Chuang, Timothy Dennehy, April Kamp Whittaker, Alexandra Norwood, Juliana Novic, and Benjamin Stanley – for expanding my understanding of urbanism and of transdisciplinary research (Chapter 7). The Social Reactors Project – Luís Bettencourt, José Lobo, Scott Ortman, and me – has been a productive, enlightening, and fun experience (Chapter 3). The Incipient Settlement Persistence Project is continuing this line of path-breaking research, and I thank Katherine Crawford, Nicolas Gauthier, Angela Huster, José Lobo, Matt Peeples, Ben Stanley, and Abigail York (Chapter 8). I have worked out the ideas in the book over many years of teaching my advanced undergraduate class, "The Earliest Cities," and I thank students in that class for listening to me rant and for asking some good questions.

Many colleagues helped me with feedback on my case studies, saving me from many small errors (and a few big mistakes!). They are Adrian Chase (Tikal), Brian Byrd (Beidha), Matt Peeples (Southwestern pueblos), Sarah Klassen and Roland Fletcher (Angkor), Rubina Raja (Jerash), Søren Sindbaek (Ribe and Fyrkat), Federica Sulas (Swahili city-state capitals), Alan Covey (Huanuco Pampa), Anna Stevens (Amarna workers compound), Alexandra Sanmark (Thing sites), Erick Poehler (Pompeii), Lisa Nevett (Olynthus), Kirstine Haase (Odense), and Vincent Gabrielsen and David Blackman (Rhodes).

For comments on individual chapters, I thank Manuel Fernández-Götz (Chapters 1, 2), René Ohlrau (Chapters 1, 2), Arlen Chase (Chapter 3), David Carballo (Chapter 4), Federica Sulas (Chapter 4), Gary Feinman (Chapters 4, 5), Christopher Morehart (Chapter 5), and April Kamp-Whittaker (Chapter 7). Cynthia Heath-Smith, Barbara Stark, and Søren Sindbaek read the entire manuscript and provided very insightful and helpful comments and suggestions; thank you!

The following colleagues helped me indirectly through background discussions on individual cities and urban traditions: Kirstine Haase, Quentin Letessen, Curtis Marean, Mads Ravn, and Søren Sindbaek. René Ohlrau and David Wengrow provided information and suggestions on specific issues. During the time I was writing this book, I benefitted greatly from discussions of early urbanism with these and other colleagues: Luís Bettencourt, Manuel Fernández-Götz, Roland Fletcher, Jack Hanson, Cynthia Heath-Smith, José Lobo, Scott Ortman, Rubina Raja, Ben Stanley, Barbara Stark, and Abigail York. I also thank Gina Deane, Amy Drew, Ditte Kvist Johnson, Christina Levisen, Mie Lind, and Leah Moyes for administrative and research help at various stages of preparation of the book. Rachel Paul copy edited the manu-script, and Sergey Lobachev of Brookfield Indexing compiled an excellent index.

The following colleagues helped me find graphics and the permissions to use them, a not insignificant endeavor! Acknowledgments for the specific figures I ended up using are provided in the captions. Thank you to Claudia Alvarado, Jens Bennedsen, Luís Bettencourt, David Blackman, Brian Byrd, Arlen Chase, Kostas Christakos, Jacques Dane, Dan Diffendale, Damian Evans, Claus Feveile, Roland Fletcher, Kirstene Haase, Luise Hilman, Willliam Iseminger, April Kamp-Whittaker, Barry Kemp, Mark Kenoyer, Carl Knappett, Rachel Kulick, Colleen Morgan, Angela O'Brian, René Ohlrau, Eric Poehler, Caroline Raddato, Rubina Raja, Margaret Cool Root, Alexandra Sanmark, Ian Simpson, Anna Stevens, Søren Sindbaek, Todd Whitelaw, and Stephanie Wynne-Jones.

UrbNet at Aarhus University supported me during the first stage of writing of this book. The Institute for Humanities Research at Arizona State University provided a book publication subvention grant, and the School of Human Evolution and Social Change helped with fees and production costs.

ONE

PREMODERN CITIES AND THE WIDE URBAN WORLD

WALKING THROUGH THE RUINS OF A ROMAN CITY SUCH AS OSTIA (Figure 1.1), you are greeted by clear signs of urbanism. Stone walls enclose living spaces that are entered from paved streets, houses are packed tightly together, and residential areas alternate with larger civic buildings such as temples, theaters, and markets. The living city of Ostia may be 2,000 years old, but its remains today are easily interpretable as a city, an urban settlement. But when one walks through the jungle in Angkor, Cambodia (Figure 1.2), it is difficult to identify the traces of urbanism. There are few streets and no surviving areas with standing house walls. In fact, one is hard-pressed to identify any houses at all or, for that matter, any buildings that are not temples. This hardly looks like an urban settlement. It is a jungle with piles of stone and a few temples. Yet Angkor in its day was the largest city (in area) ever to flourish in the ancient world, and its powerful kings ruled an extensive empire. Roman Ostia was a backwoods town in comparison to the glories of Angkor.

Effort is needed to construct a frame of reference that includes both Ostia and Angkor within the category of ancient city. The impressive variety of ancient urban forms makes this a difficult endeavor. Archaeologists often reify these concepts, attributing real existence to something – city or urban – that is a concept, not a brute fact of the real world. But even when archaeologists succeed in creating useful concepts of past urbanism, a yet greater effort is needed to bring ancient settlements and contemporary cities into the same frame of reference and draw meaningful conclusions. Many people assume ancient cities were either

1.1. Houses in the Roman city of Ostia, Domus del Protiro. Photograph by Michael E. Smith.

1.2. Stone bridge in the Khmer city of Angkor. Photograph by Roland Fletcher; reproduced with permission.

radically different from or identical to contemporary cities. Examining this idea rigorously requires archaeologists to step out of their background in anthropology or history and enter the world of contemporary social science, where most research on urbanism currently resides. I use the phrase *wide urban world* to describe this broad realm of cities and settlements, from deep history to the present.

I have been struggling my whole career to achieve these two goals – the creation of a framework to compare all kinds of ancient cities and the development of a means to link this knowledge with research on cities today. This book is a summing-up, an effort to bring together my thoughts and findings on comparative urbanism, in order to answer the questions, "What was life like in premodern cities?" and "What factors shaped urban life in the deep past?" The most important concept for understanding and explaining urban life in the past (and the present) is *energized crowding*. Energized crowding is a process that occurs when large numbers of face-to-face social interactions take place within a settlement. These interactions amplify the results of individual social interactions, resulting in a variety of social and economic changes and outcomes, both positive and negative. Energized crowding is the central concept in this book, and I explore it in detail in Chapters 2 and 3. The phrase originated with architectural historian Spiro Kostof (1991:37).

Cities are important. They concentrate economic and political activities, they influence larger landscapes and societies, and they provide an arena for the creation of institutions and processes that affect whole societies. While cities are centers of creativity and economic productivity, they are also settings for social problems, from pollution to crime and poverty. With increasingly rapid urbanization around the world today, a scientific understanding of cities and urbanism is a critical need (Bettencourt 2021; Ramaswami et al. 2018; Zhou et al. 2021). Some scholars try to achieve urban understanding by searching for power laws, fractals, and other quantitative patterns among cities today (Batty 2013; West 2017). Others focus on the economics, politics, or social processes of contemporary urbanism (Desmond 2016; Glaeser 2011; Kotkin 2006; Sampson 2012). All of these scholars have important things to say, and their work illuminates contemporary urban patterns. But their work lacks a crucial component: a deep historical perspective. When urban scholars do mention early cities, they often get the facts wrong or show a limited or misleading perspective (e.g., Bruegmann 2005; Kotkin 2006).

Archaeology provides crucial pieces of the mosaic that constitutes world patterns of urbanism. Archaeological data can now illuminate many aspects of the urban past. The findings of archaeologists, in turn, can be compared to contemporary cities to improve our understanding of cities and society today and into the future. But how is this possible? How can we know whether it makes sense to view ancient settlements as "urban"? Part of the answer lies in the realm of theories and concepts, and part lies in the findings of archaeology.

THESES ON PREMODERN CITIES

I begin with the concept of *settlement*, which has been defined by archaeologist Kwang-Chih Chang as "the physical locale or cluster of locales where the members of a community lived, ensured their subsistence, and pursued their social functions in a delineable time period" (Chang 1968:3). The focus is on the *place* where a group of people – from a few individuals to several million – lived or dwelt. Settlements last for anywhere from one day to thousands of years. The temporary campsites of mobile hunter-gatherers are settlements, as are cities. Settlements are not only the locations where people live; they are also places that concentrate activities and institutions – social, economic, political, religious – on the landscape. The primary subject matter of this book is the settlements I call *premodern cities*. By *premodern*, I mean settlements dating to the medieval period or earlier in Europe and the Mediterranean, and prior to European conquest and domination in other parts of the world. My basic definition of *city* or *urban* is a settlement where population and activities are concentrated in space (Pumain and Rozenblat 2018). I will leave this definition vague for now and return to it later in the chapter.

My use of premodern cities is quite similar to what Gideon Sjoberg (1960) calls *preindustrial cities*, but I eschew that term for two reasons. First, Sjoberg assumes the existence of a single homogeneous type of preindustrial city and describes its properties in general terms. I see more variability than Sjoberg, and I view the homogeneity or heterogeneity of my primary category as an empirical matter. Second, Sjoberg's picture of preindustrial cities draws overwhelmingly from a small set of cases (e.g., primarily historical studies of medieval European, Ottoman, Indian, and Chinese cities) that form a poor sample of the entire scope of premodern cities. Scholars after Sjoberg, moreover, have used the term *preindustrial* to refer to what historians call *early modern* – that is, postmedieval, pre–Industrial Revolution (e.g., Abbott 1974).

The following paragraphs present five theses, or fundamental principles, that describe the major outlines of my theoretical and comparative approach to premodern cities.

(1) Definitions are tools; one's definition of *city* or *urban* depends on one's goals and questions.

Scholars of cities today spend little time agonizing over how one defines the terms *city* and *urban*. In fact, they typically use the term *definition* to refer to operationalization: the measures that capture the phenomena scholars want to study. Premodern cities exhibit far more variability than modern cities in their size, form, functions, and activities; in addition, their political and economic contexts are more varied. For example, virtually all cities today exist within nation-states. But premodern cities could be part of a chiefdom, a city-state, an empire, or a weak state (Chapter 4). Cities today are embedded in a globalized, capitalist world system, whereas premodern cities could be part of a command economy, a small-scale commercial economy, or a far-flung globalized early commercial economy (Chapter 5). Because of this variability, the ways premodern cities may be defined also vary greatly. In the words of Luís Bettencourt (2021:50), "Any definition of a city requires an underlying scientific theory of what a city is and what it does." Consequently, there is no "best" definition of *city* or *urban*. This principle is often neglected by scholars of ancient cities, who may agonize over the "correct" definition of *urban*, or how to document and study the essence of cities and urbanism, which leads to my next principle.

(2) Do not reify the concepts of city or urban.

Cities and urbanism – particularly in the premodern domain – are not real things. Settlements, on the other hand, *are* real. They exist in this world. Archaeologists excavate their remains, and it is usually obvious whether a given site was a place where people resided. *City* and *urban* are categories or concepts that we apply to some settlements, when it suits our goals. If we have different goals, we may use different definitions. In the language of philosopher John Searle (1995), settlements are brute facts, while cities are institutional facts. One of Searle's examples is money. The fact that a piece of paper in my wallet has value and can be exchanged for goods and services is an institutional fact. It depends on the existence of institutions and beliefs that allow particular kinds of pieces of paper to be used to purchase things. But the physical properties of this same dollar bill – its ability to be folded or rolled up, or burned, or marked with a pen – are brute facts. They do not depend on an institutional framework or common beliefs within a community of people. There are no "brute facts" of "citiness" or "urbanity" as intrinsic attributes of a settlement, something waiting to be discovered; these are institutional facts that only make sense from a given perspective, with a given definition. The consequence of this principle is the following:

(3) The settlement should be the primary unit of analysis, not the city. We should acknowledge that some "urban" attributes and practices apply to nonurban settlements.

If settlements are "brute facts," then it makes sense to use them as a basic unit of analysis. When our research shows that a given settlement was large and complex, or served as a hub in a regional economy, then we may want to classify it as an urban settlement; in Searle's framework, this is an institutional judgment. The fact that some key features of cities also characterize smaller, nonurban settlements is a further warning about the dangers of reifying the concept of urban. Settlement scaling research shows that key quantitative outcomes of social interactions in settlements characterize both urban and nonurban settlement systems (Ortman and Coffey 2017); see Chapter 3. Similarly, comparative work on neighborhoods shows that this urban social-spatial unit is also found in nonurban settlements (Smith et al. 2015; Tuzin 2001); see Chapter 7. These findings suggest that we can proceed with analyzing settlements without agonizing over definitions or worries about whether or not they are urban.[1]

> (4) Cities and urban life are structured by the interplay between two sets of processes: centralized, or top-down, processes originate with kings, elites, and central institutions, whereas generative, or bottom-up, processes arise from the grassroots actions of individuals and households, actions that are not under the control or direction of institutions or authorities.

Urban life and organization are made up of a constant interplay of these two kinds of processes of change. My usage is based on common approaches in the social sciences outside archaeology.[2] I distinguish two types of generative processes: *Grassroots activity* refers to the intentional efforts of people to organize and coordinate their activities in pursuit of a goal (Chapter 7). *Spontaneous organization* describes actions of daily life, including social interactions, that create some kind of order or outcome that was neither planned nor created by authorities (Chapters 3 and 7). My prime example of this is energized crowding.

While both top-down and bottom-up factors are typically in play, some realms are closer to the institutional or upper domain of society, while others lie closer to the generative realm. For example, most premodern urbanites paid taxes, and taxation is primarily an activity of the state, a top-down institution. While the generative actions of individuals and groups may affect tax collection, these are typically of less importance than the top-down demands at play. Political protest, on the other hand, is primarily a generative process; nevertheless, top-down forces may affect the nature and outcomes of protests. My discussion of urban life proper is divided along these lines: Chapter 6 focuses on institutions or top-down processes, and Chapter 7 is about generative processes. This division flows from my basic definition of cities as settlements where population and activities are concentrated.

> (5) Social interactions within cities and other settlements create *energized crowding*, which is one of the fundamental forces of change in urban life.

---

[1] Perhaps ironically, this caveat has not stopped archaeologists – including me – from arguing about definitions of city and urban; see the later discussion.

[2] I wish to distinguish my usage of "top-down" and "bottom-up" from a particular archaeological usage in which "top-down" refers to studies of kings and elites, while "bottom-up" denotes studies of households. My usage, in contrast, is based on drivers of change and causal mechanisms (Chapters 3, 6, and 7).

As in the case of thesis 4, this principle also flows from my basic definition of cities. The importance of face-to-face social interaction, in the form of energized crowding, in generating social outcomes is a fundamental component of many theoretical approaches in the social sciences (Brower 2011; Glaeser 2011; Ostrom 1990; Storper and Venables 2004). This perspective has been developed into a set of formal theories with quantitative predictions, known as *settlement scaling theory* (Bettencourt et al. 2007; Pumain et al. 2006; West 2017). I have participated in one branch of this approach, which views cities as "social reactors" (Bettencourt 2013). We have extended research from contemporary cities into the deep past, revealing continuities in the role of settlement size between ancient and modern settlement systems (Chapter 3). In this book, I explore the nature and implications of social interactions for premodern cities.[3]

One response to these complexities – particularly as implied by theses 2 and 3 – would be to discard the concepts of urban and city altogether. The relevant domain of interest, in fact, is the settlement, and the ways we describe and analyze settlements vary with our goals. But given the importance of cities and urbanism in the modern world, I think it best to retain these concepts for the premodern domain as well. Most of the discussion in this book pertains to cities, towns, and urbanism (defined as follows), and I will try to clarify when the discussion also includes small or nonurban settlements. Similarly, most of the discussion applies to the premodern domain (as defined previously), but I also discuss settlements of the modern era where necessary. In particular, my discussion of voluntary camps (Chapter 3) and practical machine sites (Chapter 4) focuses heavily on modern examples; these settlements are natural experiments that allow specific urban dynamics to be observed clearly. I will discuss how contemporary cities and settlements relate to those of the distant past later in this chapter.

An additional consideration that colors how some archaeologists write about ancient cities is what I call the *urban prestige effect*. As a legacy of rigid and universalist schemes of cultural evolution popular from the 1950s through the 1970s (Service 1975; White 1959), many archaeologists assign a high value, with a high level of prestige, to the categories of cities and urbanism. This signals an unfortunate emotional association with the objects of their study (settlements). Urban sites are seen as "better" than nonurban settlements, resulting in attempts to categorize nonurban settlements as cities. Nonurban villages are not infrequently declared urban by one scholar or another, whether ancient sites like Çatalhöyük (see Case Study 2) or modern Amazonian villages (Heckenberger et al. 2008). It is almost guaranteed that complex early

---

[3] The research and publications of the Social Reactors Project are presented at www .colorado.edu/socialreactors/.

settlements – such as the Trypillia "mega-sites" – will be viewed as urban (Chapman and Gaydarska 2016a; Diachenko and Menotti 2017), regardless of the nature of the evidence; see Chapter 2. This urban prestige effect only muddies the waters of premodern settlement analysis, contributing little to our understanding of the settlements in question or to comparative urban studies.

THE DIMENSIONS OF URBANISM

The issue of defining cities has been a difficult problem for archaeologists, one I discuss at length later in this chapter. As a background to that discussion, I introduce the concept of *dimensions* to organize major attributes of settlements and cities. Dimensions are bundles of related variables. In my framework, three dimensions stand out as most important: size, urban life, and urban functions. Important cross-cutting dimensions include form, meaning, and growth. The importance one gives to particular dimensions over others influences one's theoretical approach, including one's definition of cities and urban.

The Primary Dimensions: Cities as Big, Important, and Complicated Places

(1) Big Places – Size. In a causal sense, the size of a city – its population, area, and density – is the most important of the dimensions of urbanism. Size has a major influence on the other primary dimensions, urban life and functions. Although cities today are vastly larger than those in the distant past, the role that population size plays within a given settlement system is quite similar in the present and the past, something revealed by settlement scaling research. Chapter 3 is about the size of premodern cities.

(2) Important Places – Urban Functions. An urban function is an activity or institution located within a settlement that affects life and society beyond the borders of the settlement. The presence of urban functions makes a city an important place within its region. Villages lack urban functions, whereas a political capital – by ruling a polity – has urban functions, at least in the political realm. Urban functions were first articulated by central place theory, a model of the spatial locations and sizes of market centers (discussed later). Urban functions are useful in studying regional and macro-regional social patterns because they deal with the ways a central settlement articulates with its hinterland. In this usage, if an urban shop only serves people in its neighborhood, then its activities do not constitute urban functions. But, if people travel from other settlements to use the shop, then those transactions signal economic urban functions. I discuss political and economic urban functions in Chapters 4 and 5.

(3) Complicated Places – Urban Life and Society. This is the broadest domain of urbanism, the realm of social complexity and variation. While aspects of urban life and society are included in Chapters 3–5, Chapters 6 and 7 focus intensively on urban life. The first is concerned with institutions and top-down processes that affect urban life, including social class, wealth inequality, and the role of government in providing services. Chapter 7 then focuses on generative processes in cities – those processes where individuals and households create social patterns and changes through grassroots actions, independent of the role of the state or central institutions. My discussion is organized by households, neighborhoods, occupations, ethnic diversity, and patterns of poverty and prosperity. One way of summarizing the variety of traits that make up this dimension is to note that they are markers of social complexity. Any settlement has houses, but urban settlements tend to have both large and small houses corresponding to wealth or class differences. Any settlement has economic consumption activities, but cities tend also to have markets or shops, specialists, workshops, and other economic institutions above the household level. In short, cities were the settings for social complexity in most premodern societies, as they still are today.

Cross-Cutting Dimensions: Form, Meaning, and Growth

Three additional dimensions of urbanism – urban form, urban meaning, and urban growth – are also important components of premodern urban settlements. They have less causal importance in urban dynamics, however, than the three primary dimensions discussed previously. That is, they have a smaller influence over other aspects of cities and urban life.

(1) Urban Form. This dimension includes architecture and the layout and planning of cities. Although I discuss some aspects of urban form in this book – monumentality, planning, and housing – urban form is not given a major emphasis; instead, it is treated in relation to the primary dimensions above. A comparative study of the forms, architecture, spatial layout, and planning of premodern cities is badly needed, but there is no space to address urban form comprehensively here; for a start, see Smith (2007).

(2) Urban Meaning. If one looks at the literature on premodern cities, one might get the impression that "meaning" is the most important dimension of urban analysis (Bowser and Zedeño 2009; Parker Pearson and Richards 1994; Rykwert 1988). Apart from the theoretical deficiency of such a stance (Blanton 1995; Smith 2011b), the definition of the term "meaning" employed in that literature almost ensures that archaeologists cannot recover it with confidence from past settlements (Rapoport 1990a; Smith 2007). I discuss this issue in Chapter 4, with respect to Amos Rapoport's concept of levels of meaning in the built environment.

(3) Urban Growth and Decline. Whereas archaeologists can often document the growth and decline of ancient urban settlements, there has been little theoretical or conceptual work on this topic for premodern cities. Recent publications on the persistence of early settlements – how long they lasted – are starting to address the topic systematically (Smith et al. 2021b). Urban economists have long been obsessed with urban growth (Glaeser 2011; O'Sullivan 2011). While much of the work in urban economics is difficult or impossible to apply to premodern cities (where institutions such as money, firms, industrial production, and wage labor may not have existed), specific forays of urban economists into the past have generated some useful results (e.g., de Long and Shleifer 1993; Glaeser 2021).

DEFINING CITIES AND URBANISM

George Cowgill, a leading scholar of comparative early urbanism (and my undergraduate advisor) has noted:

> It is notoriously difficult to agree on a cross-culturally applicable definition of 'the' city, but we cannot do without definitions altogether . . . . No single criterion, such as sheer size or use of writing, is adequate, and it seems best to use a somewhat fuzzy core concept rather than to try to establish criteria that will clearly demarcate all cities from all noncities. (Cowgill 2004:526)

There are innumerable definitions of *city* and *urbanism* in the literature of urban studies. Most of these are not useful for premodern times, for reasons articulated by urban anthropologist Anthony Leeds some time ago:

> Most current discussion of 'urbanism' and 'urbanization' can be shown to be ethno- and tempro-centric and based on a historically particular class of urban phenomena and urban forms of integration . . . Generalizations are then made about 'urbanism' and 'urban society' based essentially on the urban experience of the past few hundred years, apparently without the realization that all urban phenomena of the past four or five hundred years have been ineluctably affected by the expansion of the capitalist system, in short by the development of what Wallerstein calls the 'World System.' The generalizations are, then, in fact not about 'urbanization' in general but about a single form of 'urbanism' or 'urbanization,' its evolution, and its acculturational by-products. (Leeds 1979:227, 228)

Forty years later, the situation has only improved slightly. In this section, I concentrate on the two definitions most commonly used in archaeology (the sociological and functional definitions) as well as two new approaches that may prove useful (the archaeological attributes and the social interactions approaches). For a fuller discussion of urban definitions in archaeology, see

Smith (2020b). While some archaeologists strive to distinguish the city, as a settlement, from urbanism, as the larger context for cities (Graham and Isendahl 2018), my view of definitions as tools allows a more flexible approach. Just as there is no ideal definition of city or urban, there is no a priori distinction between the concepts of city and urban. In other words, I am not making a big distinction between *city* and *urban* in this book. Cities and towns are urban settlements, and my definitions of *city* or *urban* serve also to also define the other member of the pair.

Archaeological Debates on the Sociological and Functional Definitions of Cities

Archaeologists have tended to use two main definitions of cities or urban settlements: the sociological and functional definitions. Many archaeologists have used the *sociological definition* of Louis Wirth: "For sociological purposes a city may be defined as a relatively large, dense, and permanent settlement of socially heterogeneous individuals" (Wirth 1938:8). This is perhaps the most influential definition of *city* in the urban literature beyond archaeology. Emphasizing the dimensions of size and complexity (urban life), this definition fits contemporary cities in the developed world very well. Definitions both depend on and invoke theories and concepts, and the sociological definition works well with many of the approaches to theory and research on contemporary western cities (Parker 2004; Sampson 2009, 2012). These approaches, however, are difficult to apply to premodern cities. Cities were different in the distant past; in particular, they were not embedded in nation-states and the capitalist world system, two of the major forces shaping urbanism today.

While Wirth's sociological definition of urbanism works well for cities today, it does a poor job of identifying premodern cities. For example, ancient urban settlements of low population density will be excluded from urban status, yet a number of ancient state-level societies – for example, the Classic period Maya and the Khmer of Southeast Asia – were characterized by what has been called "low-density urbanism" (Fletcher 2009, 2012). Should Tikal or Angkor be excluded from urban status because their densities are not high enough?

This concern led archaeologists to adopt a second definition of *urban*, the *functional definition*. Bruce Trigger was the first archaeologist to articulate this view: "It is generally agreed that whatever else a city may be it is a unit of settlement which performs specialized functions in relationship to a broad hinterland" (Trigger 1972:577). The urban functions that identify a city can be economic, political, or religious. This definition uses only one of the dimensions of urbanism; size and complexity are left out. While Tikal or Angkor might not have populations that are sufficiently large and dense to satisfy Wirth's definition, they clearly had monumental buildings that signal past urban functions. These cities had temples larger than other settlements, suggesting that their religious influence extended beyond the settlement proper, and they had royal palaces with resident kings whose influence extended far beyond the city.

The functional definition of urbanism grew out of central place theory, which provides a group of concepts for analyzing the regional configuration of cities. Central place theory deals with the balance or tradeoff between sellers, who want to locate in common settlements to achieve economies of scale, versus consumers, who want goods and services to be offered nearby; the travel of both buyers and sellers is limited by transportation costs (Christaller 1966; Lloyd and Dicken 1977; Mulligan et al. 2012). There are a number of applications of this approach by archaeologists (Inomata and Aoyama 1996; M. E. Smith 1979). The basic procedure is to examine the size and spacing of market centers in a region, and if they conform to the predictions of the central place models, one can conclude that retail marketing activity was important in structuring the regional settlement system. I return to central place theory in my discussion of urban economies in Chapter 5. To identify a settlement as functionally urban, one must examine the entire settlement system for a region. To identify a settlement as sociologically urban, on the other hand, only requires data on the settlement itself.

In the 1970s, anthropologists broadened the concept of urban function to include features in the domain of politics and religion (Blanton 1976; Fox 1977; Marcus 1983). In the political domain, urban functions are about the control of people or territory outside the boundaries of the city. Cities with political urban functions are either capitals of a polity or else administrative centers within an empire or large polity. The territory controlled by premodern polities has been analyzed spatially using either Thiessen polygons (a model that assigns territory to the closest center) or the X-tent model. The X-tent model allows the territories of larger, more powerful centers to include the territories of lower-ranking settlements (Hare 2004; Renfrew and Level 1979) – a promising approach that should be used more widely.

The functional definition of cities has been used extensively by archaeologists, and it has stimulated more conceptual and methodological development than the sociological definition. Figure 1.3 illustrates the relationship between these two definitions. Almost any city that fits Wirth's definition will also fit the functional definition, but the inverse is not the case. Archaeologists have engaged in contentious debates about the usefulness of these two definitions. My very first publication as a graduate student championed Wirth's approach over the functional definition (Smith 1977); later I converted to the functional approach and – with the fanaticism of a convert – promoted it vigorously in a number of publications (Smith 1989, 2007). While I would like to think we have moved beyond this question, the debate does have important lessons for how archaeologists think about and analyze ancient cities, as my first case study, Tikal, shows.

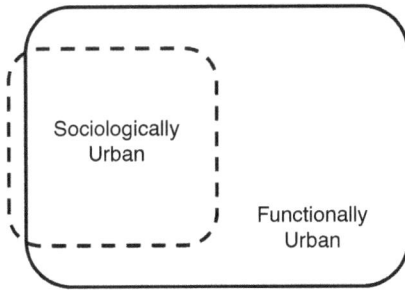

1.3. Relationship of the sociological and functional definitions of urban. Graphic by Michael E. Smith.

Case Study 1 Tikal: Urban or Not?

As one of the largest and best-studied Maya cities, Tikal has played a major role in debates about the urban status of Classic-period Maya settlements (Figure 1.4). The earliest archaeologists thought Maya settlements were basically large temples in the jungle. J. Eric Thompson (1963:48), an influential early archaeologist, called Maya settlements "ceremonial centers," empty except "for a small staff for upkeep." Peasants living in villages in the jungle supposedly came into the centers for periodic rituals, which were staged by a few priests, who were the only residents of the centers. It was assumed that there were no cities, no kings, and no written language beyond symbolic depictions of calendars and gods. This wildly inaccurate view was overturned in the 1950s and 1960s by the Tikal Project, directed by William Coe of the University of Pennsylvania (Sabloff 2003). Ek (2020) is a good overview of these and other changes in archaeological views of the nature of Maya society and urbanism.

1.4. Photo of the epicenter of Tikal during the University of Pennsylvania excavations in the 1960s. Courtesy of the University Museum, University of Pennsylvania; reproduced with permission.

Case Study 1 (cont.)

Were Maya Settlements Urban? It Depends on Your Definition. Gordon Willey, long a leading figure in Maya archaeology, declared that the Maya had been a "civilization without cities" (Willey 1962), a term that was also being applied – in error – to dynastic Egypt (Wilson 1960). The Tikal Project was one of the first to look for remains in the jungle beyond the main pyramids. A central area of sixteen square kilometers was mapped intensively, revealing a landscape of many low mounds. When excavated, these "house mounds" were found to be low platforms that supported houses made of perishable materials. In Figure 1.4, we have to assume that the forest surrounding downtown Tikal was filled with houses and house groups.

This finding set off a flurry of fieldwork and analysis at Maya sites. Numerous house mounds pointed to much larger resident populations than archaeologists had imagined. It became clear there were more people living at Tikal than could be supported by slash-and-burn agriculture, a form of traditional farming with relatively low productivity. Archaeologists discovered evidence for various forms of more intensive, productive farming that could feed the Maya populations. Excavation of palaces showed clear social classes, and decipherment of Maya writing revealed powerful kings. Some archaeologists began to talk of Maya "cities," but then an influential book by William Sanders and Barbara Price claimed these settlements were not cities at all.

Sanders and Price (1968) applied Wirth's sociological definition of *city* to Mesoamerica to support the idea that Teotihuacan (in central Mexico) was indeed a city, but Tikal and the Maya settlements were not. They published facing plans of the two settlements (at the same scale) to show how downtown Teotihuacan had houses packed closely together whereas downtown Tikal had few houses at all (Figure 1.5).[4] This conclusion was reiterated in a later article by Sanders and David Webster (1988):

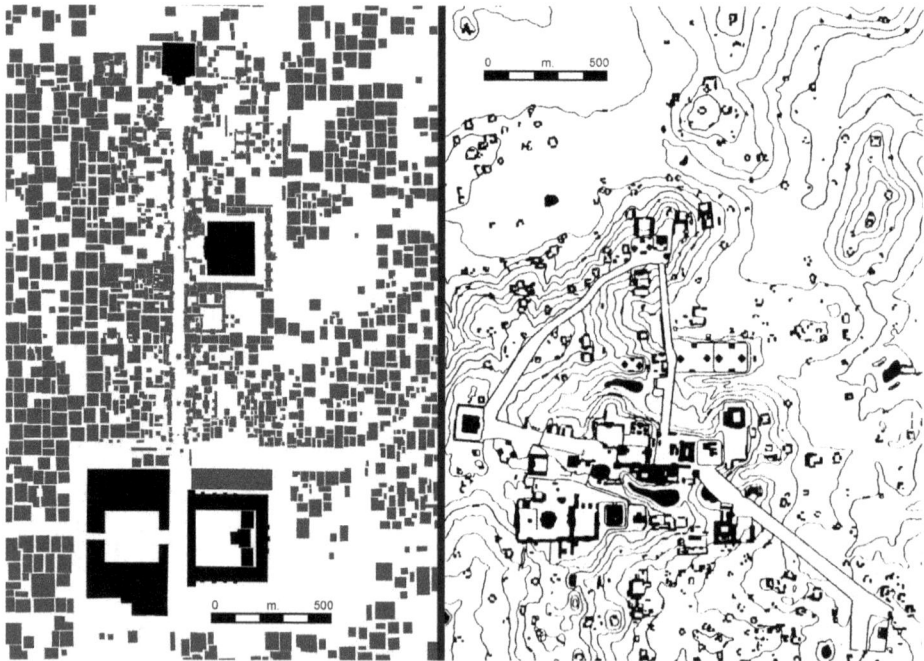

1.5. Central areas of Teotihuacan (left) and Tikal (right), shown at the same scale. Graphic by Michael E. Smith. Teotihuacan map courtesy of the Teotihuacan Mapping Project; Tikal map modified after Coe (1967).

[4] The population density of Tikal was between five and ten persons per hectare, while the density of Teotihuacan was fifty per hectare (see Chapter 3).

Case Study 1 (cont.)

Teotihuacan was a "typical city" (it fit Wirth's definition), but Tikal was too empty to be a true city. Two critiques of this paper were published. I argued for the value of the functional definition, which classified Tikal as a city (Smith 1989); Diane Chase, Arlen Chase, and William Haviland (1990) argued that at least two Maya centers were large enough to be considered urban – Tikal and Caracol – because these settlements were denser and more complex than smaller sites in their hinterlands. Arguments for the urban status of Maya cities continue today, and they are couched in terms of "low-density urbanism" (Chase and Chase 2016; Fletcher 1995; Isendahl 2012; Smith 2011a); see Chapter 3.

Comparative Insights. A cynic might think (as I did before my conversion to the functional approach) that the switch to the functional definition was a move by Mayanists to allow them to use the term "urban" for their small, low-density settlements, perhaps a manifestation of the urban prestige effect. But, in reality, the functional definition has two significant advantages over the sociological definition for premodern cities. First, it puts urban settlements into their social and regional contexts; second, it adds a far wider range of ancient societies to the ranks of "urban societies." This, in turn, allows Tikal and other low-density cities to be analyzed and compared with the broad range of premodern urban systems.

New Approaches

The Physical City and the Social City. A contrast between the physical and social aspects of cities is becoming increasingly popular in the urban literature. This is phrased in various ways, including physical city versus functional city in urban economics (Demographia 2017) and physical city versus socioeconomic city for complexity-based scaling analysis (West 2017:chapter 7). The most concise statement of this contrast – and the version that best fits premodern cities – is that of Bill Hillier (1996b:41): "Physically, cities are stocks of buildings linked by space and infrastructure. Functionally, they support economic, social, cultural, and environmental processes."

This distinction brings the challenges of urban archaeology to the fore. We excavate physical cities, but we want to reconstruct social cities. While most analyses of urban settlements must include both facets of cities, specific studies and concepts often pertain more to one domain than the other. In this section, I discuss two newer approaches to defining cities, each emphasizing one side of this division. The *archaeological features approach* is a method I devised that uses a list of material features to compare settlements within a given urban tradition.[5] This is a data-based approach, with limited theoretical significance. The *social interactions approach* defines cities as social networks anchored in the built environment: places where internal social interactions exceed interactions with outside areas. In contrast to the archaeological features approach, this approach has a strong theoretical basis but is difficult to operationalize with archaeological evidence.

---

[5] An urban tradition is a group of cities pertaining to a limited areal extent and a limited chronological interval that share key features of their form and organization.

Archaeological Features on the Landscape. For a paper on the identification of cities using archaeological data (Smith 2016b), I devised a simple method to examine urban attributes at settlements within a single urban tradition.[6] Most of the attributes correspond to the "physical city." I compiled information on the presence of key urban features and institutions at three Aztec sites I had excavated. I also included the Aztec imperial capital Tenochtitlan (Table 1.1); see the original paper for an earlier version of this table and a parallel table for Iron Age Oppida settlements. The table includes attributes organized into four dimensions: settlement size, social impact (urban functions), features of planning and the built environment, and social-economic features. The attributes are selected using three criteria: (1) each has significance in some theory or concept of urbanism, (2) each can be recovered with archaeological fieldwork, and (3) each has some significance within the particular urban tradition (Aztec settlements, in this case).

I apply crude numerical scales to highlight variation along these dimensions. The Aztec settlements in Table 1.1 illustrate a continuum from village to imperial capital, with all four dimensions – size, urban functions, built environment, and institutions – showing increasing scores at each step along the scale. The "total attribute score" is a numerical approximation of a general urban dimension for Aztec settlements. The biggest gap in the attribute score is the 400 percent jump from the village to the town. Interestingly, the activities and conditions of households at the three excavated sites were quite similar, as measured from the architecture and artifacts at commoner houses (see discussion in Chapter 7). For commoner wealth and lifestyle, the big break in this sequence is between the imperial capital and the other settlements.[7] Nadine Moeller (2016:15–26) uses a broadly similar approach by defining types of urban (and nonurban) settlements in ancient Egypt and describing the specific archaeological features of each type.

Social Interactions. In the mid-twentieth century, geographers started mapping the movements of goods and people, within and between cities (Haggett and Chorley 1969). Today, many economic geographers and urban economists define cities in terms of the spatial patterns of such interactions. Urban economist Edward Glaeser (2011), for example, provides this informal definition of cities: "Cities are the absence of physical space between people and companies. They are proximity, density, and closeness" (p. 6). He later says, "The central

---

[6] One of the tenets of cross-cultural comparative analysis is that variables and measures that make sense and lead to clarity within a cultural tradition may not work across cultural traditions. Although the features in Table 1.1 work for Aztec settlements, they may not work in other urban traditions.

[7] Unfortunately, there are insufficient excavated domestic contexts at Tenochtitlan to evaluate this idea further.

TABLE 1.1 *Urban attributes of Aztec settlements of varying sizes*

Attribute	Type of variable*	Capilco (village)	Cuexcomate (town)	Yautepec (city-state capital)	Tenochtitlan (imperial capital)
Settlement size:					
Population	M	100	800	13,000	210,000
Area (ha.)	M	1	15	210	1,350
Density (persons/ha)	M	100	50	60	155
Social impact (urban functions):		*2*	*3*	*10*	*15*
Royal palace	P/A	–	–	x	x
Royal burials	P/A	–	–		x
Large (high-order) temples	P/A	–	–	x	x
Civic architecture	S	–	1	2	3
Craft production	S	1	1	2	3
Market or shops	S	L	1	2	3
Built environment:		*0*	*8*	*9*	*10*
Connective infrastructure	P/A	–	–	L	x
Intermediate-order temples	P/A	–	x	x	x
Elite residences	P/A	–	x	x	x
Formal public space	P/A	–	x	x	x
Planning of epicenter	P/A	–	x	x	x
Social and economic features:		*2*	*6*	*8*	*10*
Elite burials	P/A	–	–	L	L
Social diversity (nonclass)	P/A	–	–	L	x
Neighborhoods	P/A	–	x	x	x
Agriculture within settlement	P/A	–	x	x	x
Imports	S	2	2	2	3
Total attribute score		**4**	**17**	**27**	**35**

Note: Table based on Smith (2016b), table 10.1.

* *Type of variable:*

 M: quantitative measurement or calculation

 P/A: presence/absence

 S: measurement scale (1: low; 2: moderate; 3: high)

 x: Present (scored as 2)

 L: Likely present (scored as 1)

theme of this book is that cities magnify humanity's strengths. Our social species' greatest talent is the ability to learn from each other, and we learn more deeply and thoroughly when we're face-to-face" (p. 250); see also Storper and Venables (2004). One urban economist has defined cities as follows: "Cities are places where a lot of human activity and interaction regularly occurs in a small space" (O'Flaherty 2005:1); he notes that his definition would include Disney World, flea markets, and a race track on race day.

Some scholars have generalized this perspective into the notion that "cities were evolved primarily for the facilitation of human communication" (Meier 1962). For planner Kevin Lynch (1981:187), "Cities may have first been built for symbolic reasons and later for defense, but it soon appeared that one of their special advantages was the improved access they afforded." He goes on to note that "more than anything else, the city is a communication network" (Lynch 1981:334).

Increases in social interactions produce energized crowding; see Smith (2019a). In urban economics and related fields, social interactions – and concomitant increases with population – are the bases for quantitative models, and the outcomes of those models can be identified and measured, for both contemporary and ancient cities (Chapter 3). Today, patterns of movement and interaction are becoming easier to measure with the availability of "big data" for many cities (Bettencourt 2014; Blei and Smyth 2017). But for archaeologists, social interactions within settlements remain difficult to measure directly.

Urban Definitions Used in This Book

Readers looking for my views on the "best" definition of cities and urbanism will be disappointed. I reiterate my first thesis from earlier in the chapter: "Definitions are tools; one's definition of city or urban depends on one's goals and questions." Here are some of the ways I employ urban definitions in this book. First, my basic definition (cities as settlements where population and activities are concentrated in space) is intended to give an idea of the scope of the book. The other definitions reviewed previously can be viewed as extensions or modifications of this basic definition. Second, I use the *functional definition* to select my sample of case studies. Premodern cities are settlements before the modern era (see the temporal definition given previously) that are the setting for urban functions within their regional and macro-regional contexts. Third, I use the *social interactions* definition for theoretical purposes. I explore this concept more fully in Chapter 2 and discuss its role in settlement scaling theory in Chapter 3. As Kostof noted, cities are places with energized crowding, even if archaeologists cannot isolate the specific activities and episodes of interaction. Fourth, the size of cities in population and/or density – part of the sociological and other urban definitions – runs throughout this book as an important dimension. Finally, I use the *archaeological attributes* approach to identify and analyze urban settlements within a specific region or urban tradition.

Archaeologists not infrequently want to know whether a particular site or group of sites in their region were "urban" or not. This desire is too often a result of the urban prestige effect (see the previous discussion). Instead of rooting around in the many definitions of urbanism (and I have not covered them all!), I would advise the following procedure: (1) Identify a series of archaeological attributes that measure some kind of complexity at sites in a region. (2) Include a range of sites, from villages to the largest sites, as I have done in Table 7.1. This is the archaeological attributes approach. (3) Finally, compare the largest or most complex of these sites to the functional or sociological definitions to see whether the concept "urban" helps advance understanding.

Rural and Urban

An important dimension of defining cities is to specify the distinction between urban and nonurban – rural – contexts within a given settlement system. Again, my views diverge from current orthodoxy in archaeology and urban studies generally. The standard view is that urban and rural are diametrically opposed contexts. Urbanism is seen as something special and different, something that produces radically new and different urban ways of life (Weber 1958; Wirth 1938). Against this notion, I follow the approach of Anthony Leeds:

> Any society which has in it what we commonly call "towns" or "cities" is in all aspects an "urban" society, including its agricultural and extractive domains ... the terms "urban" and "rural" come to stand to each other not as opposites and equivalents. Rather, the inclusive term describing the whole society is "urban" while the term "rural" refers only to a set of specialties of an urban society characterized by being inherently linked (under any technology known) to specific geographical spaces. (Leeds 1980:6–7)

This viewpoint expands the functional approach to urban definition by examining the functions or activities of all components of an urban landscape, or – as Leeds put it – an urban society. It helps avoid the problems that arise from the reification of the concepts of city and urban, and allows scholars to compare conditions and activities in urban and rural settings without a priori judgments about the nature of "urban-ness." Such reification is common in archaeological approaches that use social practice theory to identify the essence of "urbanity" as a social condition (e.g., Christophersen 2015). In addition, the more flexible approach of Anthony Leeds acknowledges that the nature and definition of settlement in periurban areas surrounding cities may be in flux, as formerly rural zones are gradually and perhaps haphazardly converted into urban residential areas (Simon 2008). Finally, Leeds's approach also helps contextualize research on urban life per se, as I explore in Chapters 6 and 7.

EXPANDING THE BOUNDARIES OF URBANISM

How should we think about settlements that show one or two of the features of urbanism but not others? For example, a large village may be high on the size dimension but not have any urban functions or evidence of social complexity. Or, a ritual site might have a strong urban function in the religious domain but lack a resident population. In line with proposition 4 above, such settlements are interesting and relevant to the subject of urbanism. I discuss three examples in this section: ritual centers, agrotowns, and semi-urban settlements. None of these settlements would be classified as urban by the major definitions reviewed above, but all have things to teach us about urbanism.

Not Quite Urban: Ritual Centers and Agrotowns

Stonehenge and other megalithic monuments in Europe are impressive places, even today. Ancient people from distant areas certainly knew about places like Stonehenge, and archaeologists assume that people came from near and far to participate in ceremonies or celebrations at these sites. This is another way of saying that Stonehenge had urban functions in the domain of religion. Yet no one would call Stonehenge an urban settlement, largely because there is little evidence for a large settlement around the monument. The nearby site of Durrington Walls (2.8 km from Stonehenge) has typical Neolithic houses, with evidence of feasting activities (Craig et al. 2015; French et al. 2012). There are remains of temporary shelters at Durrington Walls, perhaps to accommodate pilgrims who journeyed to Stonehenge. But, given the distance between Durrington Walls and Stonehenge, it is not clear whether they should be considered parts of the same settlement.

The more recently discovered site of Göbekli Tepe in Turkey appears to be a similar kind of site. It has elaborately carved monumental stone slabs, arranged into a circle (Dietrich et al. 2012). As at Stonehenge, there appears to be little evidence for an associated settlement, although settlement sites do exist in the region. Similarly, Göbekli Tepe was most likely a destination for pilgrimages. These and other similar sites (Artursson et al. 2016) can be called *ritual centers*. Their ritual role clearly affected large areas, but without an associated population, they are not urban centers. In fact, the only way to call them "settlements" at all is to include nearby temporary residential quarters.

Agrotowns are large nucleated villages of farmers that lack urban functions and have low levels of social complexity. My use of this term differs slightly from the predominant definition in the field of social history, where *agrotown* refers primarily to south Italian aggregated settlements (Blok 1969), and definitions include a long list of cultural characteristics, from the sexual division of labor to cultural codes (Colclough 2010:2–3; Curtis 2013). My usage of the term focuses on aggregated villages of farmers who have to walk out to their fields; this is close to Max Weber's term *ackerbürger* (Hansen 2006a:93–94). Agrotowns are interesting comparatively for two reasons. They are larger and denser than most villages and they can be stable for centuries, showing that processes of nucleation or aggregation do not necessarily lead to urbanization.

The Italian village of Ascoli Satriano around the year 1700 (Figure 1.6) exhibits the main features of agrotowns (Colclough 2010; Curtis 2013). Agriculture and herding were important, houses are closely packed, and the only tall buildings are the churches and an old castle. If, as is likely, the churches served the people of the village and not others, then they do not indicate the presence of urban functions. The status and size of Ascoli waxed and waned over the centuries. Three decades after this image was created, the town had grown and added many occupational specialists (clergy, merchants, and artisans). But after a century, "Ascocli's urban role was transformed from that of ecclesiastical and trading entre to classical agro-town" (Colclough 2010:9). Prominent cases of agrotowns in the distant past are the pueblos of the US Southwest (Chapter 3) and Çatalhöyük. Lawrence and Wilkinson (2015) have used the term *agrotowns* to describe the earliest aggregated settlements in northern Mesopotamia: they are villages or towns of farmers, without urban institutions.

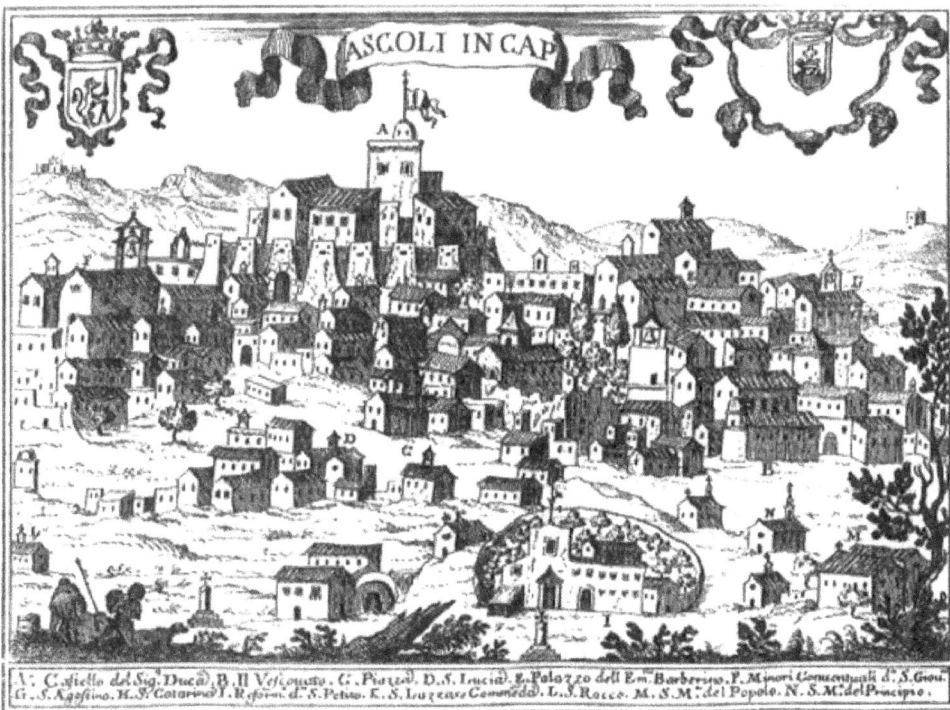

1.6. Ascoli Satriano, Italy, in 1703, an agrotown. From (Pacichelli 1703), public domain.

Case Study 2 Çatalhöyük: An Early Agrotown

When James Mellaart first excavated Çatalhöyük in the 1960s, the densely packed houses of this Neolithic settlement looked like a city neighborhood (Figure 1.7); compare this to Ostia in Figure 1.1. Owing to either a desire for publicity or a lack of comparative understanding, Mellaart made grandiose claims about the urban status of the settlement: "For already Çatal Höyük ranks, with Jericho in Jordan, as one of man's first essays in the development of town-life. Before 6000 BCE Çatal Höyük was a town, or even a city, of a remarkable and developed kind . . . . One need hardly point out that Çatal Höyük was not a village" (Mellaart 1967:15, 71).[8]

In 1993, Ian Hodder began a new project of excavations at the site. This project made heavy use of the scientific methods of "high-definition archaeology" (Chapter 8), including a variety of detailed geoarchaeological methods, cutting-edge digital technologies, and careful attention to a wide range of archaeological materials (Balter 2005; Hodder 2006, 2007). Hodder initially designed this project as a way to apply insights from postprocessual archaeology to a major site. This approach to theory rests heavily on subjective imagination, interpretation, and meaning, and avoids the kind of scientific epistemology on which the present work is built (as discussed later). Although it is too early to evaluate the empirical or theoretical results of this large and complicated long-term field project, Hodder is quite clear about the nonurban character of Çatalhöyük.

1.7. Çatalhöyük, an early agrotown. Photograph by James Mellaart. Copyright James Mellaart, with permission of Alan Mellaart.

[8] This claim received considerable publicity at the time, leading many subsequent writers (but rarely archaeologists) to parrot the idea that Çatalhöyük was the world's first city. For discussion, see Smith et al. (2014b). That Mellaart has since been exposed as a forger and fabricator of archaeological finds (Zangger 2018) does not favor continued adherence to his claims.

Case Study 2 (cont.)

Agrotown or City? Ian Hodder clearly describes the urban and nonurban features of Çatalhöyük:

> So in terms of size, we might call this settlement a 'town'. But it has few of the other characteristics that we might mean by that term. Despite careful sampling of the surface of the mound, we have not found public spaces, administrative buildings, elite quarters, or really any specialized functional spaces except those on the edge of the mound (such as lime burning) and animal penning . . . . So all there is at Çatalhöyük are houses and middens and pens. There is none of the functional differentiation that we normally associate with the term 'town'. Çatalhöyük is just a very large village – it pushes the idea of an egalitarian village to its ultimate extremes . . . . In a modern town we would expect to identify different functional areas and buildings such as the industrial and residential zones, the church or mosque or temples, and the cemetery. At Çatalhöyük all these separate functions occur in one place, the house. (Hodder 2006:95, 98, 99)

After a long history of urban claims for Çatalhöyük, starting with Mellaart's excavations and continuing to the present day (Smith et al. 2014b), Hodder's remarks are the most insightful and judicious comments on its urban status. While its population density was quite high (ca. 200 persons per ha), higher than many cities, the overall population was low; my estimate is 2,800 persons (see Chapter 3 and Appendix A). There are no identifiable urban functions at the site and few traces of social complexity above the household level. This was a nucleated village full of farmers; in other words, an agrotown. I puzzle over the question of why anyone (e.g., Taylor 2012) would claim that this site was urban, after such a clear discussion by Hodder.

Comparative Insights. Although not an "urban" settlement by any of the common definitions, Çatalhöyük is crucially important for our understanding of premodern urbanism. First, it shows that Neolithic villages could be quite densely packed, with closely spaced houses that look urban (compare Figures 1.1 and 1.7). Second, the detailed high-definition approach to fieldwork in Hodder's project reveals that a nonurban settlement can have complex household organization with elaborate aesthetic and ritual components. And third, Çatalhöyük shows that the press and the public can easily fall for inflated archaeological claims and that such ideas can have a deleterious effect on scholarship for decades (Smith et al. 2014b).

Semi-urban Settlements: Partially Urban Settlements

In 2015, I published a paper with seven students (Smith et al. 2015) that examined a number of what we called "semi-urban settlements" to show that neighborhood organization is an urban universal. We defined *semi-urban settlements* as "places where large number of people come together, whether forcibly or voluntarily, in special-purpose settlements that lack many of the features characteristic of cities" (Smith et al. 2015:173). This is not an ideal definition. The important features of these settlements become clear when they are considered under two separate categories: voluntary camps and practical machine sites.

Voluntary camps are temporary campsites, away from existing settlements, where people stay for short periods for reasons of religion or recreation.

Examples include religious revival camps, protest camps, and festival camps such as the Burning Man festival. Examples from both categories of semi-urban settlements existed in the distant past. Egyptian workers compounds (Kemp 1987) were practical machine sites, parallel to contemporary company towns. Hunter-gatherer aggregation sites can be considered as voluntary camps. Semi-urban settlements provide insights into settlement and urban processes that can be difficult to observe in ongoing urban settlements. For example, how large does an informal settlement have to be before rules and regulations are required to prevent harm and chaos? Perhaps surprisingly, the Burning Man festival provides a specific answer to this question (Case Study 7). I discuss voluntary camps in Chapter 3 as a natural experiment to examine the effects of population density on human gatherings, independent of other urban-like features.

The label *practical machine sites* is taken from the work of Kevin Lynch (1981). They are settlements established by the state or another dominant institution in order to accomplish a specific task; examples include military forts, company towns, and refugee camps. Japanese-American internment camps from World War II show some of the common features of practical machine sites (Figure 1.8). Such settlements are built in a hurry, often with an orthogonal planned layout. They tend to be isolated from existing population centers, often surrounded by a wall or fence. Compared to other cities, they lack urban functions and have a lower degree of social complexity. I discuss these settlements in Chapter 4 as a second natural

1.8. Japanese internment camp (Camp 2) at Gila River, Arizona. Courtesy National Archives, photo no. 210-G-2049M. Photograph by Francis Stewart, War Relocation Authority. Public domain. Source: Wikimedia Commons https://commons.wikimedia.org/wiki/File:Gila_River_Relocation_Center,_Rivers,_Arizona._A_panorama_of_the_northwest_section_of_Camp_Two_at_t_._._._-_NARA_-_538649.tif.

experiment, one that analyzes the effects of strong top-down administrative control on settlements.

MY BASIC MODEL

Figure 1.9 shows how these various concepts and processes fit together as an informal model of the forces that shaped urban life in the distant past. Box A contains the most important drivers of early urbanism and urban life: population size, population density, and energized crowding. In Chapter 2, I review the history of human settlements, using energized crowding as a unifying theme, and I examine population size and density in detail in Chapter 3. These forces of demography and interaction generate commonalities among early settlements. That is, they operate in a similar fashion and produce parallel effects, in different settings. The settlement scaling research I review in Chapter 3 presents quantitative evidence for the near-universal effects of energized crowding on systems of settlements.

Box B contains political and social institutions, reviewed in Chapters 4 and 5. Institutions are fundamental drivers of structure and change in premodern cities. Early political and economic systems varied widely around the world, and institutions account for much of this variation and are strong

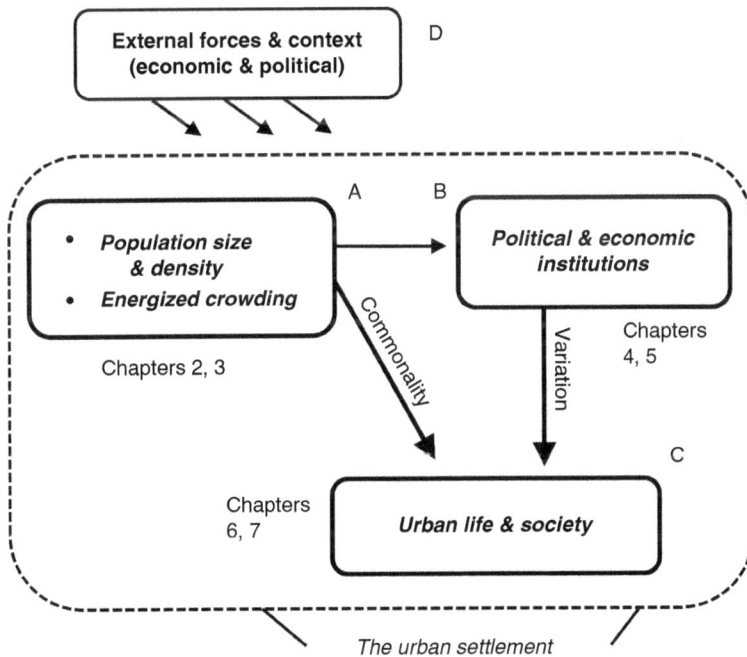

1.9. The structure of my argument. This diagram outlines some of the important factors that influenced urban life in premodern cities.

forces shaping urban life. Whereas the processes in box A lead to common-alities among cities and urban systems, those in box B generate variation. Roman cities are quite different from, say, Maya cities, largely because the political and economic institutional contexts of these societies were radically different.

Population and institutions determined the nature of urban life in premod-ern cities (box C). Some of the processes are covered in Chapters 3–5, leading up to a targeted discussion of urban life in Chapters 6 (top-down processes) and 7 (generative, or bottom-up forces). All of the processes and institutions in early settlements were strongly influenced by economic and political conditions and forces outside of the settlement (box D). Indeed, this is a central tenet of the functional approach to urban definition.

THE CONTEXT OF THIS BOOK

A New View of Cities and Urbanism

This book presents a new view of past cities and urbanism. I have been developing this perspective over the past decade and a half in my publi-cations and my blog, *Wide Urban World*.[9] My perspective includes both an empirical domain (cities around the world, in the past and the present) and a conceptual domain (the realm of social scientific concepts, applied using a rigorous epistemology). I summarize the main principles of my perspective as follows:

1. *A strongly comparative approach* that includes premodern cities, contempor-ary cities, and semi-urban settlements, through deep time and around the world. If comparison is to accomplish anything beyond a simple recognition of similarities or differences, then a rigorous comparative method is required (Smith 2012b; M. E. Smith 2018).
2. *An analytical focus on settlements and their dimensions.* It is more useful to analyze and compare specific topics or dimensions, rather than settlements as whole entities.
3. *A scientific epistemology*, as described later.
4. *A social-science perspective* that applies current knowledge and advances to better understand and explain past urban life and its determinants (discussed later).
5. *An emphasis on energized crowding and its generating mechanisms, population size, and processes.*

---

[9] The *Wide Urban World* blog is located at http://wideurbanworld.blogspot.com/.

Epistemological Context

Given that scholars of ancient cities operate from quite diverse theoretical and epistemological perspectives, I should make my own approach clear. Epistemology refers to the logic of explanation (Tilly 2008); it describes how you know what you know. My own epistemology, which derives from the philosophical approach known as scientific realism, differs greatly from the social constructivist approaches to knowledge that are common in the archaeology of ancient cities. In the words of Justin Cruikshank:

> Social constructionism is based on a relativist epistemology, which holds that all knowledge is relative to one's location within a set of social norms. This relativism motivates a radical skepticism towards all knowledge claims, especially from agents in authoritative roles, such as professionals, because social norms are taken to be imbued with power . . . . Given this, the task of research is not to uncover new truths about reality but to unmask supposedly objective knowledge claims by exposing them as symptoms of underlying power relations. (Cruikshank 2012:75)

The social-science method associated with social constructivism is known as *interpretivism*. This refers to "evidence-gathering techniques that are focused on the intentions and subjective meanings contained in social actions" (Gerring 2007:69–70). Social constructivism and interpretivism deny the possibility of the scientific study of objective social reality, a position opposite to my own realist views. These non-realist approaches are part of the movement called *postprocessualism* in archaeology, which in turn derives from an epistemological and ontological perspective – postmodernism – that emphasizes identity, meaning, discourse, deconstruction, and a multiplicity of perspectives. Post-humanist theory is one of the most common expressions of this approach among archaeologists today. Some of the prominent scholars of ancient cities who employ a social constructivist approach (often termed *social archaeology*) are Adam T. Smith (2003), Monica Smith (2003b), Christopher Tilley and Wayne Bennett (2004), Arthur Joyce (2009), Cynthia Robin (2013), and Wendy Ashmore (2015). While these works contain useful data and findings, I have not found their conceptual approach helpful in contributing to the scientific scaffolding I build in this book.

The term *science* is a dirty word for many postprocessualists (Martinón-Torres and Killick 2013). Some claim that we can never really know what happened in the past. Each city – indeed, each household in each city – was unique, and thus any search for scientific regularities is futile. For me, however, science and scientific realism (Bunge 1993; Little 2010) are the cornerstones of how I approach premodern cities. I will give two definitions of *science*, directed at different audiences. My first definition of *science* – meant to show non-scientific archaeologists what I mean by *science* – is summarized in three tenets:

1. Science is a method for gathering knowledge about the natural and social world. It gives primacy to reason and observation.
2. Science has a critical spirit. Claims or hypotheses are constantly tested through observation and experiment, and findings are always tentative, incomplete, and open to challenge.
3. Science is complex. It consists of an interconnected network of diverse evidence and theory, and its content and findings are evaluated by communities of scientists.[10]

Many scientists from the natural sciences will probably find the above definition wishy-washy. They will be less interested in how science differs from humanities-oriented fields and more interested in defining science in terms of what scientists actually *do*. For them, the following definition from biology illustrates that archaeology is indeed a science:

1. Science seeks to organize knowledge in a systematic way, endeavoring to discover patterns or relationship among phenomena and processes.
2. Science seeks to provide explanations for the occurrence of events.
3. Science proposes explanatory hypotheses that must be testable, that is, accessible to the possibility of rejection (Mayr 1982:23), rephrasing Ayala (1968:207).

A key question in evaluating whether a work is scientific or not is, "How would you know if you are wrong?" (Abbott 2004; Haber 1999; Smith 2015). Scientific theories are open to testing, and hypotheses can be proven wrong. Many postprocessualists, on the other hand, use grand theory. This is a highly abstract theory – concerning things like materiality, agency, and meaning – that can never be wrong (Smith 2017b). This feature is a consequence of the basic scientific epistemological hierarchy. At the bottom of the hierarchy are sites, artifacts, and their physical and social contexts. "Data" consist of descriptions and measurements we make of the real world. Low-level theories concern things like the formation of the archaeological record (Schiffer 1987) or reconstructions of past technological processes (van der Leeuw 2012). Middle-range theory describes theories of how society operates, based on causal mechanisms (Calhoun 2010; Demeulenaere 2011; Merton 1968).[11] Much of social science in the past few decades has concerned itself with methods for testing and evaluating middle-range theories.

---

[10] I base this definition of *science* on sources such as Wylie (2000), Sokal (2006), and Kosso (2009). See Smith (2017b) for discussion.
[11] Archaeologists should note that I am not using Lewis Binford's well-known but idiosyncratic concept of middle-range theory as propositions about formation processes (Kelly 2011).

Grand theory, at the top of the epistemological hierarchy, consists of highly abstract and philosophical propositions about how the social world operates. As a high-level construct, such theory is very comprehensive but has low empirical content. Social theories of structure and agency, for example, are abstract formulations that help scholars understand society (e.g., Giddens 1984). But they are far too abstract to actually explain specific social processes and patterns in society. Such theories are abstract perspectives that color one's interpretations, not specific propositions to be tested. Gabriel Abend's (2008) analysis of the different meanings of theory in sociology puts these claims into perspective. Two features that distinguish scientific research in the social and historical sciences from interpretivism and postprocessualism are a concern with causality and the use of quantitative evidence to make arguments. While formal and rigorous causal models (Pearl and Mackenzie 2018) are difficult to construct for the distant past, understanding is improved when archaeologists try to determine causality whenever possible.

Explicit research questions are crucial for a scientific approach to the past. Questions should be clear and anchored in one or more bodies of theory. They need to be operationalized in archaeological terms such that specific propositions can be tested with our data and found to be supported or rejected. Different research questions call for different definitions (of cities and other phenomena), which helps avoid the problem of reification of cities.

Social Scientific Context

This book presents a comparative and interdisciplinary approach to premodern cities. My interests in urbanism have expanded far beyond my disciplinary training and early professional work in anthropological archaeology. As my reading expanded to include other disciplines, I discovered two things. First, my own field – anthropology – lacked the concepts for an adequate study of cities and urbanism, modern or ancient (Smith 2011c). Second, fields from sociology to economics to urban planning have concepts and models that can help illuminate the nature of ancient cities. Lamentably, I have found that few of my archaeological colleagues – particularly the postprocessualists – even know what the social sciences are. There are claims that archaeologists need to decide whether to affiliate with the natural sciences or with the humanities (Sørensen 2017). This old "two cultures" argument (science versus humanities), popularized in the 1950s by C. P. Snow (1959), still drags on, even though the social sciences established themselves long ago as distinctive disciplines with rigorous yet distinctive epistemologies (Kagan 2009). I question the relevance of the outdated "two cultures" argument to archaeology in Smith (2017b). The present book is positioned squarely within the social sciences and the historical sciences.

I draw upon a number of disciplines to make sense of premodern cities. My theoretical approach aligns with works called "political economy" in archaeology and anthropology (Earle 1997; Feinman and Nicholas 2004; Roseberry 1988; Smith 2004). Under this umbrella, I make use of an eclectic group of theories and models, including collective action theory (Chapter 4), human behavioral ecology (Chapter 2), and complex systems theory (Chapters 6 and 7). Particularly important for this book is settlement scaling theory (Chapters 2 and 3), which is one component of a new approach to the scientific study of urbanism (Bettencourt and Lobo 2019; Lobo et al. 2020). The foundation of my approach is the generative role of social interactions among individuals within the built environment. My use of the concept of "energized crowding" comes from the intersection of settlement scaling theory with other research in the social sciences. One of my overall goals is to investigate a variant of Bruce Trigger's claim that "the most important issue confronting the social sciences is the extent to which human behavior is shaped by factors that operate cross-culturally as opposed to factors what are unique to particular cultures" (Trigger 2003:3). I would rephrase this statement to ask, to what extent were cities shaped by (1) factors that operate throughout time and around the world; (2) factors that are limited to particular cultures or areas; and (3) unique and idiosyncratic factors?

Answers to questions like this require data from many different cases, and such data need to be analyzed using comparative methods. Comparative analysis is one of three fundamental social science research strategies identified by Ragin and Amoroso (2011); the others are qualitative analysis and quantitative analysis. I have discussed the importance of comparative analysis in archaeology in other publications (Smith 2012b; M. E. Smith 2018; Smith 2020b); see Chapter 8. A key point is that comparison – in archaeology or any other realm – requires simplification (Drennan and Peterson 2012; Healy 2017). This principle is a subset of the basic tenet that "science seeks to organize knowledge in a systematic way, endeavoring to discover patterns or relationship among phenomena and processes" (Mayr 1982:23). This effort only makes sense if one is comparing cases using simplified measures and variables.

PREMODERN CITIES AND URBANISM TODAY

Present to Past: The Use of Analogy

Cities and settlements today are a source of ideas and analogies that archaeologists use to interpret ancient cities. Archaeological remains – bones, potsherds, buildings, soil, pollen, rocks, and such – provide very little *direct* evidence of life in the past. Archaeologists build arguments about ancient life and society using analogies. We start with information about material culture in contemporary or historical societies – how people use artifacts or spaces – and apply this knowledge to archaeological evidence from ancient societies, using analogical reasoning. Sometimes this has been done in a hasty or haphazard fashion; however, there are in fact clear guidelines for making these arguments more rigorous (M.E. Smith 2018; Smith n.d.; Wylie 1985). Arguments by analogy use what is known as inductive logic.

I will illustrate the use of inductive logic, or analogy, with an example. Archaeologists infer that temporary marketplaces were set up in the plazas in ancient Mesoamerican cities. Here is the basis for that inference in outline form. First, we know from ethnography and history that many modern peasant communities in Mesoamerica have open plazas that spring to life once a week as periodic marketplaces. We start by assembling contextual evidence for similarities and differences between the ancient and modern settings. The more similarities, the stronger the argument. Modern plazas are formal rectangular areas in the center of the settlement, often next to the church; the ancient plazas have a similar form and placement, although they are next to a pyramid, not a church! The modern communities are parts of regional market systems, where merchants travel among communities and set up at each one on its weekly market day. Written evidence from a few pre-Spanish communities describe the presence of similar markets and merchants. Also, analysis of household artifact assemblages from the archaeological sites suggests that goods were obtained through market exchange (Stark and Garraty 2010). Given this series of similarities between the ancient and modern features, we infer that the two sets of features had similar uses – that is, the ancient plazas were likely settings for periodic markets.

This argument began with a hypothesis (the plaza-as-market idea), which was strengthened and supported by assembling contextual and other information on the two settings. Finally, a conclusion was drawn. Inductive arguments are never absolute; they can be proven wrong but not proven correct (Copi 1982). But, such arguments can be judged as strong or weak. The more contextual and supporting evidence we can assemble, the larger the number of cases, the stronger the conclusion will be. This kind of argument by analogy underlies most of the interpretations of ancient cities in this book (M. E. Smith 2018; Wylie 1985). One difficulty in using analogical arguments in research on ancient cities is choosing among modern or historical examples for the analogy. I used twentieth-century peasant villages for the plaza analogy; had I tried to argue for markets in the past by using the architectural features of modern banks, however, the analogy would probably not have been very appropriate or useful.

Past to Present: The Contemporary Relevance of Ancient Cities

The archaeological study of early cities is at a productive stage, with better methods and concepts leading to major advances in understanding past urbanization (Fisher and Creekmore 2014; Marcus and Sabloff 2008). Archaeologists are now assembling data on ancient cities that are sufficiently rigorous and informative to be able to make comparisons with cities of the modern world. I make three arguments for the relevance of these results for scholars of contemporary urbanization: the urban trajectory argument, the sample size argument, and the laboratory argument (Smith 2010b, 2012d).

The urban trajectory argument arises from *the* major advantage of archaeological data for broader realms of scholarship: We have information on cities and societies over quite long periods in the past. Today, urban sustainability is judged by practices that people think might possibly increase sustainability in the future (Pijawka and Gromulat 2012). For archaeologists, sustainability is judged by persistence through time: Did a city last for ten years or ten centuries (Smith et al. 2021b)? If archaeologists can establish the dynamics and causal mechanisms that allowed some cities to thrive for long periods while others were more ephemeral, this knowledge could illuminate key urban issues today. Most urban scholars today, however, either pay no attention at all to premodern cities or discount their potential relevance for their research (Harris and Smith 2011). I return to the topic of urban sustainability later.

The sample size argument is a simple one: by considering ancient cities along with recent and contemporary cities, scholars increase the size of their sample of cities (for whatever purpose). Increased sample size helps distinguish unique or unusual patterns from those that are widespread. If planners are looking for examples of cities with particular traits (wide avenues, or green space, or a particular kind of neighborhood), throwing ancient cities into the mix can only improve our understanding. Most urban planners today would consider a city without streets an impossibility or absurdity. Yet many ancient cities – such as most of the Classic period Maya centers – lacked streets. Perhaps these premodern cities have lessons for the shantytowns that spring up around cities in the developing world today.

The laboratory argument focuses on the role of ancient cities as case studies – laboratories – for the evaluation of scientific hypotheses. Hypotheses devised from the study of contemporary cities can be tested against archaeological evidence if the variables can be operationalized archaeologically. Settlement scaling analysis is a good example. First worked out for contemporary cities, the quantitative predictions of the scaling models (Bettencourt 2013) were then applied to archaeological data on ancient settlement systems (Ortman et al. 2014); see Chapter 3. This exercise revealed that the processes that generate consistent outcomes in cities today also operated in past systems, thereby extending the scope of the theory – and our understanding of urbanism – considerably. I return to these three arguments in Chapter 8.

Ancient Cities and Urban Sustainability Science

This growing recognition of the relevance of ancient cities to contemporary urban studies comes at an opportune time. The fields of sustainability science (Clark and Harley 2020; Matson et al. 2016) and urban science (Acuto et al. 2018; Ortman et al. 2020a) are merging into a new discipline, urban sustainability science (Lobo et al. 2021; Ramaswami et al. 2018). This development has the potential to incorporate historical and comparative perspectives (Lobo et al. 2021), based on the argument that any general scientific model of cities or urban phenomena must incorporate the entire range of cities, through history and around the world.

One of the pressing issues in urban sustainability science is how cities will adapt to the effects of global warming (Egerer et al. 2021; Revi et al. 2014). Rising sea levels (Siders 2019), declining urban populations (Slach et al. 2019), and growing poverty and inequality (Noble and Huq 2014) are some of the consequences of climate change today. Where can scholars and policy makers find examples of cities that have dealt with shocks, stresses, and environmental changes? The archaeological and historical record is the only source of empirical evidence on how cities have adapted to – or failed to adapt to – serious challenges. The findings on early urban life reported in the chapters that follow can serve as inputs into models of urban adaptations through time.

My use of the phrase *wide urban world* is one way I try to transcend the divide that separates the distant past from the present in order to produce a broader understanding of cities, urbanism, and settlements more generally. But, any such comparisons have to be done with an appreciation of the very real differences between the contexts of ancient and modern cities. In many ways, cities today are very different from cities in the past. However, in other ways, they are quite similar. One of my tasks in this book is to explore this issue. I have written this book in part to exemplify the words of some smart and virtuous people:

> "The farther back we look, the farther ahead we can see." (Winston Churchill)

> "It's very hard to know where you're going if you don't know where you've been." (Sandra Day O'Connor)

TWO

THE PREHISTORY OF ENERGIZED CROWDING

E NERGIZED CROWDING IS A KEY PROCESS — A CAUSAL MECHANISM — that shapes the development and operation of human settlements. Ample research in economics and geography corroborates the importance of energized crowding in cities today (Glaeser et al. 2003; Storper and Venables 2004). Settlement scaling research on contemporary cities (Chapter 3) provides clear evidence not only for the dynamic role of energized crowding but also for the rather precise quantitative form of its outcomes. When my colleagues and I of the Social Reactors Project[1] extended settlement scaling work back to ancient settlements, we found similar results, including the same quantitative patterns in medieval cities, in ancient cities, and even in ancient village settlement systems. But the role of energized crowding is not universal. Hunter-gatherer settlements from the modern world do not show these effects and, in all likelihood, neither did ancient hunter-gatherer systems.

In this chapter, I trace the prehistory and history of energized crowding as a causal factor in human settlement systems. After reviewing the process in general, I turn to the settlements of hunter-gatherers. Most hunter-gatherer societies are mobile, not sedentary, and it is no surprise that the dynamics of their settlements and society are radically different from those of agricultural societies. I then look at the advent of domestication and agriculture, as they

---

[1] This research project is discussed at greater length in Chapter 3. See www.colorado.edu/socialreactors/.

relate to the early sedentary villages of the Neolithic era. Sedentarization – the process by which mobile groups settle down into year-round permanent villages – was a key development in human cultural evolution. I examine how energized crowding relates to the built environments of settlements. As suggested by Winston Churchill, "we shape our buildings and thereafter they shape us." The built environment can promote or constrain energized crowding, just as energized crowding in turn influences the built environment.

ENERGIZED CROWDING

Social interactions between individuals have social, political, and economic consequences.[2] Within a given location, the number and intensity of social interactions increase with both the number and the density of interacting people. *Energized crowding* is the process that occurs when large numbers of face-to-face social interactions take place within a settlement. The number and intensity of interactions amplify the results of individual social interactions, resulting in a variety of social and economic changes and outcomes, both positive and negative. In other words, the interactions that comprise energized crowding have generative power. My argument for the causal importance of energized crowding has three parts: (1) face-to-face social interactions have important social and economic effects in human societies; (2) the intensity of these effects is dependent on the size of the interacting group; (3) settlement scaling research provides quantitative evidence to support the first two claims. Here I discuss the first two parts of the argument; I leave the scaling research for Chapter 3.

Face-to-Face Social Interactions Have Important Social and Economic Effects

Face-to-face social interactions lie at the root of social, political, and economic structure and change. There is a growing consensus in the social sciences that this is so, but archaeologists have been slow to acknowledge the crucial role of face-to-face interactions. To take an example (elaborated in Chapter 6), nearly all social scientists agree that common participation in religious ceremonies contributes to social cohesion and solidarity among the participants. The social interactions view can be traced back to Emile Durkheim – one of the founders of sociology and anthropology – who concluded that this cohesion arises directly from the social interactions and the common physical activities of the

---

[2] Here is a technical definition of *social interactions* from an economist: "Social interactions refer to particular forms of externalities, in which the actions of a reference group affect an individual's preferences. The reference group depends on the context and is typically an individual's family, neighbors, friends or peers. Social interactions are sometimes called non-market interactions to emphasize the fact that these interactions are not regulated by the price mechanism" (Scheinkman 2008).

participants (Durkheim 1947). The coordinated physical actions of a group of people participating in a ritual, and the communication during and about such actions, are seen as the very forces that create cohesion and integration. The alternative, non-Durkheimian, view – popular among many archaeologists – is that the fundamental forces in society are the ideas in people's minds; therefore, shared beliefs in myths, gods, and concepts like social identity are what bind ceremony participants together. A large volume of empirical data, however, support the claims of the Durkheimian interaction perspective (Kertzer 1988; Turner 2003). In the words of sociologist Erik Klinenberg (2018:11), "It's long been understood that social cohesion develops through repeated human inter-action and joint participation in shared projects, not merely from a principled commitment to abstract values and beliefs."

Whereas scholars working in the Durkheimian tradition view social inter-actions as creating cohesion or social solidarity, economists have given inter-actions a more dynamic and generative role: they are a source of economic growth and change. Geographers Michael Storper and Anthony Venables (2004) identify four positive economic effects of face-to-face interactions in cities: (1) direct conversation is a communications technology that is more flexible and powerful than writing or digital media for many purposes; (2) direct social interactions build trust in social relationships; (3) such interactions help individuals evaluate the performance of others and contribute to socializa-tion; (4) face-to-face interaction is a performance that creates sociability, friendship, and other positive social outcomes.

The role of social interactions in generating change and positive outcomes is shown by research in a variety of fields of study. Economists have shown that "for many jobs, even highly intellectual jobs, working face-to-face increases product-ivity" (Glaeser and Cutler 2021:22), and this greater productivity is widespread in cities and society (Glaeser et al. 2003; Scheinkman 2008). Urban geographers have published on the numerous benefits of urban face-to-face interactions (Storper and Venables 2004). Similar results on the benefits of social interactions within settle-ments come from dual inheritance models of cultural evolution in anthropology (Henrich 2016:213–218), cognitive approaches to ancient religion (Whitehouse and Lanman 2014), structuration theory in sociology (Giddens 1984:70), and collective action research (Blanton 2016; Ostrom 1990). Here I argue that the generative role of social interactions is fundamental to the way energized crowding works. And energized crowding is fundamental to the social processes in cities and settlements. Glaeser and Cutler (2021:24) push this process back to ancient Greece – "Cities have been engendering miracles of collaborative creativity since Socrates and Plato bickered on an Athenian street corner" – but in this chapter, I show that it is far deeper historically. In Chapter 7, I discuss face-to-face social interactions and energized crowding as examples of one of the two major categories of generative processes that were important in premodern cities: self-coordination;

the other category, self-governance, refers to the deliberate collaborative grass-roots activities of the sort discussed by Graeber and Wengrow (2021). This distinction is discussed in Moroni et al. (2020).

The Intensity of Energized Crowding Increases with Population Size and Permanence

The growing population size and density of settlements, either together with or independent of processes of aggregation and urbanization (i.e., people moving into settlements), creates the conditions for increased energized crowding. It is a simple fact that the number of potential interactions increases exponentially with the number of individuals in a group (Fletcher 1995; Mayhew and Levinger 1977; Thomas and Mark 2013). As a result, the consequences of such interactions have the potential to increase exponentially as well. That is, the tangible outcomes from energized crowding can grow rapidly as the relevant population grows. In Durkheim's (2014) earliest book, *The Division of Labor in Society,* he used the term *moral density* to describe the social consequences of social interactions. In the words of sociologist Jonathan Turner: "For Durkheim, population size and growth increase material density, as do communication and transportation technologies that 'reduce the space' between individuals. Increased material density, Durkheim continues, magnifies the moral density or rates of interaction among individuals" (Turner 2003:15).

Settlements are places where energized crowding takes place. Following the logic of Durkheim, Fletcher, and other theorists, I argue that larger settlements exhibit higher rates of energized crowding than do smaller settlements. Durkheim wrote that increased social interactions lead to greater emotional arousal, particularly in ceremonies (Turner 1990). Today, social scientists focus on more mundane and tangible outcomes of social interactions. Towns or cities, for example, have been described using metaphors such as "social reactors" (Bettencourt 2013) or "electric transformers." Historian Fernand Braudel wrote that "towns are like electric transformers. They increase tension, accelerate the rhythm of exchange and constantly recharge human life" (Braudel 1981:479). Urban planning scholars Kim Dovey and Elek Pafka emphasize that this energizing feature of cities is based not solely on the density of occupation but also on the synergies of social interactions:

> Urban 'intensity' can be defined as the experience of intensive encounter in public space that may or may not emerge under conditions of density. Intensity differs from density in being a synergistic effect that is more than the sum of its parts. While density is about volumes of people, jobs, floor space and buildings, intensity is more like the 'temperature' of a city, albeit one that cannot be easily measured. Intensity is an emergent effect of the connections, alliances, interactions and differences between the people, practices and built forms that comprise the city. (Dovey and Pafka 2014:72)

Energized crowding and the effects of increased social interactions need time to develop. One-time meetings, or interactions over a period of days or even weeks, rarely have sufficient duration to create the outcomes and effects summarized later in this chapter. Scholars have yet to determine just how long the processes of face-to-face interactions need to endure before energized crowding sets in. (The voluntary camps discussed in Chapter 3 have some insights here.) My guess would be that the threshold is on the order of months — long enough to organize activities, establish routines, and set up channels for individuals to coordinate with others within a new settlement.

The Effects of Energized Crowding

The myriad results and outcomes of energized crowding can be grouped under three categories: interaction stress, community formation, and economic growth (Figure 2.1). *Interaction stress* refers to a variety of negative social outcomes at the city or community level that arise from growing populations and densities within settlements. These range from increased crime and poverty to social anomie and distrust of others. *Community formation* describes the creation of place-based socially cohesive communities. This occurs in villages (where the entire village is the community), but in larger settlements community formation occurs through the division of settlements into smaller units. Neighborhoods and local communities arise as settlements grow. When people

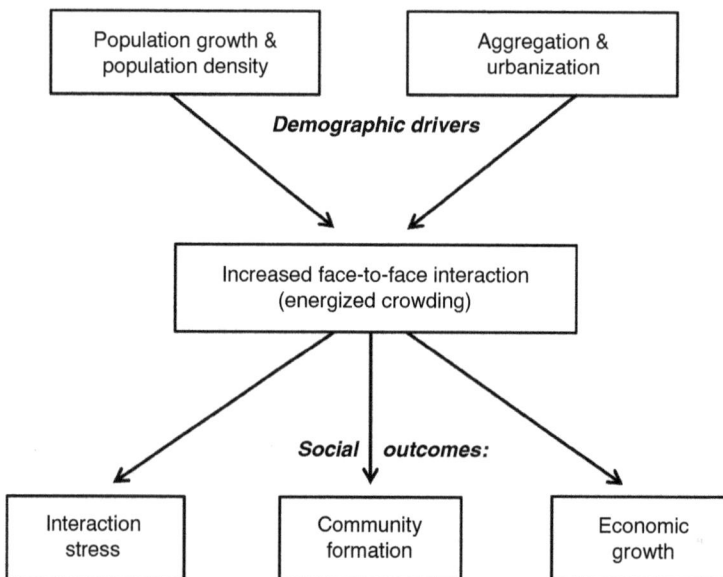

2.1. Energized crowding. Graphic by Michael E. Smith. Modified after Smith (2019a:39).

live in large, dense settlements, they invariably work to establish smaller contexts – neighborhoods – that allow them to live their lives on a scale smaller than the entire settlement. *Economic growth* refers to the increased outcomes in production and wealth that come from intensified social interactions. These three outcomes of energized crowding are explored in more detail in Chapter 3.[3]

In many ways, the positive and negative outcomes of energized crowding cannot be separated. Glaeser and Cutler (2021) remind us that "the same physical proximity that enabled Socrates to talk to Plato also enabled the flow of the Athenian plague" (p. 26) and note "the age-old urban bargain, where the city provides its choicest gifts – the interactions that bring us joy and make us rich and creative – in exchange for the risk of death by contagion" (p. 27). I now turn to the earliest human settlements, long before the processes of energized crowding emerged.

HUNTER-GATHERERS AND THE EARLIEST HUMAN SETTLEMENTS

Our ancestors lived as mobile hunter-gatherers for hundreds of thousands of years, moving their settlements periodically in order to take advantage of the wild plants and animals in a given environment. The hunting-gathering life-style has been hotly debated over the years. An older view – that these groups were constantly at the edge of starvation and death, and thus eager to adopt agriculture when they could – was replaced in the mid-twentieth century with the concept of the "earliest affluent society" (Sahlins 1972). This concept implies that hunter-gatherers would not want to adopt agriculture because their workload would increase and their health decline if they started farming. Reality, not surprisingly, is somewhere in between these polar extremes.

Can archaeologists use ethnographic studies of contemporary hunter-gatherer societies as models or analogs for the distant past? Those who answer in the negative emphasize that hunter-gatherer societies today have been influenced by nation-states and the capitalist economy. Furthermore, these societies have been forced into marginal environments that are not comparable to early times (Kelly 2013). Those who give a positive reply note that while modern hunter-gatherer societal patterns and lifeways cannot be projected directly onto the ancient past, contemporary hunting-gathering societies "do allow us to understand inter-actions under some of the conditions believed to have characterized our evolu-tionary past" (Wiessner 2014:14028); see also Boehm (2012). Here, I follow common archaeological practice in using key information about contemporary hunting groups to illuminate the settlements of our early ancestors. A major

---

[3] It is interesting to note that in a recent radical re-thinking of the nature of archaeological theory, Kristian Kristiansen (2014:21) places "interaction and networks" at "the central part, the axle of the wheel."

distinction is between mobile and sedentary hunter-gatherers. Although reality is more complicated, with a spectrum of degrees of mobility or sedentariness, I will use a simplified mobile/sedentary distinction to discuss the relevant issues.

Mobile Hunter-Gathers

Most hunter-gatherers are nomadic. They have no permanent, year-round settlements. Nearly all agricultural societies, on the other hand, are *sedentary*; that is, their villages are permanent, occupied year-round. I am deliberately leaving aside the issue of seasonal occupations and other temporary patterns of residence in villages for purposes of clarity. Archaeologists have devoted considerable attention to questions of hunter-gatherer mobility and the transition to sedentism (Binford 1978, 1983; Kelly 2013). Two central insights emerge from this work. First, sedentism is more of a continuum than a dichotomy. It incorporates questions such as: How long is a settlement occupied? How many people typically move? How often do they move? Second, hunter-gatherers have established two distinct patterns of movement, called foraging and collecting.

Figure 2.2 illustrates the foraging and collecting patterns. Foragers live in bands of some thirty individuals. They stay together over the course of a year, moving as a group from place to place. Individuals range out to gather plant food (seeds, nuts, fruits), game, and other resources, but they nearly always return to the campsite at the end of the day. The !Kung San peoples of southern Africa are a well-studied group of foragers (Thomas 1989). When they exhaust the food and water in one location, they move their campsite to a new location (Figure 2.2, A).

Collectors have a more complex settlement system (Figure 2.2, B). Their base camps may be occupied for months at a time, often for one or two seasons of the year. Smaller groups move out from the base camp and set up field camps to use particular resources. Some individuals may stay in a hunting stand along a game migration route, or a fishing camp along a river or shore, hunting or fishing for a few weeks (and typically preserving the meat by smoking). Others may go camp near an area of ripening nuts or fruit. The Shoshone of the Western United States are an example of a well-studied collector group (Steward 1941), with summer and winter base camps at different elevations to exploit seasonal resources.

The collector pattern is more sedentary than the forager pattern; more people live for a longer period in the base camps. It also looks more "urban" in its spatial complexity (Figure 2.2). These patterns of mobility have consequences for life and society. First, child spacing and reproductive fertility are important considerations. If a woman bears children too close together in age, it will be difficult to care for them while moving between or among campsites.

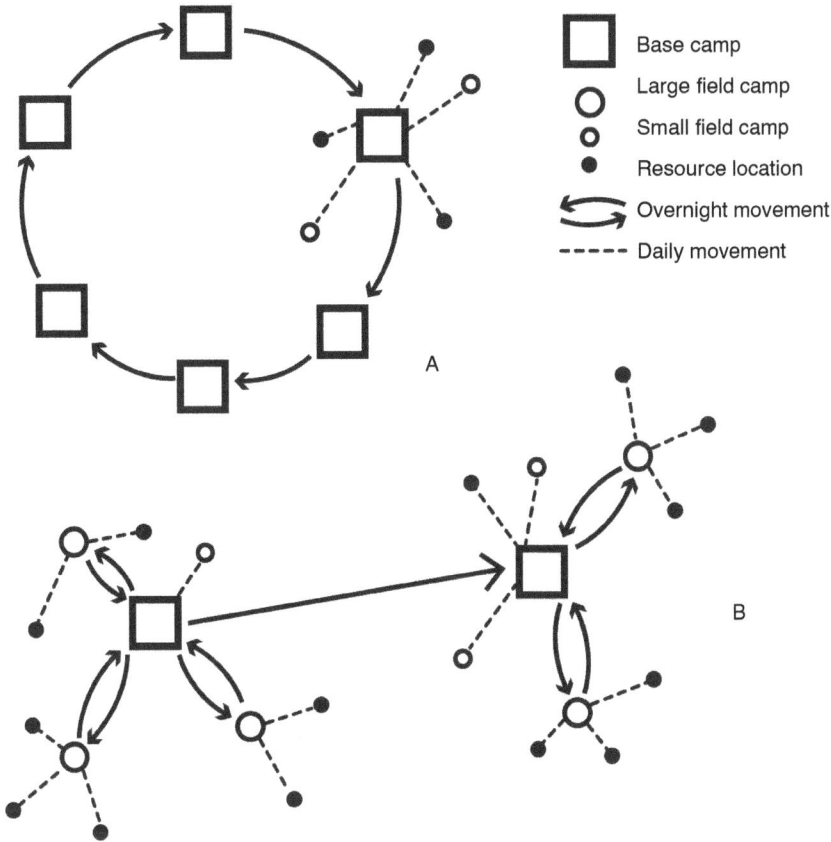

2.2. Hunter-gatherer mobility patterns. (A) foragers; (B) collectors. Graphic by Louise Hilmar, Moesgaard Museum; reproduced with permission.

Research shows that hunter-gatherers have greater birth spacing than do sedentary agricultural societies (Binford and Chasko 1976). Also, if the regional population grows too high, there may not be sufficient food for everyone. Second, mobile hunter-gatherer societies lack private property in terms of land and rarely defend territories against outsiders. It makes more sense to share hunting and gathering ranges. This pattern is predicted by a basic model of territoriality from the field of human behavioral ecology (Dyson-Hudson and Smith 1978). When key resources are abundant and predictable, they are worth defending against outsiders. This leads to the demarcation of land and defense of a territory. Other kinds of resources – those that are less abundant and/or less predictable – are better exploited without a controlled or defended territory. People can travel to find rare, unpredictable resources as needed without worrying about borders and permissions. This is a powerful model that explains many phenomena beyond patterns of hunter-gatherer mobility. For example, in comparison to most hunter-gatherer subsistence systems, just about any agricultural system creates abundant and predictable yields from land that favor protection and regulation for fields. John Bintliff (1999) explores these and additional archaeological implications of this model of territoriality.

A third feature of mobile hunter-gatherer society is lack of privacy, which has implications for settlement layout and the use of space (Wilson 1988). It is not worth the effort for mobile families to construct durable houses, and their hastily built shelters offer little privacy. Most domestic activities – food processing, cooking and eating, childcare, craft production – take place outside, often around hearths. Everybody can see what everyone else is doing. Food is shared among families in two ways. First, many groups have clear rules for doling out portions of meat among the entire band when a hunter returns with major prey, which ensures that differences among hunters in luck and skill are evened out. Second, a practice called "demand sharing" is common; anyone may ask anyone else to share some of their food or perhaps other possessions (Schnegg 2015).

Demand sharing only works in small groups where all members know one another. Hunting or gathering without fixed territories is dependent on small group sizes that have too few people for energized crowding to be much of a factor affecting life and society. There is, however, one kind of settlement where energized crowding begins to be felt: annual aggregation sites (Layton et al. 2012; Shott 2004). Many groups live in small bands most of the year but come together in large gatherings once a year for a variety of reasons. Young adults need to find mates, information needs to be exchanged, and ceremonies need to be carried out. There is trading to be done and disputes to be settled. Some of these aggregation sites are quite large and busy places for a few weeks at a time; I discuss one example in Chapter 3 – the North American Plains Societies – as a type of semi-urban settlement (Case Study 9).

Case Study 3 Pincevent: An Upper Paleolithic Base Camp

The earliest settlements excavated by archaeologists date to the Upper Paleolithic period, ca. 50,000–10,000 BCE, although individual shelters and hearths go back much further in human evolution (to 500,000 BP or earlier). The Magdalenian culture of Europe, whose subsistence was based on reindeer, flourished at the end of the Ice Age (15,000–10,000 BCE). Because of fortunate conditions of erosion and deposition after abandonment, a number of excavated Magdalenian sites are well preserved. The campsite of Pincevent, France, is one of the best-reported examples (Enloe 2003; Julien 2003; Leroi-Gourhan and Brézillon 1973).

Tents, Hearths, and Reindeer Bones. Excavations by André Leroi-Gourhan revealed at least four thin layers of Magdalenian occupation at Pincevent, each with thousands of flint artifacts and reindeer bones. Most artifacts were concentrated in clusters around hearths. The arrangement of the hearths and artifacts, with cleared areas near some hearths, suggested to Leroi-Gourhan that small tents, about three meters in diameter, had been set up next to several of the hearths, with their entrance facing a hearth. The inset in Figure 2.3 shows a reconstruction of one of these hearth-and-tent units. These tents were likely dwellings for individual families.

Case Study 3 (cont.)

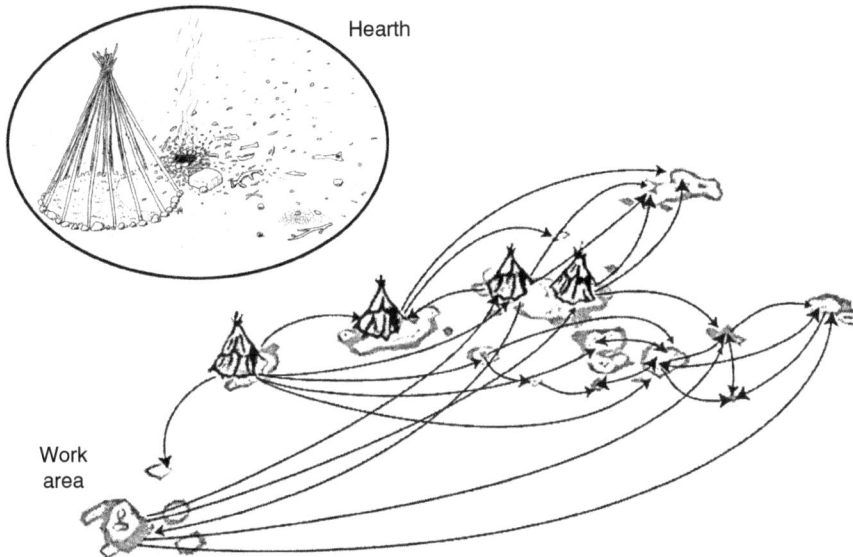

2.3. Pincevent, Upper Paleolithic hunter-gatherer campsite. Graphic by Michael E. Smith. Campsite modified after Julien (2003:109). Tent inset drawn by José-Manuel Benito. Public domain, Wikipedia Commons (https://commons.wikimedia.org/wiki/File:Pincevent_tent.gif).

Ethnoarchaeology refers to the observation of contemporary small-scale societies by archaeologists in order to learn principles to aid in the interpretation of archaeological sites (David and Kramer 2001). Ethnoarchaeological research allowed Lewis Binford (1980, 1983) to work out how hunters and gatherers discard bones and stone fragments when sitting around a campfire eating and working. The debris around the hearths at Pincevent (Figure 2.3, inset) were likely deposited by two or three people sitting around each fire (Julien 2003; Leroi-Gourhan and Brézillon 1973).

Level IV at Pincevent, shown in Figure 2.3, contained four domestic areas, each with a hearth and likely tent. Other concentrations of artifacts – lacking hearths or tents – were the locations of work areas, probably for tasks that either required extra space or left messy or unpleasant remains. Painstaking work on the artifacts from these features concentrated on what archaeologists call *refitting*. Individual fragments are compared to one another, and pieces that came from the same original block of stone or animal carcass are identified. If a chipped stone tool was produced and used at a single location, then all refits would take place within that location. When refits can be made among different locations, however, they demonstrate movement of the materials. The arrows among the different locations in Figure 2.3 show refits from two types of stone and animal bones. This is clear evidence that Pincevent was inhabited by a community of interacting individuals and households.

The animal bones and antlers show that the site was occupied in late summer and fall, but not in the spring. In the words of Michèle Julien, "The site is a genuine base camp, where several hunting groups came together to hunt reindeer during the autumn migrations" (Julien 2003:105).

Comparative Insights. Pincevent was smaller and less permanent than the other case study settlements in this book, yet its population density (33 persons per hectare) was higher than some of the political capitals (see discussion in Chapter 3). The site shows that good preservation, combined with good excavation, can reveal considerable information about hunter-gatherer life in the very distant past. Sites like these were the baseline from which later villages, towns, and cities would develop in the future.

Sedentary Hunter-Gatherers

Most hunter-gatherer societies are mobile owing to the lack of sufficient food in a given region to support a population year-round. People move in order to tap the resources of a larger area. Some hunter-gatherers, however, found those rare environments that could provide a steady, reliable supply of food, and they settled down to become sedentary. This happened in several parts of the world. The Natufian culture of the Near East, where wild wheat grew abundantly, is traditionally regarded as the earliest case. By learning to store the crop, people forged the first known sedentary society in world history, between 12,000 and 9,500 BCE (Boyd 2006). Devising tools and techniques to harvest and process wild wheat and barley, the Natufians inadvertently managed to domesticate these plants, turning them into the domesticated wheat and barley we still eat today.

The best documented sedentary hunter-gatherer societies are the villages of the Northwest coast of North America. The Kwakiutl of British Columbia are a good example (Figure 2.4). In addition to being sedentary, many features of Kwakiutl settlements and society set them off from mobile hunter-gatherers. Population size and density were higher, settlements were larger, chiefs had more power, and status inequalities were pronounced, including slavery. The economy was more complex, with occupational specialists and extensive trade.

2.4. Nahwitti, a settlement of the Kwakiutl people, sedentary hunter-gatherers, on Vancouver Island. Photograph by Edward Dossetter, 1881. Granger.

Material culture was far more elaborate, with more diversity of objects, often with elaborate aesthetic decoration (Boas 1925). These traits are typical of sedentary hunter-gatherers, as studied by ethnographers and archaeologists (Kelly 2013:243).

How were the Kwakiutl and other Northwest Coast societies able to maintain year-round settlements and many of the features of social complexity, while subsisting through hunting and gathering? The short answer is salmon. Fish – tasty and nutritious – were easy to catch on their seasonal migration upstream and smoking preserved the flesh for months. At first, these societies were seen as an exception to the grand but simplistic schemes of mid-twentieth-century cultural evolution (Service 1975). Hunter-gatherers were supposed to live in small, mobile bands with simple societies, while farmers, with rare exception, built large permanent villages with the beginnings of real complexity in the social, political, and economic realms. Archaeologists now have evidence for large, complex, sedentary hunter-gatherer societies at early dates, from several parts of the world – Japan to the Near East (Grier et al. 2006). Phrased in the language of human behavioral ecology, archaeologists came to see that "sedentism is a product of local abundance in a context of regional scarcity" (Kelly 2013:107).

A new way of thinking about these sedentary hunter-gatherers is to suggest that sedentism marked a greater transition in human society than did agriculture (Jennings 2016; Lobo et al. 2022). The traditional perspective points to domestication and agriculture as the important changes, with sedentism as a by-product of the greater productivity of farming. But the kinds of developments long held to be typical of increasing social complexity – larger settlements, inequality, division of labor – are now known to occur in societies that are sedentary yet nonagricultural. And an important part of this social transformation from mobile hunter-gatherers to sedentary societies, whether agricultural or hunting-gathering, was the emergence of energized crowding as a powerful social force. Energized crowding comes from social interactions, not from the surplus created by agriculture. In other words, settlements and their dynamics are fundamental to human societies and their changes through time. In Chapter 3, I will provide quantitative support for this assertion, from recent research on settlement scaling.

EARLY FARMING VILLAGES

When one compares the settlements and social life of Paleolithic hunter-gatherers with those of settled farming villages of the Neolithic period, the contrast is great. Unlike Paleolithic peoples, those of the Neolithic period were sedentary and *not* mobile.[4] They practiced agriculture, which typically has much higher

---

[4] I use the term "Neolithic" to refer to farming societies before the development of states and large cities. Archaeologists often use three primary traits to identify sites of the Neolithic stage: agriculture, sedentism, and pottery.

yields compared with hunting and gathering. Settlements were larger, and there were far more of them across the landscape. People lived in permanent dwellings, and they had more goods with a greater range of tools and technological items. These changes in subsistence, settlements, and technology signal fundamental changes in society, from the development of property rights in land to the beginnings of pronounced wealth inequality. The impact of people on the landscape also changed radically.

When a Magdalenian gatherer or hunter stepped outside of Pincevent to examine the surrounding countryside, he or she would have seen only rather minimal changes from human impact beyond some depletion of the animal and plant populations that the group relied on for food. By contrast, the countryside of Neolithic villages was quite different. Figure 2.5 is an idealized reconstruction of the landscape surrounding a Neolithic hamlet. The houses are larger and more permanent than at Pincevent. Nearby land is cultivated with domesticated crops. The fields are surrounded by fences to keep wild animals out, and livestock pens are fenced to keep the farm animals in and predators out. The total area of the landscape needed to feed the residents of Pincevent would have been quite large, but the area shown in Figure 2.5 includes most of the land needed to support the people living in the houses.

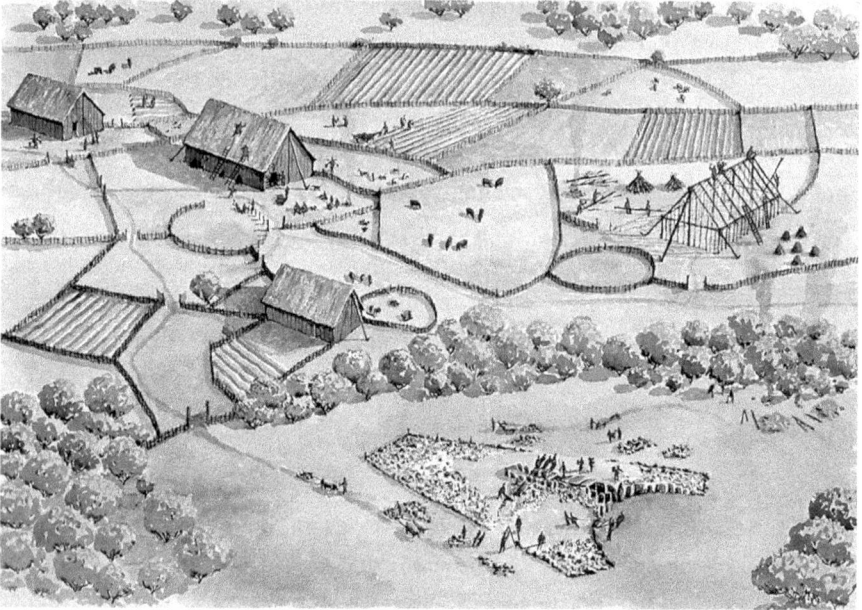

2.5. Reconstruction of a Neolithic farmstead in Ireland. Reproduced courtesy of the Queen's Crown. Copyright Department of Communities, Northern Ireland. Contains public sector information licensed under the Open Government Licence v. 3.0.

Archaeologists used to think this package of innovations developed together, at the same time – a process V. Gordon Childe (1936) described as the "Neolithic Revolution." But, as more refined data were obtained – particularly from excavations in the Near East and Mesoamerica – archaeologists realized that the various components did not develop simultaneously; in fact, the order in which traits emerged varied among regions. In the Near East, for example, sedentism came first, among the hunter-gatherers of the Natufian culture (Bar-Yosef 1998; Maher et al. 2012). These people then domesticated the major plants and animals, and after some time, the technology of pottery-making was developed (Finlayson 2013). In Mesoamerica, by contrast, crops were domesticated by mobile hunter-gatherers, who did not settle down in permanent settlements until the yields of the main crop – maize – had increased significantly. Pottery came last, but unlike the Near East, it was invented shortly after sedentism (Blake 2015; Rosenswig 2015).

These changes – from Paleolithic hunter-gatherers to Neolithic farmers – have significant implications for archaeology: (1) Neolithic villages are much easier to find than are Paleolithic campsites – there are more of them, they are larger, and they have far more artifacts and features; (2) they are easier to reconstruct, giving us a more detailed picture of life in the past.

Why Live in Town? Advantages of Dispersed Settlement

The earliest sedentary farmers probably lived in small hamlets (as in Figure 2.5) and isolated farms. Nucleated villages were not common until some time after the adoption of agriculture. Early farmers almost certainly preferred to live in a dispersed pattern, close to their fields. Proximity to fields had many advantages. It helped to keep pests away from the growing crops and contributed to a stock of knowledge of soils and local conditions that led to improved yields. It was easier to gather fuel and building materials. Farmers living near their fields did not have to spend time walking out from a dense, nucleated village (Silberfein 1989; Stone 1998). Besides, who would want to live in a dirty, unhealthy village? Larger, nucleated settlements were the homes of "small commensal rodents, feces and the absence of latrines, lack of clean drinking water, contamination from humans and animals living in close proximity in closed spaces" (Bocquet-Appel 2011:S506). Indeed, the bacterium that causes the black plague – Yersinia pestis – has now been isolated as far back as the Neolithic period in Europe (Rascovan et al. 2019). Furthermore, cognitive anthropologists have suggested that nucleated village living "must have presented significant problems of its own. Not only ecological but cognitive constraints needed to be overcome before long-term aggregations could be established" (Coward and Dunbar 2014:396). Berrey et al. (2021:15) analyze density and distance factors and conclude that "for early farmers, then, the choice between compact village and scattered-living farmstead living was a pretty even trade-off."

Indeed, skipping ahead to cities, economists have wondered why people would live in cities at all: "If we postulate the usual list of economic forces, cities should fly apart. The theory of production contains nothing to hold a city together" (Lucas 1988:38).

So, why *did* these early farmers move into villages? The most commonly-accepted reason is protection and defense. In the words of anthropologist Glenn Davis Stone (1998:84), "Defense is probably the most prevalent factor that can override the pull toward dispersion." The Southwestern United States is an area where archaeologists have studied the earliest farming villages extensively. This conclusion is common: "We suggest that, in part, the earliest villages in the Southwest formed because population aggregates provided safety in numbers and the perception of security in the context of intergroup violence or the threat of violence" (Wilshusen and Potter 2010). A similar conclusion has been drawn from studies of village formation in the developing world today (Silberfein 1989). Although some archaeologists downplay the role of warfare in early village aggregation (e.g., Peterson and Shelach 2010), most agree that it was a major driving force of the earliest sedentary villages.

Once nucleated agricultural villages developed, things started to change quickly in a number of regions around the world. Population shot up enormously, largely due to both improved crop strains (Lesure et al. 2021) and the greatly increased productivity of agriculture compared to hunting and gathering (Sandeford 2021). But sedentism itself also had important demographic implications. In a phenomenon known as the "agricultural demographic transition" (Bocquet-Appel 2011; Bocquet-Appel and Bar-Yosef 2008), sedentism led initially to a decline in birth spacing, which rapidly produced a population boom (Binford and Chasko 1976). This was followed by a surge in infant mortality, as the negative health factors noted above kicked in. Recent research has attempted to resolve this apparent contradiction between faster population growth and higher mortality rates (Page et al. 2016). Early Neolithic villages joined sedentary hunter-gatherer settlements as the first settings where energized crowding began to occur on more than an intermittent basis.

Energized Crowding and Interaction Stress in Early Farming Villages

At least two of the three outcomes of energized crowding (Figure 2.1) can be shown for Neolithic villages. *Interaction stress* developed because people were not accustomed to living in permanent groups as large as several hundred individuals. The temporary aggregation sites of hunter-gatherers could have this many people, but everyone went back to their small bands after a week or two (Chapter 3). Two tangible outcomes of interaction stress were an increased formalization of space (Fletcher 1995), and the construction of nonresidential community buildings that served to integrate the members of a village into a common whole, thereby reducing interaction stress. Examples from archaeological and ethnographic studies include dance houses, clan houses, and men's houses (Adler and Wilshusen 1990; Flannery and Marcus 2012:chapters 7, 8). People gathered in these places, and the communal focus they engendered contributed to keeping the peace in growing villages. Other changes that helped offset the negative consequences of crowding included increased privatization of space and, in the Near East, a shift from circular to rectangular houses. The new houses made it easier to hide storage facilities from outsiders and more convenient to accommodate changes in family size and structure (Flannery 2002). Another response to interaction stress was for villages to fission, with one group or faction moving off to set up a second village in a new location (Carneiro 1987).

Economic growth, the other visible outcome of energized crowding in early villages, is manifest in a number of ways. Economists Samuel Bowles and Jung-Kyoo Choi argue that the development of farming as a way of life must have been accompanied by the emergence of defined property rights in land. Their logic follows from the territorial model from human behavioral ecology outlined previously (Dyson-Hudson and Smith 1978). If farmers could not be assured continued access to their fields, then it would not be worth the effort to clear and maintain plots to cultivate year after year; therefore, property rights are required. On the other hand, the presence of a valuable and defensible resource (like farmland) is needed in order for property rights to evolve. The implication is that the two developed hand in hand. "The key event here is thus not the 'invention' of farming but the coincidence of sufficiently many individuals adopting both the novel property rights and the new technology so as to overcome the critical mass problem" (Bowles and Choi 2013:8834); see also Bowles and Choi (2019).

This property rights argument implies that complex economic institutions were beginning to develop in these early farming villages. By the time cities became common, urban institutions had proliferated to the point where they account for much of the variation in urban life among cities (Chapters 4, 5, 7). The third general outcome of energized crowding, *community formation*, occurs on only a single scale, the village itself, in early villages because of their small size. Within large settlements communities form on several scales, particularly the establishment or creation of localized place-based communities smaller than the overall settlement (i.e., neighborhoods). One of the few Neolithic examples of this process is the Central European mega-sites discussed later in this chapter.

A growing number of archaeological studies have found that settlement aggregation (often called *nucleation*) leads to changes in society and the economy (Gyucha 2019). The authors of a detailed study of changing Wendat

(Iroquois) villages through time noted, "Our conclusions suggest that settlement aggregation created social settings that led to a dramatic increase in organizational complexity" (Birch and Williamson 2013); see also Bandy (2004). Quantitative support for the emergence of economic growth as a consequence of energized crowding in early villages is provided by the settlement scaling research reviewed in Chapter 3 (Ortman and Coffey 2017); I explore the role of economic growth in Chapter 5.

Case Study 4 Beidha: From Circular to Rectangular Houses

The early Neolithic village of Beidha in Jordan was excavated in the 1950s and 1960s by Diana Kirkbride, who exposed four different occupation layers, all from the "Pre-Pottery Neolithic-B" period (8,500–6,700 BCE). Kirkbride's excavations were meticulous and covered a large area, but she only managed to publish preliminary reports and articles. Later, Brian Byrd organized and wrote up the excavations (Byrd 2005), and these are supplemented by more recent fieldwork (Makarewicz and Finlayson 2018) and detailed analyses of the data (e.g., Birch-Chapman et al. 2017; Byrd 1994).

Architectural Changes at Beidha. The occupation at Beidha is divided into six distinct chronological periods, four of which have yielded architectural plans for the small village. In three periods – A1, A2, and B2 – the houses were simple circular structures. Starting in period A2, each settlement also had at least one public building – a structure larger and different from the houses that was probably not residential in function. Cheryl Makarewicz and Bill Finlayson recently completed the excavation of a large circular public building from period A2, which they interpret as a men's house or other type of community building (Makarewicz and Finlayson 2018). In the final period, C2, house form changed radically. The new houses were two-story rectangular buildings with massive walls and interior corridors. Figure 2.6 shows the plans for periods B2 and C2. Although only a relatively small part of the village was exposed for the earliest periods, it is clear that the circular houses were constructed very closely together, with outer walls touching. Open areas surrounded by houses were probably courtyards, where various activities, including cooking, were carried out.

The switch to rectangular houses in period C2 was quite radical; no traces of the earlier circular structures remain. The new houses have a lower floor or basement excavated into the ground (see the inset drawing) and an upper story slightly above ground level. It appears that people lived in the upper story and used the lower for storage. Just as in the earlier period A2, one building stands out as much larger than the others, with a divergent plan (Figure 2.6); this may have been a shrine or other public building.

The transition from circular to rectangular buildings occurred throughout the Near East during Neolithic times (Flannery 2002; Fletcher 1995). Some perspective on this change is provided by research on contemporary traditional cultures whose members build their own houses. As shown in Table 2.1, circular houses are far more common for migratory peoples compared to sedentary peoples, and for hunter-gatherers compared to agricultural groups (Feather 1996). Probably the best explanation for this pattern has to do with the ways people figure their costs and benefits with respect to construction versus maintenance of houses. Circular houses are easy to build but hard to repair and maintain over a long period. Rectangular houses, on the other hand, are more difficult and time-consuming to build, but their maintenance costs are lower (Diehl 1992; Feather 1996; McGuire and Schiffer 1983).

The Natufian peoples, the first to become sedentary in the Near East, maintained the ancient hunting-gathering tradition of circular houses. This is not surprising, given the strength of the cultural and emotional ties that people have with their homes (Moore 2012). Even after domestication and agriculture, the first few villages at Beidha kept this tradition alive. But by period C2, households needed to store grain, and the two-story rectangular houses allowed stored goods to be kept out of view of other community members. The transition from more visible storage conditions, where everyone's goods are known to the entire community, to more secluded storage inside individual houses was one of the important transitions of the Neolithic period (Kuijt 2011).

Case Study 4 (cont.)

TABLE 2.1 *Circular versus rectangular houses in traditional cultures*

Categories	% of cultures		No. of cultures
	Circular	Rectangular	
Mobility:			
Migratory	86%	14%	14
Sedentary	22%	78%	101
Dependence on agriculture:			
Low[a]	68%	32%	28
High[a]	26%	74%	104

Note: Data from Feather (1996).

a. "Low" indicates that less than 5% of the diet is from agriculture, while "High" indicates more than 55%

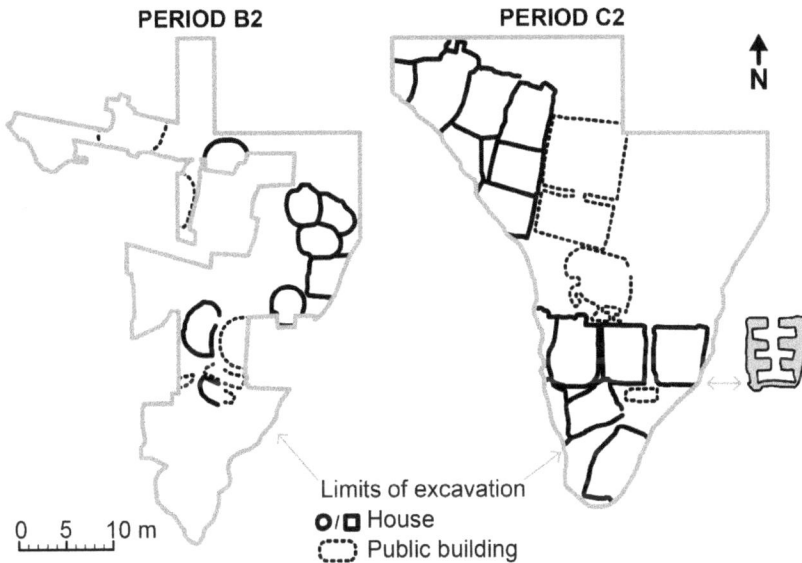

2.6. Plans of villages in Subphases B2 and C2, Beidha. Based on Byrd (2005:186, 192) and Birch-Chapman et al. (2017:10). Drawing by Patrick Fahey.

Comparative Insights. The excavations at Beidha yield a number of insights for understanding the development of early human settlements. First, the site shows an important architectural (and social) transformation at a single settlement over time. Second, it shows the presence of public buildings, important for social integration and cohesion in these newly formed villages. And third, the earliest villages could have remarkably high population densities. The 60 inhabitants in period B2 lived at a density of 300 persons per hectare, and the 180 persons in period C2 lived at a density of 600 persons per hectare (Chapter 3) – much higher than the densities of most of the cities discussed in this book. Interaction stress was probably severe at Beidha, in spite of its overall small size, and key features of the architecture of the site – public buildings and storage spaces – were likely developed in response to the stress of living in extremely high densities.

Variations on Neolithic Villages: Agrotowns and "Mega-sites"

Archaeologists have excavated Neolithic villages in many areas around the world; most were located in the open, not in a rock shelter like Beidha (Flannery 1976; Kuijt 2000; Liu 2004; Simmons 2007). While there is much variation, Neolithic villages do share a number of characteristics. They typically have between a few dozen and several hundred houses. The houses were permanent structures, arranged without any suggestion of central planning. These villages lack evidence for social classes; that is, the houses typically show only modest variation in size or quality, and there are no clear elite buildings (see Chapter 6). Many Neolithic villages do exhibit signs of wealth inequality, though (Kohler and Smith 2018). These villages often had community buildings (as discussed previously), but they lack the kinds of monumental buildings and specialized structures that mark urban functions or governmental institutions.

Against this picture of Neolithic villages, common around the world, some sites stand out for their size or their apparent complexity – agrotowns and the so-called megasites of the Trypillia culture of Ukraine and Moldova. Whereas the agrotowns of Çatalhöyük and Ascoli were basically overgrown villages (Chapter 1), the megasites are striking and unusual settlements at an early date (ca. 5000–3000 BCE). Sites such as Maidanetske (Figure 2.7) have several concentric rings of houses surrounding a large central area. The size and apparent planning of these sites (Maidanetske has 2,900 houses) has led some archaeologists to label them urban settlements, which would make this the earliest urban tradition (Chapman and Gaydarska 2016b; Gaydarska et al. 2020; Wengrow 2015). Although the sizes of the mega-sites fit within the range of both urban centers and agrotowns, they do not conform to any of the definitions of urbanism discussed in Chapter 1.

Gaydarska et al. (2020) propose a novel definition of urbanism that fits the megasites: urban sites are claimed to be those that are significantly larger than other sites in their settlement system. This is not a useful definition, and it would lead to absurdities. It would make the largest settlement in any region "urban" by definition, not following any consideration of functions or demography. These authors also use the term "low-density" to characterize these sites, in spite of their failure to calculate actual population density figures. Ohlrau (2020) makes a series of explicit and reasonable population estimates for Maidanetske, and its density (40 to 50 persons/hectare) fits within the densities of other premodern cities (Chapter 3). In fact, the density of Maidanetske is five to ten times the densities of tropical low-density cities such as Angkor or Tikal (Chapter 3). Nevertheless, just as hunter-gatherer aggregation sites have at least one urban-like trait (population density), so too do the mega-sites, and this suggests that the mega-sites can yield useful insights for the analysis of urbanism.

Based on excavations and radiocarbon dates at these sites, it appears that many houses at these sites were only occupied for short intervals. Estimates for the portion

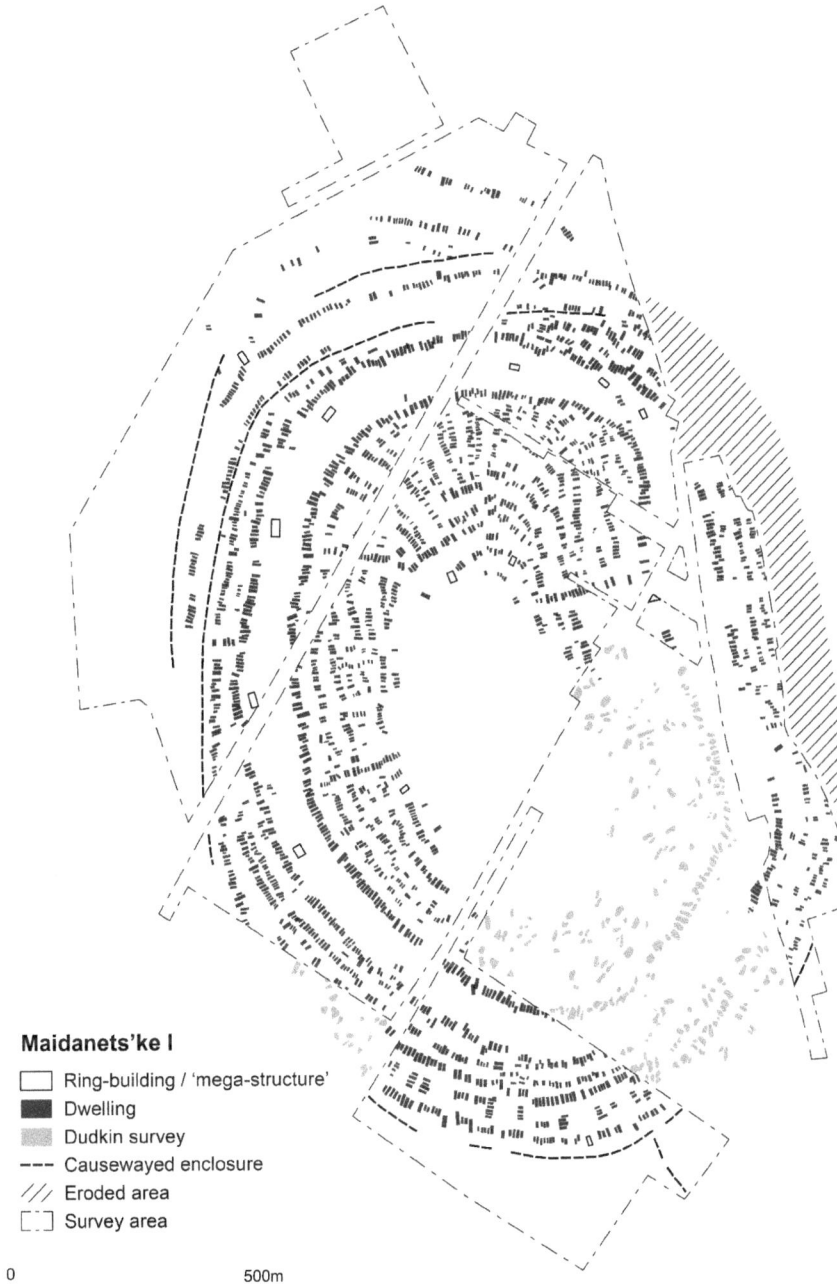

Maidanets'ke I

- ☐ Ring-building / 'mega-structure'
- ■ Dwelling
- ▨ Dudkin survey
- --- Causewayed enclosure
- /// Eroded area
- ⌐⌐ Survey area

0   500m

2.7. Plan of Maidanetske, one of the Trypillia megasites. Figure created by René Ohlrau, modified after Ohlrau (2020:fig. 24). Reproduced with permission.

of the 2,900 houses at Maidanetske that were occupied during a particular period range from about 150 houses for the earliest settlement to 1,600 houses in the period of maximum occupation (Ohlrau 2020). This leads to a population on the order of

7,000–8,000 people during the maximal extent and a density of around 40–50 persons per hectare. Similar to agrotowns, there are no monumental structures or buildings that served a hinterland (which would indicate urban functions), social classes, or political complexity. They do have large buildings that have been interpreted as "integrative architecture" (Hofmann et al. 2019); these are shown on the plan. They were likely community buildings, as discussed previously for Neolithic villages.

WHAT WE *DON'T* KNOW ABOUT THE DEVELOPMENT OF THE EARLIEST CITIES

Perhaps paradoxically, archaeologists may have a better understanding of early sedentism and the formation of the earliest farming villages than we do of the later transitions from those villages to the earliest cities. Even though early cities developed independently in six or seven different regions of the world – all of which have seen considerable archaeological research – our understanding of the rise of the earliest cities remains minimal. On the one hand, cities and states often developed in tandem, making it hard to separate the two processes empirically. On the other hand, a long-standing obsession with state formation has blinded archaeologists to the possibility that cities may have emerged before states, and this obsession continues to hinder conceptual and empirical work on how the two processes were related.

Nearly all models by anthropological archaeologists for the evolution of socially complex societies (societies with cities, institutionalized inequality, and centralized political power) have focused on the emergence of state governments. These models of the "rise of the state" tacitly assume that urbanism simply tagged along; any consideration of urbanism, or of cities as settlements, is almost an afterthought (Feinman and Marcus 1998; Flannery and Marcus 2012; Johnson and Earle 2000). In these and other works by archaeologists, "the notion of 'urban society' often seemed little more than an appendage to the concept of 'the state'" (Cowgill 2004:526). To add to the confusion, some of the foundational works on the development of states were given the label "urban," even though they included little explicit discussion of cities and urbanism per se; these include V. Gordon Childe's concept of the "Urban revolution" (Childe 1950) and Robert McC. Adam's important book *The Evolution of Urban Society* (Adams 1966). I discuss this conflation of states and cities further in Chapter 4.

This confusion of early cities with early states, which often includes the notion that they are part of the same "package" of traits that always develop in tandem, has hindered our understanding of how and why the earliest urban settlements developed around the world. A positive development is that some archaeologists have begun to suggest that urban settlements may have emerged *prior to* the first states (see the previous discussion). If so, then it is possible that urban processes may have been responsible for generating the social changes that created the first states. I build on work by archaeologists such as Elizabeth Graham (1999), David Wengrow (2015), and Justin Jennings (2016) in rejecting the idea that cities and states came as a single package (see Chapter 4). My emphasis on the generative role of energized crowding supports the possibility of pre-state urbanism; state formation increasingly appears to have been a consequence of energized crowding in the earliest, pre-state cities. While we still lack sufficient archaeological data to test this notion adequately, the findings reported in this book can be used to generate hypotheses to help guide fieldwork in the relevant regions.

My focus in this book is not on the origins of the earliest cities.[5] Rather, I concentrate on how premodern cities and settlements were organized, how they worked, and how they fit into their regional and societal contexts. A deeper understanding of these settlements will help archaeologists develop better models of how and why cities originated in the first place.

THE BUILT ENVIRONMENTS OF ENERGIZED CROWDING

High populations and high population densities work together to create conditions of crowding, which in turn generate what can be termed "interaction stress" (Fletcher 1995). This observation is most commonly made with respect to cities today. Scholarly research in two disciplines – environmental psychology and sociology – focuses on the negative individual and group effects of interaction stress; see O'Brien (2011) for a review of this literature. Interaction stress, however, also exists in nonurban settlements. The Neolithic village of Beidha – a very early, nonurban settlement – already shows two features that were most likely responses to density and stress: (1) nonresidential, integrative buildings, and (2) a shift from circular to rectangular houses with hidden storage areas. My discussion here relates to the causal arrow that points from population and energized crowding to urban life and society in Figure 1.9.

Architectural Responses to Interaction Stress

When mobile hunter-gatherers experience interaction stress, bands can split up or individual families can move to join another band, with few economic consequences. When a village (or city) grows too large and dense, on the other hand, the resulting interaction stress must be relieved in other ways. Some people may move away and found a new settlement (leaving behind cleared fields that may contain built agricultural features). Staging of more frequent and

---

[5] A further challenge to studying the earliest urban centers is that many of them are deeply buried under the later occupations of the same site; this issue is emphasized by Monica Smith (2019:58).

more elaborate rituals can help integrate the community. Social changes in the direction of increased complexity – specialization and/or the establishment of social hierarchies – can counteract interaction stress. Or, people can work to increase privacy within the settlement. Justin Jennings (2016:chapter 4) discusses these mechanisms with respect to Çatalhöyük (see Chapter 1). Many of these actions leave archaeological traces. Here, I am most interested in changes to the built environment of settlements that result from the interaction stresses that come in the wake of growing populations and densities.

We have already seen one such architectural change in early villages: the construction of specialized buildings for ceremonial or social use. The key feature of these structures is that they were used by many households within the settlement, and this gave them a role in building social cohesion among the community's residents. The creation of specialized spaces for different activities is a larger phenomenon that helped counteract interaction stress. Architectural scholar Amos Rapoport (1990b) points out that such specialization can be either spatial in nature (different places for different activities) or temporal (different activities at different times in a single location). Another kind of architectural change is the promotion of privacy for individual households, which can be accomplished by the use of larger (and rectangular) houses, or the division of residential space into public and private areas. The creation of walled house lots is yet another example (Figure 2.5). The implications of such changes for archaeology are discussed by Roland Fletcher (1995) and Susan Kent (1990). These changes in the built environment of settlement were not caused solely by population and energized crowding. They were also the result of the growing role of institutions in urban society and life (Chapter 6).

How to Promote Energized Crowding

Interaction stress is the negative face of energized crowding, and its presence typically leads to some of the architectural developments discussed previously. Community formation and economic growth are the positive faces of energized crowding, and they, in turn, lead to other kinds of change in premodern built environments. Scholars have long recognized the value of community formation and economic growth for improving urban life and prosperity (Sen 1999), and many of the built-environmental solutions have been used for millennia.

The role of face-to-face social interactions in promoting *community formation* has been a basic feature of life in sedentary settlements since Neolithic times. The special community buildings at Beidha and other Neolithic villages are an example. Just as these reduce interaction stress, they also promote the formation of cohesive social communities through positive interactions (Chapters 3, 7). These community buildings were an early example of "social infrastructure" – buildings and places where people gather to interact socially, leading to social cohesion and the development of social capital. Today, places like public libraries and open gathering spaces form the social infrastructure of cities (Klinenberg 2018), and their roles are not all that different from the community buildings of Neolithic villages (Adler and Wilshusen 1990). These insights have been incorporated into the principles of the New Urbanism movement for creating livable communities through architecture and settlement design (Congress for the New Urbanism 1996; Talen 2005); see Chapters 3 and 9.

The ways that social interactions generate *economic growth* are more diffuse and abstract than for community formation. Any feature or institution or practice that promotes social interactions within a settlement contributes to this dynamic, including the creation of social infrastructure. Open spaces where people can assemble – whether a formal civic plaza or an empty lot – are settings for the kinds of interactions that have economic implications. Specialized commercial buildings like medieval exchange buildings and guild halls, or Ottoman caravan-serai, were particularly effective interaction settings for economic purposes, although these structures developed rather late in the history of premodern cities.

City streets can be important venues for social interactions with economic outcomes. For example, the Chinese imperial capital Chang'an in the Tang period had regulations preventing people from congregating in the streets, and commerce was limited to two large official markets. But in the subsequent Song period, the restrictions on movement were lifted, commerce spilled into thousands of shops along the main streets, and the economy boomed (Heng 1999; see Case Study 16). There was a direct relationship between the way people interacted in the streets and shops, and the growth in commercial activity.

I discuss the positive and negative outcomes of energized crowding at greater length in Chapter 3 as they relate to settlement scaling theory, and I explore the nature of premodern economic growth in Chapter 5. But these patterns in the ways that population, social interactions, and the built environments of settlements intertwine turn up throughout the book.

INTO THE URBAN REALM

In this chapter, I have taken us through several major transformations in the prehistory of human settlements. This is a messy story: our ancestors did not develop from mobile hunter-gatherers to urbanites in a single, simple trajectory. Archaeologists have traditionally tracked these changes using sedentism and domestication as measures for the Neolithic revolution (Simmons 2007), and population size and social complexity as measures for the later Urban revolution (Feinman and Marcus 1998).[6]

---

[6] I will assume that Jane Jacobs's (1969) factually incorrect idea that cities preceded agriculture – promoted by some urban geographers who prefer the musings of a cult figure to empirical data (Soja 1996; Taylor 2012) – has been put to rest (Smith et al. 2014b).

Although hunter-gatherer campsites were places of intense social inter-actions (Wiessner 2014), there was little energized crowding. The populations and densities were too small and the settlements too transitory. Energized crowding requires a large population in continuous interactions over a period of months or years. Seasonal aggregation sites certainly produce energized crowding for short periods (as with the Plains Indians aggregation sites; see Case Study 9), although probably not for a sufficient interval to produce its major outcomes (Figure 2.1). A recent application of the settlement scaling framework (Chapter 3) to ethnographic data on modern mobile hunter-gath-erer groups found radically different patterns from those observed in agrarian societies (Lobo et al. 2022). Whereas larger settlements are denser than smaller settlements in nearly all known agrarian societies, mobile campsites show the opposite pattern: smaller sites are denser than large sites. On the other hand, the settlements of sedentary hunter-gatherers – including the Northwest Coast Native Americans (Figure 2.4) – scale like agrarian settlements (i.e., densifica-tion increases with size). The logical conclusion is that the transition from mobile to sedentary settlements was of fundamental importance in our prehis-tory, perhaps even more momentous for people's lives than the change from wild to domesticated resources.

People likely aggregated into the first early (Neolithic stage) villages for reasons of defense. But once stable villages grew up in various parts of the world – based on sedentism and agriculture – they proved fertile settings for the development of energized crowding. This process soon achieved a critical level in Neolithic villages, and I argue that it was the major factor that generated the development of the earliest towns and cities. The nature of these settlements will occupy the rest of this book.

Was the social transition to cities and urbanism a positive or negative development? The ways scholars and others view cities today is divided along these lines. For some, cities are places of crime, poverty, crowding, pollution, and misery; we would be better off without them. But if cities are such horrible places, why does urbanization continue at a rapid pace today? Why are rural peoples still flocking to cities when they must endure the poverty and misery of slums? The reason is that cities are places with jobs, social networks, access to resources, and opportunities for advancement (Glaeser 2011; Satterthwaite 2016). If these positive features do not outweigh the negative features, then current trends of increasing urbanization around the world make no sense at all. The most important positive trait in both contemporary and ancient cities is what economists call *agglomeration economies* – cities are places where the concentration of people and activities in specific places generates wealth and economic growth. Energized crowding is a major component of agglomer-ation economies, and it is the theme of the following chapter.

THREE

THE SIZE OF CITIES AND SETTLEMENTS

WHEN PEOPLE GATHER IN ONE PLACE – WHETHER THEY ARE ATTEN-
ding a two-day festival or living as full-time residents of a city – the
density or crowding together has powerful social effects, both positive and
negative. Larger numbers of people amplify the strength of group actions,
create a sense of community, provide more opportunities and services, and
bring about economic and social expansion. But they also generate crowding,
stress, and social problems, from irritation and anomie to crime, poverty, and
even chaos. Over a century ago, sociologist Georg Simmel (1898:834) observed
that "every quantitative extension of a group requires certain qualitative
modifications and adjustments." This is the theme of the present chapter.
Simmel's observation paves the way for an understanding of how population
size and density affect cities, settlements, and urban life.

I begin with the idea that the size of a group or a society affects many
different domains. I then consider the role of population size and density in
individual settlements. The key concept here is energized crowding
(Chapter 2). Energized crowding, and its growth as populations and densities
increase, has three main outcomes (Figure 2.1): (1) It generates *interaction stress*,
a term that covers a variety of negative outcomes of greater crowding and social
interaction within settlements. (2) Energized crowding leads to the creation of
communities. In cities, such communities take the form of neighborhoods. As
one of the only universal features of cities – throughout deep history and
around the world – neighborhoods are crucial for understanding urban life

and activities. (3) The third outcome of energized crowding is labeled *economic growth* in my diagram (Figure 2.1). I explore a recent development that permits the quantitative measurement of economic growth in cities, both ancient and modern – settlement scaling theory. This emerging body of research is based on the notion that cities are social reactors – they amplify the actions of people to create both positive and negative economic outcomes in settlements. That the predictions of settlement scaling theory are borne out in data on both ancient and contemporary settlements provides confirmation of the role of energized crowding in generating economic growth.

If population and density are so important, then why did whole traditions of low-density cities flourish in several areas of the world? Before my discussion of settlement scaling, I review low-density early cities, and then examine a natural experiment in population density: voluntary camps. A recognition of the powerful effects of the population and density of settlements – as effected through energized crowding and other processes – has profound implications for the current understanding of the development of early complex societies. Specifically, this new understanding supports the views of Justin Jennings (2016) and others that cities and urbanism likely developed *before* the rise of the first state-level societies (Chapter 2). While archaeological data in most regions remain too rough to strongly support or deny his model, the information presented below gives additional support to the new view.

WHY IS POPULATION SIZE IMPORTANT?

The notion that population growth generates effects in premodern cities is an outcome of a long tradition of research on cultural evolution in anthropology and archaeology. Early research explored the population of whole societies. The role of population growth in generating cultural evolution was analyzed by sociocultural anthropologists in the 1950s and 1960s (Carneiro 1962; Naroll 1956). Then, stimulated by Ester Boserup's (1965) work on population and agriculture, archaeologists in the 1970s debated the role of "population pressure" in generating various social changes in the past (Cowgill 1975; Morrison 1994; Spooner 1972). Archaeological consensus settled on two conclusions. First, group size is roughly correlated with ancient sociopolitical complexity (Feinman 2011; Johnson and Earle 2000). Two expressions of this correlation are shown in Figure 3.1. In the first, John Bodley (2003:56) graphs the population thresholds for various scales of sociopolitical organization; these are the vertical bars in the figure. In the second study, Ian Morris (2013:134–135) shows the size of the largest settlement in each of four kinds of political-social unit; these are the circles in the chart.

The second conclusion arising from the population-pressure debate is that population pressure alone was rarely, if ever, the sole driver of large-scale social

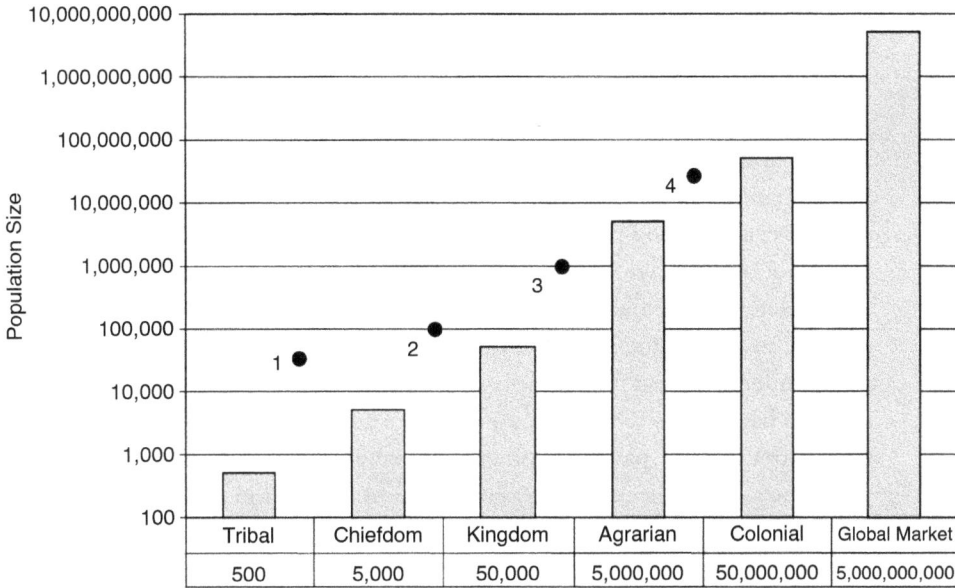

3.1. Social scale and population size. Bars: Total population of social formations. Circles: Size of the largest settlement. (1) Pre-state agricultural society; (2) Agrarian state; (3) Agrarian empire; (4) Industrial society. Bars: Modified after Bodley (2003:56); Circles: Data from Morris (2013:134–135).

change and evolution in the past. In the more limited domain of agricultural intensification and change, Robert Netting (1993) fleshed out Ester Boserup's (1965) model and demonstrated that population growth in small-scale farming communities does generate agricultural and social changes. A recent reanalysis, however, has shown the limitations of Boserup's model of agricultural intensification (Sandeford 2021).

A parallel line of analysis led historical sociologist Jack Goldstone (2002, 2017) to develop "demographic-structural theory." This model, elaborated by Turchin and Nefedov (2009), examines the joint roles of demographic variables and macro-sociological variables in generating change in human institutions. Work in other disciplinary traditions, including dual-inheritance cultural evolution (Henrich 2016; Kline and Boyd 2010) and economic history (Erdkamp 2016; Jones 2000), also shows the importance of population size for causing changes in a variety of social and cultural realms. Most of the work covered in this chapter – on the role of energized crowding in generating interaction stress, community formation, and economic growth – is based explicitly or implicitly on the notion that population growth and aggregation are major causes of energized crowding (Figure 2.1). Population and demography work to create similarities in diverse cities – that is, they work in a similar fashion, with parallel consequences. They create many of the similarities among urban centers throughout history and around the world.

If population is so important, why have archaeologists been so resistant to measure or estimate past populations? When I tout the importance of population estimates to my colleagues, I typically get replies like this: "Archaeological population estimates often rest on so many uncontrolled variables and assumptions, that they cannot be meaningfully sustained."[1] But just about *every* social interpretation of past society by archaeologists rests on similar chains (or cables) of what can be called poorly controlled variables and assumptions (Chapman and Wylie 2016). If we were to extend this evidentiary standard to other realms, archaeologists would have to pack up and go home; we would not be able to say anything at all interesting about past societies. I cannot accept this commonly offered reason for the resistance to demographic estimates by the very same archaeologists who readily employ parallel assumptions to make inferences about other past phenomena, whether social structure, religion, or economics. The reticence of my colleagues to population estimates has deeper roots.

Most directly, the anti-quantitative and anti-science turn in archaeology (Chapter 1) excluded demography and population as topics worthy of study. The broad spread of such ideas throughout the discipline (at least for the archaeology of complex societies) resulted in the omission of demography from many graduate training programs in archaeology. Beyond this, much of the hesitation to engage in population estimates from fragmentary remains probably derives from the general skepticism about the simplification required for comparative analysis (Chapter 1). Demographic reconstruction requires a complex empirical reality to be reduced to a small number of measures, and some archaeologists object to such simplification on principle. Also, an operation like population estimation requires that many uncertain parameters (e.g., household size or occupancy rate) – and the methods of their derivation and analysis – be made explicit before estimates can be generated. Again, this level of detail is avoided by some archaeologists, in favor of grand, abstract accounts of the past (Chapter 1).

Nevertheless, other archaeologists have forged on, developing methods and concepts for reconstructing past populations from survey and excavation data. It is unfortunate that it has taken several decades for early work in archaeological population estimation (Hassan 1981) to be followed up and extended (Berrey et al. 2021; Drennan et al. 2015; Ortman 2016; Whitelaw 2004). Thankfully, there are signs of a renewal of interest in rigorous population estimation (Bernardini and Schachner 2018; Chirikure et al. 2017; Hanson and Ortman 2017; Smith et al. 2019). As part of an effort to promote demographic research in the study of premodern cities, I have assembled data on the population, area, and density of each of my case studies (as discussed later).

---

[1] This quotation is from a colleague who commented on a draft of this chapter.

POPULATION DENSITY

The density of population – the number of people in a settlement (or part of a settlement), divided by its area – is another crucial piece of information about the nature of life and activities in cities and settlements. Density is a major research theme in contemporary social science and urban planning, with contentious debates about low-density suburban sprawl, the ecological and quality-of-life implications of compact cities, and the effects of urban densities on life and society today (e.g., Angel et al. 2020; Bruegmann 2005; Campoli and MacLean 2007; Talen 2005). Density is also an important part of the settlement scaling work, described later in this chapter.

For planners today, "density" is a broad category that includes a variety of different concepts (Dovey and Pafka 2014), among them the following measures:

- *Total population density* (population of a settlement divided by its area)
- *Neighborhood density* (density of a neighborhood or other delimited residential zone)
- *Parcel density* (dwelling units per area)
- *Floor area ratio* (ratio of total floor area to total plot or site area)
- *Urban footprint* (floor area per resident)

The first two are used by archaeologists and historians, and I report them in this book where possible (see Table 3.1). The final measure has also been used archaeologically, most notably in the form of "Naroll's constant," a figure of ten square meters of roofed space per person reported in an influential early study (Naroll 1962); see also Brown (1987). Angel et al. (2021; 2020) review no fewer than fourteen measures of density and develop a scheme that relates many of them in a systematic, quantitative fashion. They conclude that the total population density is the most useful measure for planners.

Archaeologists have devoted more effort to calculating and analyzing regional population density than urban density (Freeman et al. 2020; Zimmermann et al. 2009). A recent study (Berrey et al. 2021) has a useful discussion of how regional and settlement densities relate to one another. To illustrate the range of variation in the population density of early cities, I assembled plans of a standard one-hectare block within settlements (Figure 3.2). The examples are a Maya city (A), a medieval English village (B), an Aztec provincial town (C), a French medieval town (D), and a Roman city (E). It does not take much thought to conclude that the nature of urban life and society – as well as the expression of energized crowding – varied greatly among settlements with different densities. Population density is a major component of the concept of energized crowding (Chapter 2), an observation not lost on urban planners (Dovey and Pafka 2014). Before exploring these and

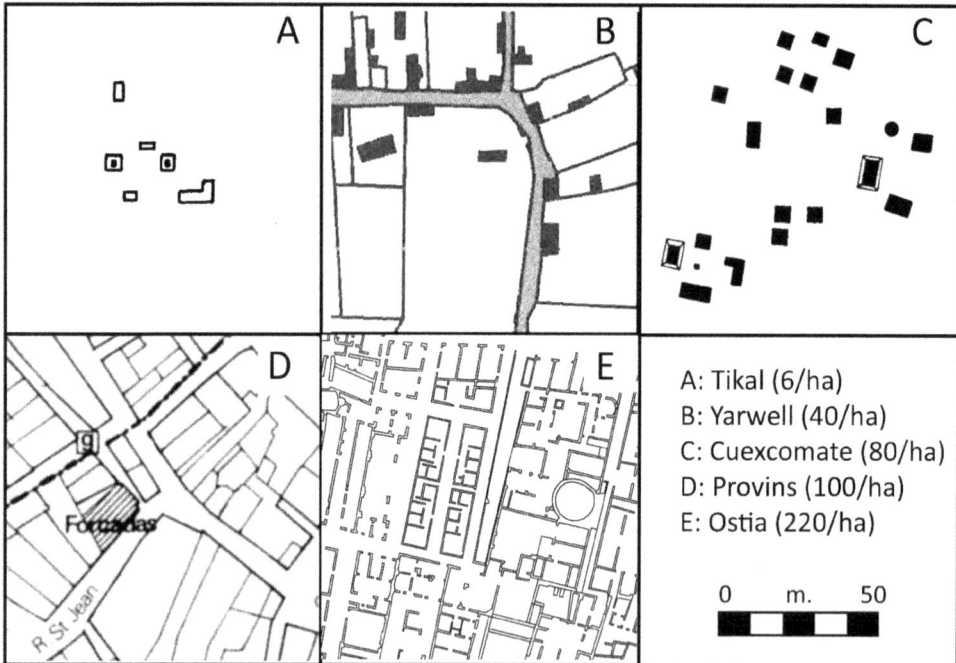

3.2. Variation in population density of premodern cities. (A) Tikal (Maya), modified after Carr and Hazard (1961); (B) Yarwell (Northamptonshire, 1778), modified after Historic England (2018:40); (C) Cuexcomate (Aztec) (Smith 1992); (D) Provins (Chatel, France, medieval), modified after Mesqui (1979:fig. 10); (E) Ostia (Roman); digitized map by Katherine Crawford, used with permission. Overall graphic by Michael E. Smith.

other consequences of energized crowding, I review one of the major negative consequences of past dense urban populations.

The Urban Graveyard Effect

The *urban graveyard effect* refers to a two-step process that operated in past cities (and in some cities in the developing world today). High disease levels led to higher mortality in cities (higher than in the countryside), which in turn led to the need for rural-to-urban migration just to maintain urban population levels. Bioarchaeologist Brenna Hassett describes the first step as follows: "In the burgeoning (Early) urban centres of the world, a triad of preconditions for epidemic infectious disease were being perfected: (1) gross poverty and associated malnutrition, which lowers immune competency and makes for a large pool of potential florid expression of infectious disease; (2) dense populations, which percolate and spread infection; and finally (3) connections to the wider world" (Hassett 2017:203–204). Historian William McNeill describes the second step: "The result, demographically, was that city populations did not sustain themselves. Too many infections were around for a stable biological balance to arise, and in addition, of course, famine and war often intervened to reduce the number of urban dwellers catastrophically" (McNeill 1979:95–96).

The urban graveyard effect was first noticed by the "father of urban demography," John Graunt, in 1662: "We must say that London is more unhealthful, or that it inclines men and women more to barrenness, than the country" (quoted in Galley 1995:448). This effect continued up until the twentieth century, although it did not stop people from migrating to cities. As Glaeser and Cutler (2021:71) put it, "America's nineteenth-century cities were far deadlier than cities in low-income countries today, and people still came by the million." Why? Because the benefits of urban living outweighed the cost of the increased disease load. "The same physical proximity that enabled Socrates to talk to Plato also enabled the flow of the Athenian plague" (Glaeser and Cutler 2021:26).

While the majority of urban historians accept the existence of the graveyard effect in cities before the modern era, it has been difficult to demonstrate this effect empirically. Historical records for medieval and early modern European cities, where the model was developed, are complicated and difficult to interpret (Galley 1995; Woods 2003a); whole collections of bioarchaeological remains that would enable archaeologists to compare disease and perhaps mortality in ancient rural and urban populations rarely comprise samples sufficiently large or systematic for such studies. For example, concerning the demography of Classical Rome, Erdkamp (2008) concludes that the urban graveyard effect did indeed operate, while Lo Cascio (2006) argues that it probably applied in some periods but not in others. Betsinger and DeWitte (2021) review much of the bioarchaeological data and find "there is no single, simple, all-encompassing conclusion" about rural-urban differences (p. 102).

In spite of these uncertainties, most demographers believe that the urban graveyard effect did indeed affect most early cities, and a comprehensive test of this hypothesis has yet to be undertaken. Accumulating evidence of the high numbers of immigrants in early cities supports the importance of the urban graveyard effect. I reviewed bioarchaeological data on immigrants in a sample of cities around the world, and in most studies more than 15 percent of individuals analyzed with chemical data were immigrants (Smith 2020c). At Teotihuacan, 32 percent of individuals in residential burials were immigrants, while 59 percent of sacrificial victims were from areas away from the city. While disease levels likely had a significant demographic effect on premodern cities, individual epidemics tended to have serious effects in the short run but minimal impact over longer periods (Glaeser 2021). In other words, cities are highly resilient to disease outbreaks.

Case Study 5 Mohenjo-daro: Dense Urban Living and Early Sanitation

Mohenjo-daro and Harappa are the two largest cities of the Indus Valley urban tradition; they flourished during the Integration Era, 2600 to 1900 BCE (Kenoyer 2012). These cities, and the overall Indus society, are fascinating from a comparative perspective. They lack obvious temples and royal burials, and it is not clear whether royal palaces were present or not (Kenoyer 1998; Vidale 2010). There is a graphic system of numerous short texts that may or may not represent a writing system (Kenoyer 1998). Craft production was carried out at an intensive level, with high skills (Miller 2000). Interestingly, the experts on this society cannot agree on some basic interpretations. Gregory Possehl (1990) accepts these large sites as cities but questions whether institutions of state government were present, while Mark Kenoyer (1998) argues that evidence of social classes (weak evidence, in my opinion) implies that a state must have been present. Regardless of the outcome of these debates, Indus urbanism does show two remarkable features relevant to our theme. First, these very early cities had dense residential zones (Figure 3.3); second, the builders of these cities worked out advanced techniques to supply water and dispose of sewage.

Housing and Sanitation. Houses in Mohenjo-daro were packed tightly together (Figure 3.3). Individual residences consisted of a series of rooms laid out around a central open patio. Such courtyard residences are quite common in the tropics and semitropics around the world, and are often called "Mediterranean style" houses. Most houses at Mohenjo-daro were built of fired brick.

Mohenjo-daro had a remarkable two-level system of water and sewage management. At the household level, many houses had wells and bathing platforms. Wells were deep circular features, lined with specially made wedge-shaped bricks. Domestic bathing platforms were built either in large multi-purpose rooms, or else in smaller, dedicated rooms. They consisted of a raised brick platform adjacent to a well. A low railing of bricks channeled water into a drain that emptied outside the house. Brick latrines or toilets (Figure 3.4) were also common. A chute channeled waste either directly into a street drain or into

3.3. Residential zone at Mohenjo-daro. It is possible that this plan includes housing that dates to different periods. Modified after Jansen (1993:42).

Case Study 5 (cont.)

3.4. Latrine at Mohenjo-daro. Copyright J. M. Kenoyer/Harappa.com. Courtesy of the Department of Archaeology and Museums, Government of Pakistan.

a cesspit. These household-level features were tied into a neighborhood-level system of both open and closed brick drains, which ran along the streets and channeled used water and effluent away from the houses. Where several street drains met, the sewage flowed into a sump chamber (cesspit) that allowed solids to settle and liquids to continue to flow.

Comparative Insights. Excavations at Mohenjo-daro show that some very early urban settlements had dense populations at both the city and neighborhood levels. The water supply and sanitation systems of Mohenjo-daro and the other Indus cities were remarkable technological achievements. Whether or not people at the time recognized the beneficial effects of these systems for health, they almost certainly served that purpose. Nevertheless, new evidence suggests that the end of the Indus cities was accompanied by – and perhaps exacerbated by – increased levels of infectious disease (Schug et al. 2013).

Especially interesting is the interplay between the actions of individual households and city authorities in designing and operating the water and sanitation systems. The street drains and cesspits were almost certainly public goods, built or organized by the authorities (see Chapter 6), whereas the domestic features – wells, bathing platforms, and latrines – were probably built by individual households for their own use. Some writers have claimed that neighborhoods such as HR (Figure 3.3) show the hand of central planning (e.g., Jansen 2010). I think they are more aptly classified as what I have called "semi-orthogonal urban blocks" – urban zones whose contiguous houses are nearly orthogonal as a result of sequential construction, not central planning (Smith 2007). If this is the case, then the Indus housing points to decentralized construction, not government planning. Mohenjo-daro and Harappa show a combination of central authority and household actions – top-down and generative processes – in an integrated system of infrastructure, at a very early period.

CROWDS, STRESS, AND COGNITIVE OVERLOAD

Ethnographer Roy Rappaport (1968:116) noticed that as the populations of villages in highland New Guinea grew, disputes among villagers increased. He coined the term *irritation coefficient* to describe escalating levels of negative social feelings and interactions.[2] This is but one example of a widespread phenomenon. As the size of a settlement or group increases, the number of potential social interactions that each individual can have increases exponentially. As certain thresholds are reached – such as Rappoport's irritation coefficient – conflict and psychological stress go up dramatically (Kennedy and Adolphs 2011). This is the negative face of energized crowding.

As discussed in Chapter 2, interaction stress arises from an overload of too many social interactions (Fletcher 1995). Numerous social scientists have discussed the negative implications of large, dense urban populations. In the modern world, interaction stress and social stress can lead to more transitory urban social relations and anomie (Mayhew and Levinger 1977), as well as psychological stress (Evans 2001). Interaction stress also contributes to larger structural effects such as poverty, crime, delinquency, and public health problems (O'Brien 2011; Spruill 2010); indeed, these negative effects of urbanization and interaction stress have been a major topic of social science research for a century or more (Blokland 2017:15–30).

In the field of cognitive cultural evolution, scholars posit that interaction stress occurs when populations cross key thresholds (Bodley 2003). *Dunbar's number* is a hypothesized constant that describes the number of individuals with which one can interact socially on a regular basis; estimates for the figure vary around 150 individuals (Dunbar 2010, 2011). Some cognitive anthropologists have hypothesized that when group size surpasses this limit, a variety of sociocultural changes occur (Coward and Dunbar 2014). The Dunbar constant and its associated cognitive approach, however, are not universally accepted in sociology and anthropology (de Ruiter et al. 2011; Wellman 2012), and a recent critique throws doubt on the whole enterprise (Lindenfors et al. 2021).

The effects of interaction stress on settlements is a major theme of Roland Fletcher's (1995) work on settlement growth. Fletcher assumes that human settlements will tend to grow – both in numbers and in density – until they reach one or both of two limits. The Interaction Limit ("I-Limit") is the maximum residential population density that people can tolerate, given our cognitive capacities; this limit is a product of interaction stress, or Rappaport's irritation coefficient. According to Fletcher, the I-Limit varies for mobile groups, sedentary

---

[2] This section is based partly on Smith (2019a).

farmers, and urban societies. The Communication Limit ("C-Limit") refers to the maximum number and density of population that can be organized effectively and integrated by a given regime of communication and transport technology. In order to transcend a particular I-Limit and continue to grow, societies must expand their C-Limit by developing innovations in the technology of communications (writing, printing), transport (horse, mechanized transport), and/or the built environment (segregation of activities, spaces for specialized activities). In Fletcher's words:

> We should expect to find an interaction limit set both by the finite capacity of people to cope with interaction and by the finite limit on a community's capacity to produce the material facilities which can mitigate aggregate interaction stress and aid communication. Because the addition of more and more people will generate markedly more potential interactive stress, more cost will be needed to control it. Therefore we should find that the maximum tolerable residential densities will decrease as community size increases. (Fletcher 1991:396)

Fletcher's model helps explain why the transition from a mobile way of life to sedentary villages was reflected not only in more permanent buildings but also in spatial arrangements that yielded greater privacy (see Case Study 4). These architectural changes increased the C-Limits of a community by reducing interaction stress and allowed communities to grow in size and density beyond former I-Limits. As noted in Chapter 2, interaction stress was reduced in early communities by the enclosure of spaces and the spatial specialization of activities in the built environment as well as by the development of integrative architectural features that promoted cohesion through group ritual.

The large volume of research by social scientists and archaeologists on social stress – conceived broadly – clearly shows its generative role in creating change in human societies and behavior. Most authors are careful to emphasize that the negative effects of population are generated not strictly by the number of people but by the number of social interactions. The level of social interactions, in turn, is a function of both population size and density, as Fletcher emphasizes. In other words, the culprit is not merely the number of people but the number of potential or actual interactions. It is through these increased social interactions that energized crowding generates interaction stress. Before turning to the socially beneficial outcomes of high population, high density, and increased social interactions, I describe two cases that illustrate specific accommodations to density-based social stress in radically different social contexts: Pueblo societies of the US Southwest and the Burning Man festival.

Case Study 6 Pueblos of the US Southwest: High Density in a Small-Scale Society

The Indigenous peoples of the Southwestern United States – modern groups and their ancestors – have been the subjects of many detailed ethnographic and archaeological studies, which have allowed impressive analyses of a variety of social and cultural phenomena (Plog 1997; Ware 2014). Of the many hundreds of documented settlements, only a few – most commonly, Chaco Canyon – have ever been called *urban*. Yet, as a group, these settlements provide insights into urban processes. Here I focus on the Pueblo societies of the late period (Pueblo IV period, 1350–1600 CE). The settlements of this period are remarkable for their dense apartment structures called *pueblos* (Figure 3.5). In my typology, they are classified as agrotowns. My discussion here synthesizes work on many individual pueblos, and the illustration (of Pecos Pueblo) shows features "typical" of pueblo settlements.

Dealing with Density in a Small-Scale Society. Western theorists who are ignorant of non-Western societies have traditionally puzzled over the question of social integration in small-scale societies: How could such groups maintain order without kings and elites to establish and enforce laws? But, as any student in an introductory anthropology class can tell you, this is not a puzzle at all. Small-scale groups have customs and practices – rooted in daily interactions and social reciprocity – that keep them going

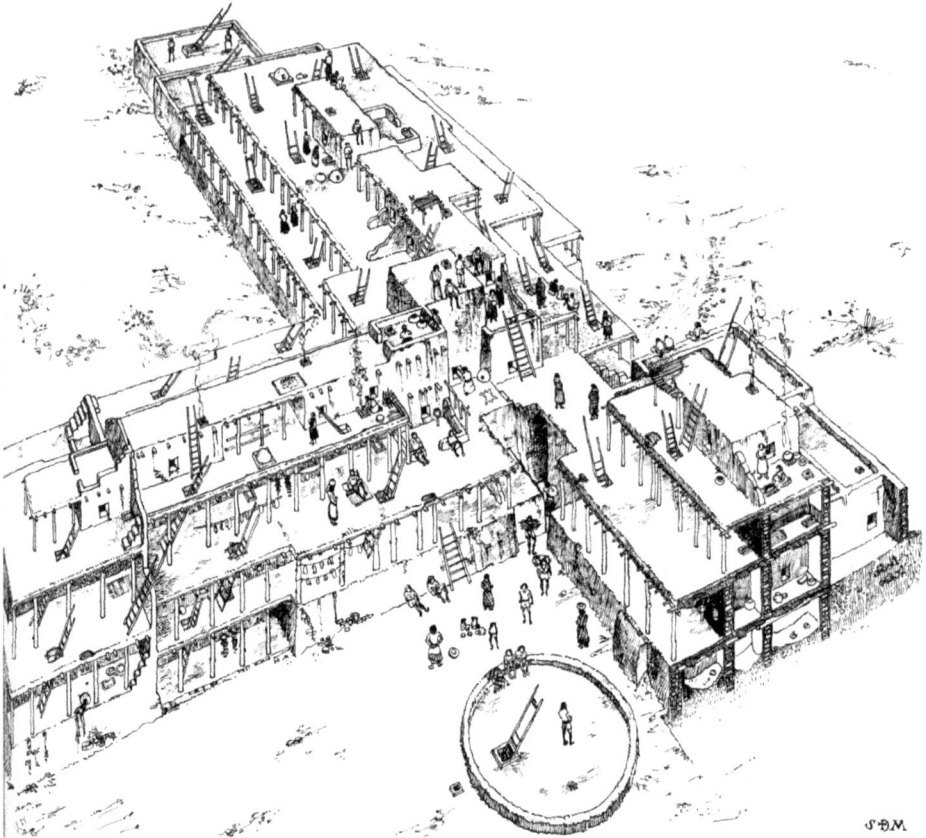

3.5. Reconstruction drawing of daily life at Pecos Pueblo, New Mexico. Drawing by Singleton Morehead, reproduced from Kidder (1958:69).

Case Study 6 (cont.)

without the need for powerful kings or bossy elites (Taylor 1982). These customs and practices have been studied extensively by archaeologists, historians, and ethnographers of Indigenous Southwestern groups.

Social integration in these groups is achieved through common participation in ceremonies. Early in the trajectory of Southwestern societies, a specialized structure, the kiva, developed as the location for many of these ceremonies (Hegmon 1989). Kivas are typically subterranean circular features; they can hold a small number of participants, who enter via a ladder through the roof (a kiva is shown at the bottom of Figure 3.5). Comparative research shows that the larger the society, the more likely that specialized ritual features such as kivas will be present (Adler and Wilshusen 1990). Other integrative ceremonies take place in plazas and open spaces (Dungan and Peeples 2018; Ortman 2012:309–311). As the Southwestern peoples aggregated into dense pueblos – most likely for protection – kivas and plazas became crucial features of the built environment.

Another practice that helped households in densely settled pueblos maintain their integrity and their social obligations was to divide large pueblos into neighborhoods (social/spatial divisions of a settlement). Southwestern archaeologists rarely use the concept of neighborhood, perhaps because of its urban connotations; however, a look at the layouts of many large pueblos (Adler 1996) shows spatially separated room blocks that almost certainly served the same role as neighborhoods in cities and towns (discussed later). Archaeologists have used concepts such as "moieties" (dual divisions of settlements) for these spatial-social units (Hill 1970; Lowell 1996), but an acknowledgment that they were neighborhoods promotes comparisons across types of societies and across types of settlements.

Comparative Insights. The late pueblos of the US Southwest illustrate the operation of a variety of "urban-like" social processes in small settlements that are almost never categorized as urban societies. These societies created agrotowns with high levels of density. Southwestern peoples built facilities to promote social cohesion: kivas were specialized ceremonial spaces; plazas were multipurpose spaces that regularly hosted ceremonies; and neighborhoods divided settlements into more manageable components. According to Fletcher, these are the kinds of features that allow settlements to grow in size. Observing such features in the pueblos does not imply we should start using the term "urban" for the pueblos; rather, these features support the point that the social interaction-based practices of human settlements cut across the traditional urban/nonurban dichotomy. This is a general point of the next case study, the Burning Man festival, a radically different kind of Southwestern desert settlement.

Case Study 7 Black Rock City: Generative versus Top-Down Processes at Burning Man

The Burning Man festival is an event held each summer in the Nevada desert. It is a celebration of art and free expression that grew from a small gathering of friends around a bonfire in San Francisco in 1986 to a bustling weeklong settlement of 60,000 by 2013, named "Black Rock City." The focal event is the burning of a large effigy of "the man," a symbol of the ephemeral nature of materiality. At the completion of each festival, the entire campsite and physical infrastructure are dismantled to be resurveyed and rebuilt the following year. The history of this event provides a dramatic illustration of a particular response to interaction stress.

Chaos and Order; Generative and Top-Down Processes. Beginning in 1997, Black Rock City was laid out in a carefully planned circular arrangement, with the effigy of "The man" placed in the center (Figure 3.6). This configuration was designed by Rod Garrett, the head of the festival's Department of Urban Planning. An important feature of the settlement is the melding of generative and top-down forces in creating neighborhoods, a situation I have written about elsewhere (Smith et al. 2015). Here, I emphasize the interplay of generative and top-down processes as outcomes of interaction stress.

Case Study 7 (cont.)

3.6. Black Rock City (setting for the Burning Man festival) from the air. Photograph by Peretz Partensky, distributed under Creative Commons Attribution-2 Generic. Source Wikimedia Commons, Creative Commons Attribution 2.0 Generic license.

Burning Man was created as a festival with artistic and anarchic ideals. Its official principles are radical inclusion, gifting, decommodification, radical self-reliance, radical self-expression, communal effort, civic responsibility, leaving no trace, participation, and immediacy.[3] Along with these values came a free-form, unorganized settlement. Before 1997, the only planning was an effort to make sure the burning of the effigy could be seen from the entire camp. When, because of its size, the festival moved from San Francisco to the Nevada desert in 1990, there were 500 participants. The festival entered a growth spurt in 1994 (Figure 3.7) and reached 8,000 participants in 1996. That was a dramatic year, as population density reached 870 persons per hectare and interaction stress overtook the unplanned, generative orientation of the festival. In the words of Larry Harvey – the founder and longtime leader of the event – "[in 1996] Burning Man was all about speeding in cars (with the lights turned off), randomly shooting guns and general 'blowing shit up'" (Harvey 2010). There was at least one serious accident that year when a car ran over an occupied tent.

   The settlement's 1996 population of 8,000, up from 4,000 the prior year, marked a tipping point. By 1997, a series of radical reforms led to the carefully planned layout that is still followed today (Figure 3.6). In a 2006 interview, Harvey noted that the causes of the change were both internal (the need for safety) and external (land managers from the Bureau of Land Management insisted on a more planned and orderly event). The festival organizers quickly set up a number of "municipal departments" to create and maintain order (Chen 2009). While the new insistence on planning and regulation would appear to be at odds with the historically free-spirited nature of the event, Larry Harvey explains the change as follows:

---

[3] From the Burning Man website: https://burningman.org/culture/philosophical-center/10-principles/.

Case Study 7 (cont.)

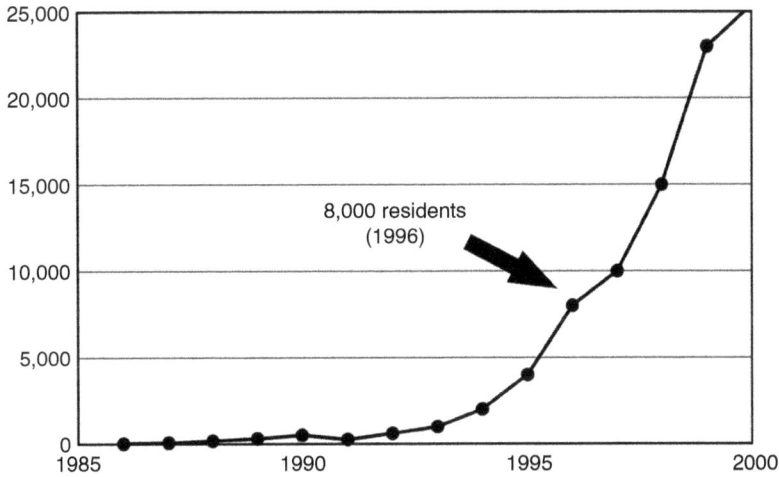

3.7. Number of participants in the Burning Man festival, showing the date when formal planning and organization was instituted. Graph by Michael E. Smith, based on data from https://burningman.org/timeline/.

"What became apparent is that all this confusion (in 1996) was limiting people's liberty, because if you live in fear, you are not free" (Fairs 2015). Since 1996, the festival has continued to grow, reaching 25,000 in 2000, 50,000 in 2010, and leveling off between 2013 and 2016 at around 67,000 (due to constraints imposed by the Bureau of Land Management).

Comparative Insights. A major theme in the literature on generative social processes is that a lack of strong top-down control does not necessarily lead to chaos; in fact, successful economic and social outcomes can follow from unregulated, local processes (Alexander 1979; Jacobs 1961; Lansing 1991; Ostrom 1990); see Chapters 6–7). But such successes are most often found in small, enduring, face-to-face communities. The experience of the Burning Man festival reinforces the notion that it is difficult to organize large, temporary populations without centralized control. Large, dense settlements may require some level of planning and coordination to be successful. Now, it is true that Black Rock City is not an urban settlement (Berg 2011); it lacks urban functions and has a low level of social complexity. But perhaps for that reason, it is a particularly clear illustration of how some settlements require planning and coordination, and that those needs arise from interaction stress, which in turn is caused by increasing population and density.

NEIGHBORHOODS AND COMMUNITY FORMATION

The formation of place-based social communities – neighborhoods – is the second outcome of energized crowding (Figure 2.1). Communities are primary sites of social interaction; indeed, a classic anthropological definition of community is "the maximal group of persons who normally reside together in face-to-face association" (Murdock 1949:79). In sociological theory going back to Emile Durkheim (Chapter 2), social interaction among multiple individuals is seen as the primary force that generates communities. When such inter-actions become routinized and occur over a period of time, they generate energized crowding. This line of thinking continues today among economists (Bowles and Gintis 2002), sociologists (Sampson 2012), and urban planners (Brower 2011). I return to this theme in Chapter 7, where I discuss the impact of generative forces on urban life.

A major spatial outcome of community formation in growing cities and towns is the generation of spatial clusters of interaction, or neighborhoods. Most likely because of interaction stress, in the form of limits – whether cognitive or social – on the numbers of social interactions people can readily handle, neighborhoods have become universal traits of cities, from the past to the present (Smith 2010a). The creation of neighborhoods and other social communities is shaped by the built environment, a relationship stressed by advocates of the New Urbanism. For example, Emily Talen (2000) proposes a causal chain that runs from the built environment, through social factors, to social interaction and the formation of communities. Energized crowding only exerts its effects in a particular place, and the specific configuration of buildings and spaces plays an important role in generating its outcomes, both positive and negative.

LOW-DENSITY CITIES

In some premodern urban traditions, population densities were far lower than most of the cities discussed in this book. The urban settlements of the Classic Maya are among the best examples of low-density cities; Tikal, for example, had less than ten persons per hectare (Culbert and Rice 1990). A common reaction to the sprawling nature of these settlements is to claim – as William Sanders did for the Maya (see Case Study 1) – that they weren't really cities at all. Yet according to the functional definition of urbanism, many Maya settle-ments had important urban functions in the realm of political administration, ritual practice, and perhaps economics. Did these cities resemble those of other, higher-density, premodern urban traditions, apart from their low densities? Or were they settlements of a fundamentally different nature?

Roland Fletcher (2009; 2011), the archaeologist who has given low-density cities the greatest comparative scrutiny, sees this kind of settlement as funda-mentally different from other cities. In Fletcher's (1995) model of settlement growth, the low density of these cities allows them to grow in area if not population while avoiding the interaction and communication limits to growth. In later publications, Fletcher (2009, 2012) compares four early urban traditions of low-density cities: the Classic Maya of Central America, Angkor in Cambodia, Bagan in Myanmar, and Anuradhapura in Sri Lanka. Cities in all four traditions have concentrations of massive stone ceremonial architecture, surrounded by large zones of sprawling settlement where farmers cultivate the fields around their houses. Fletcher and his collaborators empha-size the fragile nature of these ecosystems and they suggest that low-density cities were prone to collapse (Lucero et al. 2015), a viewpoint I challenge in Chapter 4. Fletcher directs a major fieldwork project at Angkor, where he is generating archaeological data to evaluate these features at one of the largest and least dense settlements of the ancient world.

Case Study 8 Angkor: Low-Density Mega-City

The city of Angkor was the capital of an expansive Southeast Asian empire from the ninth to fifteenth centuries CE. It is best known for its large temple complex, Angkor Wat, a major tourist destination in Cambodia today. The city presents a fascinating contrast between its oversize monumental public architecture and the surrounding dispersed, sprawling residential zones. Even after decades of mapping, the full extent of Angkor is not known; current estimates suggest an area of some 1,000 square kilometers (as discussed later), one of the largest cities in geographical area ever to exist. Even with a population estimated at 750,000, the density was quite low (8 persons/ha); see Table 3.1. For an overview of Angkor art and architecture, see Coe (2003). In recent years, the Greater Angkor Project, directed by Roland Fletcher, has mapped the site (Evans et al. 2007), and a large number of valuable technical studies are now in process (e.g., Carter et al. 2018; Klassen et al. 2021a; Klassen and Evans 2020; Lustig et al. 2018).

Temples, Reservoirs, and Farmers. For archaeologists, the term *monumental* refers to buildings that are larger than they need to be (Trigger 1990); see Chapter 4 for further discussion. From this perspective, the temples, compounds, and reservoirs of Angkor are hyper-monumental. The walled compound of the Angkor Wat temple covers 163 hectares, which by itself is larger than many of the cities discussed in this book (Table 3.1). The walls are covered with elaborate relief carvings of scenes from mythology, statecraft, and daily life, with written inscriptions in both the Sanskrit and Khmer languages. Angkor Thom is a walled city within a city, covering 9 square kilometers (900 hectares) and containing huge temples and residential areas; it may have served as a royal palace.

Even more impressive than Angkor Wat or Angkor Thom are the huge *barays*, or reservoirs. The largest, West Baray, at 7.8 by 2.1 kilometers, covers more than 16 square kilometers. The East Baray is slightly smaller. The debate about the uses of these features raged for decades: Were they ceremonial constructions meant to reflect the beauty of the monuments and symbolize various religious themes, or were they reservoirs to regulate the flow of irrigation water to the wet rice fields of Angkor? The answer, not surprisingly, is that they served both purposes. As the power of the Angkor kings grew, irrigated rice cultivation expanded, requiring construction of a massive system of irrigation canals, dams, and reservoirs (the barays). Eventually, the system failed (in part due to increases in rainfall), leading to massive flooding and destruction in the city.

One reason for the low density of population at Angkor was that much of the city was taken up by farmers living alongside their irrigated rice fields. Houses were interspersed with small reservoirs, and these units were in turn clustered around small temples with larger reservoirs (Figure 3.8). There is little common orientation or planning in these communities, beyond the requirements of the canals and rice paddies. Houses were built of perishable materials, and we know little about them today. Interestingly, the best-studied housing at Angkor is in the "gated communities" that lie within the outer walls of the major temples, including Angkor Wat (Carter et al. 2018).

Comparative Insights. Like Tikal (see Case Study 1), Angkor combined monumental temples and civic architecture with low-density, sprawling residential areas of urban farmers. These are some of the features of low-density cities, as discussed in comparative terms by Fletcher (2009, 2012). But Angkor dwarfs Tikal in both the sizes and elaboration of its temples as well as the area of its neighborhoods. For many decades, archaeologists focused on the temples and barays, producing knowledge of civic activities but

Case Study 8 (cont.)

3.8. Residential unit at Angkor, showing the house area surrounded by ponds. Photograph by Damien Evens; reproduced with permission.

little information on the other urban aspects of the city. Current mapping operations, using the latest aerial techniques, along with research on housing and spatial patterns, are bringing this huge city into the realm of comparative urbanism.

Cities of the Classic-Period Maya

Roland Fletcher stresses a variety of features that the Classic Maya cities shared with Angkor: tropical forest settings, monumental civic architecture, glorification of kings, sprawling residences of farmers, the agricultural use of water-control features, and eventual collapse and abandonment. These features justify their joint membership in his category "Low-density agrarian-based urbanism" (Arlen F. Chase and Diane Z. Chase 2016; Fletcher 2009, 2012; Lucero et al. 2015); see Graham and Isendahl (2018) for a critique of this concept. But the political contexts of Angkor and the Maya cities were radically different. In both areas, cities were political centers, created by kings for political ends. Angkor was the capital of a large empire, whereas the Maya cities were capitals of polities of varying size and extent (Martin and Grube 2008), sometimes called *city-states* (Grube 2000). Although the label *low-density cities* does capture something important about urbanism in both areas, it should not be allowed to obscure the very real differences between the Maya and Khmer cities and urban traditions.

As a city-state culture (Chapter 4), the Maya landscape during the Classic period (1–800 CE) was culturally unified but politically fragmented. Warfare, trade, and diplomacy produced a constantly changing roster of more powerful and less powerful kings. These kings promoted their authority by building elaborate temple-pyramids (Figure 3.9), organizing public ceremonies, and sponsoring battles and economic exchange. Each major city had a carefully planned epicenter that contained the royal palace, several pyramids, and usually a ballcourt and a marketplace. Kings and nobles were literate in the Maya hieroglyphic writing system. Many public texts have survived, most of which concern the history of local rulers and important ritual dates in the calendar. Most nobles and royals led a luxurious lifestyle in stone buildings in the city epicenter. Maya commoners built small houses on low platforms, arranged around patios. Each of these patio groups was home to one or more households.

3.9. Temple-pyramid known as Canaa at the Maya city Caracol. This photo shows the superstructure; the visible construction here is built on a platform 33 meters above the ground; the total height of the pyramid is 43.5 meters. Photograph by Michael E. Smith.

To return to my comparison with Angkor, no Maya king had anywhere near as much power as the kings of Angkor. As a result, Maya cities and polities were much smaller than Angkor, and their civic architecture is dwarfed by the Khmer temples and reservoirs. Whereas Khmer kings boasted of the temples and hospitals they built for their subjects, Maya kings boasted of their personal genealogy, their ritual prowess, their battles with foes, and their ties to cosmological power. And, whereas the Khmer state was involved in constructing canals and reservoirs for intensive rice cultivation, there is little evidence that the Maya governments engaged in much direct planning of, or support for, farming. As in many autocratic states (see Chapter 4), Maya commoners were on their own to conduct their basic social and economic affairs. And, as expected with such regimes, neighborhood organization was generated by local actions, not imposed or promoted by the authorities (Hardoy 1982; Smith 2011a).

VOLUNTARY CAMPS: HIGH-DENSITY TEMPORARY SETTLEMENTS

Voluntary camps are places away from major settlements where people dwell for a short time (from a few days to a few weeks) for reasons of enjoyment, pleasure, or celebration. In some definitions of urbanism, voluntary camps qualify as cities (O'Flaherty 2005:1). Most have a strong theme – religious, social, or political – that attracts people and structures the activities. These distinctive settlements are a kind of natural experiment that helps reveal the role of density in human settlements. Although voluntary camps are highly dense settlements, their small size and temporary nature prevent the establishment of energized crowding. But they do exhibit an alternative place-based phenomenon of social interaction: the creation of strong social bonds through *communitas*.

The concept of "camp" includes Voluntary camps as well as some types of practical machine sites as reviewed in Chapter 4 (e.g., Refugee camps). One of the few scholars to study the concept of camps from a broad perspective, Charlie Hailey (2008, 2009), refrains from explicitly defining the term. Nevertheless, he does present a useful three-part typology of camps (Hailey 2009):

- *Autonomy:* "Camps of autonomy confront, retreat, teach and celebrate. These {are} diverse sites of self-expression" (p. 20). Examples include summer camps, protest camps, festival camps, and camp meeting (religious revival) sites.
- *Control:* "Strategic camps of control seek to hold areas by force" (p. 240). Examples include immigrant camps, military camps, and concentration camps.
- *Necessity:* "Camps of need occur neither by choice nor, for the most part, by force. Camps of necessity certainly fall into a gray area between autonomy and control" (p. 322). Examples include refugee camps, disaster camps, work camps, migrant camps, and homeless camps.

For each of the three types, Hailey describes numerous examples; here I limit consideration to the best known of his examples. In my scheme, some of Hailey's camps of control and necessity are included as practical machine sites in Chapter 4, although homeless camps and the "Hooverville" settlements in the United States during the Great Depression would classify as Voluntary camps (Dearborn and Harmon 2012; Hailey 2009; Kusmer 2002). Hailey's category of camps of autonomy, on the other hand, corresponds well to my category, voluntary camps. Table 3.1 lists some of the major types of voluntary camps.

Table 3.1 is not at all exhaustive, and the assignment of functional category and social complexity are my own subjective judgments. Voluntary camps are places with intense social interaction and high emotion. People gather in groups that are typically small but dense. Their occupation for a period of several days to several weeks is too short for energized crowding to develop. Voluntary camps today result from a wide variety of social, political, and religious forces (Table 3.1), but they are unified in their focus on feelings and processes of *communitas*. This term refers to an unstructured but intense social experience in which a group of people – usually in an isolated location – undertake a common set of tasks or activities, resulting in strong feelings of equality and cohesion. Anthropologist Victor Turner wrote about communitas in reference to rituals celebrating rites of passage in small-scale societies. During key rituals, participants moved out of their settlement and stayed at a special temporary camp, where they were "equal individuals who submitted together to the general authority of the ritual elders" (Turner 1969:96). During rites with intense communitas, existing social divisions and hierarchies may be ignored or even reversed (Killinger 2010; Turner 2004; Turner 1969). Voluntary camps thus illustrate an alternative trajectory of community development that works

TABLE 3.1 *Types of voluntary camps*

Settlement type	Functional category	Social complexity	Urban functions[a]
Initiation camp	Ritual center	Low	
Religious camp	Ritual center	Low	
Pilgrimage camp	Ritual center	Low	
Festival camp[*]	Recreational settlement	Low	
Protest camp[*]	Political campsite	Low	
RV camp[*]	Nomadic aggregation site	Low	
Plains Indian aggregation[*]	Nomadic aggregation site	Moderate	E, P, R

Notes:
[*] Type is featured in Smith et al (2015).
[a] *Urban Functions: E: economic; P: political; R: religious.*

through the short-term intense process of communitas instead of through the longer-term and more routinized process of energized crowding. In both of these trajectories of development, a common outcome is the establishment of neighborhoods as major social-spatial units.

Voluntary Camps in the Modern World

Initiation camps. The first anthropological application of the communitas concept was Victor Turner's study of initiation ceremonies in African small-scale societies (Turner 1969). He started with Arnold van Gennep's (1960 [originally 1908]) three-part scheme for the structure of rites of initiation generally. First, initiates are separated from their everyday life in society. Second, they go through a *liminal* stage, in which they must complete a series of tests or rites. Third, the initiates rejoin society, now with a new role or status. Turner used the communitas concept to analyze the nature of the experience in the second, or liminal, stage of initiation rites. In his words, "Many of these peoples [in West Africa] have complex initiation rites with long periods of seclusion in the bush for the training of novices in esoteric lore, often associated with the presence of masked dancers, who portray ancestral spirits or deities" (Turner 1969:4).

Turner's central insight was that many social processes – from fraternity initiations to sports events to pilgrimages – exhibited van Gennep's three stages, with feelings and processes of communitas playing an important role in the liminal or separation stage.[4] Unfortunately, few ethnographic accounts of such initiations include information on the physical nature or spatial qualities of the initiation camp itself. The most extensive description I have found is John Tucker's description of an initiation camp among the Luimbi of Africa:

> The camp itself consisted of a series of rude windbreaks made of tall *osoke* grass and sticks, with various divisions serving as dormitories having the sky for ceiling, the moon and stars for lights. The initiation rite of circumcision is usually performed when the moon is half full. For beds, handfuls of leaves thrown on the ground serve, or the bare ground itself. Over the entrance to the camp and along the sides of the windbreaks is trellis-work made of braided roots, following traditional African patterns. Balls of braided bark-cloth are hung at the entrance gateway; a species of aloe is also braided and suspended to the sides of the entrance. (Tucker 1949:55)

---

[4] I still recall vividly my own process of initiation into a "secret" society within the Boy Scouts, the Order of the Arrow. After being called out publicly at a mass gathering around a bonfire, we were told to go into the woods to sleep alone, without shelter. The next day, we were brought back to a public gathering of scouts, but now as members of the Order. This event differed from most initiation ceremonies in its solitary liminal separation stage, and thus communitas was not part of the initiation ceremony.

The initiation camp serves as a kind of type case for voluntary camps, all of which exhibit van Gennep's three stages, with communitas as a prominent part of the experience at the camp itself.

Religious camps. Religious camps (voluntary camps whose primary purpose is religious worship) became popular among various Protestant denominations in the United States in the nineteenth century. A common form was the "camp meeting," held in a tent settlement in a rural, forested area (Figure 3.10). These were "outdoor revivals lasting from a week to ten days of preaching, prayer, ecstatic displays of religious conversion and intense times of fellowship" (Avery-Quinn 2017:43). In other words, the atmosphere was charged with religious fervor and communitas, and high density was partially responsible for much of the intensity of these camps In a letter of 1801, a Kentucky aristocrat expressed his wonder at the atmosphere and fervor among the 12,000 attendees at the Cane Ridge Revival: "The camp [was] illuminated with candles, on trees, at wagons, and at the tent . . . . Some feel the approaching symptoms by being under deep convictions; their heart swells, their nerves relax, and in an instant they become motionless and speechless, but generally retain their senses."[5]

3.10. Religious revival camp-meeting in the midwestern United States (Gorham 1854: frontispiece). Public domain.

---

[5] Letter from Colonel Robert Patterson to the Rev. Doctor John King on September 25, 1801, upon visiting the Cane Ridge Revival. http://www.caneridge.org/revival.html, accessed February 11, 2019. http://wideurbanworld.blogspot.com/2011/09/.

These camp meetings proved so popular that an organizational manual was published in the mid-nineteenth century (Gorham 1854). In the eastern part of the United States, camp meeting sites soon replaced their tents with small wood cottages as attendees pursued greater comfort for their summer visits. A few of these – such as Round Lake, New York – gradually transformed into permanent villages. While they no longer hold revival meetings, these villages maintain the distinctive house architecture and settlement layouts marking their origins as a religious camp (Avery-Quinn 2017, 2019; Hines 2015).[6]

Pilgrimage camps. Pilgrimage camps differ from religious camps in that they are located near a shrine or sacred place that people visit regularly. Religious camps are situated in a symbolically neutral place located away from regular permanent settlements. Pilgrimage camps are the places where pilgrims sleep once they have reached the shrine that is their destination. Most are located within permanent towns or cities that have grown up around the shrine. In the largest pilgrimage center in the world – Mecca – the camps today consist of extensive, planned neighborhoods of large, air-conditioned tents, densely packed and carefully arranged. The Mecca neighborhood of Mina contains 100,000 tents for an estimated 3 million pilgrim residents, at an astounding density of 1,500 persons per hectare (Makky 1978; Shehata and Elzawahry 2016). There is a large scholarly literature on the social aspects of pilgrimage (Palka 2014; Stoddard and Morinis 1997). While a major theme for ethnographers is the development of communitas among fellow pilgrims (Turner 2012; Turner 1969), few studies address the physical or spatial characteristics of pilgrimage camps as settlements.

Festival camps. A festival camp is the secular version of a religious camp. Today's festival camps run the gamut from enormous and widely publicized gatherings – such as Woodstock or Burning Man – to small affairs that operate on a local level (Stubbs 2005). The most extensively researched modern festival camp is Black Rock City, home of the annual Burning Man festival (Case Study 7). While all types of voluntary camps involve the creation of what Turner calls "spontaneous communitas" (the immediate feelings that arise during key types of intense social experience), Burning Man has institutionalized these processes into "normative communitas" (when communitas is organized into a lasting system). This is clear from the ten principles that guide participation in the festival (see Case Study 7). These principles "were crafted not as a dictate of how people should be and act, but

---

[6] See my blog post "Round Lake: From Methodist Camp Meeting to Modern Village," http://wideurbanworld.blogspot.com/2011/09/.

as a reflection of the community's ethos and culture as it had organically developed since the event's inception."[7]

Protest camps and RV camps. These are contemporary types of voluntary camps that are included in my study of neighborhoods in semi-urban settlements (Smith et al. 2015). Protest camps became a significant part of the political process in the twentieth century. A co-author of that paper, Katrina Johnston, studied the campsite of "Occupy Portland," a regional variant of the Occupy Wall Street movement of 2011 (Johnston 2011). The tents were separated – largely by built features of the parks – into two clusters or neighborhoods. Within each, social interactions among the residents – stimulated by common political goals – created conditions of communitas; see also De la Llata (2016).

RV ("recreational vehicle") camps are a distinctive form of settlement popular in the Southwestern portion of the United States. Most of the residents are retired couples who may spend summers in a northern area and winter in the Southwest, driving their large houses on wheels between RV sites (Counts and Counts 1996). Since 2008, many older Americans have taken to living permanently in their RV or other vehicle, a situation described in the book and movie *Nomadland* (Bruder 2017). The only such camp whose spatial characteristics have been studied is in the town of Quartzite, Arizona (Berg 2010; Bruder 2017; Simpson 2007). Because of its very low fees for RVs, this sleepy village becomes a large metropolis during the winter months. My 2015 paper with students showed that the residents and their large vehicles form clear spatial clusters, and those clusters mark zones of heavy social interaction that probably include a degree of communitas (Smith et al. 2015). These differ from the other kinds of voluntary camps in that the shelters are permanent, not temporary, although their gas-powered mobility makes their stay at any one place a temporary phenomenon.

Ancient Voluntary Camps

Stonehenge is the best-known example of a common phenomenon of the ancient world: a large public monument located far from permanent settlements. Pilgrims traveled to visit these sites, and they must have stayed overnight in places not far away. Unfortunately, these settlements – pilgrimage camps in my classification – have proven difficult to locate and study. In the case of Stonehenge, a settlement that looks like a permanent village – Durrington Walls – seems to have included houses for pilgrims. Located less than three km from Stonehenge, this site is associated with another monument (a wood-henge), but excavations suggest that Neolithic visitors to Stonehenge also

---

[7] See the Burning Man website's "Philosophical Center": www.behance.net/gallery/87323505/The-10-Principles-of-Burning-Man?locale=en_US.

stayed there, engaging in feasting and probably other communitas-building activities (Craig et al. 2015; French et al. 2012).

In other cases, archaeologists have uncovered temporary shelters at likely pilgrimage destinations. Helaine Silverman has identified the early site of Cahuachi in coastal Peru as a likely pilgrimage destination. She reports finding that "temporary housing structures made of cane and woven matting were put up and taken down leaving postholes in *apisonados* [floors]" (Silverman 1994:8); for additional studies, see Bangert (2010) or the chapters in Kristensen and Friese (2017). Unfortunately, we still lack an extensively excavated pilgrimage camp from the distant past. Another type of ancient aggregation site are hunter-gatherer aggregation sites from the Paleolithic period, as discussed in Chapter 2.

Case Study 9 Temporary Cities of the Plains Indians

After European invaders introduced horses on the North American plains, hunter-gatherer groups quickly developed distinctive horse-based bison hunting (Moore 1987; Oliver 1962). This new adaptation structured all aspects of society and life, including settlements. Like many regional groups of hunter-gatherers, these people spent most of the year in small, mobile groups. Once a year, they gathered for several weeks in large aggregation sites, and these temporary settlements took on many of the attributes of urbanism: a large, dense population, intensive social interactions, a complex division of labor. Although the social context and dynamics of these settlements differ greatly from the kinds of voluntary camps discussed previously, they do fit the definition, and they provide a striking ethnographic case of the importance of voluntary camps in a small-scale, non-Western society.

Short-Term Cities of Hunter-Gatherers. Hunter-gatherer aggregation sites differ in size and scale from the regular mobile camps in which people spent most of their time. Small camps on the Plains averaged about 6 tipis (ca. 35 people), whereas the aggregation camps averaged 40 tipis (ca. 240 persons) or more (Banks and Snortland 1995). While one would be hard-pressed to identify much energized crowding in the small mobile camps of hunter-gatherers, ethnographers remarked on the vitality and exuberance of aggregated life (Figure 3.11). The great anthropologist Emile Durkheim (1947), for example, described this contrast for the Australian aborigines; he is paraphrased by Wengrow and Graeber (2015:607) as follows: "[Durkheim] juxtapos[ed] the ordinary economic life of Australian bands – concerned mainly with obtaining food – with the 'effervescence' of their seasonal gatherings. It was there, in the excitement of the *corroboree* [a dance ceremony at aggregation sites], that the power to create society appeared to them." Anthropologist Alice Kehoe goes even further and compares the Plains aggregation settlements explicitly to urban settlements:

> Nomad peoples were constrained to adapt social affairs to ecological cycles: most of the business that in towns [in other societies] occurred over the year had to be compressed by the nomads into the few summer weeks when grass was most lush on the open plains. Trading, gambling, visiting friends from other bands, games and sports competitions, and seeking a compatible spouse or comrade were individual incentives to rendezvous in large camps. Adjudicating disputes, discussing policies and strategies for allied bands drew leaders to these camps. Above all, participation in rituals was a magnet. (Kehoe 1981:295)

Case Study 9 (cont.)

3.11. Painting of a Plains Indian aggregation site, eighteenth century, Comanche village. Painting by George Catlin. Smithsonian American Art Museum. Public domain. Source: Wikimedia Commons (https://commons.wikimedia.org/wiki/File:George_Catlin_-_Comanche_Village,_Women_Dressing_Robes_and_Drying_Meat_-_1985.66.346_-_Smithsonian_American_Art_Museum.jpg).

Comparative Insights. The exuberant activities at a Plains Indian aggregation site – and the resultant temporary energized crowding – are a particularly dramatic and well-described example of what took place at hunter-gatherer aggregation sites more generally over the centuries (Wengrow and Graeber 2015); see Chapter 2. These settlements have much to teach us about comparative urbanism. First, the general rule that settlement size predicts social complexity is clearly illustrated by the contrast between small mobile camps and aggregation sites. Second, large, socially complex settlements – with considerable energized crowding – are not limited to agricultural societies. Third, these features are not limited to permanent settlements. From this basis, it should not be surprising to learn that large aggregated tipi sites have clear neighborhood organization (Smith et al. 2015). Finally, there is a clear parallel between these aggregation sites and the Northern European assembly sites discussed in Chapter 4, showing that key aspects of the dynamics and organization of settlements cut across traditional social typologies.

Voluntary Camps and the Origins of Cities

Paul Wheatley's influential model for the origins of urbanism uses a concept like the voluntary camp as a way to understand the processes involved (Wheatley 1971). Wheatley hypothesized that people first built a shrine with sacred importance; then visitors created an associated temporary settlement with communitas (a religious camp and/or a pilgrimage camp), based on ceremonies at the shrine. Next, economic, social, and political activities were added as the site became more permanent; and the end result was an urban center in which religion provided the main integrating force. Archaeologists have shown, however, that Wheatley gave too much importance to the role of religion in generating and integrating the earliest complex settlements (Blanton 1982:432). Assyriologist Marc Van de Mieroop puts it this way:

> But people did not converge upon ceremonial centres for their spiritual leadership, and throughout the world many such centres exist in isolation. Moreover, the temple's importance in early Mesopotamia is greatly overstated, due to the archaeologists' focus on monumental architecture, and a misreading of mid-third-millennium archival records. The ideological focus provided by early cities clearly existed, but it was of insufficient strength to be the sole driving force towards urbanism. (Van De Mieroop 1997:24)

Nevertheless, the fact that some religious camps and pilgrimage camps have grown into regular settlements does suggest that at least one part of Wheatley's model makes sense. Some early religion-based settlements may have expanded into regular settlements with the addition of social complexity and urban functions.

In the modern voluntary camps, comfort and quality of life are sacrificed for a larger cause, whether religious or social. Similarly, communitas contributes to the suppression of hierarchy and social complexity in these camps. They have much to teach us about the role of generative forces in structuring human settlements and communities, a theme I explore next (see also Chapter 7).

CITIES AS SOCIAL REACTORS: SETTLEMENT SCALING AND ECONOMIC GROWTH

Economic growth is the third major consequence of energized crowding (Figure 2.1). The notion that population growth leads to economic expansion or growth dates back at least to Adam Smith's (1979) *The Wealth of Nations* (see Chapter 5). There is a new body of theory and empirical findings, however, whose greater quantitative precision is accompanied by a much wider range of application (including ancient cities). "Settlement scaling theory" is a powerful framework that predicts and explains key features of cities as quantitative expressions of a city's population. The assumptions of this approach are the following (Lobo et al. 2020):

1. Human social interactions are exchanges of material goods and information that take place in physical space.
2. The intensity, productivity, and quality of individual-level efforts are enhanced through interaction with others – that is, social networks amplify the economic and social production of individuals.
3. Any human activity can be thought of as generating benefits and incurring costs, particularly the costs of moving people and things in physical space.
4. The size, or scale, of a human settlement is both a consequent and a determinant of the overall economic and social productivity of the settlement.
5. Human effort is bounded – that is, there are upper limits on the amount of time and energy that individuals can put into their activities.

Using these assumptions as a foundation, Luís Bettencourt (2013) constructed a quantitative model that uses population to predict the densities of cities, as well as their levels of social and economic production, within particular urban or settlement systems. The parameters are quite simple: movement (distance) has a cost, and social interactions have benefits. This is an example of a "spontaneous order" process – that is, a complex system (a settlement, or urban society) has features that derive from social interactions without strong imposition of rules from authorities, and without the interacting individuals necessarily deliberately trying to achieve or create those features (Bowles 2004:57–58; Cronk and Leech 2013:156–161). In urban planning, spontaneous order has been called "self-coordination" (Moroni et al. 2020); see the discussion in Chapter 7.

Empirical Scaling Patterns

The development of settlement scaling theory began with observations of contemporary urban systems. The existence of regularities in the sizes of cities within a given urban system has been recognized for many decades (Jefferson 1939). City size in many urban systems conforms to a power law distribution (a specific distribution with many more small values and fewer high values than the normal distribution), known as Zipf's law, or the rank-size rule (Adamic 2011). In these systems, the second largest city has half the population as the largest city, the third largest has one-third the population, and so on (Mitchell 2009:chapter 17). Archaeologists have used Zipf's law to investigate ancient settlement systems, under the label of "rank-size analysis" (Drennan and

Peterson 2004; Johnson 1981; Smith 2005a); many of these studies have focused on cases where an urban system deviates from the rank-size rule, such as urban primacy (the label for systems in which the largest settlement is larger than predicted by the model). The Zipfian distribution is remarkably widespread in both ancient and contemporary cities, but the forces that generate the pattern remain elusive to scholars (Bettencourt 2021; González-Val et al. 2014). Deviations from a rank-size or Zipfian distribution, where one city is much larger than predicted, are thought to arise when political forces dominate economic forces in generating urban growth and change (Ades and Glaeser 1995; de Long and Shleifer 1993); see Chapter 4. The regularities of settlement scaling, however, go far beyond examining the distribution of city sizes.

The approach to scaling described here – known as *settlement scaling theory* (Lobo et al. 2020) – originated at the Santa Fe Institute, a research center for the science of complexity and complex adaptive systems.[8] Geoffrey West and colleagues had first established a quantitative, network-based understanding of the long-known scaling of metabolism with body weight in the animal kingdom (West 2017; West et al. 1997). West and a group of colleagues then began a search for power-law regularities in city size by examining how a series of quantitative urban variables could be predicted by knowing the sizes of cities in particular urban systems (Bettencourt et al. 2007; Bettencourt et al. 2010; Pumain et al. 2006). Empirical studies of contemporary cities identified a series of striking regularities. The quantitative patterns of greatest interest are expressed by a parameter called β, which is the exponent of the power law. There are three types of relationships between urban variables and city population: (1) *Linear scaling*, in which β is equal to 1; the quantity in question increases at the same rate as population; (2) *Sublinear scaling*, in which β is less than one; the quantity increases at a lower rate than population; and (3) *Superlinear scaling*, in which β is greater than one; the output increases at a rate greater than population.

Several urban measures exhibit sublinear scaling, with highly regular quantitative expressions. The area of a city, for example, increases with population with a β of 2/3 (0.67). This means that area grows less rapidly than population. Another way to say this is that the per capita area decreases with city size; that is, larger cities are denser than smaller cities. Similarly, the total length of urban infrastructure (roads, cables, etc.) increases with population with a β of 2/3. This makes sense; if city A is twice as large as city B, city A does not need twice the surface area or length of roads since some of the increased traffic can use the

---

[8] See the Santa Fe Institute website, www.santafe.edu.

existing roads. In the language of economics, infrastructure and area exhibit economies of scale with respect to population. The remarkable thing about these relationships is their regularity across urban systems (Bettencourt 2013).

More surprising than sublinear scaling are cases of superlinear scaling. A wide range of measures of social output – from income, wealth, and innovation to crime and poverty rates – exhibit superlinear scaling with city population. In other words, within an urban system, larger cities on average not only have more wealth or crime than smaller cities; they also have *higher per capita rates* of these measures than smaller cities. This is a very different relationship; superlinear scaling signals the presence of increasing returns to scale (Cesaretti et al. 2020), which is an important kind of economic growth (see Chapter 5). Remarkably, most measured superlinear variables scale with population with a β of 7/6.

Figure 3.12 illustrates the three kinds of scaling with respect to the area-population relationship. In superlinear scaling, area increases more rapidly than population, leading to settlements that are less dense; linear scaling has an even

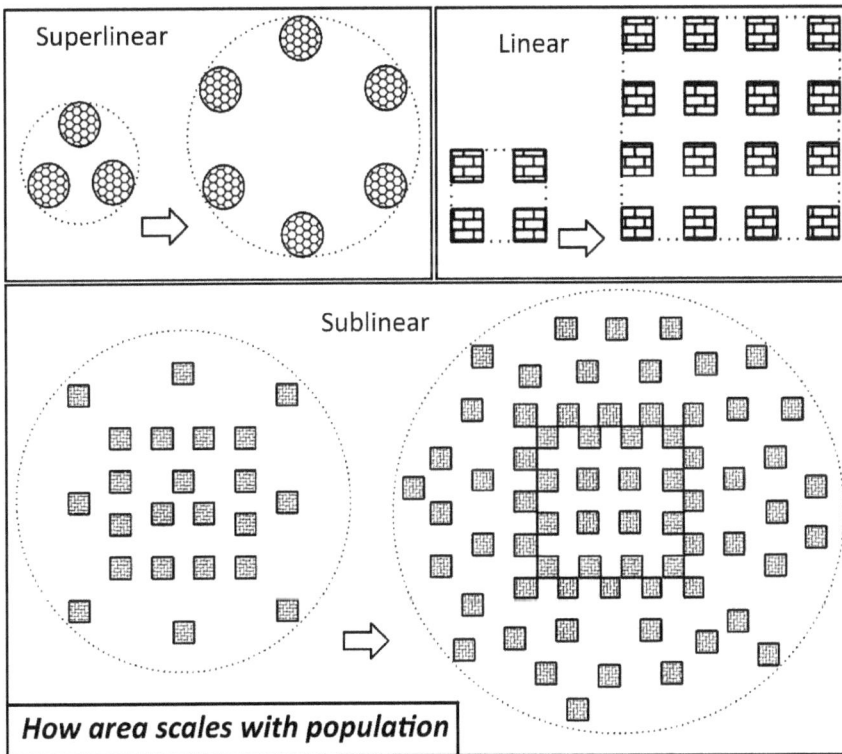

3.12. Three patterns in the way settlement area scales with population. Modified after Birch-Chapman et al. (2017:8).

growth of the two variables, and sublinear scaling means that area increases more slowly than population. The result of sublinear scaling of area with population is that larger settlements are denser than smaller settlements.

The Social Reactors Model

The data on sublinear and superlinear scaling in contemporary cities accumulated during the early 2000s (Bettencourt et al. 2007; Pumain et al. 2006; West 2017). In 2013, Luís Bettencourt published a quantitative model that uses a small number of variables (based on the assumptions listed above) to predict the empirical findings (Bettencourt 2013). His model is based on the number of people in a settlement, the distances they move on a daily basis, the probabilities they will encounter other people, the average output or productivity of each person, and the increase in outputs caused by social interactions. A basic assumption is that each social interaction generates economic benefits, which could be increased information for the individuals, or some kind of productive collaboration.

The scaling model is a type of network model in the sense that personal interactions establish social networks, which can be said to generate outcomes. The built environment acts to promote or hinder movement and interaction. The quantitative expression of these variables (for the formulae, see Bettencourt 2013) produces ideal or theoretical findings that predict quantitatively just how urban measures should scale with city population (within a given settlement system). In fact, the empirical data match the predictions rather closely. In Bettencourt's words, "These results also suggest that, despite their apparent complexity, cities may actually be quite simple: Their average global properties may be set by just a few key parameters" (Bettencourt 2013:1438). This theoretical system is based on the nature and number of social interactions as determined from the population of a settlement. In other words, energized crowding lies at the base of the model.

Bettencourt calls his model the "social reactor model" of urban dynamics. Superlinear scaling indicates that the actions of individuals in cities yield per capita outputs greater than would be predicted by linear scaling alone. Cities are social reactors, and the bigger they are, the greater their per capita output. This model is a kind of micro-foundation for one of the major insights discussed in this book: the notion that population and energized crowding generate change in human settlements. Or, looked at from another perspective, the dynamics of energized crowding provide a social-science framework for Bettencourt's quantitative model of urban scaling.

Expansion of the Framework to Premodern Settlement Systems

Figure 3.13A shows superlinear scaling of gross domestic product with population in US cities today. Power law distributions are typically graphed by first transforming the variables into logarithms, which produces a linear pattern amenable to analysis with linear regression methods. The scaling coefficient, β, is the slope of the fit line. In the figure, the dashed trend-line marks a β of 1.0, or linear scaling. In this case, the β for GDP is 1.13; the relationship is superlinear. The confidence intervals of the data include the predicted slope of 7/6, or 1.167.

Once the behavioral mechanisms and empirical findings of scaling regularities within systems of modern cities were established, an obvious question (obvious to archaeologists, at any rate) was whether this approach would also yield fruitful results for cities before the modern era. The basic assumptions of the social reactor model do not depend on contemporary economic institutions such as the capitalist global economy, wage labor, firms, or advanced financial institutions. These are not microeconomic models that rely on utility functions or maximization, features difficult to apply to ancient economies. Because of the generality of Bettencourt's model, there is no obvious a priori reason why they should not hold for early or non-Western settlement systems. The next task was therefore to gather data to test the scaling models for past urban systems. The logic is that if the data of past settlement systems conform to the predictions, then we can infer that the processes that generate the predictions did indeed operate in the past. While it is impossible to rule out alternative models altogether, at this point there is no known quantitative model – apart from Bettencourt's – that makes similar predictions that match urban data.

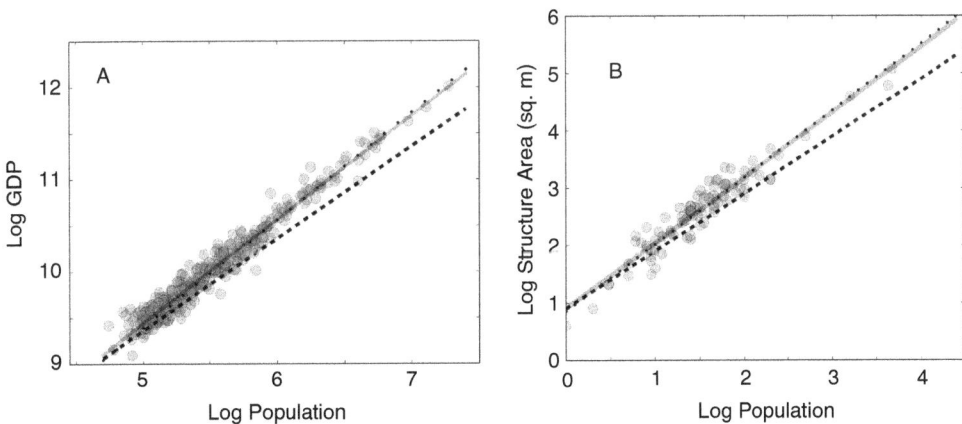

3.13. Superlinear scaling of social and economic outputs with population. (A) US cities, gross domestic product; (B) Ancient house size, Mantaro Valley, Peru. The dashed line shows linear scaling (β=1.0). Graphic by Luís Bettencourt, used with permission.

Scott Ortman assembled the first set of archaeological data to evaluate scaling models in the distant past. Working together with Bettencourt and José Lobo at the Santa Fe Institute, Ortman showed that both site area and wealth (using house size as a proxy for wealth; see Chapter 7) in the Aztec period Basin of Mexico scale with site population at the rate predicted by Bettencourt's theory (and as found empirically for contemporary cities); see Ortman et al. (2014, 2015). Given these initially promising results, the "Social Reactors Project" was formed in 2014 by Luís Bettencourt, José Lobo, Scott Ortman, and myself, in order to explore the scaling models and other quantitative urban expressions in both ancient and non-Western societies.[9] Our results to date have confirmed the presence of similar scaling regularities in a number of early urban systems, including city areas in medieval Europe (Cesaretti et al. 2016) and the Roman Empire (Hanson and Ortman 2017), and wealth in the Inca-period Andes (Ortman et al. 2016). Figure 3.13B shows the scaling of wealth against population for the latter region, resulting in a β identical to that reported for contemporary economic output.

Recent research has now extended these findings to the settlement systems of small-scale farming groups that do not qualify as "urban" in most senses of that term. Two separate village settlement systems in prehistoric North America – Mandan and the ancient Pueblo system – exhibit superlinear scaling of wealth and population (Ortman and Coffey 2017), and a number of twentieth-century peasant settlement systems in Mesoamerica and the Near East show the predicted sublinear scaling of area with population (Cesaretti 2016). These studies are summarized in several publications (Lobo et al. 2020; Ortman et al. 2020b; M. E. Smith 2019a); the close match between observed archaeological values for β and the predicted values is striking. While these patterns characterize nearly all of the settlement systems we have analyzed, there are two kinds of settlement systems where they do not hold: the campsites of mobile hunter-gatherers, and the Classic-period low-density cities of the Maya.

Among mobile hunter-gatherers, larger base camps are *less dense* than smaller base camps. First pointed out by Polly Wiessner (1974), this pattern is now documented for a large sample of mobile hunter-gatherers, whose dynamics of settlement diverge radically from those found among settlements in agriculturally based societies (Lobo et al. 2022). It seems that the potential economic benefits of densification – typical in agricultural settlement systems – are too weak to overcome the strong ecological forces leading to residential dispersion. Maya settlement systems resemble mobile hunter-gatherer systems in one respect: larger settlements are less dense than smaller settlements. Yet the

---

[9] "The Social Reactors Project: Human Settlements and Networks in History," University of Colorado Boulder, www.colorado.edu/socialreactors/.

Maya centers are functionally urban, displaying many of the characteristics of urban, state-level societies.

We recruited a group of Mayanists with quantitative data on settlement systems to examine this apparent anomaly (Smith et al. 2021c). We found that by redefining the relevant spatial units, the Maya system falls into line with other agrarian settlement systems. In most systems, the area of a settlement – the urban zone – is the spatial unit within which energized crowding takes place to create the scaling regularities: people live and interact within the urban zone. For the Maya, the expected scaling results come about when the measured urban zone is reduced to the epicenter, and the interacting population is expanded to the hinterlands of settlements. Thus a spatially more extensive population came into the city and created energized crowding in the epicenter, leading to the expected sublinear scaling for area and superlinear scaling for household wealth. The lower population density in Maya cities created a situation of lower levels of social interactions, but the larger relevant population interacting in the city center had similar scaling outcomes to most agrarian settlement systems.

The ongoing work of the Social Reactors Project has identified a number of striking regularities in the size-based properties of cities and settlement systems. This research has a number of implications for the stories of premodern cities told in this book:

1. Premodern settlement systems scale very much like contemporary urban systems.
2. The scaling relationships hold for state-level urban systems, for noncommercial economies (the Inka; see Chapter 5), and even for non-state village settlement systems.
3. The first two implications point strongly to the existence of fundamental and profound regularities in the structure and dynamics of settlement systems through the ages.
4. Energized crowding – social interactions driven by population size – is one of the casual, or generative, dynamics of settlement scaling.
5. Size is important. These results give strong support to my contention that the size of a settlement is one of its most important and influential attributes.

SETTLEMENT SIZE DATA

Size of the Case Study Settlements

Because of the importance of city size for the arguments in this book, I have assembled data on the population, area, and density of as many of my case studies as possible (presented in Table 3.2). The sources of these data are

TABLE 3.2 *Sizes of case studies, by settlement type*

#	Case	Loc	Type	Settlement			Neighborhood		
				Pop	Area	Dens	Pop	Area	Dens
Villages:									
4	Beidha, level B2	Old	V	60	0.2	300			
4	Beidha, level C2	Old	V	180	0.3	600			
Agrotowns:									
2	Çatalhöyük	Old	A	2,800	13.6	206			
6	SW pueblos (mean)	New	A	523	6.2	84			
Towns:									
11	Swahili city-state capitals	Old	T	925	15	62			
20	Ribe	Old	T	600	14	43			
Cities, New World:									
1	Tikal	New	C	7,000	1,127	6			
10	Cahokia	New	C	12,700	1,800	7			
12	Huanuco Pampa	New	C	13,500	200	68			
18	Otumba	New	C	10,700	220	49			
22	Yautepec	New	C	13,300	209	64			
26	Teotihuacan	New	C	100,000	1,876	53			
Cities, Old World:									
5	Mohenjo-daro	Old	C	33,500	259	129	432	2.6	166
8	Angkor	Old	C	903,800	300,000	3 *	1,700	68	25
15	Persepolis	Old	C	6,500	120	54			
16	Chang'an	Old	C	1,000,000	8,400	119			
17	Knossos	Old	C	16,000	70	229			
19	Jerash	Old	C	14,400	85	169 *			
21	Rhodes	Old	C	15,000	300	50			
23	Ado Ekiti (Yoruba)	Old	C	9,100	240	38			
24	Pompeii	Old	C	9,900	60	165			
25	Olynthus	Old	C	4,000	50	80	270	1.7	159
27	Odense	Old	C	2,660	39	68			
28	Ur	Old	C	12,000	96	125 *			
Practical Machine Sites:									
13	Amarna workers village	Old	S				360	0.5	720

(continued)

TABLE 3.2 *(continued)*

#	Case	Loc	Type	Settlement			Neighborhood		
				Pop	Area	Dens	Pop	Area	Dens
29	Fyrkat	Old	S	156	1.1	138			
Campsites:									
3	Pincevent	Old	TC	20	0.7	29			
7	Burning Man, 1996	New	TC	8,000	9.2	870			
14	Thing site	Old	TC						
9	Plains aggr site	New	TC	5,600	201	28			

* The population has been calculated from the area and a density constant. See Appendix A.

described in Appendix A. The figures listed under "Settlement" pertain to the entire extent of the settlement, typically as measured by an expert. In some cases, I had to calculate the populations myself; the details are in the appendix. The figures under "Neighborhood" are for a single residential neighborhood of a city, or for an independent settlement that corresponds to a neighborhood (e.g., the Amarna workers compound, Case Study 13). Because the area of a neighborhood typically leaves out any large open areas in a settlement, neighborhood density is almost universally higher than settlement density.

The purpose of the data in Table 3.2 is to illustrate the variation in population size and density among the case studies of this book. This is not a good sample for wider analysis. I picked the case studies to illustrate specific (nonquantitative) points, with no effort to be inclusive or representative. I did use one broader selection criterion: I selected at least one case from each part of the world. The variation among these cities apart from size – different political forms, economic systems, and other factors – is far too great for the size data from the case studies to be meaningful for questions, such as, Were imperial capitals larger than city-state capitals? Were cities in highly commercialized economies larger than those with less commercialized systems?[10] An adequate database of premodern city size to address these and other questions would be of great value, especially given the readiness of economists and other non-archaeologists to use patently bad data on ancient city size to reach likely specious conclusions about the past.[11]

[10] Indeed, the total size variation is too large for reasonable analysis; the standard deviation for all six categories exceeds the mean, and for total population, the standard deviation is three times the mean.

[11] See my blog post, "Why Would a Journal Called 'Scientific Data' Publish Bad Data? The Chandler/Modelski City-Size Problem," *Publishing Archaeology*, https://publishingarchaeology .blogspot.com/2016/06/why-would-journal-called-scientific.html.

TABLE 3.3 *Comparison of Old World and New World cities*

Location	No. cases	Median population	Median density[a]	Largest city	Population
New World	6	13,000	51	Teotihuacan	100,000
Old World	12	13,200	100	Chang'an	1,000,000

Note: Data from Table 3.1.
[a] Persons per hectare.

In spite of these qualifications about the size and representativeness of my sample of case studies, one pattern stands out as likely significant: the largest premodern cities in the Old World (such as Chang'an, with one million or more residents) were larger than those in the New World, a pattern that has long been evident to scholars. But, perhaps surprisingly, the median population size for the two regions is almost identical (Table 3.3), while the median density of Old World cities was twice that of New World cities.

Urbanization Levels

Although the term *urbanization* is often used as a generic label for processes of urban growth and/or expansion, it has a technical definition: "the proportion of the total population concentrated in urban settlements" (Davis 1968:3). When people note that more than half the earth's inhabitants now live in cities, they are, in fact, talking about the level of global urbanization. Urbanization is an important comparative measure that can reveal much about the nature and importance of cities in different contexts (Bairoch 1988; de Vries 1984; Woods 2003b). Higher urbanization levels can be promoted by a variety of factors, including economic growth, technological innovation, and increased rural-to-urban migration (Jedwab and Vollrath 2015; Woods 2003b; Wrigley 1990).

Archaeologists presenting data from regional settlement pattern projects have occasionally calculated urbanization levels (Sanders et al. 1979), but they have generally skipped over the technical issues necessary to discuss comparative urbanization levels with confidence. Most basically, the urbanization level one calculates from a given set of regional settlement size data is a direct reflection of the cutoff size one uses to label a settlement urban; higher thresholds lead to lower urbanization values, and lower thresholds produce higher values. I discuss this and other methodological issues of comparing urbanization levels, and present data from the Aztec Empire, in Smith (2017a) and Smith et al. (2021a); de Vries (1990) provides a more detailed discussion focused on historical demography.

SIZE IS IMPORTANT

The importance of city size for urban life and social dynamics – both within cities and in society generally – has been known to modern scholarship at least since Simmel's (1898:834) remarks (discussed previously). But, as early as the fourteenth century, Ibn Khaldun observed, "The more numerous and the more abundant the population in a city, the more luxurious the life of its inhabitants" (Bosker et al. 2013:1418). Johannes Müller (2013:2) lists seven "societal spheres" that are strongly influenced by group size and population density: economic activities, specialization and division of labor, architecture, political organization, horizontal networks, commodity exchange, and creation of identities. Sociologists and anthropologists have tended to emphasize the negative social consequences of city size, which I describe under the label of interaction stress. Community formation as an outcome of urban growth has been addressed by sociologists and urban planners. Economists, on the other hand, have focused their attention on the implications of city size for economic growth.

The settlement scaling research is a new, interdisciplinary approach that captures both the positive and negative aspects of urban growth in a single model of widespread application. That nearly identical scaling results have been reported for ancient and modern urban systems, for commercial and command economies, for both non-state (and non-urban) village societies, and for states is nothing short of remarkable. This research supports my claim that many "urban-like" processes are also found in non-urban systems. As I argue in Chapter 1, these results suggest that "cities" may be an artificial category, with "settlements" being the more natural unit for comparative social-science analysis. This is also why we call the scaling work *settlement scaling theory*, instead of *urban scaling theory*.

A further implication of the findings discussed in this chapter is that energized crowding and related processes – the ways people interact within settlements and the changes that are generated by such interactions – are some of the most important forces in creating change in society. This notion can be applied to Justin Jennings's (2016) suggestion that cities and urban settlements were created before the development of the earliest state governments. In his words:

> I have argued that much of what we think of as civilization is better conceived as the sporadic, often unintended, by-products of rapid settlement aggregation. People, using skill sets largely developed in a world of small-scale agriculturalists, mobile pastoralists, and hunter-gatherers, tried to solve the wide array of novel problems that occur as a result of increasing population size and density. (Jennings 2016:273)

Research by Jennings goes against the prevailing view in which the earliest states brought about the creation of cities (Adams 1966; Feinman and Marcus

1998). The arguments in Chapters 2 and 3 of this book support Jennings. People first aggregated into settlements for defensive or environmental reasons (as described in Chapter 2) and only later – after permanence was reached – did the resulting energized crowding lead to the development of the political hierarchies and social inequalities at the heart of early state societies.

In my view of premodern cities, urbanism, and society, size – both population and density – is perhaps the single most important measure one can make of human settlements. Many of the urban dynamics discussed in this book – particularly the nature and contours of urban life – were heavily influenced by the number of people and the population density of settlements (Fletcher 1995). The reason why I assembled the city sizes in Table 3.2 is to stimulate my colleagues to take population seriously. If archaeologists can continue to estimate populations from sites found in survey (Drennan et al. 2015), and apply population methods to excavated and mapped sites (Hanson 2016), the growth in our understanding of premodern cities, urbanism, and society in general will expand tremendously. Such data can be used for settlement scaling analysis, comparison of urbanization levels, and a variety of other tasks. Beyond the realm of urban life, population – as measured by energized crowding and its outcomes – also has more indirect effects. These operate through the effects of size on the political and economic dynamics of cities, the subject of the next two chapters. I begin with the relationship between states and cities.

FOUR

STATES, CITIES, AND POWER

W HEN THOMAS HOBBES WROTE IN THE SEVENTEENTH CENTURY that human life in nature was "solitary, poor, nasty, brutish and short," he set political philosophy onto an unproductive path that still has a negative influence on our thinking today. Hobbes claimed that only with the development of an autocratic state could people achieve a successful and satisfying existence. Without a powerful king, who would keep the forces of chaos away? Who would prevent the "war of all against all" that Hobbes attributed to life in the state of nature? Any student of anthropology can identify the problems with Hobbes's claim. Humans lived for tens of thousands of years on earth before the institutions of states came about during the Urban Revolution. And thousands of human groups continued to live without the state in the thousands of years since the Urban Revolution.

Hobbes, like many parochial European thinkers, was largely ignorant of the nonstate societies that flourished around the world. If the discipline of anthropology has learned anything at all in its first century and a half, it is that people in small-scale societies can get along just fine without kings and elites telling them what to do (Graeber and Wengrow 2021). Life is anything but solitary, poor, nasty, brutish, and short among hunter-gatherers and small-scale agriculturalists (Suzman 2017). Yet the Hobbesian vision that small-scale societies lived in chaos, that people needed kings and laws to make society safe and secure, lives on in contemporary political science and economics; for example, see North et al. (2009). In a strong critique of Hobbes's views on early human society, Karl

Widerquist and Grant McCall (2017) compare anthropological findings to works in contemporary political philosophy. In the words of Maeve McKeown (2019:284), those authors show that "the difference between philosophy and anthropology is that anthropologists looked at the evidence and (for the most part) realized they were wrong. Philosophers didn't bother."

Just as small-scale societies do not need kings and elites in order to flourish, I argue that cities do not need states in order to grow and flourish. But the converse is not true. States clearly do need cities. Without urban settlements, kings, elites, and the institutions of government can only operate on a very small scale. Polities that are small and weak can exist for a time with only rudimentary urban settlements, but in order to grow and thrive, states require cities or towns. They do not necessarily need large, dense settlements that fit Wirth's definition of the city, but they need places where the personnel and institutions of rule and administration can work. Among the outcomes of such work are political urban functions: political activities and institutions that affect a larger hinterland.

This chapter explores political and administrative institutions and activities that affected early cities and urban life; these are shown as external forces in Figure 1.9. I begin with a discussion of the relationship between cities and states. Do all states have cities? (Answer: Probably.) Do cities exist outside of states? (Answer: Yes, without a doubt.) I then review variations in the power and scale of state societies – from the weak states of feudalism to powerful empires – and show how this variation influences the cities in a society. I next turn to governance – the degree of collective or autocratic rule in a region – and show how this influences cities. I then use the category practical machine sites as a natural experiment to examine some of the specific ways that political administration creates and influences urban form and dynamics. I close the chapter with a short review of the ways various political forms and processes create top-down urban planning. Most of this chapter is about polities and forms of government; in other words, the focus is on top-down forces within premodern cities. I defer discussion of power, coercion, and ideology – how political power and government affect individuals and households – until Chapter 6. Unlike population processes, which serve to create commonalities among different cities, political institutions and forces create variation. The great variety of premodern political forms and systems and dynamics reviewed in this chapter created much of the variation we see among early cities around the world. Urban life can only be understood in relation to the polity and political dynamics of its encompassing society.

CAN CITIES AND STATES LIVE WITHOUT ONE ANOTHER?

Ever since V. Gordon Childe formulated his concept of the "Urban Revolution" (Childe 1936, 1950), archaeologists have associated (or perhaps

I should say "confused") cities with states. For Childe, the Urban Revolution was a label for the development of the earliest state-level societies, not a label for the development of cities per se. In fact, cities are one of ten new institutions claimed by Childe to develop together as a package and create a new way of life. Our understanding of Childe's influential model has changed over the years (Smith 2009), and only a few archaeologists still see his various traits – things like specialized production, writing, a state form of government, and social classes – as developing together, all at the same time; see Jennings (2016) for discussion.

The first cracks in Childe's model that cities and states developed together in ancient times came when archaeologists saw that settlements in Egypt (prior to the New Kingdom) and the Classic Maya lowlands seemed too small to call cities. Egypt was labeled a "civilization without cities" (Wilson 1960), a phrase that was immediately applied to the Maya as well (Willey 1962). While Egyptologists soon recognized that it was not productive to label early Egyptian settlements as non-urban in character (Kemp 1977; Moeller 2016), Mayanists entered a period of debate about the urban status of their settlements (Chapter 1).

The consensus now is that it would be difficult, but not impossible, to maintain a state form of government without some kind of urban center. Nevertheless, the inverse question (Can cities exist without states?) is more controversial. It should be clear from the first three chapters that my approach to urbanism allows cities and towns to flourish in the absence of state organization. Before exploring this idea further, I should make it clear what I mean by *state*.

What Is a State? Do States Need Cities?

The word *state* is used in two ways in the social and historical sciences. My usage in the above paragraphs is typical of archaeology and anthropology, where *state* refers to a type of society that is larger and more complex than tribes or chiefdoms or small-scale societies. The influential comparative archaeologist Robert McC. Adams defined states as "stratified, politically organized societies based upon a new and more complex division of labor" (Adams 1966:2). In his famous list of ten features of the Urban Revolution, Childe (1950) was referring to states in this sense.

In fields like political science, social history, and sociology, on the other hand, *state* refers to the political and administrative institutions that govern a state-level society. Charles Tilly, for example, defines states as "relatively centralized, differentiated organizations the officials of which more or less successfully claim control over the chief concentrated means of violence within a population inhabiting a large, contiguous territory" (Tilly 1985:170). It is in this sense that Marxists can discuss the state as a mechanism of exploitation, or economists can debate the roles of the state and the market in particular domains. Because scholars in this tradition rarely address what anthropologists call non-state societies, their usage of "state" makes sense.

In archaeology, where the rise of state-level societies – and the nature of their state institutions – have long been important research topics, the use of a single term for different concepts can only cause confusion. In this book, I will use the term *government* to refer to the administrative institutions involved in ruling or administering a state-level society. States are the kinds of polities that developed out of smaller, less complex polities such as chiefdoms.

Can states exist without cities? Almost all definitions of states include the requirement that they control a territory, which is governed by a ruler or another institution. If the government is based in a fixed location, then that location must – by the functional definition – be a city. It is a place whose activities and institutions affect an area beyond the city. But what if a king moves around the landscape, residing for periods of time in different locations (Bernhardt 1993; Geertz 1977)? If such a king – for example, Charlemagne (McKitterick 2011) or Alfred the Great (Roach 2011) – is able to exercise his power or administrative duties in each place, should we classify them all as urban places? Perhaps they all, together, constitute sequential, temporary manifestations of the capital. Or perhaps we should reserve that label for the most permanent and urban-like of the court locations. Charlemagne's itinerant court would set up at monasteries, palaces of local nobles, and even temporary campsites, but he built a cathedral and established his formal capital in Aachen. Charlemagne spent more time in other places, however, whose populations surged when the royal entourage was in residence, perhaps including tent cities (McKitterick 2011) or temporary pit houses of the type that has been documented for Scandinavian church towns (Jørgensen et al. 2011).

The itinerant royal court was common in Anglo-Saxon England and other parts of early medieval Europe (Bernhardt 1993), and it has been documented in medieval Inner Asia (Atwood 2015), the foreign Liao Dynasty in China in the tenth and eleventh centuries (Twitchett and Tietze 1994), Java (Geertz 1977), Mughal India (Sinopoli 1994), and Ethiopia from the sixteenth through the twentieth centuries (Horvath 1969). As I discuss later, these fascinating temporary capitals are an example of the "City as a practical machine" model (Lynch 1981). Even the settlements where the royal court resided temporarily do not fit Wirth's definition of *urban* because they are not permanent, but they do fit – if only for a short while – the functional definition of *urban* (Chapter 1). A rural monastery or noble's residence could serve as a temporary capital (i.e., a temporary city). The mobility of these places worked against economic growth, however; there was not sufficient time for energized crowding to establish itself as a generator of growth and change. Against arguments to the contrary that point to mobile or dispersed capitals (Christie 1991), I conclude that states do indeed need cities but – for states with little economic growth – permanent capitals are not necessary. But what about the converse? Do cities need states?

Cities without States?

Four main lines of research and evidence support the idea that cities can exist and thrive in the absence of a state form of society or state institutions of government. First, archaeological findings suggest that the earliest urban settlements may have preceded the earliest states. Jennings (2016) provides the most complete statement of this position. He examines six early urban centers – Cahokia, Harappa, Jenne-jeno, Çatalhöyük, Tiwanaku, and Monte Albán – and makes the claim that in only two cases (Tiwanaku and Monte Albán) did state-level societies develop out of early cities. In the other four cases, the interaction stresses of urban life were too great, and these urban centers collapsed without their enveloping societies developing into states. For Jennings, these earliest cities were chaotic and unstable. People had an aversion to hierarchy, based on their earlier experiences in smaller-scale societies without social classes (Taylor 1982), and therefore they opposed the imposition of state institutions and control. Jennings's argument is attractive (see also Jennings and Earle 2016), but the archaeological evidence from these cases is not yet sufficiently refined to confirm or reject his model as a general pattern with confidence. Perhaps the clearest evidence of a pre-state urban settlement is the site of Nekhen in Hieronkopolis (Moeller 2016:81–103).

The second kind of evidence that cities can exist without state governments consists of cases where cities and urbanism continue in "dark ages" times, after the collapse of states. Several authors have pointed to cases of this in world history (Hansen 2008; M. L. Smith 2003a). Perhaps the best archaeological evidence comes from sites such as Ayn Asil in Egypt, whose urban traits spanned both the centralized Old Kingdom and the politically decentralized dark ages of the First Intermediate Period. As Moeller (2016:241–243) shows, this urban settlement had a continuous occupation from the Early Kingdom to the Middle Kingdom periods, with continuities in craft production, public cult, and use of a palace structure.

Third, there is a growing scholarly trend showing that many urban features are created, not by kings, elites, or other authorities, but rather by the actions of people independently of hierarchical institutions. This moves us into the realm of the economic activities and functions of cities, to be discussed in Chapter 5. The settlement scaling research described in Chapter 3 verifies this conclusion about the importance of bottom-up processes and social interactions, or energized crowding. A wide range of studies in many disciplines come to parallel conclusions (Alexander 1979; Batty 2013; Birch 2013; Jacobs 1961). I explore this topic in more detail in Chapter 7.

While this research supports the notion that cities may not need state institutions to flourish, it does not provide much direct evidence for cities in the absence of states. Fortunately, the literature on chiefdoms – the fourth line of research on cities without states – does provide that evidence. Chiefdoms are hierarchical polities that are smaller and less complex than states (Drennan and Peterson 2006; Earle 1997, 2021; Grinin and Korotayev 2011).[1] The two key identifiers of states are political centralization and institutionalized social inequality (Adams 1966:2). Chiefdoms are ruled by a chief whose power and control are less than the power and control of a king or other state ruler, and the institutions of government are more rudimentary than in states. But chiefdom leaders do have more power and authority than leaders of tribal or small-scale farming societies. Wealth inequality and social ranking are present in chiefdoms (Smith et al. 2018), but they are not institutionalized into rigid social classes.

The chiefs who rule chiefdoms collect tribute or taxes and exert a level of control over a population that typically resides in an area larger than the immediate settlement. The chief's actions, and the associated institutions and their supporting built environment, therefore constitute political urban functions. In addition, many chiefdom centers have prominent temples and other religious structures that probably served the residents of both the center and the hinterland. Consequently, chiefdom centers are urban settlements by the functional definition of urbanism. The great Mississippian city of Cahokia is a clear example of a capital of a large and powerful chiefdom. Cahokia is larger and more socially complex than most chiefdom towns, and thus it is not a typical case. But it does have the advantage of being one of the most extensively studied chiefdom centers in the world.[2]

EMPIRES, CITY-STATES, AND WEAK STATES

The variety of political forms before the modern era, and outside the Western tradition, is tremendous. I present a typology designed to simplify that variation and illustrate how political forms relate to urban forms. I then review two case

---

[1] Chiefdom is a contested concept in archaeology. The major critique of chiefdoms (Pauketat 2007) objects to the way certain twentieth-century anthropologists used the chiefdom concept. Beck (2009), Carneiro (2010) and Grinin and Korotayev (2011) point out problems with Pauketat's ideas, and reaffirm the usefulness of chiefdom as a societal type.

[2] It also has the personal advantage of being the setting for my student training in archaeological fieldwork in the 1970s.

Case Study 10 Cahokia: Chiefdom Capital

Cahokia was the largest ancient urban center in North America north of Mexico, and its central building – an earth pyramid called Monks Mound – is one of the largest pyramids in the world. Early perceptions of this site and its associated Mississippian culture were biased by the myth of the mound builders. This was a racist notion that Native Americans and their ancestors were not capable of constructing large mounds, and therefore the mounds must have been built by some other race. Archaeologists soon figured out this was false; the native peoples encountered by European expansion across North America were the direct descendants of the Mississippian peoples. Cahokia is now recognized as one of the best preserved and best excavated chiefdom centers in the Americas (Milner 2005; Pauketat 2009). Cahokia was located in the largest expanse of the floodplain on the Mississippi River, and the peak of its development came between 1100 and 1300 CE (Pauketat 2009; Tainter 2019).

Chiefdom Urbanization. Although archaeologists once hesitated to call Cahokia an urban settlement, that trend has reversed in the past decade, with terms like *city*, *urban sprawl*, and *metropolitan area* becoming common among specialists (Lawler 2011). Although the size (1.5 square km) and population (20,000) of Cahokia dwarf other North American sites (Benson et al. 2009), its density was in the lowest tier of cities considered in this book. Evidence for political urban functions is not hard to find at the site (Figure 4.1). A large wood structure once stood on the top of Monks Mound. It is not clear whether this was a residence (of a chief), a temple, a council house, or a building that combined multiple uses. Most archaeologists see Cahokia's leader as having some kind of political control in the region, both in the dense concentration of settlements in the immediate floodplain area and places more distant. A separate kind of political urban function was defense. A large wood palisade (Figure 4.1) enclosed the central ceremonial area and some houses, and people from surrounding sites may have gathered inside the palisade if the city was attacked. The public plazas in front of Monks Mound were settings for ceremonies and other activities that constitute energized crowding.

4.1. Cahokia, reconstruction painting. Cahokia Mounds State Historic Site; painting by William R. Iseminger; reproduced with permission.

Case Study 10 (cont.)

Monks Mound likely had a religious urban function of some sort, and the many smaller temples (rectangular mounds today) also point to major ritual activity at Cahokia. Since the number and size of the Cahokia temple mounds are lacking at nearby settlements, these features probably served religious urban functions. Another example is a circular arrangement of posts – known as the *woodhenge* (on the left side of Figure 4.1) – that seems to have been used for astronomical observations with religious significance (Iseminger 2010). Evidence for extensive craft production has been found at Cahokia (Muller 1997; Pauketat 1997), although it is not clear whether the products (primarily lithic tools and shell ornaments) were destined for export or not.

Comparative Insights. Twenty years ago, the term *urban* as a label for Cahokia seemed iconoclastic, but today an urban interpretation of the settlement has become widespread. Mesoamericanist John Clark has said, "If you found this [Cahokia] in the Mayan lowlands, there would be no doubt this was a city" (Lawler 2011:1619). I agree. The implications are that cities are present in chiefdom societies, and thus cities can thrive outside of state-level societies, and in the absence of state governments. My interpretation thus concurs with Justin Jennings (2016), for whom Cahokia was a city whose polity did not develop into a state.

studies that show the relationship between the nature or type of a state and its cities: Swahili city-state culture and a provincial capital in the Inka Empire.

Types of Polity and Their Capitals

A polity is a territory or group of people ruled by a government that is largely autonomous from other polities. By *government*, I mean a set of institutions that exert political power and have an administrative role in society. States and empires are clearly polities, as are societies with weaker power and less-developed administrative structures such as chiefdoms and feudal societies. There was tremendous variation in premodern polities, and this variation is important for understanding the nature of urban life through history. I offer a simple typology of agrarian polities (Figure 4.2) to address this situation. (I use the concept of agrarian polities to exclude both non-agricultural and modern industrial polities.[3]) This scheme organizes the variation in agrarian polities along two axes: the size of the territory controlled and the level of centralized power of the regime. These two dimensions are my own relative judgments, not absolute measurements. In other words, a large city-state in one region might have a larger territory than a small empire in another.

---

[3] The high level of variation in political forms and dynamics through history makes definition and comparative analysis difficult. For more discussion, see Hansen (2000b) or Tilly (1992). Alternative typologies of premodern state forms include those of Eisenstadt (1963), Trigger (2003), and Tilly (1992). These are all useful for some purposes, but they fail to capture the kind of variability that relates strongly to city size and form. My table serves to organize a complex body of material; it is not meant as a rigid statement about the nature of the world.

Territory size

	Small	Large
High	City-states	Territorial states & empires[a]
	Indirect-rule empires	
Low	Weak states[b] & chiefdoms	

Centralized power (vertical axis label: High at top, Low at bottom)

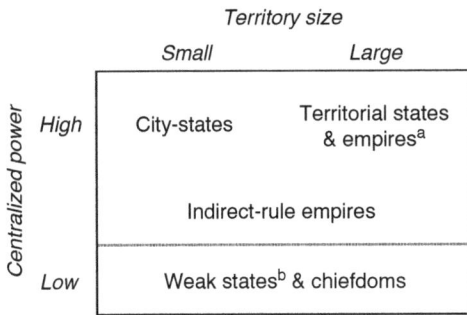

a Includes direct-rule empires, patrimonial states, the
    Asiatic mode of production, Trigger's territorial states.
b Includes feudal polities, segmentary states, and
    theater states.

4.2. Typology of premodern states. Graphic by Michael E. Smith.

Chiefdoms and Weak States. In simplistic comparative schemes, such as the band-tribe-chiefdom-state typology of 1960s cultural evolution (Sanders and Price 1968; Service 1975), chiefdoms and what I call *weak states* are not classified as true states, which in turn implied that such societies could not have urban settlements. As part of my effort to broaden the scope of comparative urbanism, however, it is important to include them when considering variation in urban forms. The *weak state* category includes feudal polities and the kind of small pageant-based states that anthropologists have called segmentary states (Fox 1977; Southall 1988); the latter category includes theater states (Geertz 1980) and galactic polities (Tambiah 1977). While some of these polities could be quite large in extent, all are characterized by a low level of centralized political control. In many cases, the power of these petty kings was based on charismatic power; the king himself was the central focus, and part of his authority derived from being seen in person by nobles and commoners alike. The king may have traveled around his kingdom or else hosted major theatrical pageants where he paraded through the capital (Geertz 1977, 1980).

Cities in weak states reflect the nature of the polity. For Charlemagne and other Early medieval kings who moved their court regularly (discussed previously), multipurpose, permanent, cities simply did not develop. Nevertheless, the temporary capitals probably exhibited energized crowding at a limited scale, and they certainly had political functions. Similarly, the Mughal emperors of India moved a huge entourage – up to 300,000 persons (if the eyewitness accounts are believed) – around the kingdom (Sinopoli 1994). Although sometimes regarded as a powerful empire, the Mughal patterns of kingship have been labeled "patrimonial," a weak state form of kingship (Blake 1991). In some weak-state settings, archaeologists have found various urban features (churches, palaces, meeting places) distributed across the landscape. This was the case in eighth-century Anglo-Saxon England, a period that preceded

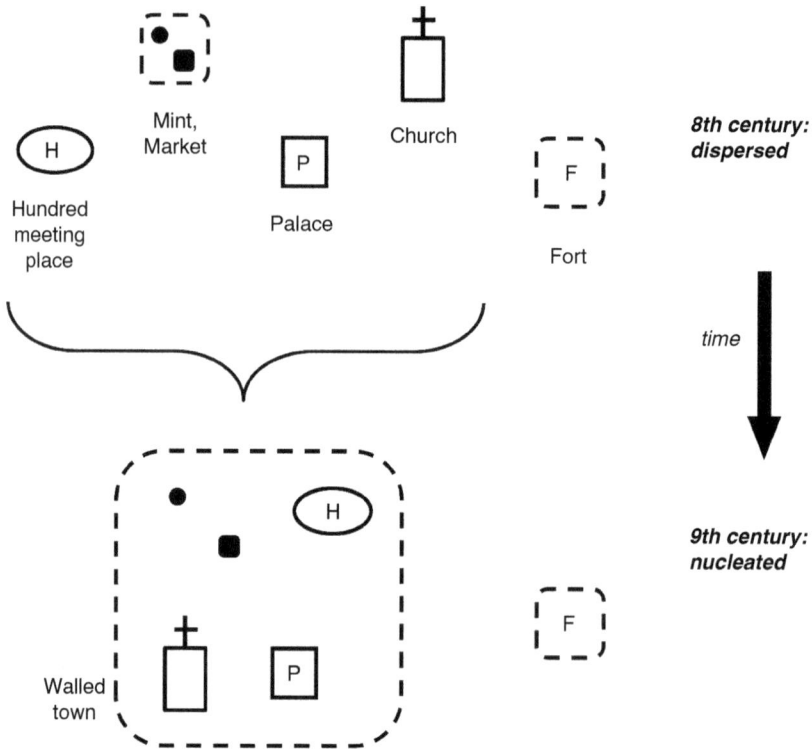

4.3. Aggregation of urban features over time in Anglo-Saxon England. Graphic by Michael E. Smith, based loosely on Hill (1988:202) and Aston (1984:199).

aggregation and urbanization (Blair 2018). Then in the ninth century, these features were concentrated into walled towns such as York (Figure 4.3).

The (permanent) cities of many segmentary states reflected the importance of performance and show in their royal political dynamics. The towering temples of Maya cities were paired with plazas and specialized civic buildings, all designed to show off the king and his court. The oversized and often highly decorated civic architecture belies the fact that political power was only partially centralized in these cities. On the other hand, one might say that the exuberance of temples and civic architecture was a public statement that weak kings felt obligated to make to the world (see my discussion of middle-level architectural meaning later in this chapter). The ritual authority of these petty kings often extended further than their political authority. Nevertheless, their urban world – the number of people in their capital – was typically quite small, given the very low population densities of cities such as Tikal, Cahokia, and Angkor. Richard Fox (1977) uses the term "regal-ritual city" for these settlements. They clearly functioned as urban places in the political and religious realm, but few would satisfy Wirth's definition of *city*.

Indirect-Rule Empires. The contrast of direct versus indirect rule is a useful way to characterize premodern empires (Gerring et al. 2011). In the former system, the imperial regime takes steps to incorporate conquered subjects directly into the polity. They may be granted the rights of citizens, including special consideration for taxation. Direct-rule empires typically send armies and bureaucrats to the provinces to administer the territory, and they may build cities, roads, and other public facilities in provincial areas. The Inka Empire is a well-documented direct-rule empire, and much of the Roman Empire (particularly in Gaul and Britain). Indirect-rule empires, on the other hand, rely on provincial control through local elites. They operate like an organized-crime protection racket; their message to subjects is, "Pay your taxes and we will leave you alone." The Aztec and Athenian Empires used indirect control, as did the Roman Empire in the eastern provinces.

It is hard to identify clear and consistent differences between the capitals of direct-rule and indirect-rule empires. The former probably had more facilities for administrators and bureaucrats. On the other hand, the provincial cities in these two kinds of empires differed radically, a theme taken up in the Inka case study later in this chapter.

City-States. City-states are polities that have a single capital city – often no larger than a town – that rules a small agricultural hinterland. One of the most interesting features of these polities is that they almost never exist alone; instead, they flourish in large regional systems that Mogens Hansen (2000c) calls "city-state cultures." This consists of an area that is unified culturally and linguistically, but fragmented politically. Classical Greece is the basic model for a city-state culture, but this kind of system was quite widespread in the ancient world. Hansen assembled thirty examples (Hansen 2000a) and showed how they conform to his basic model. City-state cultures were dynamic political landscapes. Individual city-states interacted constantly with one another, in ways both friendly (trade and marriage alliances) and antagonistic (conquest and domination). When one city-state succeeds in dominating its neighbors, the result can be a small empire; this happened with Athens in Classical Greece and Tenochtitlan in Aztec Mexico.

The capitals of city-states, not surprisingly, were small settlements. They are usually the only urban center in the polity. In a study of Aztec city-state capitals (Smith 2008), I found that the second-largest settlement in each city-state was – on average – about one-tenth as large as the capital. Because of the constant interactions among polities in city-state cultures, the capitals usually shared basic elements of urban form and institutions. They were potent places for the operation of energized crowding and its effects.

Territorial States. This category (Figure 4.2) includes large powerful states that fit a number of existing political typologies. I take the label from Trigger

(2003), who contrasts territorial states with city-states. Other labels include Max Weber's (1950:chapter 12) "patrimonial state" (Mann 1986:171–191), the Marxist concept of the "Asiatic mode of production." I also include the category direct-control empires (Gerring et al. 2011) here.

These large and powerful states tended to have large and complex capitals, but it is hard to generalize about their form or structure. Because of the large size of the polity, only a small portion of the total population resided in the capital, and this fact must have contributed to the higher levels of wealth inequality, and the frequency of more autocratic regimes, among territorial states as compared to city-states (Hansen 2008; Trigger 2003:131–141) The capital cities of major empires and territorial states were typically primate cities, in that they were far larger than any other city in the polity. In research on city-size distributions (Chapter 3), this is known as a *primate distribution*, and it is found where politics dominates economics as a major determinant of urban size and dynamics (Ades and Glaeser 1995; de Long and Shleifer 1993). It is not surprising that Greg Woolf (2020:401) has noted that in the ancient Mediterranean region, all of the largest cities were imperial capitals. The concept of *world city* has been used to describe these large, cosmopolitan, imperial capitals whose influence covered vast areas (Edwards and Woolf 2002; Smith 2020c).

A distinctive type of territorial-state capital is the disembedded capital. This is a new city, founded on neutral ground, to serve as capital of a large polity whose existing cities have entrenched political elites and institutions (Joffe 1998). The rulers want to free the capital from particular localized interests. Modern examples of disembedded capitals include Washington, DC, Brasilia, and Canberra. The pharaoh's capital of Amarna in New Kingdom Egypt is the clearest premodern example (Joffe 1998; Kemp 2012). As a new ruler promoting a new religion, Akhenaten founded Amarna in a new location, at least in part to escape the entrenched power and interests of the priesthood, which was rooted in existing capital cities.

Case Study 11 Swahili Cities: Trade and Urbanism in a City-State Culture

The Swahili city-state culture flourished along the East African coast between about 900 and 1500 CE (Figure 4.4). These cities were wealthy trading ports that served as intermediaries between the African interior and the busy Indian Ocean trading system (Abu-Lughod 1989). I focus on two of the best-excavated sites: Kilwa (Chittick 1974; Wynne-Jones 2007) was a large town at the south end of the Swahili system (Figure 4.4), and Shanga (Horton 1996) was a village at the northern end of the system (Figure 4.5).

Intensive Commerce in Small States. Long-distance trade was important along the East African coast going back to Roman times at least. Around 1000 CE, the Indian Ocean trading system expanded in size and intensity. Local coastal villages on good harbors grew into towns and cities, and state governments were formed. Although many separate languages were spoken initially, the Swahili language soon spread as part of the development of the city-state culture (Kusimba et al. 2017). Civic buildings and large houses were built of blocks of coral, finished with plaster, while smaller houses were constructed of wattle and daub. Swahili cities shared a basic architectural inventory of stone buildings: houses, tombs, mosques, and

Case Study 11 (cont.)

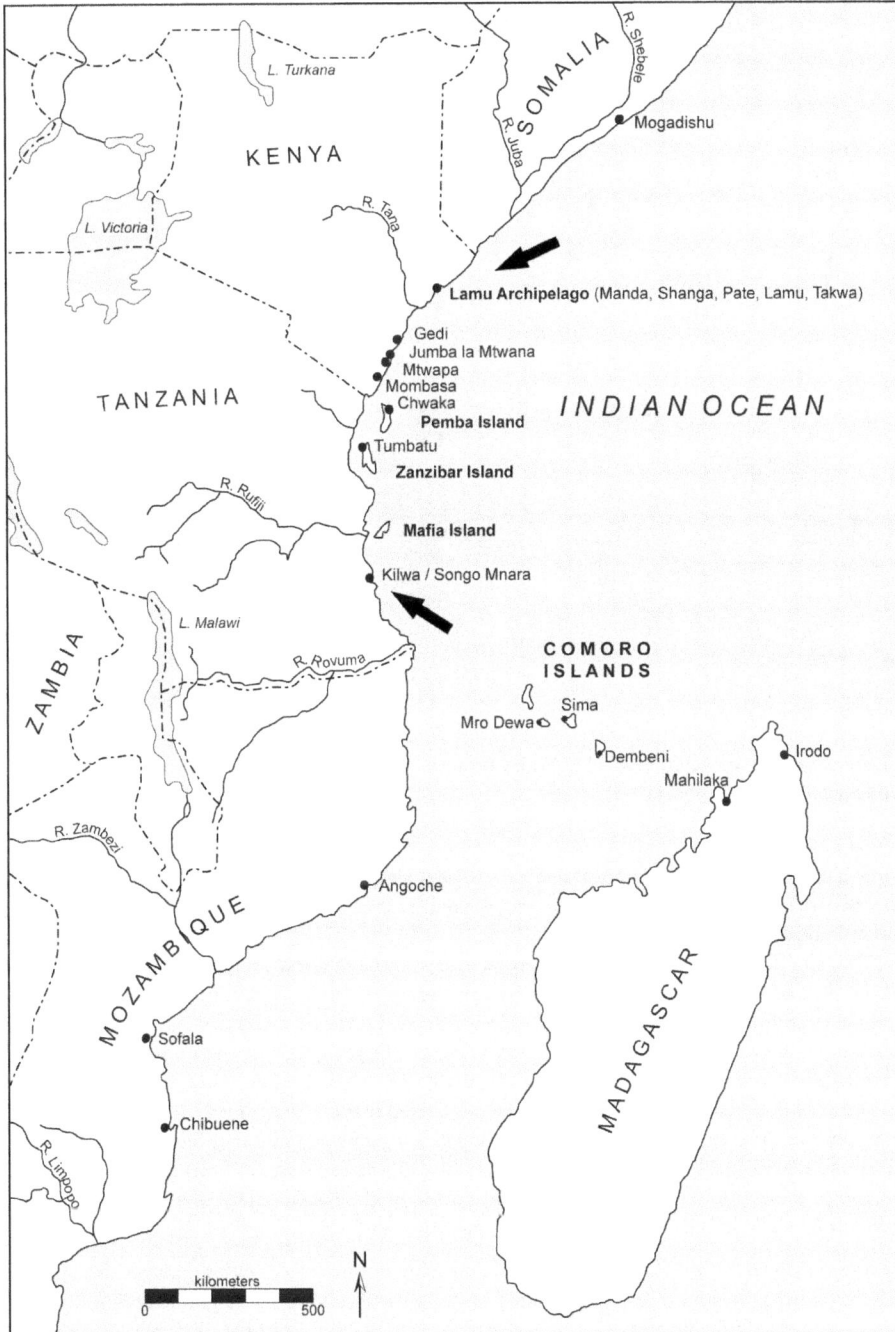

4.4. Map of Swahili city-state capitals along the East African Coast. Map by Stephanie Wynne-Jones; used with permission.

Case Study 11 (cont.)

4.5. Plan of Shanga, a Swahili town. (A) Friday mosque; (B) Western mosque; (C) Eastern mosque. Modified after Horton (1996:31–31).

a town wall. Cities like Kilwa had multiple elite palaces and large mosques. Villages like Shanga were composed of stone houses and mosques, but they lacked features such as a city wall, elite palaces, or large tombs with markers.

The Swahili cities exported a long list of products. From the interior, they received and shipped out ivory, timber, and iron. Northern parts of the Swahili area provided frankincense and myrrh, while gold and copper came from southern areas. Local exports included turtle shell and iron. Gold, obtained from the inland city of Great Zimbabwe via the port of Sofala (Figure 4.4), was the most lucrative export, underwriting the commercial and political development of Swahili city-states. Iron working was also of great economic importance. Archaeologists have discovered that this was a major industry on the coast prior to 1000 CE and continued in importance during the city-state period. Many Swahili settlements had vast areas of industrial-scale smelting outside the walls, with smaller-scale smithing in town. The active economies of these cities provided ample opportunities for the development of energized crowding, which in turn helped stimulate greater economic growth.

Comparative Insights. The Swahili cities illustrate the main features of a city-state culture: small but rich capitals, interacting intensively with one another, in a setting of cultural and linguistic uniformity. They also show very clearly the importance of trade in the creation and flourishing of city-state cultures. As Mogens Hansen noted in the conclusion of his comparative study of city-state cultures, "one of the major results of the present investigation has been to demonstrate the close connection between city-states and trade, and they emphasize long-distance trade as one of the essential links which could hold together the different city-states of a city-state culture" (Hansen 2000b:615).

Provincial Cities in Empires

Most of my discussion of cities and state forms has focused on capital cities. But the influence of political forms and functions on cities is also felt in the provincial cities of empires. In fact, direct-control and indirect-control empires had radically different provincial urban patterns. This can be seen through my comparison of provincial cities in the Aztec (indirect control) and Inka (direct control) empires. I will then focus specifically on an Inka case study – Huanuco Pampa (Case Study 12) – to provide more insight into provincial administration in a direct-control empire.

Urban buildings in the provinces of both the Inka and Aztec empires showed architectural similarities with their capitals, but the origins and nature of that similarity were radically different. In the Inka case, the types of buildings, settlement layouts, and construction methods linked provincial cities to the capital, Cuzco. Agents of the Inka Empire deliberately designed provincial cities to look "Inka" in style by copying Cuzco patterns; this was part of their imperial control strategy. The best-known example is Huanuco Pampa, discussed later.

In the Aztec case, the indirect-control empire had little interest in provincial cities, and it made no effort to plan or build or modify them. It is clear, however, that the style of the central temple in the provincial city of Cuauhnahuac (at the site of Teopanzolco, in the modern city of Cuernavaca) was almost identical to the style of the central temple in the imperial capital Tenochtitlan. A sign for tourists at the site even claims that the Cuauhnahuac temple was copied from the temple in Tenochtitlan. My own research shows, however, that the Teopanzolco temple was built some two centuries before the founding of the city of Tenochtitlan! The imperial rulers revived an archaic temple style that had been popular centuries earlier at Teopanzolco and other early Aztec cities. Thus the architectural similarities between capital and provinces had nothing to do with imperial expansion or strategy; it arose from the fact that both the capital and the provinces were part of a widespread cultural tradition within which architectural styles had spread long before the expansion of the Aztec empire (Smith 2008).

Case Study 12 Huanuco Pampa: Provincial Capital in a Direct-Control Empire

The Inka Empire is a fascinating case for comparative study, for a number of reasons. In addition to its status as a direct-control empire, the Inka economy was one of the few noncommercial economies among the empires of antiquity (Chapter 5). The lack of a system of writing meant that imperial administration was a complex operation. The Inkas used the *quipu*, a device with knotted strings, to keep track of quantities of goods, people, and animals. The political and economic structure of the Inka Empire shaped the nature and layouts of cities, and the best known of these is Huanuco Pampa (Figure 4.6). This city was built in a new location and then occupied for just a generation or two by

Case Study 12 (cont.)

bureaucrats and others brought from distant areas. After Francisco Pizarro conquered the Inka empire in 1532, most of the residents of this city went home, with only very minor later occupation before Craig Morris carried out mapping and excavations in the 1970s (Morris 1972; Morris et al. 2011; Morris and Thompson 1985).

Provincial Architecture and Infrastructure. A sure sign of a direct-control empire is a surge of construction activity in the provinces, directed by the empire. The Inka case is particularly spectacular in this regard; imperial bureaucrats supervised the construction of thousands of kilometers of roads, rope bridges over deep canyons, and inns along major highways (Hyslop 1984, 1990). Whole cities like Huanuco

4.6. Plan of Huanuco Pampa and Inka administrative center. Plan by Delfín Zúñiga. From *Huánuco Pampa: An Inca City and Its Hinterland* (Morris and Thompson 1985:54–55); Thames and Hudson, reproduced with permission.

Case Study 12 (cont.)

Pampa were built as administrative hubs. Some buildings used a distinctive style of high-quality masonry that achieved a close fit between often irregularly shaped stones, without the use of mortar. The Spanish conquerors marveled that the stones were set so closely that it was impossible to insert a knife blade between them. This was the Cuzco imperial style, and its presence in the provinces sent a clear message: the empire is here. As an Aztec specialist, I marvel at the Inka provincial infrastructure; the Aztecs, with their program of indirect control, did none of this.

Huanuco Pampa is full of typical imperial buildings, particularly the long, narrow halls called *kallanka*. These were used for what Morris (1972) called "state hospitality." Chiefs and leaders from the region were invited to wine and dine with Inka administrators, who were able to convince them to go along with the new higher level of exploitation under the empire. This must have been quite a task. The empire appropriated any empty lands, as well as lands that had belonged to villages. Aside from having some of their lands confiscated, the villagers had to pay imperial taxes – in labor. This was a noncommercial economy, run by the state. People contributed not by paying taxes in the form of goods, but by working on state lands and projects; they built roads and bridges or maintained temples or inns. Even though this was a strong empire with a command economy (Chapter 5), there were spaces and opportunities for the development of energized crowding. Our work on settlement scaling in another part of the Inka empire revealed the same sorts of economic outcomes that are found in commercial economies (Ortman et al. 2016).

One of the key urban features at Huanuco Pampa and other Inka administrative cities were rows of storage facilities. These were stone buildings with a long row of single-room storage chambers. An early postconquest drawing of Inka storehouses (Figure 4.7) shows the bureaucrat in charge (with a khipu, looking nervous), reporting to the highest imperial official, the Emperor himself (identified by his

4.7. Inka storehouses, with the bureaucrat in charge showing his quipu to a high imperial official. Drawing by Felipe Guaman Poma de Ayala, drawing no. 132, reproduced by permission, Royal Danish Library.

Case Study 12 (cont.)

earspools and mace-head). Their primary contents were maize and potatoes, harvested from the imperial lands by local villagers. Storehouses stretched out in long lines along the slopes above the city.

Comparative Insights. Craig Morris (1972), the excavator of Huanuco Pampa, was my professor when I was an undergraduate at Brandeis University. He coined the apt phrase *compulsory urbanism* to describe Inka provincial capitals. Many of the "residents" were people brought in from elsewhere, paying their imperial taxes by working in the city. When their stint was done, they went back home; and when the empire crumbled before the Spaniards, the entire city was abandoned. This makes it an ideal archaeological site: the entire city plan is visible on the ground surface for mapping (Figure 4.6), allowing targeted excavations to investigate specific questions. One of the truly great urban sites of the ancient world, Huanuco Pampa shows us that states – particularly direct-control empires like the Inka polity – do indeed need cities in order to function.

COLLECTIVE AND AUTOCRATIC GOVERNANCE

In a paper titled "War Making and State Making as Organized Crime," Charles Tilly (1985) noted that states (governments) do two things: they exploit people, and they provide services. Most of this exploitation takes the form of transfers of wealth from people to the government (taxes), but other forms include restrictions on freedom and livelihood from laws and regulations. The balance between exploitation and services varied tremendously among ancient governments, a topic to which we now turn. The trade-off between exploitation and services can be insightful for any state-level society, from the Urban Revolution to the present day. Indeed, a large part of contemporary political ideology on both the left and the right hinges on what people think is a proper balance between exploitation and services in their own local or national context.

Outdated Views of Ancient Kings and Kingdoms

There is a false story about ancient governments that remains popular among both scholars and the public. It goes something like this. All ancient state governments were ruled by cruel autocratic tyrants who strived to control all aspects of life in their realm. These kings used forced labor (slaves and serfs) to construct large monuments like the Egyptian pyramids. People were exploited and downtrodden, with little self-determination and certainly no voice in the way their polity was run. And then the Greeks invented democracy! Unfortunately, this nice-sounding story is more fantasy than reality. Figure 4.8 shows a propagandistic image in which Ramses II smites his enemies in an almost cartoon-like manner, compared to a body of deliberating Athenians engaged in democracy. The cartoon-like view of ancient despotism has been labeled "oppression theory" by Richard Blanton (2016:chapter 7).

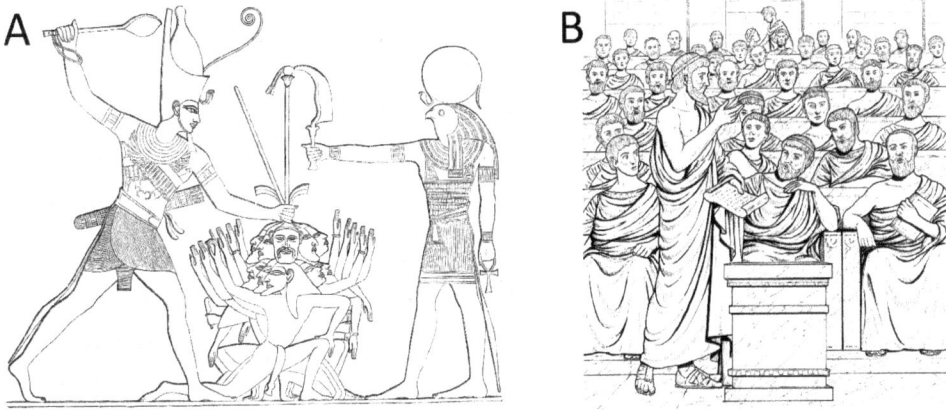

4.8. Propagandistic images of autocratic (A: the Egyptian pharaoh Ramses II, smiting his enemies) and collective (B: the Athenian senate) regimes. (A) Woodcut relief from Abu Simbel, from Anton Springer, History of Art Picture Sheets, 1888. (B) Idealized image of the senate of Classical Athens. Vital Imagery Ltd.; reproduced with permission.

What is wrong with this story? First, there is little evidence that ancient monuments were built with slave labor. Workers were paying their taxes through *corvée labor*, a form of labor tax common in premodern states (Booth 1998; Scheidel 2015). Second, large monuments can be constructed without cruel overseers and without states or elites. Megalithic monuments such as Stonehenge provide a striking example, as do cases of major monumental construction among small-scale groups in recent times. In Figure 4.9, for example, a group of workers from a weak state in Indonesia around 1900 moves a very large stone without coercion. The third problem with the story recounted previously is that the Greeks were not unique in establishing a democratic or collective government in the ancient world; in fact, many ancient governments were more collective than autocratic, and their rulers did not attempt to control the lives of their subjects.[4]

Collective and Autocratic Regimes

One of the major works helping overturn the old and faulty view of ancient despots is the book *Collective Action in the Formation of Premodern States*, by Richard Blanton and Lane Fargher (2008). These scholars assembled a sample of thirty early state societies documented by history and ethnography. By painstaking analysis of source material, they report a spectrum of political forms that can be arranged on a scale that runs from autocratic to collective.

---

[4] The idea of an all-powerful state that controlled everything, known as *statism*, was once common in the social sciences generally. For critiques and historical discussion, see du Gay (2012) or Mitchell (1991).

4.9. Moving big stones in a weak state, Nias Island, Indonesia, 1915. Photograph by Ludwig Borutta. Tropenmuseum, Amsterdam, Collectie Stichting Nationaal Museum van Wereldculturen. Creative Commons Attribution-Share Alike 3.0 Unported license. Wikipedia Commons (https://commons.wikimedia.org/wiki/File:COLLECTIE_TROPENMUSEUM_%27Het_verslepen_van_de_steen_%27Darodaro%27_voor_de_gestorven_Saoenigeho_van_Bawamataloea_Nias_TMnr_1000095b.jpg#mw-jump-to-license).

Their quantitative scale results from adding together the scores on three subsidiary scales for each society (Figure 4.10):

- *Bureaucratization:* The extent to which the actions of government are bureaucratized in specific ways that promote collective action; this is a more restricted meaning than bureaucracy in general. Blanton and Fargher use five measures: feasibility of commoner appeals and complaints, degree of tax farming, detection and punishment of official agency, office holder recruitment, and degree of salaried officials (Blanton and Fargher 2008:165–171).[5]
- *Control over principals:* The degree to which the ruler ("principal") can be influenced and even deposed by citizens or a council. The measures Blanton and Fargher use are monitoring of principal behavior, principal adherence to a moral code, role of high officials or advisory council, restrictions on principal's control of

---

[5] Blanton and Fargher's concept of bureaucracy and bureaucratization is much more restrictive than Max Weber's sociological definition of bureaucracy; see the discussion in Chapter 5.

	More autocratic	**More collective**
	←	→
Scale:		
Bureaucratization	Low	High
Control over principals	Low	High
Public goods provision	Low	High
Causal force:		
Revenue source	External	Internal

4.10. Scale of collective versus autocratic (less collective) governance. Graphic by Michael E. Smith, based on information in Blanton and Fargher (2008).

material resources, restrictions on principal's control of ideological resources, and principal's standard of living (Blanton and Fargher 2008:203–206).

- *Public goods provision:* The level to which public goods such as infrastructure and keeping the peace are provided by the regime. Blanton and Fargher use many measures, including the provision of roads and bridges, public water supplies, public safety, and a redistributive economy (Blanton and Fargher 2008:133–138). I discuss public goods in Chapter 6.

Blanton and Fargher provide a detailed description of the original data and their methods of coding and analyzing the data. They show that the major sources of revenue for a regime largely determine the extent to which it exhibits autocratic or collective practices. In a nutshell, rulers who rely on collecting taxes from their subjects must treat them well (by providing public goods and some degree of popular control over leaders); otherwise, their subjects will rebel, leave the polity, or shirk their taxes and responsibilities. On the other hand, rulers with external sources of income (such as taxes on trade or exploitation of foreign populations) have few incentives to treat their subjects well. They can exercise autocratic rule and not worry about whether their subjects are happy or not. Blanton and Fargher are following a line of analysis pioneered by political scientist Margaret Levi (1988) that looks at government as a form of negotiation between ruler and subjects. Their work has been followed by papers refining and extending their analysis, including attempts to apply it to Mesoamerican archaeological cases (Carballo 2013; Carballo et al. 2014; Fargher et al. 2011; Feinman and Carballo 2018; Stark 2021).

At the most autocratic end of Blanton and Fargher's scale are several African (Nupe) and Indonesian states (Aceh); twelfth century England under Richard II is not far behind as an autocratic government. The most collective society in their sample is Classical Athens, with Ming China, Republican Rome, and the Aztecs as slightly less collective. The middle ground is occupied by the Ottoman Empire and the African city-state cultures of the Swahili and Yoruba societies.

One fascinating result of their analysis may seem counterintuitive at first. They find that the most autocratic regimes interfere the least with their subjects. Local communities are not a major source of revenue, so it is not worthwhile to try to organize or control them. Collective regimes, on the other hand, *do* interfere in people's lives. They need to count people and keep track of who has paid taxes and who has not. Such regimes use bureaucratic procedures to keep a much tighter rein on their subjects. The goal is not to control their lives; it is to extract tax revenue efficiently. This adds a new criticism of the old and erroneous view of ancient rulers: ancient despots did *not* try to control their subjects, but democratic regimes *had to* control people in order to survive. This finding has important implications for the nature of cities in autocratic versus collective states.

Blanton and Fargher (2011) suggest that cities in more collective regimes will have denser populations and a more complex road system, and that they are more likely to use orthogonal planning. Their evidence for these suggestions, however, is quite thin. Perhaps the most dramatic effect of regime type on cities is in the public visibility of rulers. Most autocrats advertise themselves with statues, paintings, and texts in public areas, many of which survive archaeologically. They not only have large and sumptuous palaces, but they commonly build impressive royal tombs. In more collective regimes, on the other hand, there is much less focus on the person and personality of the ruler, and in many cases it may be impossible to identify rulers from the material record (Blanton et al. 1996; Carballo and Feinman 2016). I develop this idea more fully below.

The nature of regimes also has a visible effect at the neighborhood level (Fargher et al. 2019). Collective regimes typically engage in some form of planning and organization in urban neighborhoods. This can take the form of planned layouts (e.g., orthogonal grids) or the presence of civic architecture in neighborhoods (Fargher et al. 2011; Stark 2021). Because autocratic regimes do not tax their subjects, they feel no need to organize neighborhoods or provide services. The unplanned narrow and winding lanes of Ottoman or medieval European cities are examples of the lack of interference in neighborhoods by autocratic regimes. Finally, the type of regime likely influenced the level of wealth inequality in ancient cities (Kohler et al. 2018); I take up this topic in Chapter 6.

Blanton and Fargher's study is an important work on variation in ancient state organization, and their autocratic-collective scale has numerous implications for premodern urban life. I want to re-emphasize the counterintuitive dimension they have identified: collective regimes interfered more directly and extensively with the lives of their subjects, whereas autocratic regimes left their subjects to their own devices. In other words, institutional forces impinged on households and neighborhoods more directly and strongly in collective regions, leaving less room for generative forces. In autocratic regimes, the lower level of institutional control and services granted generative forces greater scope in organizing households, neighborhoods, and urban life. In a recent study of collective and autocratic polities in the past and present, political scientist David Stasavage (2020) proposes a theory different from Blanton and Fargher's taxation model to explain the variation in governmental forms. For Stasavage, democracy was common among small-scale societies and early states around the world. But when it became easier for officials to track agricultural production, this led to autocratic regimes and/or the development of an independent bureaucracy to collect taxes and information on subjects. He traces a number of developmental sequences around the world where democracy alternated with autocratic rule over time. Regardless of whose causal theory is correct, Blanton and Fargher's account is easier to operationalize with archaeological data.

In a recent interdisciplinary urban research project, my colleagues and I gathered systematic data on a sample of twenty-three premodern cities as documented by historical and archaeological data. One of our variables is a scale of governance, running from 0 (fully autocratic) to 100 (fully collective). While our study was modeled on Blanton and Fargher in some respects, we measure governance of cities, not of entire polities (Smith et al. 2016; Stanley et al. 2016). For each city, we coded a series of variables that were scored as 0, 1, or 2. We then added up the scores for a city. I standardized the scores to run from 0 to 100. Our results are shown in Table 4.1. Four of the cities in the sample of that project are included as case studies in this book: Chang'an, Teotihuacan, Ado Ekiti, and Tikal. Another ten of the cities in Table 4.1 are very similar to specific case studies in this book; they are from the same urban tradition and match up in size and function. The cities in both samples run the gamut from very strongly collective urban rule to strongly autocratic rule. I explore the linkages between this governance scale and urban life more fully in Chapters 6 and 7; see Appendix B for details on the methods of coding for the data in Table 4.1.

KEVIN LYNCH AND THE CITY AS A PRACTICAL MACHINE

Kevin Lynch, one of the most influential scholars of urban planning in the twentieth century, first defined the category "The City as a practical machine" (Lynch 1981:81–88). These are residential settlements built by a powerful institution for a specific practical purpose. Lynch's examples include colonial cities (Ancient Greek colonies, and Spanish colonies in the New World), Roman military camps, and some gridded Egyptian and Roman cities. These settlements are built quickly in ways that allocate land and resources efficiently. They are usually placed so as to isolate the settlement from its surroundings for reasons of efficiency and control. My use of the city as a practical machine

TABLE 4.1 *Scale of governance for selected premodern cities*[a,b]

City	Tradition	Case study[c]	Governance Score	Population
Cities with strongly collective governance:				
Chester	Medieval	(~27)	100	4,000
Ostia	Roman	(~24)	90	50,000
Montreal	Early modern		90	15,000
Chang'an[b]	Chinese imperial	**16**	83	1,000,000
Empurias	Roman	(~24)	79	3,500
Kyoto	Japanese imperial		79	100,000
York	Medieval	(~27)	79	11,000
Teotihuacan	Mesoamerican capital	**26**	75	100,000
Cities with moderately collective governance:				
Lamu	Swahili	(~11)	60	9,000
Aleppo	Ottoman		57	110,000
Cairo	Ottoman		57	210,000
Arroy Hondo	Southwestern Pueblo	(~6)	50	1,230
Bhaktapur	Newar		50	40,000
Ilesha	Yoruba		50	35,000
Monte Alban	Mesoamerican capital		50	22,500
Poshuinge	Southwestern Pueblo	(~6)	50	1,338
Pumpu	Inka	(~12)	50	4,700
Cities with moderately autocratic governance:				
Zanzibar	Swahili	(~11)	43	25,000
Ado Ekiti	Yoruba	**23**	33	9,000
Caracol	Maya	(~1)	25	100,000
Xochicalco	Mesoamerican capital		25	11,850
Cities with strongly autocratic governance:				
Kahun	Dynastic Egypt	(~13)	0	5,000
Tikal	Maya	**1**	0	62,000

a   This sample of cities is from the project Service Access in Premodern Cities (see Appendix B).
b   Cities in bold font are case studies in this book.
c   Case study numbers in parentheses indicate cities similar to a case study.

model is both more restricted and broader than Lynch's original formulation. I limit consideration to semi-urban settlements, which leaves out the colonial cities Lynch discusses. On the other hand, I expand his concept to include a far broader range of nonpermanent settlements (Table 4.2), from company towns to refugee camps to medieval assembly sites. The table provides examples of the various categories of practical machine sites; it is not an exhaustive list of all such settlement types. The entries in the table for "Functional category" and "Social complexity" are my informal judgments.

These practical machine sites provide clear examples of top-down, central planning. In fact, they can be seen as a kind of natural experiment in which central planning is used in the absence of many other urban features. These settlements are set up – by a state or other political or economic institution – to serve a specific practical purpose that requires a resident population. There is

TABLE 4.2 *Types of practical machine sites*

Settlement type	Functional category	Social complexity	Urban functions[a]
Permanent:			
Fortress	Military settlement	Low	P
Company town[*]	Labor settlement	Moderate	E
Workers compound[*]	Labor settlement	Low	E
Temporary or variable occupation:			
Mining or lumber camp	Labor settlement	Low	
Refugee camp[*]	Displaced persons camp	Variable	
Disaster camp[*]	Displaced persons camp	Variable	
Military camp[*]	Military settlement	Low	
Internment camp[*]	Detention center	Low	
Concentration camp	Detention center	Low	
Cyclical occupation:			
Itinerant capitals	Temporary capital	High	E, P, R
Medieval assembly sites	Temporary capital	High	E, P, R

[*]   Type is featured in Smith et al (2015).
a *Urban functions: E: economic; P: political; R: religious*

usually a low level of social complexity or social variation in these sites (Table 4.2). With the exception of the political settlements that were cyclically occupied, most practical machine sites lack urban functions. Fortresses do have political urban functions; their military features (barracks full of soldiers, weapons, military organization) affect a hinterland. But, these sites are partial settlements that can be seen as a functionally specific part of an urban landscape. Because of the low level of economic activity, their small size, and the forces of central administration, processes of energized crowding in these settlements operate on a much lower level than in more permanent settlements. This limits the activities, growth, and vibrancy of practical machine sites, which usually suits the interests of their sponsoring or controlling institution.

Types of Practical Machine Sites

In Table 4.2, I divide practical machine sites into three categories, based on the length and temporal pattern of their occupation.

Permanent. To say that a settlement is *permanent* does not necessarily mean that it will last forever (or even for centuries). I use this label for settlements that are established with the goal of enduring for a period of a year or more. Not surprisingly, these are the type of ancient practical machine sites whose remains have endured the longest for archaeologists to locate and excavate. The Aggersborg Viking *fortress* (Figure 4.11) is a good example. This is one of a series of Viking ring-forts (called Trelleborg-style fortresses) established by king Harald Bluetooth in the late tenth century CE. Harald was the first king to

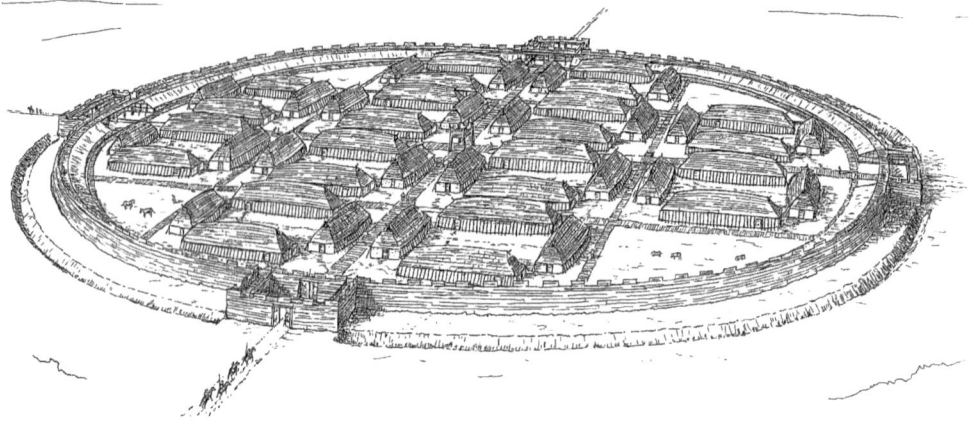

4.11. Viking ring-fort at Aggersborg (Roesdahl et al. 2014, 184). Drawing by Edward Clark. From Brown et al. (2014).

unify Denmark and built these fortresses in a time of crisis, "primarily to control a country ready to revolt" (Roesdahl 1987:226).

This reconstruction drawing of Aggersborg is based on extensive excavation and mapping (Roesdahl et al. 2014). It shows one of the key traits of the permanent practical machine sites: geometric spatial planning. The fort controlled a key maritime passage in the northern part of Harald's kingdom in Jutland, Denmark. If fortresses like this had low social complexity and limited urban functions, what is the justification for considering them urban at all? First, fortresses often had a high population density. The Aggersborg fortress had a density of 140 per hectare, and Fyrkat, another Viking ring-fort discussed in Chapter 8, had a density of 110 per hectare. Roman forts were also quite densely settled. Second, some of these sites – such as Roman fortresses – were clearly divided into spatial zones that correspond to neighborhoods (Smith et al. 2015).

Company towns are specialized settlements built and run by a particular economic corporation or other powerful institution, for a specific economic purpose (Crawford 1995; Dinius and Vergara 2011; Garner 1992). In the nineteenth and twentieth centuries, a corporation would typically own all the houses and businesses, creating a dependent relationship between the company and the resident labor. In this sense, company towns covered a wide range of settlements, from industrial zones such as Pullman, Illinois, to mining villages and lumber camps. I limit the use of the term *company town* to permanent, long-lasting settlements, and classify mining and lumber camps under temporary sites. To reinforce the dependency of labor and enable surveillance and control, company towns were spatially isolated from surrounding areas. In some cases, ethnically or functionally specific neighborhoods within company towns were also spatially isolated from one another; the oil town of Abadan in Iran shows this pattern (Smith et al. 2015). The *workers compound* is a direct ancient analog of the modern Company town; I discuss an Egyptian case study later in this chapter.

Temporary or Variable-Length Occupation. This category consists of practical machine sites set up for a special purpose whose planned use is a few years or less (Table 4.2). Their institutional sponsor can be a corporation (in the modern world), the state (ancient and modern times), or another major institution. These settlements are often called *camps* because of their hasty construction, often with tents or other insubstantial shelters. But, unlike most modern concepts of the camp (Hailey 2009), social life in some of these places could be quite controlled. *Military camps* and *concentration camps* have highly regimented social patterns, reflected in highly standardized and regulated spatial organization. *Internment camps* have similar regimented spatial layouts, but life was less controlled and regimented.

The Japanese-American internment camps built in the western United States during World War II show standardized, regimented layouts, similar to military and concentration camps (Figures 4.12, 1.8). The internment camps consisted of quickly built standardized wood structures, arranged following a standard plan. At the Granada Relocation Center (Figure 4.12), each block of twelve barracks had three public buildings: a mess hall/kitchen, a recreation building, and a bathhouse/laundry. Once the internees arrived at this rather regimented-looking settlement, however, most aspects of their lives were allowed to develop in a generative fashion, with little central control (beyond the requirement of staying in the camp). In fact, ethnographic, historical, and archaeological research shows that social interactions led to the development of neighborhoods with social cohesion (Burton et al. 2002; Kamp-Whittaker and Clark 2019; Smith et al. 2015; Spicer et al. 1969).

Refugee camps show a spectrum of regimented planning; those laid out in advance tend to have well-structured hierarchical spatial plans, including neighborhood organization (Corsellis and Vitale 2005). The sponsoring institution is typically a nation-state or the United Nations. Refugee camps assembled in a rush show less standardized planning, although when occupied for some time various groups typically create spatial neighborhood patterning (Agier 2011). Agier compares refugee camps to Wirth's definition of the city and concludes that they provide an analogy for the origins of cities, before permanent housing and infrastructure were established. Speaking of many twentieth-century refugee camps, Agier says "camps can lead to towns, and the history of wars and population movement has already offered several examples of this. This transformation will signal the end of the camps and the beginning of resilient towns" (Agier 2011:187). Similar observations could be

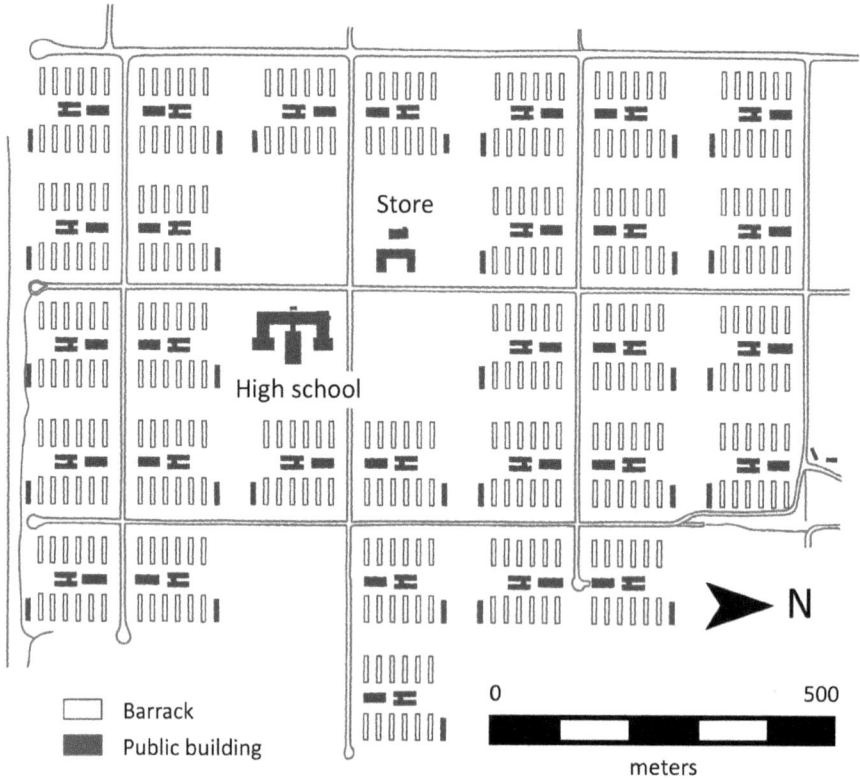

Store

High school

Barrack
Public building

0   500

N

meters

4.12. The Granada Relocation Center, Colorado (Amache) National Historic Landmark. Graphic by April Kamp-Whittaker using data from the University of Denver Amache Project and Jim Casey, based on a map in the National Archives, item 27813676; Reproduced with permission.

made about mining and lumber camps: many grew into fully functional towns and cities, while others did not (Bell 1984; Lucas 1971).

Cyclical Occupation. Itinerant capitals and medieval assembly sites help us understand the relationship between urbanism and political dynamics in early times. As discussed previously, states need cities but not necessarily permanent capitals. Although these settlements diverge from other practical machine sites in their social complexity and urban functions (Table 4.2), it makes sense to consider them in the present category. They were deliberately created by an institution – the king – to serve practical purposes (conduct administrative business and show off the king's authority), and they were not permanent settlements. Itinerant capitals are one of the most fascinating types of urban centers in the premodern world, and a systematic comparative analysis is badly needed. Until then, the most useful general works to date are Bernhardt (1993: chapter 2), Geertz (1977), and Fletcher (1991). The next two case studies – the Amarna workers compound and assembly sites – illustrate permanent and cyclical practical machine sites.

Case Study 13 Amarna Workmens Compound

Amarna – the new Egyptian capital founded by the pharaoh Akhenaten – was a disembedded capital, founded in a location away from existing bases of power in order to free politics and administration from entrenched local elites and interests (Joffe 1998). Ancient disembedded capitals are important not only for their insights into political dynamics but also because some of them are fantastic archaeological sites. Like the Inka provincial capital Huanuco Pampa (Case Study 12), Amarna was founded on new ground, built in a hurry, and then abandoned after only a few decades. Later occupation was minimal. Because of the combination of limited occupation, good preservation, and the historical importance of Akhenaten, archaeologists have been working intensively at Amarna for over a century (Kemp 2012). While Amarna is a fascinating city in many respects, here I concentrate on just one part of the city, the so-called workmen's village.[6]

A Company Town in Ancient Egypt. The Amarna workers compound (Figure 4.13) is a walled area set off from the main residential areas of the city by about a kilometer of desert. Unlike most housing in Amarna, the houses in this compound are standardized in size and form, with a highly regular layout. It can be interpreted as a neighborhood within the larger city (Smith et al. 2015), which is how Egyptologists interpret the settlement (Kemp 2012). The common label "workmen's village" (Kemp 1987) therefore does not imply that this is a rural village outside of Amarna. It has been clear to archaeologists that the Amarna workers compound must have been built and maintained to serve a specific purpose. The most common interpretation is that it provided housing for tomb excavators, specialized workers whose lives and activities were managed to some degree by the state. Under the Egyptian command economy (Chapter 5), many people were provisioned with bread and beer produced in state workshops (Samuel 1999). The discovery of animal pens in the grounds adjacent to individual

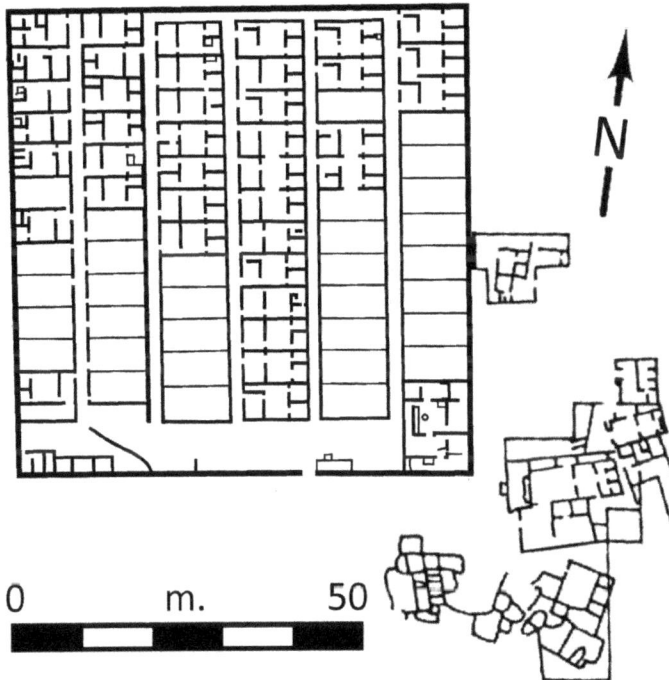

4.13. Workers compound at Amarna, Egypt. Image courtesy of Barry Kemp.

---

[6] This kind of settlement has as long history in dynastic Egypt. Moeller (2016:chapter 5) discusses examples going back to the Old Kingdom period.

Case Study 13 (cont.)

houses expands this view by showing that even in a command-based redistributive economy, individual households raised some of their own food; that is, generative processes exist even within the structure of a powerful institution like the Egyptian state (see Chapter 7).

A second Egyptian worker compound (there are four or five in total) that has been excavated and extensively studied is Deir el-Medina (David 1986; Lesko 1994). This walled compound was less carefully laid out than at Amarna. The houses were nearly as standardized, but the entire compound was less regular in form. Deir el-Medina housed craft workers and others who labored on the tombs in the Valley of the Kings. Barry Kemp, the head excavator at Amarna, has suggested that the workers from Deir el-Medina were moved as a group to populate the Amarna workers compound (Kemp 2012:295–296). Recent fieldwork suggests that a second outlying neighborhood of Amarna, called the Stone Village, may also be a specialized settlement for laborers on quarries or tombs (Stevens 2011, 2012). This presents a fascinating contrast with the main worker compound in that the Stone Village has a less imposing wall, and the houses are less regular and regimented. This may suggest two distinct forms of labor organization for tomb workers at Amarna.

Comparative Insights. The Amarna workers compound is a direct ancient analog of the company town of the nineteenth and twentieth centuries.[7] A powerful institution (the state) built and maintained a walled residential area to house its laborers and keep them isolated from the rest of society. When considered together, the Amarna workers compound and the Stone Village show that even a powerful autocratic regime with a command economy can support divergent patterns of urban layout and labor organization. I now move to a very different kind of settlement with very different social implications; nevertheless, it too conforms to the category of practical machine site, although one with cyclical occupation.

Case Study 14 "Thing Sites" and Assemblies in Northern Europe

For more than a thousand years, local governance in much of northern Europe was handled by assemblies of notable individuals. Affairs of government and conflict resolution (as well as economic, religious, and social activities) were carried out when people gathered at a set place. This account, penned around 900 CE to describe the life of a saint over a century earlier in Saxon Germany, gives an idea of the nature of these events:

> In olden times, the Saxons had no king but appointed rulers over each village; and their custom was to hold a general meeting once a year in the center of Saxony near the river Yser at a place called Marklo. There all the leaders used to gather together and they were joined by twelve noblemen from each village with as many freedmen and serfs. There they confirmed the laws, gave judgment on outstanding cases, and by common consent drew up plans for the coming year on which they could act either in peace or war. (From the *Vita Lebuini Antiqua*, quoted in Ehlers 2015:315)

In Scandinavia, these assemblies were called a "Thing" (Sanmark 2017; Semple and Sanmark 2013). They clearly marked a form of governance more collective than most ancient societies; decision-making was broadly-based, and personal participation and deliberation were important. But while some would call this form of government "democratic" (Thing Project 2018), Alexandra Sanmark (2017) points out that much of the planning, organization, and power were in the hands of elites. She also shows that there were two or three levels of these assemblies, from local to high-level, more restricted events. For a recent political analysis, see Stasavage (2020:chapter 5).

---

[7] This was the conclusion of the senior honors thesis of Bridgette Gilliland (2011).

Case Study 14 (cont.)

Problems of Studying Cyclical Assembly Sites. People attending a Thing or another Northern European assembly stayed for a week or more in temporary shelters. Archaeologists have located very few remains of these, but "booths" (shelters with turf walls and a canvas floor) have been excavated in association with Thing sites in Norway (Storli 2010) and Iceland (Sanmark 2017). The most important activity was the public assembly itself. Figure 4.14, a 1932 poster for Swedish schools, shows a Thing assembly at Gamla Uppsala, home of Swedish kingship since the sixth century CE (Ljungkvist and Frölund 2015). A king or other important figure sits on the left, and the central fenced area is surrounded by nobles and lords, who are negotiating over a war or battle. The main audience sits on the "Thing mound," a feature that still stands at Gamla Uppsala today. But that is about all that remains archaeologically of Thing assemblies at the site.

These assembly sites are urban in having – for a short period – high social complexity and urban functions (because the activities there affected a larger area). But they leave only scant traces. Most assembly sites today have only a named hill or perhaps a rune stone to mark them. The Thing site of Arundshög in Sweden (Figure 4.15) has more intact features than most. There is a large mound (probably for the audience, as in Figure 4.14), five ship settings (set stones arranged in the shape of a ship, sometimes with human burials), some smaller mounds, rune stones, and several other standing stones. Unfortunately, the direct markers of the actual assembly space and any shelters that may have been present rarely preserve archaeologically. At Arundshög, the assembly area is delineated by the wooden monument, the watercourse, and the wetlands. This combination of natural and constructed features is typical of Thing sites, many of which have been identified by place names and early court documents, not by excavation (Baker and Brookes 2015; Gleeson 2015; Sanmark 2017).

4.14. Painting of a Thing event at Gamla Uppsala. Painting by Swedish artist Ollie Hjortsberg in 1932 and used as a poster in Swedish schools.

Case Study 14 (cont.)

4.15. Thing site at Arundshog, Sweden. Photo by Daniel Löwenborg. Reproduced with permission.

Comparative Insights. Northern European assembly sites are highly urban settlements – full of people and activity – that last for only a week or two each year. This is a unique kind of urbanism, and one whose housing, population, and social dynamics remain very poorly understood. In many ways, the Thing sites are comparable to Plains Indian aggregation sites (Case Study 9).

ANCIENT GOVERNMENTS AND URBAN PLANNING

Early rulers and governments used urban planning to make statements about their power, their legitimacy, and the relationship of the regime to the cosmos. Sometimes archaeologists can read these messages, and sometimes we cannot. The planning of premodern cities is a big topic (Moore 1996; Smith 2007), and here I will focus on just one aspect: How did the principles and forms of urban planning promote the political functions of premodern cities? That is, how did city design and layout promote the power, control, and longevity of ancient governments?

The most widespread and fundamental principle of urban planning in premodern cities is what I call the *epicenter planning* model. Planning scholar Jorge Hardoy first described this model as follows:

> The essential nature of pre-Columbian urban planning was not concerned with the periphery of cities, with the low-density and unserviced suburbs.

> The housing of the poor classes was self-built with segregation, the elite living
> in or around the central square .... Town planning only reflected concern
> about the physical characteristics and the quality of the environment in the
> central districts of major towns where the elite and its immediate collaborators
> lived .... The housing of the poor classes was self-built with perishable
> materials, not very different from rural shelters. (Hardoy 1982:22; see also
> Smith 2007)

Therefore, the question about power and planning concerns civic architecture within the urban epicenter, and not the layout of residential zones. Cases where entire cities exhibit central planning – such as classical and modern cities with orthogonal grid layouts – have different social implications (Grant 2018).

Monumentality and Levels of Meaning in the Built Environment

A productive approach to the relationship between planning and political functions is illustrated by Amos Rapoport's model of levels of meaning in the built environment (Rapoport 1988, 1990a). Table 4.3 shows Rapoport's three-part scheme.

High-level meaning describes cosmological and supernatural symbolism that may be encoded in buildings and city layouts. These are usually esoteric religious ideas only understandable to a literate elite. High-level meanings are culturally-specific and idiosyncratic concepts, which means they typically cannot be reconstructed by archaeologists in the absence of written texts (Flannery and Marcus 1993). This reduces the usefulness of comparative analysis for major parts of ancient religion, for two reasons. First, without texts, it is very difficult to reconstruct myths, symbols, and other nonmaterial aspects of religion, except occasionally in situations with exceptionally rich visual records. Second, such ideas are almost always culturally specific (prior to the rise of the major Axial Age religions, Christianity, Judaism, and Islam),

TABLE 4.3 *Levels of meaning in the built environment*

Traits	Low	Middle	High
Domain	How people use the built environment	Communication of social and political messages	Religious symbolism and esoteric concepts
Audience for messages	All users	Subjects of the regime and potential subjects	Literate elite
Universality	Universal, cross-cultural	Almost universal	Culturally specific
Major themes	· Movement	· Power	· Cosmology
	· Access	· Identity	· Mythology
	· Privacy	· Status	· Worldview
	· Expected behavior	· Durability	· The sacred

Source: Rapoport (1988, 1990); Smith (2007)

which means that knowledge from one case cannot be applied to interpret another case. Archaeologists can rarely reconstruct the myths, beliefs, and symbols that lie behind temples and other religious buildings in early cities, which is one reason why ancient religion does not play a larger role in this book.

Scholars know (from texts) that in some ancient urban traditions – particularly Chinese imperial capitals and cities in India and Southeast Asia – high-level meanings about the structure of the cosmos were deliberately expressed in the design of cities (Steinhardt 1990; Wheatley 1971). In other traditions, including Mesoamerica, there is little evidence for the incorporation of cosmological principles in city layouts. This concept, however, has been dangerously attractive to archaeologists, leading to numerous speculative accounts positing cosmo-logical influences on planning. I criticize these speculative accounts for Mesoamerica in Smith (2003; 2005b).

Middle-level meaning refers to deliberate messages about identity and status communicated by the designers and constructors of buildings and cities. A major theme concerns monumentality and power; kings used large buildings to show off their power and control. Bruce Trigger (1990:119) has defined monumental architecture as buildings that are far larger than they need to be: "Its principal defining feature is that its scale and elaboration exceed the requirements of any practical functions that a building is intended to perform." In addition to large buildings, monumentality in many ancient urban traditions was expressed in long, broad streets, orderly layouts, large plazas, and the use of symmetry and formality in the design and placement of buildings (Lynch 1981; Rapoport 1990a).

The construction of towering pyramids and other huge structures demon-strates the ability of the government to carry out large projects, the ability of the ruler to convert disorder to order, and the ability of the state to force individuals to conform to societal needs (Blanton 1989). Because these messages and features are not difficult to understand, middle-level communication operates in similar ways in most premodern states. We may not be able to identify the specific god worshiped in an ancient temple (i.e., the high-level meaning of the temple), but we can understand the middle-level messages and their effect on residents and visitors to an ancient city. In other words, without texts or exceptionally rich visual remains, archaeologists are destined to have an impov-erished view of the beliefs of ancient religions (no gods, myths, or complex high-level messages). But we *can* create reliable knowledge about the practices of those religions.

The tall monuments of many premodern cities can offer clues to the nature of the city. José Lobo and I have proposed two broad types of cities across history; we call them *political cities* and *economic cities* (Smith and Lobo 2019).

In political cities, politics and government are the dominant institutions, and economic factors take a backseat in terms of the operation and growth of the city. In economic cities, by contrast, production and exchange activities predominate. This is a very simple classification, but it does identify some important variations in premodern cities. Cities that are dominated by huge palaces and temples are often political cities in this scheme, while those with major economic roles but lacking the showy architecture with its middle-level messages of power and durability are economic cities. I explore middle-level meanings in some political cities in the case studies that follow.

Low-level meaning describes the ways in which the built environment channels and interacts recursively with behavior and movement. Rapoport's concept captures Winston Churchill's famous observation that "we shape our buildings, and thereafter they shape us." Low-level meanings have to do with movement and access through a city or building, settings of privacy and openness, and the understanding of expected behavior in a place. At this level, the basic principles might be human universals, but the way they operate in a given context is culturally specific (Hall 1966).

Rapoport's concept of middle-level meaning of the built environment is crucial for understanding the political functions of premodern cities. In early states, power was often fleeting and needed frequent reinforcement. This is most obvious in the weak states discussed previously, but even powerful emperors often felt the need to show off their power, or to re-assert their legitimacy, and they often used buildings and cities to do this. Premodern cities were not just places where ancient governments happened to be based; their forms and functions were created out of deliberate political programs of power and ideology (see the discussion on power, ideology, and domination in Chapter 7). This is nowhere clearer than in the great Achaemenid (Persian) capital Persepolis (See Case Study 15).

Were Early States Fragile?

A number of archaeologists have begun to make the claim that – in spite of the imposing buildings and spaces in early cities – these governments and cities were actually very "fragile." One part of this claim is the notion that tropical low-density cities and their governments were prone to collapse because of their fragile environment (Fletcher 2019; Lucero et al. 2015). Another version is Norman Yoffee's claim that most early cities and states were fragile by their very nature. He asserts that many ancient cities "were 'fragile' in spite of the indisputably great power of kings and their courts" (Yoffee 2015:522). For Yoffee, fragility appears to mean that their encompassing states were not "well integrated" (p. 556). In an edited volume, he begins with a programmatic claim: "We contest the notion that ancient societies

Case Study 15 Persepolis: Monumentality to Show Off the Emperor's Power

The ruined city of Persepolis in Iran is one of the most impressive ancient urban sites today. The heart of the city consisted of a large platform, fourteen hectares in size, upon which sits a series of palaces and other structures with monumental columns, many of which survive today. Persepolis was built by the Achaemenid emperors (most likely Darius I, who ruled from 522 to 486 BCE, and his successor Xerxes I, 485–465 BCE). The design of the platform, palaces, and monumental stairways showcased the power of these kings, who had monumental reliefs carved to show them as powerful and influential rulers (Figure 4.16). The Achaemenid Empire had a strongly autocratic government, and Persepolis illustrates some of the main characteristics of the capitals of such polities.

Showing Off Power. The large palaces of Persepolis, with their towering stone columns, exemplify the ability of monumental architecture to communicate messages about power, durability, stability, and legitimacy. The fact that we are still impressed by these structures today, even in their ruined and partial state, shows that this kind of middle-level meaning transcends specific cultural traditions. Carved stone reliefs, like that shown in Figure 4.16, present a similar message, although with greater specificity. The emperor Darius I sits on a throne, receiving visitors from a foreign area. Darius and his minister are depicted at a larger scale than the other figures, emphasizing the glory and magnificence of the king.

Public inscriptions that glorify Darius are presented in three languages (Old Persian, Elamite, and Babylonian), to make sure everyone understood; nonliterate visitors could get the message from the pictorial reliefs alone. One such text lists twenty-five countries that were subject to the emperor. Should we view such ancient proclamations as simple descriptions of political organization (the emperor was great and powerful), or are they better seen as grandiose ideological claims that may or may not be accurate? It is hard to say, although such public glorification of the king was a common thread in the public messages (middle-level communication) of ancient autocratic regimes.

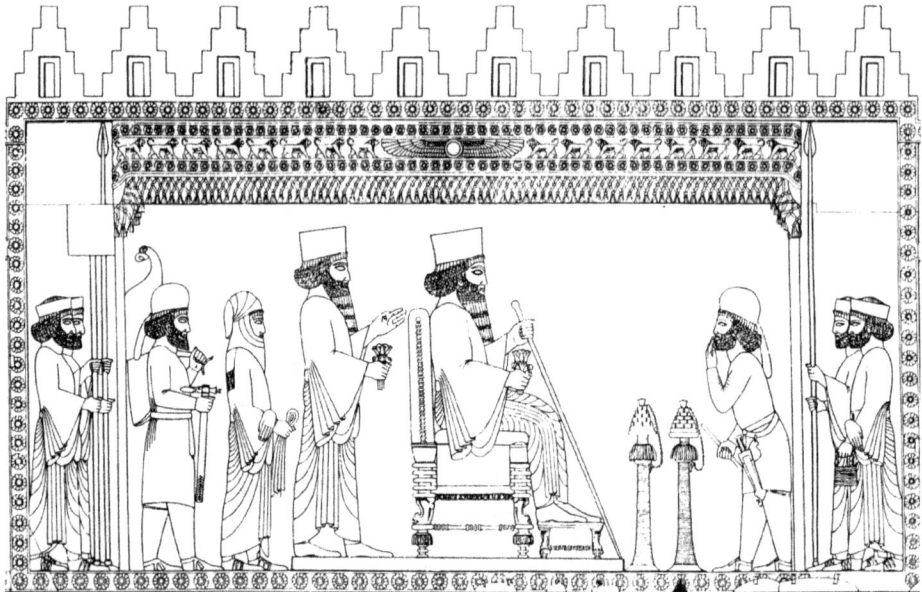

4.16. Persepolis Apadana, North Stair, Original Central Panel. Modified after Root (2015:22). Reproduced with permission.

Case Study 15 (cont.)

A major find from excavations at Persepolis was a series of cuneiform texts that describe the economic and social life of the city. These are called the *fortification tablets* because they were recovered in one of the defensive walls. Many of these suggest a command economy (Chapter 5), with individuals receiving standardized rations from the government (Hallock 1969). One text gives insight into the chaotic nature of corvée labor projects. A weary low-level supervisor tries to explain to his superiors why a canal had not been excavated on time. He complains that his workers kept running away, in spite of being housed in a secure location. He had to run after them to bring them back. Furthermore, he was left with only 80 percent of his original crew, and many of the remaining workers were children and old men (MacGinnis 2003). While the public inscriptions are scenes of power, order, and magnificence, this private administrative text reveals a specific kind of generative force – a harried official trying to deal with unruly and unenthusiastic labor gangs to simply get the work of the city done.

Comparative Insights. Similar monumental buildings and inscriptions exist at other, even more ancient, Near Eastern imperial capitals, from Nineveh to Babylon, but Persepolis stands out for the good condition of its ruins today. These were created by powerful autocratic rulers who used various techniques to communicate middle-range meanings for visitors. Until someone excavates the houses of commoners, however, our understanding of generative processes at this magnificent capital will remain limited to a few scattered texts.

Case Study 16 Chang'an: Planning and Neighborhoods in the Largest City in the World

Chang'an was founded as a new imperial capital for the Tang dynasty (ca. 600–900 CE). It quickly grew to a population of one million (Table 3.2), making it the largest city in the world at that time. As part of a remarkable millennia-long tradition of imperial city planning, Chang'an shared a series of principles of design, layout, and symbolism with earlier and later capitals (Steinhardt 1990). Chang'an was planned from the start as a very large walled city with straight avenues connecting to gates in the defensive walls. Like other capitals, Chang'an's builders oriented the city to the cardinal directions, and the entire city was viewed as a cosmogram – that is, a built symbol of the structure of the cosmos. Later sources tell us that principles of magic and divination had been used to select the site for the city (Wheatley 1971).

Closed and Open Neighborhoods. The basic principles of urban layout at Chang'an included a monumental defensive perimeter wall, a strict orthogonal grid, and the use of walled compounds to divide the city into functional and residential areas (Figure 4.17). As in other Chinese capitals, a central feature was the walled administrative compound, the "palace city." Commerce was limited to two large central markets. The southern part of the city (shown on the map as a low-density area) contained gardens and orchards, with only a few residences (Heng 1999; Xiong 2000).

Most of the large rectangular zones were walled wards or districts (see Figure 7.6B) divided into 16 sectors or neighborhoods of 3 to 3.5 hectares; these were then further subdivided into lots with houses, residential compounds, and other buildings. The walled wards and neighborhoods were in part a response to the population density in Chang'an. The city's density of 119 persons per hectare was high, especially considering that the city included some 29 square kilometers of open land in the southern portion of the city. Neighborhood densities ran as high as 200 persons per hectare (Table 3.2).

Each walled ward had one to four gates that were locked and guarded at night. Officials beat drums when the gates closed in the evening and opened each morning. At night, residents needed a permit to leave their ward. This kind of regulation of daily life is more typical of collective than autocratic governments (see the previous discussion), and thus it is no surprise that Chang'an had one of the highest collective scores in the Urban Services sample (Table 4.1).

Case Study 16 (cont.)

At the end of the Tang period, life in Chang'an changed drastically in two ways. First, the tight control over neighborhoods and movement came to an end. The gates were destroyed, curfews were no longer enforced, and people could move freely throughout the city. Second, commerce escaped from heavy oversight by the regime. Trade had previously been limited by decree to the two large marketplaces. After the change, shops sprung along the main streets, which quickly filled with people enjoying their newfound freedom of movement (Heng 1999). Both changes increased the opportunities and intensity of energized crowding in Chang'an.

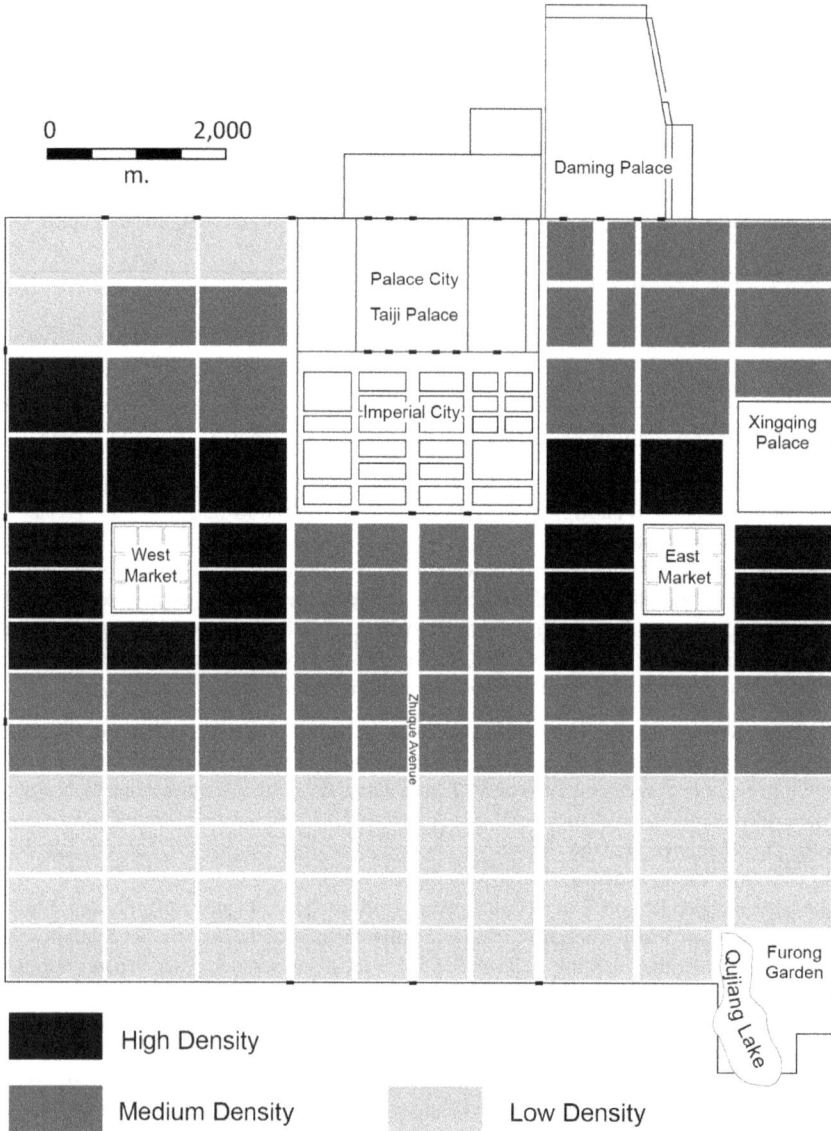

4.17. Plan of Chang'an, showing variation in density. Source: Heng, Chye Kiang, "Visualizing Everyday Life in the City: A Categorization System for Residential Wards in Tang Chang'an." *Journal of the Society of Architectural Historians.* Copyright 2014 by the Society of Architectural Historians. Published by the University of California Press. Reproduced with permission.

Case Study 16 (cont.)

Comparative Insights. Chang'an has several lessons about life in early cities. First, the large and dense urban population required subdivision into smaller units, the wards, and neighborhoods (as predicted by Roland Fletcher's model; see Chapter 3). Second, tight control of people and movement was coupled with tight control over commerce, and both of these systems broke down at the same time, leading to a major reorganization of urban life. Third, a strong ruler could make statements about his power and control – middle-level communication – that did not involve depictions of himself or massive texts about his glory.

---

were in any way social wholes" (Yoffee 2019); indeed, fragility is said to be "an inherent property of early cities and states" (Yoffee 2019:3).

Yoffee's concept of "fragility" for early cities and states seems more of an ideological position than an empirical claim. Following my scientific realist epistemology (Chapter 1), a claim of "fragility" for ancient states would require three things: (1) a formal definition of fragility; (2) operationalization of that concept for archaeological data; and (3) empirical data showing that some states or cities were more fragile than others. The chapters in Yoffee's (2019) edited volume provide none of these. Indeed, the lack of a formal definition of the central concept of a book is surprising and casts doubts on the entire enterprise. To my mind, a concept like fragility suggests a temporal element: the notion that early cities and states did not last for very long. If they were fragile, they collapsed quickly. Yet some of the so-called fragile states, such as Angkor and the Maya city-states, flourished for more than five centuries. So, perhaps the contributors to Yoffee's volume have another definition of fragility in mind. But the simple fact is that we have little idea how many years or centuries early states and cities persisted (Smith et al. 2021b). Until someone gathers data on this, it seems premature to label cities and states as short-lived, long-lived, fragile, or durable.

CITIES, STATES, AND GOVERNMENTS IN DEEP HISTORY

Persepolis and Chang'an present a fascinating contrast. Both were imperial capitals, places from which powerful emperors ruled huge territories. In both cases, the emperors used the built environment to express (middle-level) messages of power and accomplishment. But, these messages were radically different, as befits the differences between these cities and their social contexts. The Achaemenid rulers built large and sumptuous palaces and temples, with oversize reliefs glorifying the king, claiming he was unique and powerful. The Tang rulers of Chang'an, on the other hand, built a much larger city whose regularity of layout and organization mirrored that of the cosmos. The emperor judged himself not by his personal power and glory, but by the extent to which his rule was in tune with the supernatural. Much of the difference between Persepolis and Chang'an can be explained by their forms of rule: autocratic versus collective (Blanton and Fargher 2008). While I cannot provide a numerical score for the degree of collective governance at Persepolis, it almost certainly belongs in one of the more autocratic categories in Table 4.1; Chang'an, on the other hand, is near the top (more collective) end of the scale.

This distinction between autocratic and collective polities or cities had profound implications for the nature of life in early cities. The average commoner residents of Chang'an were probably more prosperous than their counterparts in Persepolis, but subject to greater regulation and interference in their daily activities. Prime evidence for this are the walls and gates between neighborhoods and wards, curfews, and regulation of commerce. These differences in governance and the built environment created divergent opportunities for energized crowding; this was almost certainly more intensive in the cities of more collective regimes. But, the autocratic/collective distinction is not the only political factor that had a strong influence on urban life in the distant past. The size and strength of the polity (Figure 4.2) also exerted an influence. Consider Charles Tilly's observation that states do two things – exploit people and provide services. More centralized states extracted more taxes than weaker states, and they in turn provided more public goods – from defensive walls to streets and canals. Moreover, these had a strong effect on patterns of urban life. The ways that urban life was impacted by these political variants illustrate the point I make in Chapter 1 that political and economic institutions created much of the variation in early cities and urban life.

Anthropologists have shown that Thomas Hobbes was wrong in claiming that life was chaos before the invention of states and elites and laws. Thousands of small-scale societies thrived for millennia without the state. Now, comparative urbanism can add cities to this equation: cities can also exist – and thrive – in the absence of a state government. The inverse, however, is not true: states cannot exist for long in the absence of urban centers where the power of the state – including political urban functions – can be created and expressed from a physical location on the ground. What is missing from this account is the role of economic institutions and processes, the topic of the following chapter.

FIVE

MARKETS, CRAFTS, AND URBAN LIFE

EARLY ALL CITIES TODAY ARE ORIENTED AROUND ECONOMIC activity. To urban economists and many other scholars of contemporary urbanism, cities whose primary focus lies in the economic realm seem normal. Chapter 4, on the other hand, shows that political functions were crucial in most premodern cities. Is this a real distinction between two types of cities – economic cities today versus political cities in the past – or is reality more complicated (Smith and Lobo 2019)? To answer this question, we need to take a close look at specific economic practices and institutions in cities from a variety of historical and cultural settings.

How did economic practices and institutions affect urban life in the past? In most cities before the modern era, craft production, exchange, and other economic activities were prominent, but they took widely divergent forms. The small-scale household business was the most common commercial unit throughout history. A Roman relief of the Hadrianic period (Figure 5.1) shows a butcher at work. While the viewer's attention is drawn to the butcher on the right side, his wife – on the left side – is also at work, writing on a tablet. This was a family business, one of the numerous such operations that made up a good part of the Roman economy.

I begin this chapter with two concepts: economic growth, and the distinction between market economies and command economies. These themes unite the two spatial strands of urban economics – urban functions (how cities affect a hinterland), and local activity (economic activity within the city, as it

5.1. Relief of a Roman butcher shop. Replica in the Ashmolean Museum, Oxford University. Photograph by Caroline Raddato; used with permission.

affects residents). I then move on to examine the urban economy under three headings: the regional economy, craft production, and exchange. In contrast to the political dynamics covered in Chapter 4, where most of the discussion focused on kings and elites, most (but not all) of the economic dynamics of premodern cities were fueled more by generative processes – that is, energized crowding was a major force in early urban economics. In Chapter 6, I return to urban economics to explore how economic activities and institutions shape society and the experience of life in premodern cities.

ECONOMIC GROWTH AND ECONOMIC URBAN FUNCTIONS BEFORE CAPITALISM

An Approach to Ancient Economies

I employ a pragmatic, empirical approach to economic activities and processes in the cities of the past. I borrow insights from both anthropology and economics, while rejecting the extreme ideas within these disciplines. A useful starting point is what economic historian Peter Temin (1980) calls "modes of behavior." He lists three such modes: *customary behavior* (including both behavior based on long-held traditional customs, and behavior based on what one has done previously); *command behavior* (when people follow orders in a hierarchical setting); and *instrumental behavior* (rational or self-interested behavior). People follow these modes of behavior depending on the social setting and specific circumstances of an individual or a relationship; see Table 5.1. Temin analyzes how these modes match up with three large-scale

TABLE 5.1 *Modes of behavior*

Mode	Institution	Form of sociality	Moral principle
Customary	Communities	Communal sharing	Communism
Command	States	Authority ranking	Hierarchy
Instrumental	Markets	Market pricing; Equality matching	Exchange
Temin (1980)	Temin (1980); Bowles and Gintis (2002)	Fiske (1991)	Graeber (2011)

ideal types of institutional structures: communities, states, and markets. The correspondence between these two schemes is a general one, not simple and deterministic. Thus, while instrumental behavior may be the most common mode in a market setting, markets are also settings for customary behavior, and instrumental behavior is found in many nonmarket settings. These same three institutional structures are identified by economists and complexity scientists Samuel Bowles and Herbert Gintis (2002) in a study that contrasts the capacities of communities with those of states and markets. As a simple correlation with concepts used throughout this book, communities are settings where generative processes flourish, while states are settings where institutional forces predominate. Markets combine the two; institutions of exchange and production frame and shape behavior, while many – but not all – economic settings promote and reflect generative actions of urban residents.

Table 5.1 also includes parallel schemes from two social anthropologists. Alan Fiske (1991) has proposed a scheme for comparative analysis that classifies social relationships and interactions into the "elementary forms of sociality." Finally, David Graeber (2011:chapter 5) describes three moral principles of human society, which he calls *communism*, *hierarchy*, and *exchange*. These correspond rather closely to Temin's three modes of behavior. People normally engage in all three modes, typically at different times and in different settings. The most obvious implication of this scheme – and of the research that accompanies the categories in Table 5.1 – is that human social behavior is complex and cannot be modeled with any single type of behavior or principle. More relevant to the economic functions of past cities, this scheme shows the conceptual inadequacy of many past approaches to ancient economies.

Archaeologists and historians wasted considerable time and effort pursuing scholarly debates that seem trivial – and even silly – in light of these modes of behavior. In anthropology, the "formalists" argued that economic models designed for the contemporary capitalist economy can be applied directly to all non-Western and early societies. Leaving aside the question of whether such economic models adequately explain the economy today (e.g., Gintis 2006), the very real differences between the contemporary economy and those of the distant past cannot just be ignored. The opposing "substantivists," led by Karl Polanyi, went too far in the opposite direction, suggesting that non-Western and ancient economies are so radically different from Western economies today that they require a distinct noneconomic approach to understanding (Polanyi et al. 1957). This argument was paralleled by a debate in classical studies between the "modernists" (a formalist approach, based on analogy with the modern economy) and the "primitivists" (substantivists). For useful discussions of these debates, see Wilk and Cliggett (2007), Earle (2002), Scheidel et al. (2007), or Feinman and Garraty (2010).

Some models from economics can be applied easily to some ancient economies in some situations. Moreover, some ancient economic processes are amenable to analysis using the tools of economists, while others are not. A priori judgments on these issues are often a recipe for biased and limited accounts, as in the scholarly debates mentioned previously. The settlement-scaling model described in Chapter 3, for example, is an appropriate model for ancient cities because its assumptions are easily met by past settlements and society. This and other models discussed below require at least a weak conception of rationality. Philosopher of science Lina Eriksson (2011) has identified three kinds of rationality in the social science literature of rational choice theory. Weak views of rationality invoke only the first kind: rationality as instrumental behavior. People generally know what is good for themselves and their family or group, and act accordingly; social behavior is rarely erratic and irrational. The stronger types of rationality – self-interested agents and calculative or strategic reasoning – are not required for economic models (Gintis et al. 2005), even though they are often invoked by political scientists (Eriksson 2011).

Economic Growth in the Past

The first question economists and economic historians ask of past cities and societies is, inevitably, "Was there economic growth?" (e.g., North 1981). This obsession with growth can be frustrating for archaeologists, who find it difficult, and often impossible, to identify and analyze economic growth given the data at our disposal. Nevertheless, economic growth is an important concept for ancient urban life. Economists concluded long ago that growth is a prerequisite for economic prosperity. Indeed, this is one of the principal conclusions of Adam Smith's (1979) *Wealth of Nations*: expansion of the market and increasing division of labor generate economic growth, which creates prosperity. Not surprisingly, economists call this kind of growth "Smithian growth" (discussed later). Given that kings, elites, and other wealthy individuals in premodern times were not going to redistribute their wealth to the poor, economic growth may have been the only way to generate the resources to improve the lives of non-elites.[1]

Most discussions of economic growth concern intensive growth. This refers to increases in economic output per capita. Extensive growth, in contrast, describes increasing output that originates simply from the growth of population. That is, economic production and exchange must grow when populations increase, but this does not necessarily produce changes in per capita rates. Discussions of intensive and extensive growth can be found in Goldstone (2002), Erdkamp (2016), or Jones (2000). The views of economic historians range from the notion that there was no (intensive) economic growth at all prior to the Industrial Revolution (Clark 2007), to the position that economic growth did indeed characterize some ancient economies, such as Republican and Imperial Rome (Erdkamp 2016), and Classical Athens (Ober 2015). In the words of Jack Goldstone:

> Growth and prosperity were not monopolies of the modern or Western (or even "capitalist") worlds. Rather, at many times and places in history opportunities were created and seized, most often under conditions of amplified cultural and commercial exchange and the renovation and extension of political institutions, to innovate, raise productivity, and provide sustained population growth and urbanization simultaneously with rising and high levels of per capita income. (Goldstone 2002:377–378)

The results of settlement scaling research (Chapter 3) support this latter position. Superlinear scaling (Figure 3.11) may provide evidence of intensive growth, brought on by social interactions and energized crowding within settlements. There is thus a close link between economic growth and urban growth. Another term for intensive economic growth is "increasing returns to scale" (Krugman 1991; Romer 1986). Economist Brian Arthur defines this as follows: "Increasing returns are the tendency for that which is ahead to get further ahead, for that which loses advantage to lose further advantage. They are mechanisms of positive feedback that operate – within markets, businesses, and industries – to reinforce that which gains success or aggravate that which suffers loss" (Arthur 1996:100).

Ancient economic historians can now, for the first time, discuss the presence and nature of Roman economic growth based on empirical data, although agreement has not yet been reached (Erdkamp 2016; Jongman 2012; Scheidel

---

[1] Recent critiques of the idea that growth is required for prosperity in the contemporary world (Dalziel et al. 2018; Jackson 2009) have not gained widespread acceptance among economists, and their phrasing in terms of the modern capitalist economy prevents their usefulness for studies of precapitalist economies.

2009). A minority view is that this emphasis on intensive economic growth is misplaced, because extensive growth was far more widespread in antiquity, and provides a more compelling account of the Roman economy (Bang 2016). Nevertheless, archaeological data are starting to contribute to the study of intensive economic growth in the distant past (Morris 2004; Ober 2015; Ortman and Lobo 2020; Stark et al. 2016). What was the relationship between economic growth and cities in the past? Of the various types of intensive growth identified by economists (Acemoglu 2009; Joffe 2017; Jones 2000), the one most relevant to ancient urban economies is Smithian growth.

Smithian Growth

Smithian growth is the term for intensive economic growth achieved by an increase in the division of labor and/or in the extent of the relevant market or exchange system (Goldstone 2002; Kelly 1997; Persson and Sharp 2015:chapter 2). It may be contrasted with *Promethean growth*, which refers to intensive economic growth driven by technological innovations or a switch to more efficient fuel sources (Jones 2000). Most economists see population growth as a prerequisite for Smithian growth. Figure 5.2A shows a model of economic growth (as measured by per capita income) proposed by two economic historians (Persson and Sharp 2015:68).

One of the mechanisms of increasing returns is called *learning-by-doing* (Arrow 1962), which refers to "improvements in productive efficiency arising from the generation of experience obtained by producing a good or service" (Beaudry 2008:125); see also Duranton and Puga (2004). In Figure 5.2A, Smithian growth is created by a combination of an increased division of labor and the operation of learning-by-doing. An increasing per capita income is the outcome of Smithian growth. This diagram also shows a countervailing process, known as the Malthusian trap. In this process, population growth surpasses economic growth, leading to diminishing returns to scale, which then decreases per capita income. Those economists who deny the operation of intensive economic growth in the past (as discussed previously) argue or assume that Malthusian processes overwhelmed Smithian growth. Erdkamp (2016) is an excellent discussion of this issue in reference to the Roman economy.

The second diagram in Figure 5.2 (B) is my own summary of the drivers of Smithian growth, based on the sources cited above. Smithian growth occurs when productivity per worker increases, and this usually requires an increase in specialization. Such expansion in the division of labor typically requires increasing exchange at the regional or long-distance levels. An expansion in the scale of the economy – either the demographic scale or the spatial/social scale – is another contributor to Smithian growth. Overall, an increase or

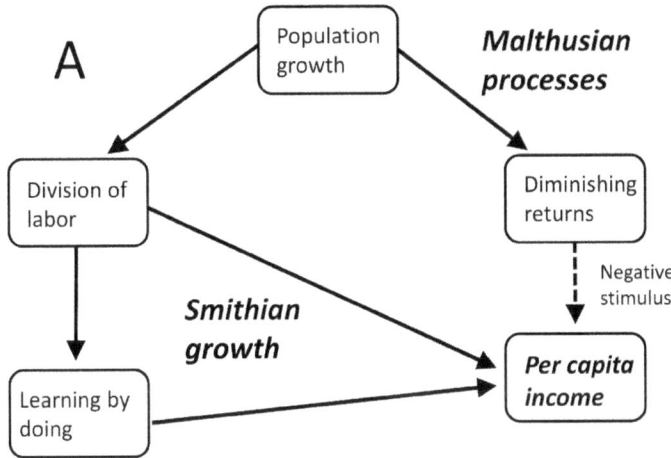

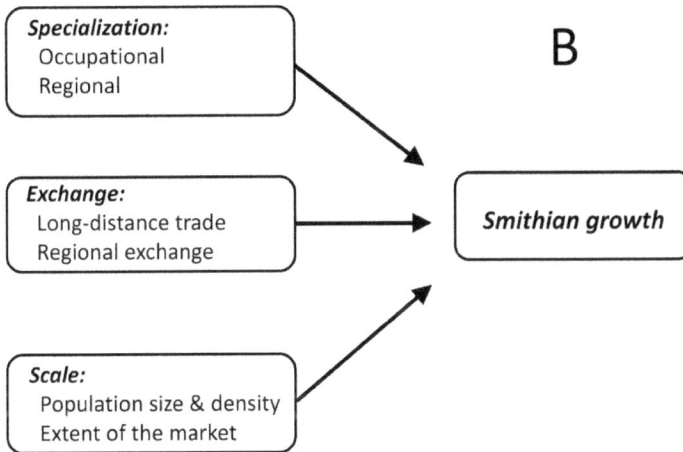

5.2. Smithian growth models. Graphics by Michael E. Smith. (A) Modified after Persson and Sharp (2015:68).

expansion in several of the drivers listed in Figure 5.2 – reinforcing one another – can generate Smithian growth.

Given that it is quite difficult to identify direct evidence of Smithian growth with archaeological data, how is this relevant to ancient urban economics? First, Smithian growth is implied by the results of the settlement scaling work described in Chapter 3. Second, the analysis of economic growth in the deep past will become more prominent in the future, particularly with improving methods to analyze and quantify production and exchange systems. Guillermo Algaze (2018) has proposed Smithian growth as an important process in ancient Mesopotamia, and Ortman and Lobo (2020) have operationalized an archaeological model of Smithian growth – based on settlement scaling – for pueblos in the US Southwest. It will be important for archaeologists to have a grounding in the relevant concepts and models, which do not require complex econometrics. Third, Smithian growth requires an expansion of economic urban functions. While occupational specialization or urban population growth can occur solely within the bounds of a city, most of the drivers of Smithian growth involve an expansion in regional economies, which implies the operation of economic urban functions. The scheme presented in Figure 5.2 furnishes an organizational framework for part of this chapter.

Broadening the Concept of Growth

For many historians and social scientists outside of economics, the concept of economic growth has two drawbacks: it seems to be limited to the modern capitalist economy, and it ignores important noneconomic practices and phenomena, such as culture (Polanyi et al. 1957; Sahlins 1972). I have dealt with the first objection above; there is no inherent reason why intensive growth could not have happened in the distant past, and archaeologists and historians are now developing the data and methods to study this. The second objection misses the mark, however; this objection is like criticizing a political concept for not dealing with religion, or a social concept for ignoring economics. Nevertheless, recent scholarship has tried to broaden the concept of growth.

In an extension of Blanton and Fargher's (2008) work on collective and autocratic governance (Chapter 4), they have developed the notion of a broad process of social and economic growth they call the "coactive causal process" (Blanton 2016:248–259). They identify five key processes – commercialization, standard of living, urbanization, population growth, and intensification of production – as tending to co-occur and reinforce one another. These combine into two pathways of growth, one driven by collective action and the other by urbanism and markets. When the coactive causal process takes hold in an area, a major outcome is the development of more collective polities (Chapter 4). Institutional economists and social historians have developed other schemes that show how the operation and interaction of key institutions lead to improvements in social welfare (Acemoglu and Robinson 2012; Prak 2018), but these seem less applicable to premodern societies (Huff 2013) than the coactive causal process.

MARKET ECONOMIES AND COMMAND ECONOMIES

Ancient commercial economies were a glaring blind spot in Karl Polanyi's influential substantivist view of early societies. Polanyi defined ancient commercial exchange out of existence by insisting that only capitalist economies had markets and commercial institutions, whereas precapitalist economies were organized solely around redistribution and reciprocity. We now know that Polanyi's strong adherence to this viewpoint led him to distort historical evidence in order to shore up his theory (Smith 2004). However, now that we can acknowledge that many ancient economies did indeed have money, merchants, markets, and entrepreneurial behavior, it is important also to recognize the existence of noncommercial, state-run economies in the deep past. In this section, I explore the nature of commercial institutions among ancient urban economies. For an overview of the variation in ancient economies, see Hirth (2020). As I argue in Chapter 1 (Figure 1.9), this variation in ancient economic institutions and practices was a major force shaping the differences in urban life among early cities and urban traditions.

Markets and Commercial Exchange

Marketplaces were important settings for exchange in many premodern cities. The Aztec markets greatly impressed the Spanish conquistadores and visitors. In addition to the massive and busy central imperial market of Tlatelolco, each city-state capital sported a weekly market (Berdan 2014; Smith 2008) As in many premodern and contemporary rural systems, most Aztec markets were periodic, meeting once each five-day week. This allowed merchants to travel among markets and extend their area of sales, and it gave consumers access to a greater range of goods than would be available at a permanent daily market or shop (Lloyd and Dicken 1977). Market days in periodic market systems are times of bustling activity, celebration, and heightened social interaction (de la Pradelle 2015; de Ligt 1993; Skinner 1964). As such, they are prime settings for the operation of energized crowding.

Busy marketplaces, however, do not necessarily signal economic urban functions. If the markets – or shops – exclusively serve the retail needs of the local urban population, then they do not contribute to economic urban functions. I discuss markets and shops as facilities used by urban residents in Chapter 7. When exchange at an urban marketplace links up with regional or long-distance networks – often through wholesale merchants – then we are dealing with urban functions. Marketplaces were only one place where commercial exchange may have occurred in early cities. In the early modern Netherlands, for example, commercial transactions took place in the central market square, at periodic fairs, in commercial halls and shopping streets (lined with shops), at street stalls, and with itinerant peddlers (Stabel 2008). Prior to the European Renaissance, commercial exchange in most areas was limited to fewer locations, including a central marketplace or market building. Nevertheless, marketplace exchange was only one of many commercial institutions in premodern societies.

TABLE 5.2 *Commercial Institutions*

1	Imported goods	9	Foreign merchant residents
2	Retail marketplaces or shops	10	Written accounting system
3	Entrepreneurial merchants	11	Bills of exchange/letter of credit
4	Money	12	Wholesale markets
5	Private property in land	13	Wage labor
6	Standardized weights/measurements	14	Commercial partnerships
7	Coinage (metal)	15	Banking
8	Wholesale infrastructure	16	Commercial loans

One way to examine variation in the nature of ancient economies is to focus on their level of commercialization. Nonmarket, command economies have very low commercialization, whereas early modern northern Europe had a high level. I have defined *commercialization* as follows: "Commercialization is a synthetic concept that includes several related aspects of economic process: the extent to which a price-making market allocates commodities and the factors of production; the prominence of entrepreneurial activity; and the pervasiveness of institutions such as money, marketplaces, credit, and banking (Neale 1971; Smith 1976b)" (Smith 2004:78–79).

Table 5.2 is a list of commercial institutions found in premodern economies. These features approximate a Guttman scale, which means the presence of a particular institution – say, coinage – is usually accompanied by all of the institutions ranked lower on the scale, but may or may not also include the higher-ranked features. As one moves up the numerical commercialization scale, the institutions take on greater importance as economic urban functions. That is, imported goods or money often pertain to local exchange and may not greatly influence the hinterland, whereas banking or commercial exchange are more likely to influence other settlements in the region or beyond.[2]

Table 5.3 shows how these commercial institutions are distributed among the case studies in this book. Cities toward the top of the scale have a greater number of commercial institutions and therefore can be described as more heavily commercialized than cities lower on the scale. The data used to assemble this commercialization scale are discussed in Appendix A.[3] As a general observation, cities with more heavily commercialized economies engage in higher levels of production and exchange, and this is related to their higher levels of energized crowding.

[2] This scale was developed by the project "Service Access in Premodern Cities" (Smith et al. 2016; Stanley et al. 2016).

[3] The coding of the case studies for commercial institutions is described in Appendix A. These are my personal judgments, based on published sources and interviews with experts on individual case studies. In the absence of additional research and validation, this should not be viewed as a rigorous data set suitable for reanalysis.

TABLE 5.3 *Level of commercialization, case studies*

		Score	Commercial traits (see Table 5.2):															
			1	2	3	4	5	6	7	8	9	10	11	12	13	14	15	16
Highly commercialized economies:																		
24	Pompeii	16	x	x	x	x	x	x	x	x	x	x	x	x	x	x	x	x
21	Rhodes	14	x	x	x	x	x	x	x	x	x	x		x		L	x	x
11	Swahili	13	x	x	x	x	x	x	x	x	x	x		x	x	x		
27	Odense	13	x	x	x	x	x	x	x	x	x	x	x	L	x	x		
16	Chang'an	11	x	x	x	x	x	x	x	x	x			x		x		
19	Jerash	11	x	L	x	x	x	x	x	x			L	x			x	
15	Persepolis	11	x	x	x	x	x	x	x	x				x	x	x		
Moderately commercialized economies:																		
25	Olynthus	10	x	x	x	x	x	x	x		L			x		x		
28	Ur	9	x	x	x	x	x		x			x	x		x			
29	Fyrkat	9	x	L	L	x	L	x	x		L					L		
14	Viking thing site	8	x	x	x	x	x	x	x							x		
8	Angkor	7	x	x	x	x	x		x					x				
20	Ribe	7	x	x		x	x	x	L	x								
18	Otumba	6	x	L	L	x	L				L							
22	Yautepec	6	x	L	L	x	L				L							
Somewhat commercialized economies:																		
23	Ado Ekiti	4	x			x	L	L										
26	Teotihuacan	4	x	x	L						x							
1	Tikal	2	x	x														
5	Mohenjo-daro	2	x					x										
17	Knossos	2	x					x										
7	Burning Man																	
Uncommercialized economies:																		
2	Çatalhöyük	1	x															
3	Pincevent	1	x															
4	Beidha	1	x															
6	SW Pueblos	1	x															
10	Cahokia	1	x															
12	Huanuco Pampa	1	x															
13	Amarna Work vill	1	x															
9	Plains aggre site	1	x															

Key:
x   Trait was present
L   Trait was very likely present

Command Economies

A command economy is one where major economic activities are administered directly by the government, in place of relying on markets or independent entrepreneurs. The phrase was used initially to contrast the economies of Nazi Germany and the Soviet Union with the dominant capitalist economy (Ericson

2008), but the concept has existed in anthropology for some time (Stark and Garraty 2010). This was, in fact, how Karl Polanyi interpreted *all* ancient state-level economies. Now that we recognize Polanyi's errors on this subject, however, it is important to understand that markets and commercial institutions are far from universal in early state societies. The three best-documented examples of ancient command economies are Dynastic Egypt, the Inka (and probably other pre-Inka societies) of the Andes, and the Bronze-Age palace economies of the Aegean (Minoan and Mycenean). While there may have been small-scale localized markets in these systems, the emphasis on state control – coupled with the absence of money – limited the extent of commercial exchange. Goods were transported by state agents, not by entrepreneurial merchants.

A large and active bureaucracy is one of the salient features of ancient command economies. Without independent merchants or producers, an army of scribes was needed to run the economy. In Weberian sociology, bureaucracies are characterized by professional workers whose task is specialized by job, such that the occupant of the position should not make a difference in how the job is done. The procedures are public knowledge, and written records are kept (Kiser and Baer 2005; Swedberg and Agewall 2005:19–20). The most bureaucratic ancient economies were in Egypt (Figure 5.3) and Peru. For example, the Egyptian king Senusret I ordered an expedition to quarry stone in the desert. The crew consisted of a single noble (a herald named Amemy), 8 scribes, 80 officials (lower-ranking scribes), 18,700 laborers, plus millers, bakers, and brewers to supply food for the crew (Kemp

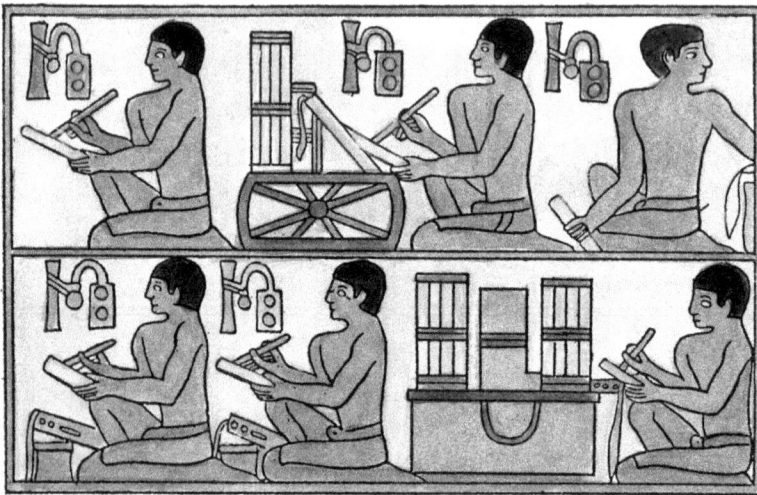

5.3. Egyptian scribes at work. Depiction of a relief from the tomb of Ti, Sakkara, Egypt. Granger.

2006:181). Inka bureaucrats, identified by their large ear flares, managed the storehouses and other parts of the state economy (Figure 4.6, Huanuco Pampa). Large state-sponsored storage facilities, like those at Huanuco Pampa or Knossos (discussed later), are usually the sign of an uncommercialized economy (Smith 2012c). Other material signals in command economies are the lack of marketplaces or shops (Moeller 2016:382), and the location of craft production facilities adjacent to palaces.

Beyond the presence or absence of specific features of urban infrastructure, early command economies had many more state-founded settlements than did societies with more commercialized economies. This situation is clearest for dynastic Egypt. In Nadine Moeller's (2016:15–26) analysis of urbanism before the New Kingdom, the majority of her types of urban settlements – and the vast majority of urban sites overall – were state foundations. An informal comparison of state formations in Inka and Aztec societies – parallel imperial, urban societies with radically different economies – supports my contention. The major works on urban settlements outside of the imperial capitals (Hyslop 1990; Smith 2008) reveal two major differences. First, there were more types of state foundations in the Inka case: administrative centers (see Case Study 12, Huanuco Pampa), inns, and fortresses. Second, two types of state foundations – royal estates and sanctuaries – are represented by only single examples in Aztec society, as compared to many examples in the Inka case. In command economies, the state controls more than just the economy; it also dominates the urbanization process. The following case study looks at a particularly well-known city in an ancient command economy.

Case Study 17 Knossos: Bronze-Age Palace Economy

The economies of the Bronze-Age Mycenean and Minoan societies (1700–1200 BCE) are often described as *palace economies*; this is a synonym for my concept of command economy. Archaeological excavations have revealed the size and centrality of royal palaces in these societies, and the palaces typically contain major storage facilities. Texts in the early Greek script Linear B describe palace agents who administered the production and distribution of goods. Early versions of the palace economy model were based on Polanyi's concept of redistribution. More recent analyses have confirmed the role of the palace in controlling much of the economy, but without the unnecessary baggage of Polanyi's model. Scholars now acknowledge the localized, small-scale operation of other exchange methods, such as markets (Christakis 2011; Earle 2011; Parkinson et al. 2013). Knossos has one of the lowest commercialization scores (2) of any city in a state-level society (Table 5.3).

The Palace Economy of Knossos. Knossos was the largest settlement on Crete during the Minoan period (Whitelaw 2004, 2017). The famous palace was excavated by Sir Arthur Evans in the early decades of the twentieth century and remains a major tourist attraction today. Although many elements of the reconstruction of the palace owe more to Evans's imagination than to archaeological reality (Brown 1983), the basic plan of the palace is generally accepted as valid (Figure 5.4). This palace shares features of form and layout with other Minoan palaces (Letesson and Knappett 2017; McEnroe 2010). Among their distinctive features are blocks of long, narrow rooms used for storage. Ceramic storage jars known as

Case Study 17 (cont.)

pithoi – some quite large – were common at Minoan sites (Figure 5.5), and the storage rooms were likely filled with these jars (Christakis 2008).

In his excavations of the Knossos palace, Evans recovered numerous clay tablets with inscriptions. These list a variety of products – from grains and wool to fruits and oil – whose production and distribution were managed by palace bureaucrats. Wool textiles, for example, were produced in the palace, from sheep owned by the palace. This was a top-down, administered economy in which economic transactions at smaller settlements were linked directly to the palace bureaucracy in Knossos (Bennet 1985). How did this command economy affect cities and urban life on Crete? To begin with, people had limited autonomy or agency in handling their basic economic affairs. The wealth that flowed within the system was used strategically by the king to reward followers (Christakis 2011), which means that the command economy was a major force in the development of wealth inequality. The economy

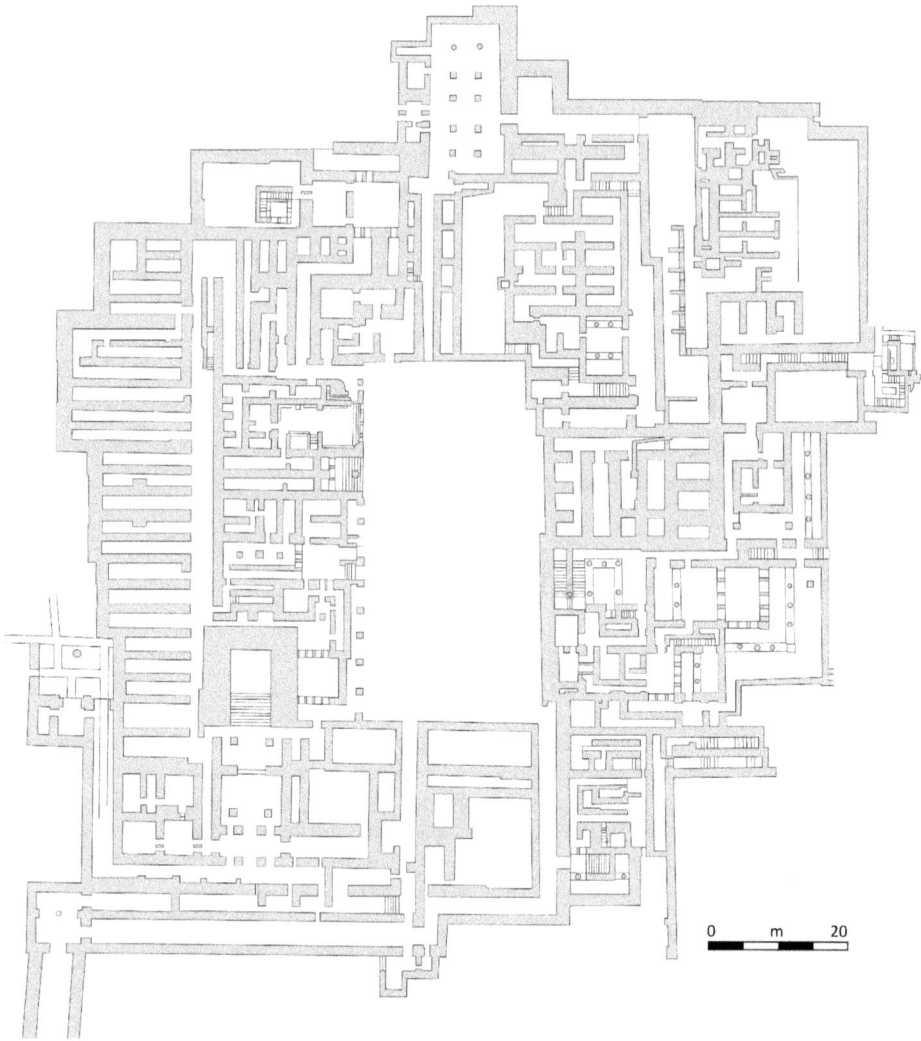

5.4. Plan of the palace at Knossos. Drawing by Phoemela Ballaran, based on a map in McEnroe (2010:70), reproduced with permission.

Case Study 17 (cont.)

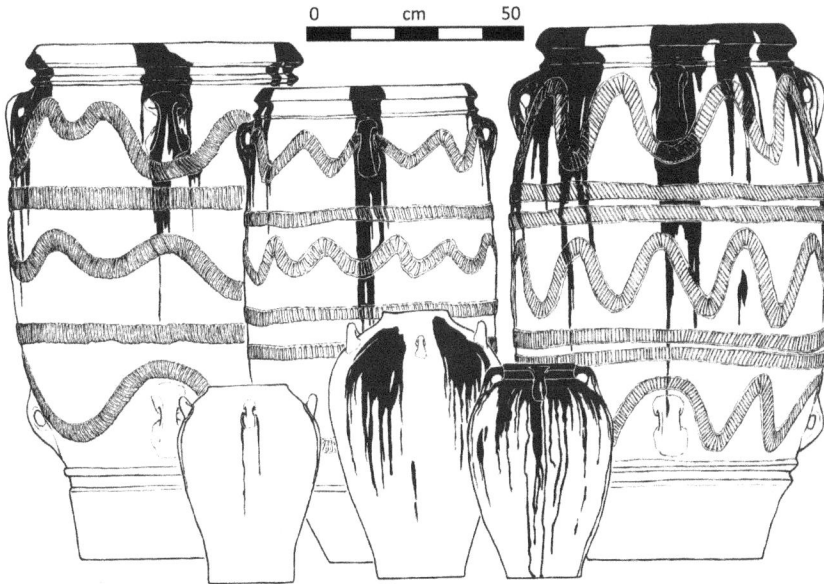

5.5. Storage jars (*pithoi*) from Knossos. Modified after Christakis (2008:figure 3).

structured the nature of urban functions, since political control was strongly concentrated in Knossos and the other palace centers such as Malia and Gournia.

Comparative Insights. Late Bronze Age Knossos gives us a picture of a command economy – a type of economy rare in the history of state-level societies around the world. While this economy was highly bureaucratic, by necessity, it was also a dynamic and vibrant economy, producing a variety of goods and engaging in exchange with neighboring Minoan polities and with foreign states around the Mediterranean. The economy determined the size and activities at royal palaces such as Knossos, and these in turn affected life in these cities and their hinterlands.

URBAN CRAFTS AND THE DIVISION OF LABOR

Adam Smith famously observed that "the division of labor is limited by the extent of the market" (A. Smith 1979:book 1, chapter 3). For premodern cities, the "extent of the market" has two components: the size of the area (and its population) covered by a given exchange system and the degree of penetration of marketing into the whole economy (i.e., the level of commercialization). As the case of Knossos shows, however, even a noncommercialized command economy does have specialists; they work for the state, however, rather than for themselves. Adam Smith's observation that the concentration of craft producers in a settlement was a mechanism of urban growth has been explored by both economists (Duranton and Puga

2004; Jacobs 1984) and archaeologists (Hanson et al. 2017; Kenoyer 1998; Láng 2016). Croix et al. (2019), for example, argue that the concentration of different specialized craftspeople in the trading emporium of Ribe (Case Study 20) allowed the production of complex goods beyond the ability of any one specialist to create, which in turn stimulated commercial exchange, leading to the growth of the settlement.

Craft Production and the Division of Labor

The "division of labor" is a broad concept in the social sciences that includes a number of separate dimensions of society and the economy (Becker and Murphy 1994; Durkheim 2014; Freidson 1976). The most common of these dimensions is *labor input*: Do individuals work full-time or part-time at a given occupation or task? Unfortunately, for archaeologists, this can be very difficult to identify in the deep past. It may not be hard to identify the traces of craft production in a domestic context, but to determine whether the producer was a full-time specialist or a farmer working part-time on the craft may be difficult.

For this chapter, I focus on a second dimension of the division of labor: the *scale of production*. While various measures of production scale leave archaeological traces, one of the clearest is the size and nature of production facilities (Costin 1991). D. P. S. Peacock (1982), in an ethnoarchaeological study of traditional ceramic production in Mediterranean societies, presents a useful typology of the scale of production facilities in that area (Table 5.4). This scale ranges from crafts produced at home for domestic use (not for exchange) to large-scale dedicated facilities. Another relevant dimension of the division of labor is what Costin (1991) calls *social context* of production. A basic distinction in social context is between independent producers, who work for themselves and sell their wares in the market or shops, and attached producers, artisans who work directly for a patron, whether an individual or an institution. For the former, their livelihoods are more directly under their own control, and their economic activity is a generative process within cities (Chapter 7). Attached producers, on the other hand, have less control over how they do their work; their work is more strongly influenced by top-down institutions (whether king, priest, or noble).

In Aztec cities, makers of utilitarian goods such as pottery, stone tools, textiles, and basketry were independent producers, whereas those who made luxury goods – stone sculptures, jewelry, featherwork, gold metallurgy – were attached to a noble patron. Independent producers set their own schedule and production regime, while attached producers created objects required by a noble or institution. Aztec attached producers also made some items

TABLE 5.4 *Scale of Mediterranean ceramic production*

1	**Household production:**
	Production in the home, for domestic use
	Nonspecialized
2	**Household industry:**
	Production in the home, for exchange
	Part-time producers
	Hand production, turntables, simple kilns
3	**Individual workshops:**
	Production in a dedicated facility, for the market
	Main source of income
	Potter's wheel and kilns
4	**Nucleated workshops:**
	Clustering of individual workshops into a single complex
	More permanent facilities
	Greater standardization of products
5	**Manufactory:**
	Large-scale workshops, capital investment required
	High volume of output
	Labor is specialized by task; products are standardized
6	**Special forms:**
	Estate production
	Institutional production

Note: Based on Peacock (1982).

independently that they were allowed to sell in the market (Smith 2012a). Not surprisingly, attached specialists tended to reside in cities, whereas independent specialists – although more numerous in town – also plied their trade in rural areas. The scaling research outlined in Chapter 3 shows that in most regional systems, the level of the division of labor (the number of specialists and number of trades) increases with settlement size.

THE REGIONAL ECONOMY

Cities exist in an intimate relationship with their immediate hinterland, if only because this is where their food comes from, as well as the labor for major construction projects. A crucial question for urban economies is why rural farmers would want to bring or sell their food to people in the city. Regional exchange systems do more than just supply towns with food; they help structure the economy and society in both the city and its hinterland. One cannot understand urban life in the past without considering the regional economy (de Ligt and Bintliff 2020; Skinner 1964; Smith 1976a).

Although archaeologists often use the term *region* colloquially, I prefer a more technical definition: a region is the hinterland of a high-order central place. That is, *region* refers to the area in which exchanges of goods, information, and labor are concentrated around a central place or city, or perhaps around a group of nearby cities (Lloyd and Dicken 1977; Murphey 1982). When these exchanges are focused on a central settlement, they constitute urban functions. The concept of economic urban functions originated in the spatial study of market regions, using central place theory (Christaller 1966). As noted in Chapter 1, the retail economic functions first analyzed by central place theorists were expanded by anthropologists to include political and religious

---

Case Study 18 Otumba: Aztec Craft Center

Outside of the imperial capital, Tenochtitlan, most Aztec cities had low levels of craft production. Nearly all utilitarian goods were produced by independent part-time producers; these were usually farmers, working in the off-season. One of the more important craft industries was the production of textiles of cotton and maguey fibers (Huster 2019). Producers of utilitarian goods worked out of their homes and sold goods in the market. This corresponds to Peacock's Household industry category (Table 5.4). Otumba differs from other Aztec urban centers in its greater number of craft goods, and the possibility that the production of some crafts was organized on a larger scale, that of individual workshops. After the Aztec capital Tenochtitlan – which I infer to have a likely commercialization score of 8 – Otumba has one of the highest commercialization levels (6) of any New World city. The reason for this may be that Otumba sits on one of the major geological sources of obsidian in central Mexico. One can speculate that obsidian working was the first craft to develop at the site and that other crafts were added later. On Aztec urban crafts in general, see Berdan (2014) or Smith (2012a).

Surface Collections and Craft Workshops. Otumba is an unassuming site to visit today. One advantage, compared to other Aztec cities, is that the colonial and modern occupation only cover a relatively small part of the Aztec city. As a result, the Aztec site has been extensively plowed and disturbed. There is no standing civic architecture at all. But these conditions make Otumba an ideal place to carry out intensive surface collections, an important method for studying ancient cities (Johnson and Millett 2012).

At Otumba, the plowed fields have higher levels of craft production debris than most sites in Mesoamerica. To investigate the nature and level of craft industries at Otumba, Deborah Nichols and Thomas Charlton directed a program of intensive, systematic surface collections at the site (Charlton et al. 2000; Nichols 2013; Nichols et al. 2000; Parry 2001). They collected all visible artifacts in over one thousand squares of five by five meters, spread out across the site. There is a clear tendency for the debris from individual production types to form clusters (Figure 5.6).

Most craft production at Mesoamerican sites corresponds to Peacock's category of household industry: farmers engaged in craft activities during the dry season when they had little work in the fields (Hirth 2009). Although there have been only a few test excavations at the Otumba production locations, it is likely that at least some of these mark facilities on the level of Peacock's individual workshops. First, the artifactual remains of crafts are particularly dense and varied. Lapidary production areas, for example, yielded production tools (perforators and polishers), premanufacture blanks, and partially finished products such as beads and earspools. Second, Otumba is the only Aztec site with spatial clustering of textile production debris. Most Mesoamerican textiles were produced by women, spinning and weaving by hand at home. The dense concentrations of large spindle whorls, used to spin maguey thread, suggests that Otumba was the setting for production above the household norm; that is, individual workshops.

Comparative Insights. Otumba yields several insights for our knowledge of premodern cities. First, the concentration of production debris in surface collections indicates a higher level of craft production than in most Mesoamerican cities. Yet the fact that the craft facilities at this major Mesoamerican craft center were likely limited to a few individual workshops shows that urban economies in this area were less

Case Study 18 (cont.)

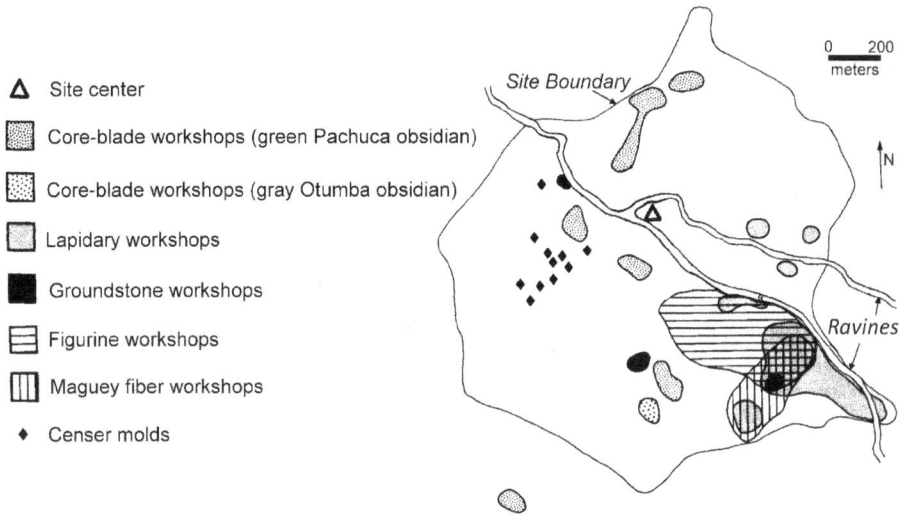

5.6. Plan of the Aztec city of Otumba, showing craft production locations. Modified after Otis Charlton (1994:fig. 8.1), reproduced with permission.

highly commercialized, and had a lower division of labor, than many ancient cities in the Old World. Otumba's score on the commercialization scale (Table 5.3) is 6, lower than the average Old World score of 8.2. Finally, the Otumba research validates the method of intensive surface collection as a method for studying the spatial distribution of activities within urban sites.

Case Study 19 Jerash: Commercial Expansion at an Islamic City

Jerash (or Gerasa), known today for its Roman architecture and orthogonal city plan, is a site that has attracted generations of archaeologists and tourists. As recently as 2011, it was claimed that the site was abandoned after capture by Arabs (Gates 2011:404). But excavations reveal a significant Islamic occupation in and around the buildings of the Roman period (Rattenborg and Blanke 2017; Simpson 2008). Contradicting older accounts of the decline of Jerash and other Near Eastern cities under Islamic rule, new finds point to a busy and prosperous commercial city at least until the impact of an earthquake in 749. My case study focuses on the early Islamic period, between ca. 630 and 749. Whether the city was largely destroyed by the earthquake, or showed resilience in its aftermath, remains a topic of current debate among archaeologists working in different parts of the city (Lichtenberger and Raja 2015; Rattenborg and Blanke 2017).

Crafts and Markets after the Roman Period. Craft production not only continued to flourish in Jerash after the Roman period but also may have increased. Excavations of the post-Roman occupation revealed several "industrial" work areas with pottery kilns and piles of sherd wasters indicative of workshop production (Lichtenberger and Raja 2015; Rattenborg and Blanke 2017). One interesting find is that over 99 percent of the ceramics (in a fully quantified sample from one excavation) were produced locally (Romanowska et al. 2022). But was ceramic production an economic urban function? To answer this question, we need to know whether the ceramic products of Jerash were exported or not; this research has not been done yet.

Case Study 19 (cont.)

Other large-scale crafts in the early Islamic period include glass production (Barford et al. 2018) and tile mosaics. A recently excavated house contained a large interior stone trough filled with tens of thousands of unused stone tesserae (Figure 5.7), intended for mosaic production (Lichtenberger and Raja 2017; Wootton 2017). This and other nearby houses had been abandoned quickly after the earthquake, with many objects left in their original positions.

Another kind of evidence for expanded commercial activity in the Islamic period is the construction of new shops in the commercial center, at the crossroads of the two major avenues of the city. Figure 5.8 shows this area, the *tetrakionion*, with both the original Roman buildings and the Islamic additions (Simpson 2008). The perimeter of the tetrakionion was initially lined with shops, but these were expanded out into the public space in the Islamic period, probably to create larger facilities with back storerooms. New rows of shops were also created along the main north-south avenue, the *Cardo*, as well as along the walls of the newly built congregational mosque. These small single-entrance structures resemble shops in other early cities (Chapter 7), and finds of coins, storage jars, and imported objects support this interpretation. The lack of excavation outside Jerash makes it hard to say whether or not these shops served a clientele beyond the urban residents – that is, did they serve an economic urban function?

Comparative Insights. Jerash was an important commercial center in both the Roman and Islamic periods. Prior suggestions that the city and urban life declined in the Islamic period have been discredited by recent excavations, particularly by projects that apply a high-definition approach to the analysis of archaeological materials (Barford et al. 2018; Lichtenberger and Raja 2017; Stott et al. 2018). Islamic Jerash was highly commercialized (with a score of 11), and fieldwork illustrates the conjunction of diverse markers of a commercial economy, such as shops and high-volume craft production.

5.7. Tesserae found in a trough in an early Islamic house (trench P) at Jerash. Courtesy of the Danish-German Jerash Northwest Quarter Project.

Case Study 19 (cont.)

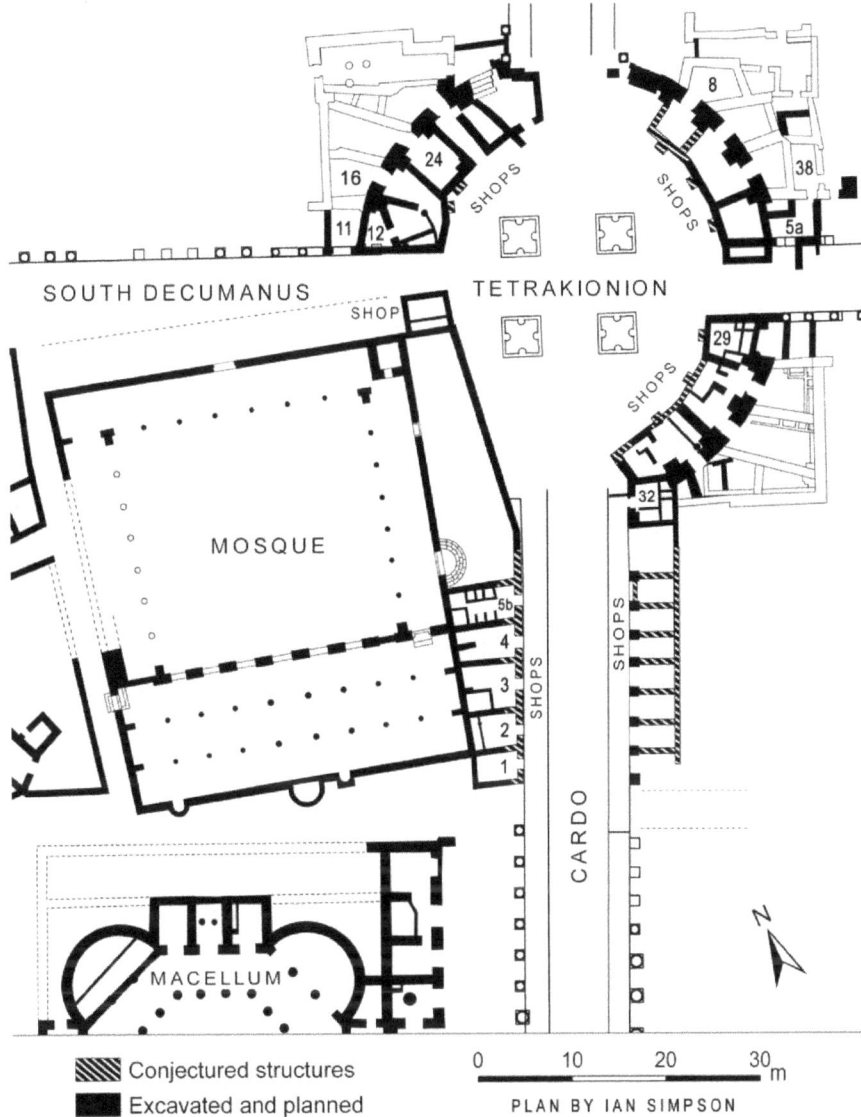

5.8. Islamic market and shops at Jerash. Modified after Simpson (2008:124).

urban functions. One of the building blocks of central place theory is the observation that small cities tend to have small hinterlands, and large cities have large hinterlands that include the hinterlands of smaller cities (Lloyd and Dicken 1977; Mulligan et al. 2012). The larger cities in an area (or, more technically, the higher-order central places) have more urban functions than the smaller settlements – more shops or merchants, a wider variety of goods and services, more bureaucrats, more temples, and larger civic buildings; as a result, they also have higher rates of energized crowding. The hierarchy of city sizes in an area is matched by a nested hierarchy of urban hinterlands. If we are to understand the spatial and social context of a city, we need to understand its region. This includes the nature of exchanges within the region, the nature of the regional settlement hierarchy, and the population who grows the food and provides the labor or taxes for a city (Berrey et al. 2021; Trigger 1972).

Peasants, Intensification, and Urban Food Supply

The term *peasant* refers to rural farmers who are integrated into a state society yet have little voice in local or regional governance. They differ from tribal farmers in that they are required to pay taxes and/or rent to landlords and governments. In the words of anthropologist George Foster, "Peasants have very little control over the conditions that govern their lives" (Foster 1967:2). Similarly, peasants differ from farmers in developed nations today both in this lack of control, and in their greater isolation from wider economic and cultural dynamics. Peasant agriculture today typically employs lower levels of farm mechanization and higher levels of traditional practices. Nevertheless, even if peasant households strive for self-sufficiency, they need to participate in their regional economy, if only to garner cash for rent and taxes. Both sets of payments serve to link peasants to a city.

Peasant farmers produced most of the food consumed in premodern cities. In many premodern states, urban elites owned the farmland. Peasant farmers in some settings paid their rent in food (e.g., through a sharecropping arrangement), and in other cases, peasants paid rent in money. This required them to sell some of their goods to obtain cash for rent and tax payments. Thus, both agricultural land rent and taxes stimulated peasants to sell food in urban markets (Smith 1974). In command economies, taxes could not be paid in the form of money, so they were paid in labor and/or food and other goods.

The definition of *peasantry* given previously – focusing on a lack of resources and control with respect to landlords and the state – is meant to position the peasantry within the structure of society. While these restrictions on peasant participation in society were very real, two domains permitted peasants enough agency and self-determination to achieve prosperity and a high quality of life: smallholder intensification and market systems. Agricultural intensification refers to processes by which farmers invest additional labor or energy into subsistence in order to achieve higher yields on the land (Kirch 1994; Sandeford 2021; Turner and Doolittle 1978). Smallholder intensification is a social pattern among households that accounts for much of the peasant intensification in premodern societies (Netting 1993).

There is a large literature on intensification in premodern societies. For my argument in this book, two features of intensification are crucial. First, all state-level societies in the past relied upon intensive agricultural methods in order to produce sufficient food for their large populations. The most common methods were hillside terracing and canal irrigation. The walls, dams, and canals required by these methods required more labor than basic rainfall agriculture, but, in return, these methods produced far higher yields on the land. These built features are often called "landesque capital" (Håkansson and Widgren 2014; Sen 1959); they represent investments in the landscape for long-term intensive agricultural production. Most farming in early societies was not under direct elite or state control. When kings or nobles wanted to increase their income, they just raised taxes (kings) or rents (noble landlords) on the peasants, who turned to intensification in order to produce the needed extra crops. Farming in command economies, on the other hand, was subject to greater management and supervision by state bureaucrats.

The second major feature of intensification is that it can serve as an avenue to prosperity for peasant households. Netting's (1993) model of smallholder intensification is crucial here. This is a social-economic pattern widespread in ancient and recent commercial economies. Its main features are the following:

1. Farms are small and located close to the residence.
2. Farmers have secure access to their plots, either through ownership or usufruct.
3. Labor is provided by household members.
4. Farmers have intimate knowledge of local soils and conditions.
5. Cultivation is intensive (high labor and high yields).
6. Technology is simple.
7. Land is improved with terraces or other forms of landesque capital. (Netting 1993)

When peasants engage in smallholder intensive agriculture, they have the potential to advance economically and achieve prosperity (depending on local environmental, economic, and political conditions, of course). My excavations at the Aztec sites of Cuexcomate and Capilco in Mexico furnish a good archaeological example of such prosperity among smallholders practicing intensive agriculture (Smith 2016a); see discussion in Chapter 7. Peasants are important for cities because their activities and conditions affected life in cities, and because they grew the food for urban residents. I now turn to the regional economies that linked rural and urban settings.

Regional Market Systems

Utilitarian craft items – ceramic vessels, household tools, and other items – circulated through markets. Peasants from the countryside obtained the goods they did not produce themselves at markets. They either exchanged food for such goods, or else they sold craft goods produced at home. Under conditions of population pressure and poverty in the countryside, a common strategy of peasant households through the ages has been to engage in part-time craft production to augment their income. This link between rural craft production and poverty has been identified by historians and ethnographers in many settings (e.g., Arnold 1985; Thirsk 1961), and it has been proposed for some archaeological cases as well (Smith and Heath-Smith 1994).

Regional exchange systems – based around a central urban marketplace – can be quite busy and complex. Figure 5.9 shows just a few of the movements of goods, raw materials, and people that characterized the regional economic system around a typical Oppida settlement. The Oppida were low-density, walled, urban sites in Iron-Age Europe; some of them were described by Julius Ceasar during his conquest of Gaul (Fernández-Götz 2018). The diagram shows three local systems – villages or small subregions – tied into the regional system around an Oppida. This kind of busy regional exchange system grew up around most premodern cities.

Research by anthropologist Carol Smith (1976b) shows that the nature of a regional exchange system plays a large role in shaping not only the regional economy but also the nature of social classes and inequality. Smith defines three types of premodern regional exchange system: (1) *Direct exchange* is her term for noncommercial exchanges, as in a command economy or a small-scale village system. (2) *Solar market systems* are small, self-contained systems in which nearly all exchanges are between the central town and the hinterland; there are few exchanges with other nearby markets. Social classes in these closed regional systems are called *estates*: strong elite-commoner differences, urban-based elites, and little class mobility. (3) *Interlocking central-place market systems* occur in highly commercialized economies with a high volume of exchange both within and between nearby market systems. Elites tend to reside in both urban and rural settings, and social mobility is high.

Carol Smith's scheme is important for understanding how regional exchange systems influence the nature of society and life in cities and their regions. It reinforces my claim that one cannot understand a city and

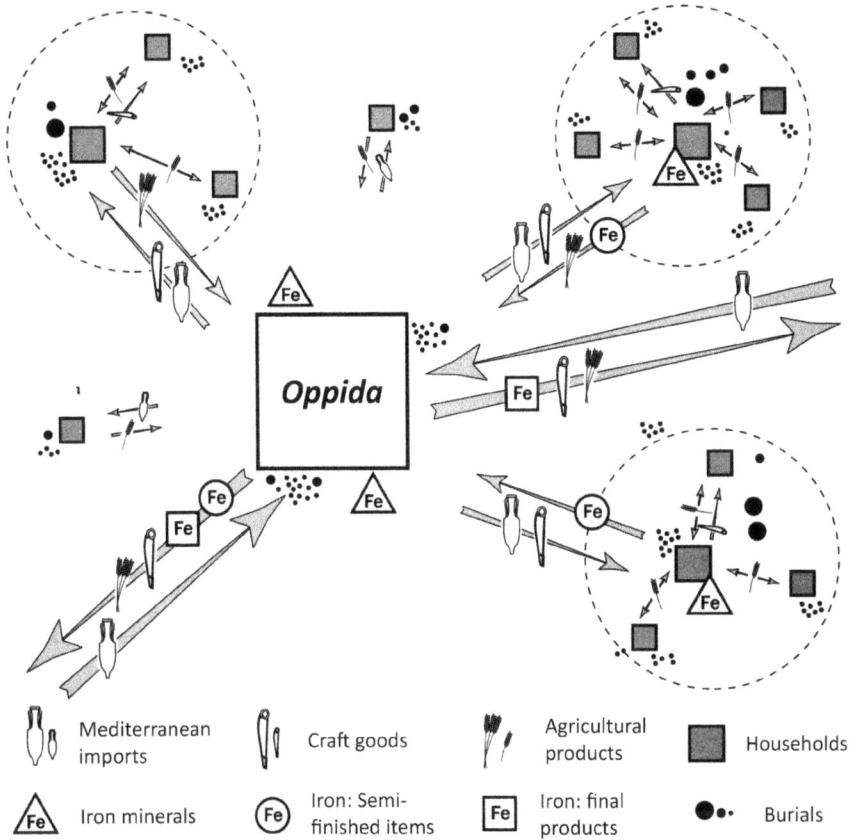

| ⚱ | Mediterranean imports | 🗡 | Craft goods | 🌾 | Agricultural products | ⬛ | Households |
| ▲Fe | Iron minerals | Ⓕe | Iron: Semi-finished items | Fe | Iron: final products | ●•· | Burials |

5.9. Regional exchange system based in an Oppida. Modified after Fichtl (2005:179).

its urban society without taking into account the regional economy. In all but the least commercialized systems (e.g., command economies), regional markets not only help get food to urbanites but structure the nature of society and economy in both the city and its associated peasant population.

LONG-DISTANCE COMMERCE AND ECONOMIC NETWORKS

The study of the long-distance exchange of goods is both a success story and a cautionary tale in the advancement of archaeological methods. In addition to the long-standing practice of identifying imported goods based on their style and form, archaeologists now have a wide variety of chemical methods that use trace elements (elements present in minute amounts) in pottery, stone, and other materials — as well as mineral and pigment identification — to identify the place of origin of imported goods. Unfortunately, the development of models and concepts of exchange has lagged behind the adoption of methods of source analysis (Smith 2004); most studies continue to report their results and then apply simplistic post-hoc arguments to account for them. Until this field advances conceptually, our understanding of the relationship between long-distance commerce and urbanism will remain at a low level.

Politics and Economics of Long-Distance Commerce

Goods can be moved to an urban (or other) settlement over long distances using several different mechanisms. The simplest has been called *down-the-line exchange* (Renfrew 1975). Goods move from one settlement to the next, carried "down the line" by a sequence of exchanges between individuals. Eventually, some items end up far from their point of origin. This process is usually found in small-scale village societies that lack professional merchants and other commercial institutions. Far more common in states and cities is the *movement of goods by professional agents*. Entrepreneurial merchants, who assume the risks of commerce and reap the profits, are the best-known type of such agent (Hirth 2016; Ogilvie 2011). In command economies, state functionaries are the agents of long-distance exchange.

It is useful to distinguish economic movements of goods from administrative or political movements. In Frederic Pryor's (1977) scheme, the latter are known as *transfers* (one-way transactions, such as taxes, where goods and services are given without a direct return), and the former are *exchanges* (balanced transactions where goods or services are exchanged for other goods or services of equal value). While transfers do have economic consequences for cities and urban life, they operate quite differently from exchanges. For example, foreign goods that move into a capital city by taxation may enrich only a small group (the royal family, or leading elites), or their benefits may be spread more widely among the urban population, depending on the nature of governance (Chapter 4). But goods arriving through commercial exchange are more likely to create wealth and economic benefits for a larger number of people who are not part of the government or ruling coalition (Jacobs 1984).[4]

---

[4] One of the negative consequences of the adoption of Karl Polanyi's substantivist ideas by archaeologists stems from his failure to distinguish exchanges from transfers. This led a generation of archaeologists to subsume political transfers (such as taxation and other redistributive institutions) under the label of economic processes, hindering our understanding of both government and the economy.

As archaeological methods for identifying long-distance exchange have improved, it has become clear that some ancient cities were far more invested in such exchange than others. Furthermore, high levels of trade do not necessarily signal a highly commercialized economy; the latter requires a series of economic institutions and practices that go far beyond the fact of exchange. This point is made by the next two case studies. The Viking trade center Ribe had a moderately commercialized economy but a very high level of exchange, while the Hellenistic city of Rhodes had both very high levels of trade and a strongly commercialized economy. Both case studies illustrate the value of the concept of network for the analysis of long-distant exchange (Brughmans and Poblome 2016; Raja and Sindbaek 2018; Sindbaek 2013).

Case Study 20 Ribe: Viking Emporium

The withdrawal of the Roman Empire from northern Europe brought a decline in urban economies (Ward-Perkins 2006). Roman provincial cities had combined strong political and economic urban functions, and the end of imperial rule was disastrous for cities and towns. Then, a new kind of generative settlement arose in the seventh century CE around the North and Baltic Seas: the *wic* or *emporium* (Hill and Cowie 2001; Pestell 2011). These were trading centers with few or no political urban functions. They grew rapidly through exchange with areas as far as Africa and Byzantium. Then, as more powerful states developed, the emporia declined. Ribe, on the west coast of Jutland in Denmark, has been the location of major excavations. Depending on one's definition of the Viking period (Croix 2015b), Ribe can be considered either a pre-Viking or an early Viking trade center.

Ribe's Trade and Generative Urbanism. In the words of Stéphane Lebecq (2012:16), the earliest emporia "were created out of nothing and in the middle of nowhere. The only requirement was a safe landing site for ships." Most of these sites had a harbor, but they lacked defensive walls prior to the mid-ninth century. They have yielded many imported goods and considerable evidence of craft production.

Ribe was excavated several times from the 1970s through the 1990s. A new multiyear project using high-definition methods was initiated in 2017 (Sindbaek 2016, 2018). Although most of the emporium site is covered by the medieval settlement of Ribe, archaeologists have found sufficient open area in the town for horizontal clearing. In the emporium, individual wood houses were set on long rectangular lots perpendicular to a street. This was to become the most common plan in medieval European towns. Although archaeologists initially suggested that the houses were temporary, seasonal structures, perhaps even tent-like, careful analysis of the excavated deposits showed that these were permanent houses (Croix 2015a), a finding confirmed in the more recent excavations.

Ribe was founded in the eighth century CE and grew to become a major trading center during the ninth century. The use of high-definition chronological methods allows the chronology of crafts and imports to be reconstructed almost year by year during the eighth and ninth centuries (Philippsen et al. 2022). Figure 5.10 shows an artist's reconstruction of Ribe at this time. This was a small and relatively dispersed settlement lacking any public architecture that would signal political or religious urban functions. The economic urban functions, on the other hand, are impressive. Ribe was a major hub for maritime trade networks. Imported goods included tesserae from Italy; glass beads from the Islamic Middle East; beads, quern stones, and pottery from Germany; and stone, pots, and iron from Norway (Feveile 2012). Finds include Roman coins and gems that had evidently been in circulation for several centuries. Figure 5.11 shows some of these imports.

Case Study 20 (cont.)

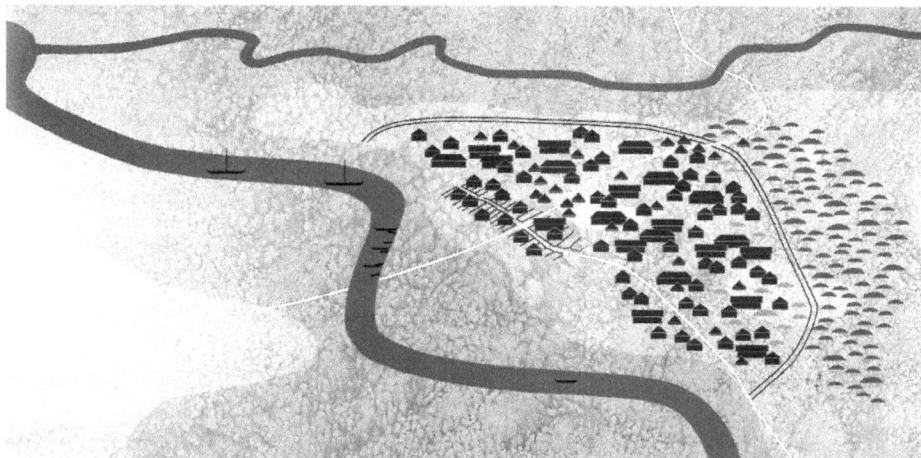

5.10. Ribe, reconstruction of the town, circa 825 CE. From Claus Feveile, *Viking Ribe: Trade, Power and Faith*, 2013. Illustrator: Flemming Bau. Reproduced with permission.

5.11. Local and imported craft items from excavations at Ribe. The brooch and clay mold at the left and some of the glass beads were produced in Ribe. The items on the right were imported from the Carolingian and Frankish regions. The beads are a mixture of Mediterranean imports and local products. These items are sitting on a quern made of basalt from the Rhine area. Photo courtesy of Claus Feveile; reproduced with permission.

Case Study 20 (cont.)

Trade was not the only economic activity prominent in Ribe. Crafters produced objects of glass, amber, and high-quality iron, as well as bronze and silver (Figure 5.11). Small silver coins known as *sceattas* – often no larger than one centimeter in diameter – were used throughout the emporia trading network, and coins manufactured in Ribe have been excavated at other emporia sites. Craft production areas were located on house lots, often within the house. In Peacock's typology (see Table 5.4), these would correspond to Individual workshops.

Comparative Insights. The merchants and crafters of Ribe engaged in considerable commercial activity, creating a clear record of imports and manufactured goods. This high level of commercial activity can be attributed to two main conditions. First, Ribe's location on the North Sea was ideal for maritime trading. Second, the lack of political control enabled commerce to thrive. Mats Mogren (2013:79) has suggested, "We must understand settlements like Ribe, Reric, Ahus, and others, as founded by self-organizing groups of traders and craftsmen." In the language of this book, Ribe and the other emporia were founded, and then thrived, through generative processes with a low level of political control. Another insight from Ribe is that the volume of trade is independent of the level of commercialization. In spite of an impressive suite of imports and craft goods, Ribe's commercialization score of 7 is low for an Old World city; this is a consequence of the specialized trading function of this settlement. I now turn to a Hellenistic Mediterranean city – Rhodes – whose volume of trade and commercialization were both on a much greater scale than Ribe.

Case Study 21 Rhodes: Colossus of Mediterranean Trade

Although perhaps best known for a statue (the Colossus of Rhodes, one of the seven wonders of the ancient world), for my purposes this Hellenistic city-state's primary importance lies in the sophistication and volume of its maritime exchange system. After the decline of Athens in the fourth century BCE, Rhodes took its place as the top maritime power in the eastern Mediterranean. The Rhodian navy helped its merchants establish a lucrative system of trade. These merchants were responsible for a series of innovations in commercial practices, making Rhodes the most highly commercialized urban economy prior to Late Republican Rome.

Commercial Innovations and Five Harbors. The island of Rhodes, 1,400 square kilometers in area, was home to several city-states. Rhodes, with no fewer than five harbors, was the largest city and most powerful of these polities. Conditions on the island were ideal for grape cultivation, and Rhodian wine was traded widely around the Mediterranean (Lund 1999; Rauh 1999). Merchants set up a profitable program of exchange with Alexandria in Egypt, trading wine for grain. In the words of ancient Greek historian Diodorus Siculus, the people of Rhodes "derived the majority of their revenues from the merchants sailing to Egypt and . . . in general their city was sustained by that kingdom" (quoted in Gabrielsen 2013:67).

The Rhodian wine trade can be traced rather precisely because one handle of each amphora used to carry the wine was stamped with the seal of an official in Rhodes. Many thousands of these amphora seals have been recovered at Hellenistic sites around the Mediterranean. Over 100,000 are known from Alexandria alone (Figure 5.12); see Lund (1999, 2011). This is an unprecedented level of imported goods for the ancient world.

Contemporary writers were impressed with the Rhodian navy. Quoting from Diodorus Siculus again, "Rhodes had reached such a peak of power that it took upon its own, on behalf of the Greeks, the war against the pirates and cleared the sea of that scourge" (Gabrielsen 2013:67). To service both the navy and merchant shipping, maritime infrastructure grew up around the harbors of Rhodes (Figure 5.13). By suppressing piracy, the Rhodian navy contributed to the success of the city's maritime trade. In the

Case Study 21 (cont.)

5.12. Amphorae from Rhodes excavated from Alexandria. These are being studied by a team from Ege University, Izmir, directed by Gonca Cankardeş-Şenol. Photograph by André Pelle, Archives CEAlex; reproduced with permission.

language of economics, military activity lowered the transaction costs of maritime trade (Gabrielsen 2013).

Another reason for the commercial success of Rhodes is found in a number of commercial innovations. Previously, long-distance trade in the Mediterranean had been handled by individual merchants, traveling from city to city with their merchandise. The Rhodian merchants began to specialize in their tasks, with some handling the assembly of wine on Rhodes, others journeying with the cargo on ships, and still others stationed in Alexandria. They did this by forming partnerships and promoting wholesale trade (Gabrielsen 2005, 2011, 2013). It is no surprise that Rhodes had the most highly commercialized economy of any city prior to Republican Rome (Table 5.3).

Comparative Insights. Rhodes was one of the most prosperous Hellenistic cities in the Mediterranean (Berthold 1984:38–58). Compared to the smaller and later emporium of Ribe, Rhodes enjoyed several economic advantages. First, the Mediterranean sea trade could reach a far greater population than trade in the North Sea. Second, the Mediterranean cities had histories of state-level governments and commercial economies going back centuries, and these provided a platform for commercial and technological innovation (Woolf 2020). Finally, the Rhodian state and navy worked together with merchants to promote commerce. Unlike cities under contemporaneous Mediterranean monarchies, such as the

Case Study 21 (cont.)

5.13. Shipshed for repair of ships in Rhodes. This is a military installation, but similar facilities were used for commercial vessels. Blackman et al. (1996:387, fig. 16).

Ptolemies of Egypt or the Seleucids of the Near East, political urban functions in Rhodes did not dominate economic urban functions.

ECONOMIC ACTIVITIES AND URBAN FUNCTIONS

I began this chapter by showing that many scholarly approaches to ancient economies are biased and in error. Karl Polanyi (and the substantivists in economic anthropology and the primitivists in classics) ruled out ancient commercial exchange by definition, a wildly inaccurate view. But his opponents – the formalists and modernists – went to the other extreme and assumed that the institutions and practices of the modern capitalist economy could be found in all types of ancient and nonwestern society, another serious error. Perhaps because of the unproductive debate that ensued from these absurd positions, conceptual advances in understanding ancient economies have been slow. No one wanted to continue fighting old, unproductive scholarly battles, yet few archaeologists were willing to venture out into new conceptual territory. As a result, scholarly under-standing of the economic role of premodern cities – and the effect of economic patterns on urban life – have been held back.

I argue that the level of commercialization – the strength and abun-dance of commercial institutions and practices – played a major role in shaping urban life in the past. Premodern cities – like most cities through history – were embedded in their regional context. Cities affected life in the hinterlands, and regional economic systems affected urban food supply and prosperity. The information available about the case studies in this book (Table 5.4) suggests that cities and economic systems in the Old World were generally more highly commercialized than those in the New World. Although the unrepresentative nature of my sample makes this interpretation tentative, the most highly-commercialized New World economy – that of the Aztec imperial capital Tenochtitlan – would score only a level of 8 on the scale (Nichols et al. 2017).

Regardless of the variation and importance of the level of commercialization in ancient urban economies, fundamental demographic processes operated in a similar way in all ancient (and modern) settlements. As I show in Chapter 3, the number of people in a settlement had regular effects not only on population density (within a given urban system large settlements are denser than small settlements) but also on economic productivity. The scaling relationships that provide supporting evidence have been observed in the New World and the Old World, in commercial and command economies, and even in non-state village systems of settlement (see Chapter 3). It is now time to focus directly on the top-down (Chapter 6) and bottom-up (Chapter 7) forces that constitute urban life proper.

SIX

TOP-DOWN INSTITUTIONS AND THE SCALE OF URBAN LIFE

WHEN I EXCAVATED AN AZTEC URBAN SETTLEMENT (YAUTEPEC, a city-state capital; Case Study 22) after previously excavating a town and a village not far away (Cuexcomate and Capilco), I was surprised to find that household activities and conditions were almost identical at the three sites. Families at all three sites lived in small houses built of adobe brick, with thatched roofs and stone or dirt floors. They carried out the same types of domestic activities: food preparation and serving, domestic rituals, and small-scale cotton textile production. All households had ready access to imported goods, including cutting tools of imported obsidian and imported decorated ceramic serving vessels from a variety of locations around central Mexico (Smith 2016a). The artifacts of domestic life showed few differences between rural and urban contexts. Yet there was no doubt that Yautepec was far more urban than the other sites: it was larger, it had urban functions, and a higher level of social complexity (Table 1.1).

I am no longer surprised by these results. In some settings, urban life can be quite similar to rural life, while in others it can be very different. This situation is clarified by sociologist Alan Latham, who suggests we should view urban life as "generative of ways of living with others – rather than seeing it as a distinctive way of being, in and of itself" (Latham 2009:892). That is, larger numbers of people in a settlement affect the conditions of living and working. The distinction between urban and nonurban life is a matter of degree, not kind. Latham's perspective goes against much scholarly writing on cities and urbanism. For decades, ethnocentric social scientists, generalizing from contemporary western cities, tried to show how urban life differs radically from life in the countryside (e.g., Redfield 1941; Wirth 1938). This perspective contributed to my initial surprise at my excavation results. Lathan's perspective, however, dovetails nicely with Anthony Leeds's (1980) views that rural and urban are not opposed concepts, but rather functionally-distinguished settings within a larger urban society (see Chapter 1). As places with more people and more economic and/or political institutions and activities, cities show more effects of population size and density – stronger forces of energized crowding – than do smaller settlements within the same urban system. This perspective also fits well with my attempt in this book both to avoid the reification of the concept of "urban," and to extend the scope of urban-like processes to non-urban settlements for some kinds of analysis (Chapters 3, 4).

Any consideration of urban life needs to examine activities, conditions, and institutions at a variety of social-spatial scales. Figure 6.1 outlines my approach to urban life. All activities and processes within settlements are built on a foundation of face-to-face social interaction. These interactions bring about generative processes, which are often called bottom-up forces. I explore some of the large-scale consequences of such generative processes in my discussion of settlement scaling in Chapter 3. Human social interactions take place at – and have consequences for – different social and spatial scales. I include four such levels in Figure 7.1: the household, neighborhood, urban services, and class structure. Sitting analytically above all of these levels are urban institutions. These institutions (e.g., the state; temple organizations; guilds) set many of the parameters or structures within which urban life is carried out. Their actions

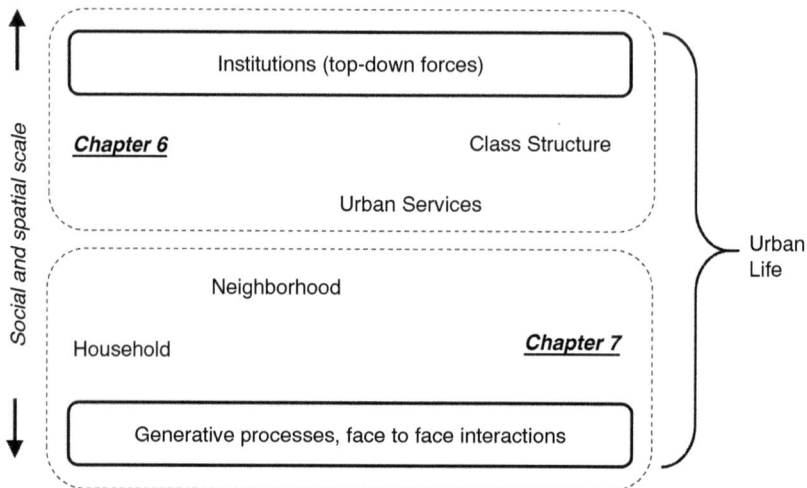

6.1. Conceptual diagram for the major institutional and generative forces shaping urban life. Graphic by Michael E. Smith.

can be labeled as top-down in nature. My distinction between institutions and generative processes is analogous to the structure/agency dichotomy as described by Anthony Giddens (1984) and other social theorists. While such concepts – structure and agency, institutions and generative processes, top-down and bottom-up forces – help scholars make sense of complex societal settings like cities, they are not explanatory concepts themselves. We need middle-range theory (Chapter 1) to supply more concrete causal and explanatory accounts of urban life. I explore the distinction between top-down and bottom-up forces in more detail in Chapter 7.

Urban life consists of all of the elements shown in Figure 6.1 and more. I divide my discussion between two chapters. The present chapter starts with the top portion of this diagram: top-down urban institutions. I focus on a series of activities, practices, and features that operate at the level of the entire settlement, including systems of social inequality and the role of government in structuring urban life. Chapter 7 continues my discussion of urban life at the scales of the household and the neighborhood. On this level, generative processes are paramount in structuring life and society.

Latham's (2009) article poses two of the fundamental questions concerning urban life. First, why do people aggregate into cities and settlements? His answer fits well with research in settlement scaling theory, as described in Chapter 3: "Through specialization, the unexpected mixtures, the concentration of resources, and the challenges of living in a dense, heterogeneous environment, urban life creates a productive dynamic that transcends the sum of its parts" (Latham 2009:893).

This "productive dynamic" is what I am calling energized crowding. Latham's second question is, how do cities manage to generate order despite their size and heterogeneity? Part of the answer lies in the political and economic systems and institutions reviewed in Chapters 4 and 5. But the bulk of the answer to this question lies in the realm of urban life. Specifically, urban order is generated and maintained by two sorts of forces: top-down institutions (the topic of the present chapter) and generative processes (Chapter 7).

URBAN INSTITUTIONS

My perspective on institutions combines two broad approaches that are sometimes seen as opposed. The sociological approach sees institutions as durable social structures. They consist of sets of social practices and material resources that serve either a general societal need or else the interests of specific groups (Scott 2001; Turner 2003). The economics approach, on the other hand, sees institutions as rules. In the words of economist Douglass North, "Institutions are the rules of the game in a society, or, more formally, are the humanly devised constraints that shape human interaction" (North 1990:3).

These two approaches to institutions are described by sociologist Toby Huff as follows: "Whereas economists tend to look at the small structures of rule formation as institutions, sociologists and other social scientists view institutions as large structures that solve major societal problems, such as the family, the legal system, the polity, the military, or perhaps the stock market" (Huff 2013:56).

The institutions-as-rules perspective is more dynamic and used more widely in the social sciences than the sociological viewpoint of institutions as social structures. Institutional scholar Elinor Ostrom elaborates on some of the advantages of the economics view as follows:

> A different field opens when institutions are defined as "the sets of working rules that are used to determine who is eligible to make decisions in some arena, what actions are allowed or constrained, what aggregation rules will be used, what procedures must be followed, what information must or must not be provided, and what payoffs will be assigned to individuals dependent on their actions." (Ostrom 1990:51)

For archaeologists, it is difficult or even impossible to get at such working rules. The most common approach to institutions has been to focus on the structures, resources, and individuals – rather than on the rules – for specific types of institutions, such as forms of government and types of states (Chapter 4), or market systems and merchant organizations (Chapter 5). A group of archaeologists has recently advocated for the development of an institutional approach within archaeology (Bondarenko et al. 2020; Holland-Lulewicz et al. 2020). Unfortunately, they ignore the two main approaches to institutions, and instead define institution in terms used by social scientists for *organization*, a distinct concept. For these archaeologists, institutions are "organizations of people that carry out objectives using regularized practices and norms, labor, and resources" (Holland-Lulewicz et al. 2020:1). In sociology organizations are "stable associations of persons engaged in concerted activities directed at the attainment of specific objectives. It is thought to be a decisive characteristic of such organizations that they are deliberately instituted relative to these objectives" (Bittner 1965:239); see also Greif (2006:31) or Stinchcombe (1965). The concept of organization lacks the major attributes of institutions. Institutions are more enduring, typically with broader scope, than organizations.

The approach to institutions I find most useful for ancient cities is a deliberate synthesis of the sociological and economic approaches. The analyst who comes closest to my perspective is economist Geoffrey Hodgson (2006, 2007), who defines institutions as rules ("systems of established and embedded social rules that structure social interaction") but draws from the sociological tradition to situate institutions within social structures. In addition to institutions, social structures include groups, organizations, laws, demographic structures, and sets of social relations that are stable or durable through time (Stinchcombe 1965). Institutions structure behavior through a process philosophers of science call "reconstitutive downward causation" (Fleetwood 2008:250; Hodgson 2006:7). In this line of analysis, "institutions are simultaneously both objective structures 'out there' and subjective springs of human agency 'in the human head'" (Hodgson 2006:8). They arise not through instantaneous rational calculation or logic, but rather through negotiations and tensions between social groups (Ogilvie 2007; Ogilvie and Carus 2014).

David Soskice et al. (1992) also combine the economic and sociological approaches to institutions in a way that is congenial for archaeology. These authors identify four key features of institutions:

1. Institutions (like all of society) are marked by a division of labor.
2. Institutions are longer lived than their members. They thus contain persons of different generations.
3. Institutions are hierarchical. They contain, then, both senior and junior members, with juniors desiring to attain senior rank.
4. Institutions are rule governed.

The second feature is crucial for archaeology: institutions persist for long periods of time, and this not only gives them greater causal importance than more ephemeral groups, organizations, or structures, but it also leads to the creation of buildings, artifacts, and other material remains that increase the ability of archaeologists to study institutions. A related feature of many institutions that aids in their archaeological – and historical – analysis is their association with particular spaces. These can include dedicated buildings (e.g., guild halls, workshops, and palaces) or regularly-used spaces (e.g., periodic markets held in plazas).

In Chapters 4 and 5 I discuss a number of urban institutions in the realms of politics and the economy. In a polity, the government is an institution, and governments are built from a number of constituent institutions. Kingship is an institution, as are systems of corvée labor, taxation, and the military. Marketplaces, shops, workshops, guilds, and regional marketing systems are all institutions, as is money.[1] All of these institutions are built on a foundation of face-to-face social interactions, operating at one or more spatial scales, at varying temporal rhythms, to create more durable physical and social remains (Figure 6.1). Once in existence, they tend to influence urban life as unitary, high-level forces.

---

[1] Recall my discussion in Chapter 1 of John Searle's (1995) use of money as an example to distinguish brute facts from institutional facts.

In terms of impact on urban life, three patterns of institutional variation discussed in Chapters 4 and 5 stand out as particularly important. First, the distinction between command economies and market economies makes a big difference. These economic systems structured access to goods as well as opportunities for urbanites to become involved in generative economic activities like independently organized craft production and commerce. Second, the continuum of autocratic versus collective regimes established many of the parameters of urban life. Collective regimes had a much heavier institutional load compared to autocratic regimes. Because autocrats provided few public goods, people were forced into grassroots activity in order to obtain water or protect their neighborhoods (Abu-Lughod 1987); see Chapter 7. Finally, the type of polity influenced the nature of capitals and urban life. The smaller size and typically more collective rule of city-states, when coupled with a highly commercialized economy, led to greater generative economic activity, whereas the converse conditions in imperial capitals led to the flourishing of elite-oriented material culture, often produced by attached specialists. In these and other cases, the deep variability of institutions and their effects in premodern societies created and promoted variation in the forms, functions, and activities of early cities.

In this chapter, I discuss urban institutions that have not been covered in previous chapters. These fall into two categories: (1) inequality and social class and (2) aspects of city governance that most directly affect urban life. My focus is on central, top-down institutions: those created or promoted by political authorities and/or elites to promote their own interests. In the words of institutional economists Daron Acemoglu and James Robinson (2012), these are extractive political and social institutions (see the later discussion in this chapter). Such top-down institutions are often associated with the ruling regime – that is, they may be promoted by political authorities, and they may function as part of the structure of governance. But other kinds of institutions – inclusive institutions to Acemoglu and Robinson (2012) – can be created by generative processes, which can solidify over time into structural features that play a big role in shaping urban life in the past and the present.

SOCIAL CLASS AND WEALTH INEQUALITY

Prior to the Industrial Revolution, social inequality was pervasive and pronounced in most state-level societies, and it had a strong influence on the nature of life and society in premodern cities. I review social inequality under three headings: social class, the distribution of wealth, and quality of life; I defer the latter topic until Chapter 7.

Thinking about Social Class in Premodern Cities

The population of most premodern state societies was divided into two social classes: a small and wealthy elite class, whose members controlled most of the resources in society (including government), and a mass of commoners who were subservient to the elite in various ways, and to varying degrees (Bottomore 1965:18; Lenski 1966; Trigger 2003:145). Social class was an institution that structured many aspects of life in early cities. Elites made up only some 2 or 3 percent of the population in most early states (Bodley 2003:91–101; Lenski 1966:219), but their influence on urban life was enormous. The institutions of social class are crucial for understanding life in premodern cities.

I take a sociological approach to the issue of class, grounded in works by Lenski (1966), Tilly (1998), and Trigger (2003). I follow Lenski in viewing *class* as "an aggregation of persons in a society to stand in a similar position with respect to some form of power, privilege, or prestige" (Lenski 1966:74–75). When a class is legally defined, with rights and duties established by law, it is called an *estate* (Smith 1976b). Elite classes in many societies are estates, but commoner classes rarely are. Furthermore, when an elite class is both legally defined and hereditary, it is called a *nobility* (Bloch 1961:238). An *aristocracy* is an elite class in a society without these restrictions (Brown 1988).

Nearly all premodern societies had two social classes – elite and commoner (Sjoberg 1960:109–110; Trigger 2003:145; Williamson 2010). Although some authors have claimed that early cities had a "middle class" of economic specialists intermediate between elite and commoners (Hicks 1999; M. L. Smith 2018; 2019:chapters 8, 9), they have been unable to furnish evidence that supports their claim.[2] Those who propose the unlikely "middle class" view fail to appreciate that each class – elite and commoner – typically had significant internal variation in wealth, power, and status. There were high- and low-ranking lords, and commoners were often divided into slaves, landless laborers, or serfs (Figure 6.2) and "free" commoners. Nevertheless, the division between the two classes was usually deep and pervasive.

In ancient societies with a significant number of slaves – such as the Roman Empire – slaves formed a separate social class, below the other commoners (Bang 2009; Scheidel 2008). Occupations for Roman slaves included both household tasks (servants, secretaries) and hard labor by large gangs of slaves (in mining and agriculture). In other premodern systems, the number of slaves

---

[2] Before I accept the presence of a "middle class" in premodern cities, I would want to see a trimodal distribution of house size or some other wealth measure, or at least an argument that is based on quantitative evidence of some sort, rather than on first principles and speculation. See my views on the strength of arguments in Smith (2015). Mayer (2014) argues for the existence of a Roman middle class, based on textual evidence, but his claim is rejected by nearly all of the reviewers of the book.

6.2. Lord giving alms to a beggar, woodcut from 1569, London. Public domain. Wikipedia Commons (https://commons.wikimedia.org/wiki/File:Woodcut_Giving_Alms_to_a_Beggar .jpg).

was lower than in the Roman Empire, and their economic contributions were primarily at the household level. In Aztec society, for example, slaves were domestic servants, helping with farming or with the production of textiles (Smith and Hicks 2017). In this case, one can consider slaves as the bottom rung of the commoner class, rather than as a separate class of their own.

Social inequality and class structure were regarded as the normal state of affairs in most premodern societies. In Trigger's words, "Inequality was regarded as a normal condition and injustice as a personal misfortune or even as an individual's just deserts rather than as a social evil ... . The general pervasiveness of inequality ensured that its legitimacy went unquestioned" (Trigger 2003:142).

A key question about early class systems is the possibility of social mobility into or out of the elite class. Such mobility is much more common for aristocracies than for estates or nobilities. When the elite is a form of closed class, as with nobilities, but merchants or other commoners can advance their position by accumulating wealth, conflict is inevitable. For some theoreticians of class (including Karl Marx), a true social class must have "class consciousness" – that is, the members must be aware of their social position and act together to preserve or advance their conditions (Collins 1988:152).

In premodern societies, elites typically did have class consciousness – particularly estates and nobilities – but commoners as a group rarely recognized or acted as a class-based interest or group (in part because elites worked hard to prevent commoner class consciousness or action). Slaves likely recognized other slaves as belonging to a common group, but, except for occasional slave rebellions, they rarely acted in concert with slaves from widespread areas.

The practices of wealth inequality – and their effects – were interwoven throughout the social world of premodern cities, affecting urban life in countless ways. This pervasiveness is shown by Charles Tilly's (1998, 2001) model of durable inequality. Durable inequality consists of unequal social patterns – such as class divisions or differential ranking of groups of persons – that persist over long periods. Tilly identifies four causal mechanisms that account for the persistence of inequality. A causal mechanism is a social process, activity, or event that works to bring about or maintain a pattern or condition within society. Causal mechanisms are the "nuts and bolts" of how society works (Bunge 2004; Elster 1989).

Exploitation is Tilly's first and most powerful mechanism of durable inequality (these are discussed here in their order of importance). He defines this carefully; exploitation exists when a group of dominant individuals control a resource, enlist others in producing value from that resource, but exclude those others from benefitting from their effort. Early elites typically controlled two crucial resources: agricultural land and the institutions of government. By working the land and paying their taxes in goods and (corvée) labor, commoners were supporting the elite and thus being exploited. The second mechanism, *opportunity hoarding*, is defined as "confining the use of a value-producing resource to members of an ingroup" (Tilly 2001:366). Craft and merchant guilds are prime examples; they limit participation in key economic activities to a small group, in order to benefit that group (Ogilvie 2011).

Emulation, for Tilly, is the process by which structures and practices that reinforce inequality are transferred or imported from one social context to another. For example, the Aztec priesthood adapted hierarchical principles of class inequality to their own system of governance, in order to promote and maintain inequalities in the priesthood (Smith 2021a). Tilly's fourth and least powerful mechanism, *adaptation*, consists of the ways that people develop day-to-day routines that ease the process of living in an unequal world. In his words, "In coping with unequal situations, moreover, victims themselves improvise routines that involve them in the reproduction of inequality, even slaves acquire interests in the predictability of their masters' behavior, in conformity that will increase their chances of emancipation, and in the segregation that affords them opportunities for mutual aid" (Tilly 1998:98).

If one were to posit adaptation as the primary cause of inequality, this would amount to blaming the powerless for their condition. But in Tilly's analytical scheme, adaptation is the least influential causal mechanism, operating to lock in systems of inequality created by exploitation. This approach holds promise for understanding ancient systems of inequality; for a case study, see Smith (2021a).

The institutions of inequality – including the causal mechanisms that create and maintain them – are not abstract social forces, relevant only to the debates of scholars. Every time a peasant tilled his field, or an urbanite lined up for his or her week of corvée labor, or a household member purchased something from a guild-based crafter, they were participating and reinforcing the very structure of those institutions. These are very real forces that acted in all areas of the city, at all levels of the social hierarchy.

The archaeological study of social class and wealth differences has expanded greatly in the past decade. New methods are being developed, and archaeologists are studying, measuring, and counting a variety of kinds of material remains to reconstruct past systems of inequality. Class differences can be analyzed using the size and elaboration of houses (big, fancy palaces compared to small, simple houses), differences in mortuary treatment (elaborately constructed tombs, even pyramids, versus simple graves), variation in diet and health quality as measured from the human skeleton, and artistic production (e.g., portraits, sculptures, and literary texts for the elite). While the difference between Versailles and a Paris slum hovel in the eighteenth century was extreme and obvious, cities without strong class differences might not show such stark differences. In fact, we get a better idea of class structure by comparing commoner houses or graves with those of nonroyal elites. Kings and emperors almost always have over-the-top luxurious residences, whether or not elites and commoners are greatly differentiated.

To illustrate these points, I assemble data on the relative sizes of houses in five cities in central Mexico, plus pre-European Bali (Table 6.1); I defer for now the justification for using house size as a measure of wealth. For each city, the average commoner house size is set to 1, and the size of the larger houses are expressed as multiples of the commoner size. For example, in the Aztec imperial capital Tenochtitlan, noble houses are – on average – ninety-two times as large as commoner houses, whereas at Teotihuacan, noble houses are only four times as large as commoner houses. Not surprisingly, written documents show strong class differences in Aztec society (Tenochtitlan and Yautepec), whereas at Teotihuacan many archaeologists see a more egalitarian society with prosperous commoners (Case Study 26). Indeed, the noble house I excavated at Yautepec is smaller than the average commoner house at Teotihuacan! I explore this seeming contradiction later; these two cities are case studies. Elites are present in nearly all premodern cities. In fact, this is one of the universals of cities through the ages: if a society has class divisions and an elite class, then some or all members of the elite class will reside in an urban settlement.

TABLE 6.1 *Magnitude of wealth differences (house size) between social classes*

Settlement	Type	Source	Commoner house (avg. size)	Commoner house	Noble house	Palace of local king	Palace of emperor
Tenochtitlan	Imperial capital	1	26	1	92		980
Cuexcomate	Small town	2	23	1	34		
Yautepec	Local capital	3	28	1	14	197	
Xochicalco	Local capital	4	110	1	9	54	
Teotihuacan	Imperial capital	5	417	1	4		73
Bali	(Not given)	6	(Not given)	1	5	60	560

Note: Commoner house size is in square meters. The remaining figures are ratios of the mean values for each social category, with commoner means set to 1 (i.e., noble houses in Yautepec are fourteen times larger than commoner houses).
Source: (1) Unpublished data from Edward Calnek; (2) Smith (1992); (3) Olson and Smith (2016); (4) Hirth (2000:137); (5) Smith et al. (2019); (6) Bodley (2003:56).

Case Study 22 Yautepec: Wealth and Class in an Aztec City

Yautepec was an Aztec city-state capital (1100–1519 CE) in a provincial area of the Aztec Empire. In the 1990s, I directed a fieldwork project at Yautepec to excavate houses and reconstruct patterns of social class (Smith 2016a; M.E. Smith 2019b; Smith et al. 1999). With a population of approximately 13,300 and a density of 64 persons per hectare, this was a midsized Aztec city. Although we only managed to locate and excavate the architectural remains of seven houses, we did excavate an additional eight residential midden deposits. A very large royal palace at the site was partially excavated by another project (see Smith 2008).

Housing and Social Class. I was surprised when the commoner houses and domestic artifacts at Yautepec turned out to be almost identical to those at the rural Aztec sites I had excavated previously. This was not the only similarity among the sites, though; the class composition of the town of Cuexcomate matched the lower part of the class structure at Yautepec. Cuexcomate had some 130 commoner households and one noble household in its final stage. The commoner houses were smaller at this site than at Yautepec, and the one noble's residence was larger than the noble house I excavated at Yautepec (Table 6.1).

Some premodern cities show a continuum in the size of houses, making it difficult to draw clear class distinctions from house size alone. Yautepec (Figure 6.3) and Cuexcomate, however, both show clear and deep differences between the mass of small houses and a few larger and fancier elite structures (Table 6.1). My interpretation of these patterns as marking social classes is based on more than house size. The small houses were built at the level of the ground, whereas the large houses were elevated on platforms. The large houses also made much greater use of expensive and elaborate architectural materials, including cut stones and lime plaster (concrete) floors and walls. On this basis, I interpreted the two kinds of houses as marking different social classes.

The next step was to see whether the class differences were also reflected in the artifacts associated with the houses. At these sites, people threw their trash out back, behind the house (even the nobles did this), so it was easy to compare the artifacts from the excavated houses. We focused on the kinds of domestic

Case Study 22 (cont.)

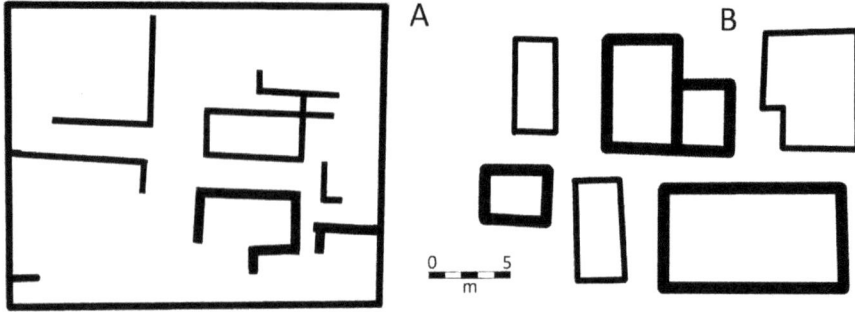

6.3. Houses excavated by the author at the Aztec city of Yautepec. (A) Noble residence; (B) Commoners' houses. Graphic by Michael E. Smith.

objects most likely to reflect wealth differences (Smith 1987). My student Jan Olson tested and statistically confirmed the hypothesis that artifact types differed between social classes (Olson 2001; Olson and Smith 2016). The noble-commoner differences are not dramatic. Commoners, in fact, had access to all of the types of exotic and valuable goods we excavated, from bronze tools to jade beads to fancy painted ceramics, but the noble middens had *more* of these things.

Some historical documents from immediately after the Spanish conquest support my archaeological interpretation of social classes at Yautepec. A census from the town of Molotla, located somewhere within the political territory of Yautepec, describes the household of a midlevel noble named Molotecatl. Molotecatl owned 600 units of farmland immediately after the Spanish conquest; he farmed 372 units himself (with servants and helpers), and rented out the remainder to commoner households. The ratio of his holding to the average holding of the commoners is 16:1, quite close to the noble-commoner house size ratio for Yautepec (Table 6.1).

Comparative Insights. The Yautepec case shows that it is possible to identify and analyze class structure based on the size and other features of residential architecture. Furthermore, it shows that class structure is also expressed in the quantities of key types of domestic artifacts. While the argument can be made that the commoners of Yautepec were relatively prosperous and successful economically (Smith 2016a), their prosperity paled in relation to that of the people of Teotihuacan (Case Study 26), some one thousand years earlier.

Wealth Variation

An alternative approach to wealth inequality is to examine the distribution of wealth in ancient cities and societies, without worrying about class. In this chapter, I have already used the size of a house as a measure of the wealth of its inhabitants. Some archaeologists like to point out that the size of a house is dependent on many variables in addition to wealth: family size, domestic cycle, or cultural norms that favor showing off one's house versus norms that promote the concealment of wealth and status (Cutting 2006; Hayden and Cannon 1984). Considered quantitatively and comparatively, however, there is a large body of ethnographic and historical evidence that – on average – the size of a house is strongly predicted by household wealth, within a given premodern society (see reviews in Kohler et al. 2017; Olson and Smith 2016). This allows archaeologists to use house size as a proxy for wealth.

For the study of inequality in premodern cities, the wealth distribution approach has advantages and drawbacks compared to social class analysis. The big advantage is that we can draw on methods developed by economists and demographers that allow wealth distributions to be summarized by a single value and compared across contexts. The most common such measure is the Gini index, which ranges between the values of 0, complete equality, where every household has the same wealth, and 1, complete concentration, where a single household controls *all* of the wealth (Milanovic 2011; Milanovic et al. 2011). Use of the Gini index allows direct comparisons among premodern cities, as well as between premodern, historical, and contemporary cities and contexts. Archaeologists are now working out the methodological details of this kind of analysis, dealing with questions such as: Is house size best measured as floor area, or as the volume of construction? How do measurements of inequality based on house size relate to measurements based on burial goods? Or, can ancient house size data be compared directly to modern financial wealth (or income) data? (Kohler and Smith 2018; Kohler et al. 2017).

Table 6.2 presents Gini scores for some of the case studies in this book, with a few other settlements added for comparison. The wealth proxy here is the size (area) of houses. A major lesson of these data is that the level of wealth inequality varies considerably, within and between settlements. The level of inequality is not predicted by the population of a settlement. Nevertheless, when relationships like this are examined within a specific urban tradition, clear patterns emerge. For example, within central Mexico, there is a strong relationship between settlement types and settlement population (Kohler et al. 2018); see Table 6.1. Also, for Mesoamerica as a whole, settlements in societies with more collective governments have lower inequality than settlements in societies with autocratic governments (Kohler et al. 2018).

The ability to make comparisons – such as those in Table 6.2 or between ancient and modern conditions – is the main advantage of using a measure like the Gini index to examine the distribution of wealth. But this advantage comes with a cost: the simplification involved in calculating a single index ignores many features that are fundamental to understanding inequality and its social context. This is where class analysis has a big advantage: it incorporates a much wider range of information, and thus provides a clearer view of the extent and significance of ancient inequality. These two approaches are complementary, and together they provide a richer and more complete picture of ancient social inequality. Additional components of social inequality – quality of life and prosperity – will be discussed with generative processes in Chapter 7.

TABLE 6.2 *Gini (wealth inequality) measures for selected settlements*

Settlement	Gini[a]	Population[b]	Case study	Source[c]
Forager villages:				
Jerf el Ahmar	0.13	20		1
Bridge River	0.20	125		1
Agricultural villages:				
Tell Sabi Abyad (Neolithic)	0.30	40		1
Mesa Verde area (Neolithic)	0.36	45	~5	1
Capilco (village in a state)	0.16	21		1
Practical machine sites:				
Kahun	0.68	500		1
Amarna workers compound	~0.00	360	19	5
Towns:				
Cuexcomate	0.48	240		2
Heuneburg	0.57	270		1
San Jose Mogote	0.25	1,000		1
Cities:				
Ado Ekiti	0.42	1,670	23	4
Yautepec	0.21	1,900	22	2
Pompeii	0.54	2,200	24	1
Tikal	0.63	7,000	1	1
Cahokia	0.27	12,700	9	1
Caracol	0.60	17,860		3
Teotihuacan	0.34	100,000	26	5
Mesopotamia (various)	0.40			1

a   In cases with multiple Gini values, I use the highest value.
b   Where the sources give households, I multiply by 5.
c   Key to sources: (1) Kohler et al. 2018; (2) Smith et al. 2014; (3) Chase 2017; (4) Service Access Project; (5) New research by the author.

THE ROYAL PALACE AS AN URBAN INSTITUTION

A royal palace was not just the seat of government in premodern cities (Chapter 4); it was also a multipurpose institution whose presence in a city had an impact on urban life. Royal palaces are notable for the wide variety of activities that took place within their walls. I draw on a comparative study by James Sheehy (1996), who examined the nature of activities in a sample of sixteen premodern royal palaces from around the world.

Sheehy identifies five types of spaces within royal palaces. (1) *Residential/domestic areas* are found in all sixteen palaces in his sample. Not only the king and his family, but other family members, court officials, guards and servants, and staff typically live in the palace. Most royal palaces have (2) *ritual or ceremonial areas*. Temples, ancestor shrines, and spaces for oracles or other specialists are common. (3) *Administrative areas* are found in all royal palaces. Such spaces include council chambers, reception areas, and law courts. (4) *Markets and workshops* are located within, or adjacent to, most palaces in Sheehy's sample, and (5) *other special-purpose spaces* are also common. All cases but one have a public assembly area, and some have a space for the tomb of the king, or some kind of educational facilities. Based on Sheehy's analysis, it is clear that urban residents who are not part of the palace staff would come to the palace regularly for a variety of reasons, and this made the institution of the royal palace a major influence on urban life (beyond its role as a political center). A good picture of how this worked is provided by the royal palace in the Yoruba city of Ado Ekiti.

Case Study 23 Ado Ekiti Palace

Yoruba cities of West Africa provide a wealth of information on urban life in the premodern era. Yoruba city-states flourished from the sixteenth century CE until they were incorporated into the British Empire in the mid-nineteenth century (Peel 1983, 2000). British and other European travelers, merchants, and soldiers described government, life, and society on the verge of annexation. Yoruba cities, in particular, have been the target of scholarly research based on those sources (Krapf-Askari 1969; Peel 1983). Today, archaeology is beginning to contribute to the growing picture of Yoruba cities and urbanism (Usman 2003).

Urban Life and the Palace. Nigerian geographer G. J. Afolabi Ojo pieced together early accounts of Yoruba palaces, together with observations of the few surviving examples (Ojo 1966b). The palace of the city of Ado Ekiti, with its surrounding wall containing the "King's forest," is located in the center of the walled city (Figure 6.4, A). In the minds of urban residents, all roads led to the palace, whose walled area was 10.9 hectares in size. The centrality of the palace within the city had both a political/symbolic meaning (the king as the center of society) and a practical meaning (the main market of the city was located at the palace gate). Some

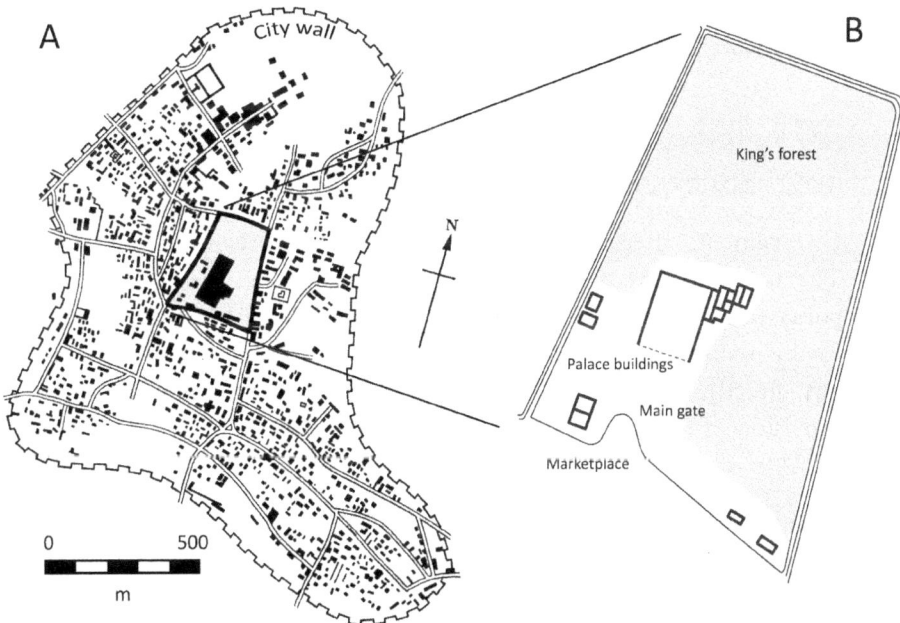

6.4. Royal palace in Ado Ekiti, a Yoruba city. (A) City plan; (B) Royal palace plan.
(A) Modified after Krapf-Askari (1969:182) and Ojo (1966b:31). (B) Graphic by Louise Hilmar, Moesgaard Museum; reproduced with permission, based on Ojo (1966b:43).

Case Study 23 (cont.)

sources describe the market as being located inside the walled palace compound (Ojo 1966b:35), and others put it immediately outside the gate (Figure 6.4, B); perhaps it expanded to cover both areas.

The palace consisted of six connected courtyards (Figure 6.4, B). The first courtyard one would enter was by far the largest. It was used for public gatherings. People would come to witness key ceremonies and hear proclamations by the king or officials. The king would host important travelers or visitors in special apartments constructed within the confines of this courtyard, and this was where the most important attached craft workers and artists would reside. The large courtyard was the only place where the public was allowed to see the king, who was considered sacred and powerful, far above the realm of normal people. In fact, the entire palace was considered sacred, and people were not allowed to touch the walls.

The next two courtyards were for the royal family and the chiefs. First came the courtyard where the princes and princesses relaxed, followed by an administrative courtyard for the chiefs. These were local officials who administered a specific area for the king. Their dedicated courtyard was where the king met with the chiefs and where new chiefs were installed. At this point, one entered the inner palace zone. This began with the residences of eunuchs, oracles, and diviners who worked for the king. Next came the main residence of the king and his wives. Finally, the innermost – most restricted – courtyard was the kitchen, where food for the royal family was prepared.

The king was considered the owner of the main marketplace of the city. He gave the command to open the market each day, and the market and king were linked by a ritual bond. Many urban residents were employed as palace staff, and some – notably crafters and artists – lived within the palace compound. The palace in Ado Ekiti, as in other Yoruba cities, was therefore a major institution in the life of the city, affecting residents in many ways.

Comparative Insights. The palace of Ado Ekiti gives us a picture of how a royal palace was integrated into the life of the community. Rather than being closed off to the public, the palace was instead a place where people came, on a regular basis, to take care of normal business. Two features of palace life promoted energized crowding in Ado Ekiti: the market held at the palace gate and the periodic gatherings in the main courtyard.

GOVERNMENT AND THE PEOPLE

Governments affected the lives of premodern urbanites in many ways. The nature of the regime (autocratic versus collective) and the type of polity (city-states versus empires) obviously played big roles (Chapter 4). In this section, I discuss two ways that premodern governments reached out directly to their constituents: public ideological messaging and the provision of services.

Propaganda, Ideology, and Religion

Public propaganda and ideology were important strategies of legitimation for ancient rulers. Most premodern societies had beliefs about the sacredness of the ruler and the duty of people to support the regime. Autocrats, in particular, broadcast these ideas through public art (Case Study 15, Persepolis), religious texts, and orations at ceremonial events (DeMarrais et al. 1996). These ideas were typically phrased in supernatural terms, with messages such as "If you disobey the regime, you are also disobeying the gods, and you will be punished" (Trigger 2003:250). Did people believe, or internalize, these messages? Were they the basis of the legitimation of ancient rulers? This notion − that belief in and adherence to ideology were the reason people paid taxes, fought in wars, and obeyed the regime − may seem unlikely, but many archaeologists evidently believe it (e.g., Brumfiel 1998; Emerson 1997:21−23; Halperin 2009). One might say that the propaganda of ancient kings was so effective that it is still working today!

The notion that ideological justification upheld ancient regimes is part of what social scientists call the "dominant ideology thesis" (Abercrombie et al. 1980). This theory holds that people supported regimes − and failed to rebel or resist when exploitation was severe − because they believed the propaganda of the rulers. The Durkheimian social interaction view of society (Chapter 2) − which attributes social action to interactions, not beliefs − is opposed to the dominant ideology thesis (Eagleton 1991; Kertzer 1988; Trigger 2003). In the words of Terry Eagleton (1991:34):

> If people do not actively combat a political regime which oppresses them, it may not be because they have meekly imbibed its governing values. It may be because they are too exhausted after a hard day's work to have much energy left to engage in political activity, or because they are too fatalistic or apathetic to see the point of such activity.

As a Durkheimian, I find it more reasonable to view the propaganda and ideological messages of ancient rulers as tools to integrate the elite class and deflect challengers to the regime, not to secure the obedience of commoner subjects (Abercrombie et al. 1980:3; Paynter and McGuire 1991). Supernatural and political symbols − and their manipulation in ceremonies and other practices − helped elite classes achieve cohesion and bound them to the ruler. The supernatural power typically claimed by ancient rulers was not a direct source of political power, but it did play a role in the legitimation of rulers (Kurtz 1978; Wolf 1999), particularly in more autocratic regimes (Blanton 2016).

A related way that early rulers likely benefitted from the encouragement of particular ideas among commoners is the inculcation of pride in the accomplishments of their own city. In early colonial Mexico, for example, the construction of a Christian church often became a rallying point around which the commoner laborers sought to outdo their peers in other towns (Lockhart 1992). This kind of pride in monumental civic architecture has been suggested as a source of community cohesion in other early cities (Cowgill 2003; Westenholz 2002). Timothy Pauketat (2000) has developed a similar argument for Cahokia, but with the idea that commoners were duped by the rulers. But, to my mind, this kind of attachment and pride in civic accomplishments comes about through social interactions and fulfillment, not through the specific mental or ideological content of a dominant ideology.

If propaganda and ideology were insufficient to induce people to go along with ancient exploitative regimes, what are the alternatives? Ideology is often contrasted with coercion and violence as alternative means of achieving order and obedience. By itself, coercion has rarely been a stable and effective means of getting people to go along with an unpopular regime. The best analysis of compliance, by political scientist Margaret Levi (1988), combines ideology and coercion into the concept of *quasi-voluntary compliance*. "Quasi-voluntary compliance rests on norms but is backed by material incentives and by coercion" (Levi 1988:68). This concept is one of the conceptual foundations of Blanton and Fargher's (2008) analysis of collective and autocratic regimes in premodern states (Chapter 4). In sum, while ancient regimes promoted various supernatural ideological messages to urban residents, these messages – by themselves – played only a minor role in binding people to the ruler.

Urban Services

One difference between urban and rural contexts in a given system is the greater self-sufficiency of peasant households compared to city dwellers (see Chapter 1). Because of the greater population, density, and division of labor in cities – compared to rural villages – urban households found it hard to take care of many basic needs and activities on their own (Boone and Modarres 2006:96–97). In the city, for example, tools that rural peasants regularly produce themselves, at home, typically must be purchased in shops or markets; water that is easily available to peasant households must be brought in using infrastructure for urban domestic needs; and ceremonial activity that satisfies the needs of peasants typically expands in urban setting to require specialists and dedicated buildings.[3]

Many of the objects that urbanites cannot produce or create on a domestic basis can be purchased in a market or shop (or provided by the regime in a command economy). But services in premodern cities are often provided by the government or some other institution. Many urban services are what economists call *public goods* – goods or services that benefit most or all urbanites

---

[3] A parallel relationship has been observed for household activities compared to city size in the Roman Empire. "The range of functions [activities] performed by each individual declines with city size, even as the range of functions performed by the group overall expands" (Hanson et al. 2017:10).

6.5. Medieval city wall. Micklegate, York, UK. Photograph by Chabe01, distributed under Creative Commons Attribution-Share Alike 4.0 International license. Wikimedia Commons (https://commons.wikimedia.org/wiki/File:Remparts_Porte_Micklegate_Tour_Sadler_York_1.jpg).

and are hard to restrict to only a few consumers or users. According to public goods theory in economics – going back to Adam Smith – these goods are difficult for the market to deliver, and therefore the government or another institution must step in to provide them (Blanton and Fargher 2008; Levi 1988; Ostrom 2005).[4] In the modern world, important public goods are territorial defense, law enforcement and the administration of justice, infrastructure, education, and disaster mitigation. For premodern cities, the list is somewhat different, although elements of these modern public goods are relevant for premodern cities. Other urban services – such as markets and shops – may be provided by local grassroots actions rather than by an institution; these are not public goods.

The defense of a state's territory is often at the top of the list of public goods in the modern world. In premodern times, most individual cities were responsible for their own defense, leading many to construct enceintes, or defensive fortification walls (Figure 6.5). These could be a major expense. The city of Perugia, Italy, spent one-third of its budget on defense in the years after 1300 CE, whereas only 8 percent was spent on other public works (Cipolla 1993:44).

---

[4] Technically, the key characteristics of public goods are that they are *not*: (1) subtractable (i.e., use of a public good by one person does not prevent simultaneous use by other persons); or (2) excludable (i.e., it is hard or impossible to exclude someone who has not paid for a good or service from use of a public good).

The prominence of medieval city walls in Europe has misled many – including the great sociologist Max Weber (1958:81) – into thinking defensive walls were so important that they should be part of the definition of a city. To the contrary, most premodern cities around the world lacked walls (Tracy 2001); indeed, defensive walls are extremely rare in some urban traditions, such as Mesoamerica. Furthermore, premodern city walls often had a symbolic function in defining urban space and creating cohesion, whether or not they also had a military purpose (Connah 2000; van der Graaff 2018).

Roads, bridges, canals, and other elements of physical infrastructure were public goods in many premodern cities. Local or central governments typically provided these urban services. Educational or medical facilities were urban services in some cultural traditions, and these were sometimes provided not by governments, but by religious institutions or private charity groups (Kuran 2001; van der Heijden et al. 2010). Educational facilities were often limited to particular social categories in premodern cities (ethnic, class, gender), and thus urban services could form part of the institutional framework for social inequality.

My colleagues and I investigated the relationship between urban service provision and social inequality in a sample of twenty-three historical and archaeological cities (see Chapter 4 and Appendix B for a discussion of our project and sample). We plotted the physical locations of three types of service facilities – markets or shops, temples or shrines, and public gathering spaces – in relation to neighborhoods. Using straight-line walking distance as our measure of access, we found major differences among the cities in access to service facilities (Dennehy et al. 2016; Stanley et al. 2016). Not surprisingly, we found the best access to services in cities with more collective regimes and cities with more commercialized economies.

Religion as an Urban Service

Several aspects of religion in premodern cities can be considered a public good: open to consumption by all members of a community, such that its use by one person does not detract from its use by others. As such, religious buildings and activities in cities were settings for urban services. Rao (2008), for example, labels temples and their associated rituals "symbolic public goods." I begin with anthropologist Anthony Wallace (1966), who studied the nature of religious cults across the spectrum of non-Western societies. While many societies had individualistic, shamanistic, and communal cults, cities and states were the settings for what he called *ecclesiastical cults*. These religions were characterized by a series of traits that are rare in non-state societies: full-time religious specialists, a hierarchically organized priesthood, close linkages between church and state, gods that were interested in morality, and temples integrated into the social, economic, and political life of the community.

Much public religious activity in cities focused around state cults. In an earlier book, I developed the idea that Aztec state religion can be considered a public good. By constructing and supporting temples and ceremonies, "Aztec kings furnished their subjects with supernatural protection, personal satisfaction and emotional fulfillment, and feelings of identity with the community and the city" (Smith 2008:194). The architectural evidence consists of temples, plazas, ceremonial ballcourts, and shrines, all built by the kings of city-states for their subjects. What about religious activities on a smaller scale? Many urban temples and shrines operate on a neighborhood level; they were used by local residents, and may or may not have been connected to the state religion.

Neighborhood temples and shrines were one subject of the comparative service access research project (Stark et al. n.d.). Most of the twenty-three cities in our sample had such facilities distributed throughout the city.[5] We found that in 35 percent of the cities, neighborhood temples were built and maintained by the state; in other cities, they were built by private individuals (26 percent) or by a central religious or social institution (26 percent). In most cities, people had ready access to these features. While people might have had to walk considerable distances (1,000 metres or more) to attend a ceremony at the main city temple downtown, they could get to their local shrine easily and quickly. In the most autocratic regimes (the two lower categories in Table 4.1), neighborhood temples and shrines were built by the state. In the cities with more collective regimes, however, private individuals and institutions were more likely to be responsible for the neighborhood features.

Case Study 24 Pompeii: Who Paved the Streets?

The city of Pompeii, on Italy's Gulf of Naples, was a midsized Roman city. Founded prior to Roman times, the city expanded and flourished under the emperor Augustus, until it was destroyed and buried by ash from an eruption of Mount Vesuvius in 79 CE. The remains have been under near-continuous excavation for almost three hundred years, revealing some of the most spectacular finds of any premodern city. The extensive architectural remains provide detailed knowledge of Roman houses, streets, and temples. Many masterpieces of al fresco mural painting and mosaic floor art have been recovered. In the mid-nineteenth century, archaeologist Giuseppi Fiorelli realized that voids in the consolidated ash were hollows where people and animals had died in the eruption, and he began the process of injecting plaster into the voids to create replicas of individual people and dogs who died in 79 CE.

---

[5] Neighborhood temples and shrines can be classified as intermediate-level service facilities. High-level facilities – the central large temples and civic buildings – tend to be larger than lower-level facilities, and they serve a larger base of individuals. Low-level religious features are those used by families in households (see Chapter 8).

Case Study 24 (cont.)

6.6. Street in Pompeii, whose repaving was terminated by the eruption of Vesuvius. The front portion (A) was recently paved, and unprepared paving stones sit ready to be finished and laid (B). Poehler and Crowther (2018:597). Image available at https://works.bepress.com/eric-poehler/97/. Reproduced with permission.

Given the high degree of preservation and extensive fieldwork at Pompeii, many aspects of urban life can be reconstructed to an incredibly detailed scale, from the gardens of the wealthy to neighborhood bars and brothels, from cosmetics and perfume to the toolkits of artisans (Beard 2008; Berry 2007; Laurence 2007). Here, I describe a recent study that uses the stones of the streets of Pompeii (Poehler and Crowther 2018) to draw conclusions about the provision of street paving, an important urban service in many premodern cities.

Paving the Streets. Eric Poehler and Benjamin Crowther analyzed the paving stones in the several miles of streets of Pompeii. A variety of types of evidence allowed them to isolate individual *paving events*, or episodes when a segment of a street or streets was paved as a unit. The evidence included the type, size, and arrangements of stones, and patterns of wear. Older streets in Pompeii have deep ruts in the stone made by cart traffic. When a rut ends abruptly at the break between two sections of street, it is clear that the side without ruts was laid down in a paving event at a later date than the side with the ruts. The street called the Vicolo delle Conciapelle (Figure 6.6) was apparently in the process of being repaved when the volcano erupted. The central portion of the street has been newly paved ("A" in the photo), and an unpaved section lies beyond. A pile of new paving stones (B) sits on the sidewalk. The curb stones (C) were produced by splitting old paving stones.

Poehler and Crowther use their evidence to ask whether street paving in Pompeii was carried out as an urban service, under the direction of municipal officials, or whether individual property owners took care of their own segments of streets. Their analysis shows that areas pertaining to a paving event typically extended far beyond the façades of individual buildings, often including intersections. Furthermore, the paving of Pompeii streets was consistently uniform in material and

Case Study 24 (cont.)

stonework. Although wealthy property owners sometimes did repair the street in front of their houses, the evidence suggests that street paving was indeed a municipal urban service. Poehler and Crowther compare the Pompeii evidence with comparable remains from the plank streets of medieval Oslo, where archaeologists found "difference in the pattern of the planking corresponding to different house plots" (Jørgensen 2008:556), suggesting that street construction and repair were done by households and were thus not a public service. Poehler and Crowther's conclusion for Pompeii is supported by historical documents showing that paving was a very expensive activity. Roman streets were, on average, 16 Roman feet wide (4.72 meters). The cost of a single linear Roman foot of road (16 square feet) cost 2.8 times the daily bread consumption rate of commoners (Poehler and Crowther 2018:599–600).

Comparative Insights. There are innumerable topics for which Pompeii offers more detailed insights into urban life than most premodern cities. The example of street paving is just one small part of the known past of Pompeii. It is especially interesting, however, in allowing us to address an important topic for urban life that is poorly understood for the distant past: Who built and maintained urban infrastructure before the modern era?

INSTITUTIONS, FREEDOM, AND COERCION IN PREMODERN CITIES

A growing trend in economics and economic history has been to explain the divergent historical trajectories and conditions of nations today in terms of positive and negative institutions. Anthropologist Mary Douglas phrases this distinction as follows: "A benign institution would be one that permits members to cooperate to their mutual advantage. Perverse would be a system of rules which benefits the short-term interest of a few at the expense of the longer term and wider interests of the majority of the community" (Douglas 2013:46). The best-known account of this approach is the book *Why Nations Fail: The Origins of Power, Prosperity, and Poverty* (Acemoglu and Robinson 2012). The central concept is a contrast between inclusive and extractive economic institutions.

Inclusive institutions favor mass participation and allow individuals to flourish without heavy repression. "Inclusive economic institutions foster economic activity, productivity growth, and economic prosperity" (p. 75). Extractive institutions, on the other hand, "are designed to extract incomes and wealth from one subset of society to benefit a different subset" (p. 76); these institutions lead to poverty, underdevelopment, and misery for the nonelite members of society. Other parallel accounts include Avner Greif's (2006) analysis of early medieval and modern merchants and the book *Violence and Social Orders* by Douglass North, John Wallis, and Barry Weingast (2009); for them, an open order society is one with inclusive institutions, and closed order societies are those with extractive institutions. The parallels with Blanton and Fargher's contrast between collective and autocratic regimes (Chapter 4) should be clear.

While this line of analysis is becoming increasingly popular (Acemoglu and Robinson 2019), it has been criticized for its sloppy concept of "inclusive," which can refer to a variety of processes, some detrimental to all but the wealthiest in a society (Ogilvie 2021).

While much of the work by economists on these topics sounds limited and simplistic to anthropologists and historians, it is clear that the nature of institutions has profound effects both on the individual level and on the broader level of social and economic patterns. I want to close this chapter by extending this general perspective into the realm of premodern cities. Sometimes institutions conspired to generate freedom and other positive outcomes for urban residents. The eleventh-century German phrase "City air makes you free" (*Stadtluft macht frei*) initially referred to a legal principle that granted a serf freedom if he or she could manage to live in a city – away from the master – for a year and a day.

This phrase also has a broader meaning; it is often used to refer to a series of rights and freedoms given to cities and their residents in medieval Europe. With growing commercial power, cities were granted royal charters with key concessions and rights: the right to hold a market, to host a guild, or to mint coins, freedom from customs duties, or the right to have cases tried in a local judicial court (Lilley 2002:44–55; Richardson 2003). For some economic historians, the freedoms that developed in European medieval towns were the source from which later individual rights and freedoms developed in European societies (Young 2017). The freedoms of medieval towns did not develop by accident, nor did they originate in some kind of special European or Bourgeois spirit, as argued by McCloskey (2010). They were the product of a particular conjunction of institutions that operated in and on urban settlements, starting in the early medieval period (Ogilvie 2011, 2019).

In other cases, institutions created conditions of coercion and misery for urban residents. Perhaps the clearest examples are cases where modern nation-states have forced nomadic or seminomadic peoples to settle down in houses and communities that do not accommodate indigenous lifeways or cultural practices. For example, the Israeli government has forced many nomadic Bedouin peoples to settle in permanent communities (Falah 1985; Meir 1997). Early attempts that tried to enforce European-style orthogonally planned villages with standard housing units were a failure, leading to defections and violent conflicts. Earlier mission settlements in Africa and the New World were even more coercive, using newly settled villages to forcibly convert Indigenous people to Christianity, while destroying much of Indigenous culture (Legesse 1998; Lindsay 2012).

The Bedouin settlement program had a positive outcome – in at least one area – when state bureaucrats decided to ask the Bedouins what kind of (permanent) settlement they would want to live in. The Bedouin wanted defendable neighborhood units that replicated tribal or subtribal groups, and individual family lots with flexible housing that could accommodate demographic changes in family size and structure. When these choices were honored, the settlement program had much greater "success," in that it led to fewer conflicts and less disruption of traditional values and practices (Meir 1997; Stern and Gradus 1979).

These processes also operated in the deep past, but they are difficult to study. In a case of "compulsory urbanism" (Morris 1972), the Inka Empire founded new administrative cities in key provincial locations. They forced people from a variety of different areas – some quite far away – to move to the city to handle administrative tasks. The best-studied example is Huanuco Pampa (Case Study 12). One signal of the "artificial" nature of this settlement is that when the Inka Empire collapsed with the arrival of Francisco Pizzaro, Huanuco Pampa was abandoned and people went back home. Was life difficult and miserable for the forced immigrants under Inka rule? This is difficult to judge with current archaeological data.

These cases reinforce my central point: that institutions – whether part of the state, a religious organization, or some other realm – had a strong role in structuring the nature of life in premodern cities. Institutions were also crucial in shaping the long-term trajectories of cities through time. When a city lasted for many centuries, it must have had the kinds of institutions that allowed it to adapt to stresses and shocks from the environment and society. The study of the determinants of settlement persistence is still in its infancy (Smith et al. 2021b), yet this is one area where data on premodern cities might usefully inform research on urban climate-change adaptations today (Glaeser 2021; Smith et al. 2021b).

The institutions described in this chapter are, for the most part, the "top-down" forces that established the structure within which people lived out their lives in premodern cities. But this does not mean that life was necessarily determined, or even strongly structured, by institutions. There is not much support for the old "statist" views of society (Chapter 4) that posit the central regime as controlling – or even trying to control – all aspects of life and society in ancient times. I next turn to generative processes to explore the role of "bottom-up" forces that sometimes operate together with urban institutions, at times independently of them, and sometimes in opposition to them (Figure 6.1).

SEVEN

GENERATIVE FORCES AND URBAN LIFE

U NTIL THE PAST DECADE OR SO, ARCHAEOLOGISTS GAVE LITTLE attention to the role of generative forces in the past. For many (including myself!), the state was the only thing that mattered for understanding cities and urban life. This "statist" attitude was rampant: the state was all-powerful, the only actor worth considering (see Chapter 4). Today, most scholars recognize that the state was not the only institution that influenced urban life in the past. There is a growing recognition that the actions of people working together, apart from the state or other institutional contexts, contribute greatly to the contours of urban life and society (Blanton 2016; Borck and Sanger 2017; Graeber and Wengrow 2021). These grassroots actions in cities, when undertaken by groups of people, can be called *generative forces*. They generate – or create – order and enduring structures within cities, and they bring about change from the bottom up, as contrasted with the state and other central institutions, which regulate society and generate change from the top down. My separation of top-down and bottom-up forces in this chapter and the last is somewhat artificial. The distinction is not a dichotomy; many processes combine top-down and bottom-up actions, and there are forces and actions at intermediate levels.

Generative processes, labeled "self-organization" by Moroni et al. (2020), occur in two distinct forms. The first are processes of *self-coordination*. These occur when people carry out the basic activities of daily life, interacting with others, which can lead unintentionally to outcomes that have some level of organization that influences the actions and conditions of people. Energized crowding is a major type of self-coordination, as is the structure of order within markets as influenced by an "invisible hand" (A. Smith 1979). The result of this kind of process is often called "spontaneous order" (Cronk and Leech 2013:156–161; Nadeau 1998). The fact that this line of analysis has sometimes been used to promote extremist free-market capitalist ideologies (e.g., Hayek 1944) should not blind us to its more general relevance to social and urban analysis; see Bowles et al. (2017) and Cronk and Leech (2013) for discussion.

The second type of self-organization identified by Moroni et al. is *self-governance*. This occurs when people intentionally organize themselves and create methods of group decision-making in order to achieve a common objective. Neighborhoods, guilds, and many voluntary associations are examples from early cities. The term *grassroots activity* is often used for these processes (Mehaffy 2008). Research in the tradition of academic anarchism puts grassroots activities at the center of the ways societies are organized and change (Graeber and Wengrow 2021; Ward 2000). It is not uncommon for organizations created by grassroots activity, such as a merchant guild, to become solidified into an institution that plays a structuring role in a premodern city (Ogilvie 2019). Most of the generative processes described in this chapter are examples of grassroots activity.

A number of examples of generative processes of both types are covered in Chapters 4 and 5. In terms of politics and government, some kinds of polities and some kinds of regimes promote or favor greater grassroots activity, whether supporting or resisting the state. In the economic realm, market economies promote generative activity. Independent crafters create their own working conditions and make their own production decisions; these are generative actions. Markets allow consumers more latitude, or freedom (Sen 1999), to follow their own goals; in command economies, on the other hand, many economic decisions are made by officials and bureaucrats.

Archaeologists have only recently begun to explore how top-down and bottom-up forces operated in past societies (Altaweel 2015; Blanton and Fargher 2008; Chase 2019). Some archaeologists describe these two categories as types of scholarly approaches rather than as types of force or process (Furholt et al. 2020; Ur 2020). An extreme example is to use the label *top-down* to categorize any study of elites or rulers, and *bottom-up* to describe any study of households. This idiosyncratic approach limits the usefulness of these concepts and helps isolate archaeology from the other social sciences. Both kinds of process operate in almost any society, and at multiple levels within a society or city. For example, top-down and bottom-up forces both operate at the household level. I align my approach with standard research on these topics in the social sciences in order to benefit from their insights (Cronk and Leech 2013; Easterly 2008; Laborde et al. 2018; Moroni et al. 2020).

In this book, I give little attention to a particular kind of generative force that some archaeologists consider to be ***the*** dominant process shaping life in early cities – social identity (Joyce 1991; Magnoni et al. 2014; Robin 2013; M. L. Smith 2014). For these and other authors, social identities such as ethnicity and gender are viewed as an attribute of individuals that strongly influences – even determines – their ways of thinking and behaving. These archaeologists conflate the different types of social identity discussed in the social sciences – categorization, self-understanding, and group cohesion (Brubaker and Cooper 2000). They also tend to ignore the fact that it is often very difficult – or even impossible – to reconstruct past social identities with confidence. With proper attention to rigorous guidelines of method and theory, archaeologists can reconstruct past identities in some contexts (Hu 2013; Peeples 2018). While many of the generative processes discussed in this chapter – household and neighborhood activities, specialized occupations, or striving for quality of life – may have involved the activation of social identities of some sort, these urban social processes can be analyzed adequately without speculating about the possible natures or expressions of past social identities.

GENERATIVE FORCES AND THE TENSIONS OF URBAN LIFE

Generative forces describe the actions of people to create livable urban space and to solve their own problems apart from any top-down planning or organization. These forces are most prominent at the levels of the household and neighborhood, and sometimes small corporate groups.[1]

Generative Forces in Urban and Settlement Planning

Jane Jacobs, a towering intellectual figure in urban studies, claimed that livable cities – places with safe, vibrant neighborhoods as well as productive economies – were created, not by the actions of central planners, but by generative processes. The actions of individual residents, living their lives as they please while interacting with both friends and strangers in public settings, generated the conditions that make urban life a positive experience, and that make cities creative and productive places (Jacobs 1961). The social interactions she describes are examples of energized crowding. Jacobs was reacting against the kind of sterile, lifeless modernist cities being promoted by the emerging field of urban planning in the mid-twentieth century (Page and Mennell 2011).

---

[1] I should note that my approach is broader than a particular usage of the label "generative approach" in the social sciences, which refers to a specific program of agent-based modeling of human societies (Epstein 2007).

Jane Jacobs was part of a larger movement that promoted the values of "generative methods in urban design" (Mehaffy 2008). In the field of architecture, proponents of this movement located generative forces in the wisdom of traditional communities, outside of the control of the state and the modern world economy. The most influential architect in this area was Christopher Alexander:

> We begin with that part of the language [a language of design] which defines a town or a community. These patterns can never be "designed" or "built" in one fell swoop — but patient piecemeal growth, designed in such a way that every individual act is always helping to create or generate these larger global patterns, will, slowly and surely, over the years, make a community that has these global patterns in it . . . . We do not believe that these large patterns, which give so much structure to a town or of a neighborhood, can be created by centralized authority, or by laws, or by master plans. (Alexander et al. 1977:3)

Planner Besim Hakim studied the development of such generative community principles over time in the Near East (Hakim 1986, 2008, 2014). He summarized how this approach to community design differed from centrally planned communities in a diagram, shown here in Figure 7.1. In Hakim's generative model, diverse households and communities gradually develop "meta-principles" based on local usage and long periods of negotiation and experience. In systems with top-down planning, on the other hand, a central authority attempts to create uniformity by standardizing the diverse units (Scott 1998). This is shown in Hakim's diagram as an attempt to enforce a single shape (the circle) on the diverse actors. The creation of "timeless" urban forms in the traditional settlements studied by Christopher Alexander and Besim Hakim — or the busy interactions on modern urban sidewalks described by Jacobs — are examples of spontaneous organization. Attempts to recreate these forms or processes today, however, can

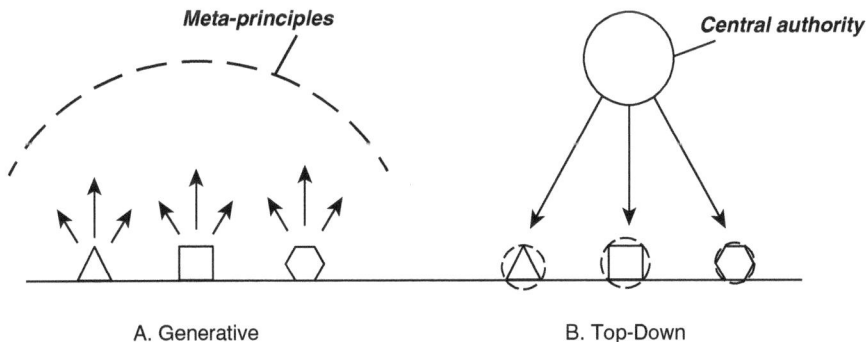

7.1. Besim Hakim's model of generative versus top-down planning principles. Modified after Hakim (2008:26).

be either top-down actions (if done by planners or authorities) or grassroots activities (if enacted by residents).

In considering generative versus top-down factors in early urban layout and structure, it is important to keep two spatial contexts separate: the central epicenter of a city and the residential neighborhoods that surround the central area. In Chapter 4, I discuss the epicenter planning model in which the civic architecture in the urban epicenter was centrally planned, whereas the residential zones were created by generative processes; in fact, I identify this as the most widespread principle of urban layout and planning among premodern cities (Smith 2007). It is also important to distinguish the initial planning and creation of an urban space from its subsequent patterns of use. The changes and modifications that can occur between construction and later use introduce complexities into the use of settlement plans to analyze activities and dynamics. One setting where these two contexts often diverge is formal open space. Formally arranged open spaces (such as plazas and parks) are almost always the creation of central planning. These are rarely if ever present where generative forces predominate in the initial layout of urban land (Pojani 2019; UN-Habitat 1982:chapter 2). While such spaces may be built by rulers for processions, parades, or ceremonies to support their power, they can then be taken over by grassroots protests and other generative activities. Tiananmen Square in Beijing is a striking contemporary example. In the sections that follow, my focus is on residential zones, not the formally planned civic architecture of the epicenter.

Generative Actions at the Community Level

The process of "energized crowding" (Chapter 1) is a prime example of a spontaneous-order type of generative force. Created when people interact in large or dense settlements, the outcomes of energized crowding impact life in cities (Figure 2.1). As discussed in Chapters 2 and 3, *interaction stress* describes many of the negative effects of crowded urban life – irritation, conflict, cognitive overload, and a lower quality of interaction with fellow urbanites – while *economic growth* describes the positive economic effects, including increased productivity and the resulting improvements in the quality of life. The third major outcome of energized crowding is *community formation*.

Communities and their associated patterns of sharing, cooperation, and other customary practices are one of the modes of behavior I discuss in Chapter 5 (Table 5.1). People's actions in marketplaces and shops – another mode of behavior in Table 5.1 – are not under central control, and their separate, individual activities can lead ultimately to changes in exchange, production, and consumption, often through the action of energized crowding. But the generative actions of communities are quite different from those associated with markets. Economists Samual Bowles and Herbert Gintis (2002) emphasize two key differences between markets and communities: social interactions in markets tend to be anonymous, while community interactions are personal, and markets are places with ephemeral social ties while social relations in communities are enduring. For premodern cities, I would relax the anonymous and ephemeral features of markets somewhat (Mintz 1961). Nevertheless, the personal and enduring nature of community social ties is one of the reasons why neighborhoods – communities within larger settlements – are a universal feature of cities throughout history. I return to Bowles and Gintis's analysis of communities in my discussion of neighborhoods later in this chapter.

While governments and other institutions are needed to provide urban services and other public goods for urban residents (Chapter 6), they are not very good at organizing life on a local basis. For this, the generative processes associated with households and neighborhoods do a much better job. The interplay between institutions and generative processes is one of the fascinating dynamics of urban life. Even when a settlement is established with regimented central planning, the actions of residents over time create generative forces that structure interactions and life on a local scale. This has been documented in Japanese internment camps in the United States (Kamp-Whittaker and Clark 2019); an ancient example is the Greek city of Olynthus.

Case Study 25 Olynthus: Generative Processes in a Centrally Planned City

The system of orthogonal planning exhibited by Classical and Hellenistic Greek cities was attributed by Aristotle to Hippodamus of Miletus (498–408 BCE). Whether this individual originated grid planning in Greece or not (Shipley 2005), the planning tradition associated with his name produced striking layouts in many Greek cities (Wycherly 1962). Olynthus is one of the best cases of Hippodamian planning. It was rebuilt or expanded in grid format in 432 BCE, and then Phillip II of Macedon destroyed the city in 348 BCE.

The short life of Olynthus is a boon for archaeology. A densely packed neighborhood of some forty-five houses was excavated on the North Hill of the site in the 1930s by David Robinson, who published fourteen volumes of detailed descriptions of the houses and their artifacts (Robinson 1929–1959); see Figure 7.2. These volumes allowed Nicholas Cahill to digitize the information decades later and analyze it according to contemporary methods and concepts. His report is one of the most complete analyses of ancient urban housing and home life ever published (Cahill 2001). Ongoing research directed by Lisa Nevett is greatly expanding the studied area of the site, with important results (Nevett et al. 2020).

Adjusting to Urban Conditions. The houses in the excavated North Hill neighborhood (Figure 7.2) were laid out in blocks of ten houses, each house approximately seventeen meters on a side. Greek urban houses had a common suite of rooms that included an open courtyard, a covered veranda (*pastas*), a male meeting room (*andron*), as well as a kitchen, sleeping rooms, workspaces, and a bathing room (Nevett 2010; Wycherly 1962). These room types are readily identifiable at Olynthus from the floor plan and associated artifacts. Many of the houses had a second story. There has been some remodeling of walls and doors (Cahill 2001), which complicates the reconstruction of the original plans.

Two adjacent houses in Block A, labeled houses Av9 and Av10, show what these structures were like (Figure 7.3). House Av10 (the southern house) yielded a sales inscription, stating that "Dionysium son of Ithryas bought this house, together with the storeroom and all the things that bring income" (Cahill 2001:117). It is not clear what was meant by the storeroom, but the income-generating parts were two, and possibly three, shops on the east side of the house, plus a piece of olive crushing equipment (see

Case Study 25 (cont.)

7.2. Excavated neighborhood at Olynthus. (Gerster 2005), p. 50. Copyright Estate Georg Gerster, Switzerland, www.GeorgGerster.com.

discussion of shops in Chapter 5). Two of the shops had large numbers of coins. The north shop was probably run by the household, since it opened into the house as well as onto the street. The south shop may have been rented out, since it did not connect to the house. More than sixty loomweights were recovered in this house, but they could not be traced to specific rooms. This house showed only minor obvious remodeling.

House Av9, on the north side, had been extensively remodeled. The central area around the courtyard was fashioned into four weaving rooms (as shown by concentrations of loom weights) arranged around the remaining small patio area. One shop opened only to the street, one opened to both the street and the house, and the shop in the northeast corner did not have any preserved doorways.

While an initial glance at this North Hill neighborhood (Figure 7.2) gives the impression of a series of standardized houses, in fact each house had its own distinctive arrangement of rooms (Figure 7.3). The size and shape of houses were standardized, and the initial layouts were likely standardized too. Cahill notes that "variations in house design are due to later modifications" (Cahill 2001:195). As people lived in these houses, they modified them to fit their changing social and economic needs.

Comparative Insights. The Olynthus houses show us that – even in a city with standardized and centrally planned housing – there was considerable opportunity for independent, generative activity by individuals and households. To see this today required two stages of archaeological work: an initial meticulous excavation with excellent recording and publishing of finds, and a contemporary problem-oriented reanalysis of those data to address details like activity differentiation by room and architectural remodeling.

Case Study 25 (cont.)

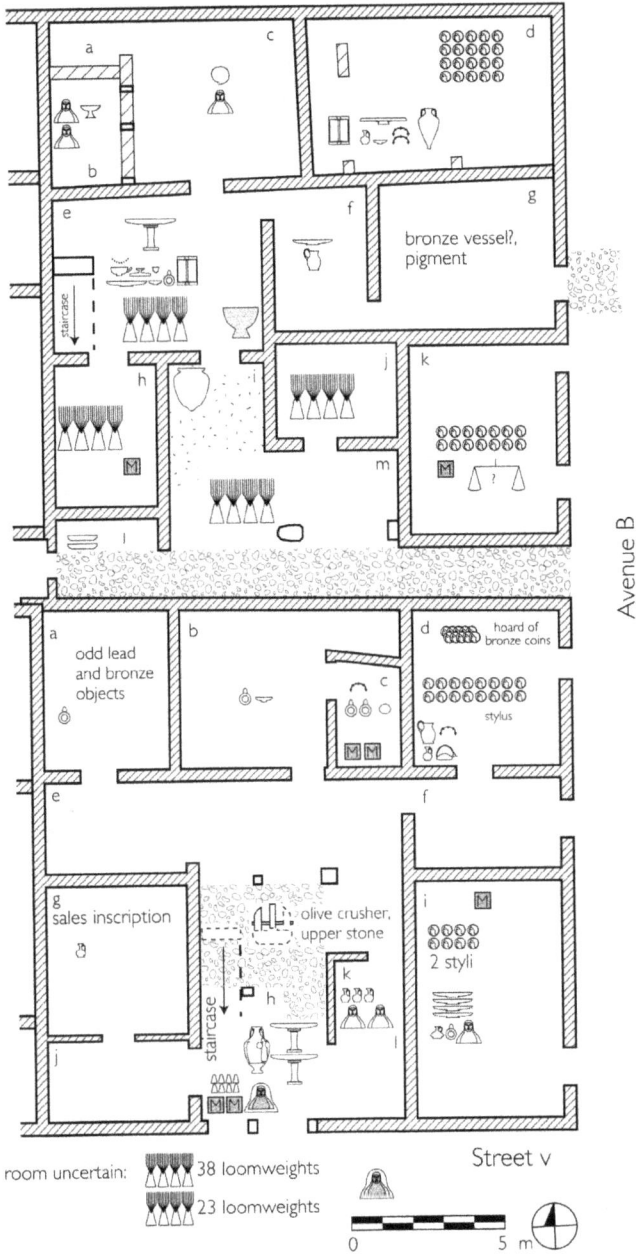

7.3. Houses with shops at Olynthus, showing modifications of what was probably an initial identical layout. Cahill (2001:114). Reproduced with permission.

Confirmation of the strength of the kind of generative processes evident in the Olynthus houses comes from some extensively-excavated settlements in Egypt. Urbanism in dynastic Egypt was a state-controlled activity, probably to a greater extent than in any other ancient urban tradition.

Case Study 25 (cont.)

Yet even in a centrally-planned neighborhood of even greater uniformity than Olynthus – at the Middle Kingdom site of Tell el-Dab'a – people made individual modifications to their houses. Nadine Moeller (2016:258) notes, "The alterations did not all occur simultaneously and in the same manners within the whole site, which is good evidence for individual decision-making in this matter."

URBAN HOUSES AND HOUSEHOLDS

Social scientists who work at the domestic level have found households a better focus for their research than families. A family – whether nuclear or extended – is a kinship group, whereas a household consists of the people living together in a dwelling. Many households are indeed families, but the presence of non-kin within a house is quite common cross-culturally. Servants, slaves, tenants, boarders, and other non-family members typically contribute to the activities and life within a household. In the 1970s and 1980s, anthropologists and social historians started focusing scholarly attention on households, their variation across cultures, and their changes through time. The book, *Households: Comparative and Historical Studies of the Domestic Group* (Netting et al. 1984), marked the maturity of the new anthropological/historical perspective on the household. The contributors moved attention away from the *structure* of households (kinship) and instead focused on *what households do* – that is, their activities and functions. They singled out five common functions of households: production (labor in agriculture or other sectors), distribution and consumption within the unit, transmission and inheritance of resources, reproduction and socialization, and co-residence (Wilk and Netting 1984).

Household Archaeology

Archaeologists were quick to jump on the household bandwagon (Flannery 1976), excavating houses all over the world. While our data has little to say about kinship, we typically recover considerable information on several of the five basic household functions. "Household archaeology" became a major focus within the discipline (Wilk and Rathje 1982), a trend that remains strong today (Smith 2016a). Indeed, the household archaeology approach has been responsible for many of the advances in understanding urban life in the distant past, including research on exchange and craft production (Chapter 5), social class and wealth inequality (Chapter 6), and studies of urban crafts occupations and professions (see the discussion that follows).

The practice and results of urban household archaeology vary greatly depending on the population density of the settlement. Low-density cities have a tremendous advantage, particularly in urban traditions where domestic trash is simply tossed out into the yard. At some Classic Maya sites, for example, any excavation behind a house-mound will encounter a midden of trash discarded by the residents of that structure. I found the same situation at the Aztec sites I excavated, in both rural and urban contexts (Smith 2016a). In contrast, densely occupied cities with closely packed houses needed a system of trash disposal, whether organized by an institution or by residents. The archaeological remains of dense cities like Olynthus, Pompeii, or Teotihuacan give little indication of just where all the household trash ended up. Excavators of houses in dense cities must be satisfied with three kinds of deposits: (1) what we call *fill* – reworked deposits that often contain some domestic refuse along with earth and stones; (2) tiny objects that were lost, perhaps ground into the floor; or (3) things left behind when a house was abandoned. It is important for archaeologists to distinguish these different types of deposits before analyzing household artifacts. The study of how deposits were formed, known as "formation processes," is an important part of household archaeology (Schiffer 1987).

Urban House Form

The size and spatial configurations of houses and compounds give us clues about the lives and conditions of urban households in the distant past. In Figure 7.4, I present a typology of urban housing for premodern cities, based on Smith (2014). For nonelite urban residents, the choice of a housing type depended on three main considerations: the density of occupation in a city (How much open space is available? How expensive is urban land?), the nature of political organization and central planning (Did the authorities build houses, or was it left to individual households?), and cultural traditions (things like family structure, preferred house types, and cultural norms of space use); see Rapoport (1969) I use the term *dwelling* to refer to the building or space where a single household resided (Tipple et al. 1994). I will review these five types of urban housing in turn.

(1) The individual house is a house surrounded by a yard or lot. This form was most common in past low-density cities, as well as in many cities and suburban areas today. Archaeologists have found that in early villages (and some cities too), the material remains of a household typically extended beyond the house

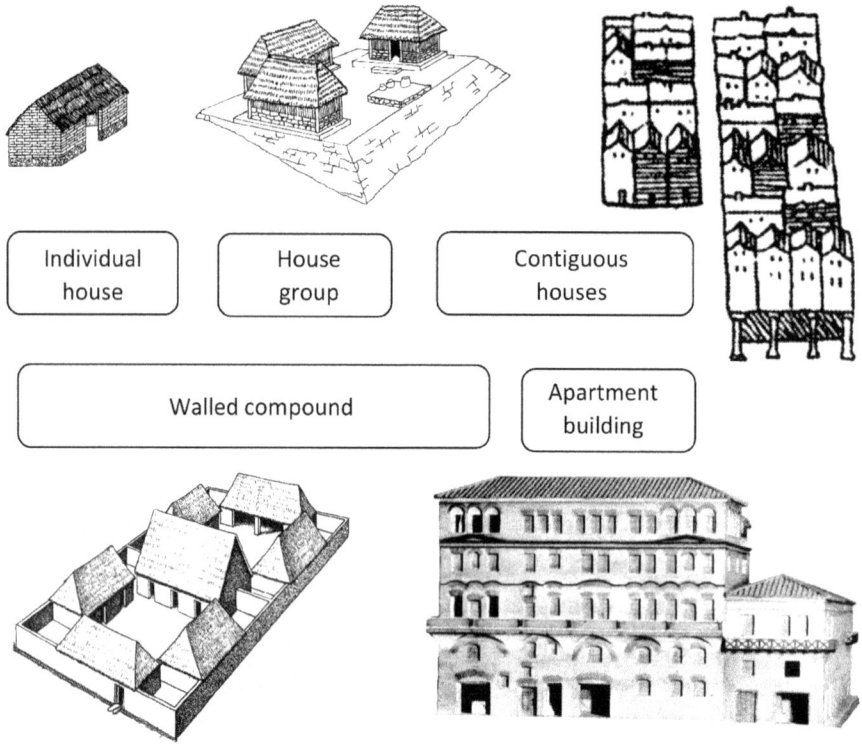

7.4. Typology of urban housing. Population density increases from left to right. Figure modified after Smith (2014:201). Not to scale. Clockwise from top left: Aztec peasant house (Michael E. Smith); Maya patio group, modified after Lohse (2007:21); Paris in 1550, Truchet map; Roman insula in Ostia (modified after an internet image); Inka kancha, modified after Gasparini and Margolies (1980:190).

structure to include adjacent features such as ovens, storage facilities, and burials (Flannery 1976; Jongsma and Greenfield 2003). Such features are present in low-density cities but rare in dense cities where space is at a premium.

(2) The house group consists of several structures grouped around a common area. Such groups were common in cities in Mesoamerica (Flannery 2002) – where they are called *patio groups* or *plazuela groups* – and some parts of Africa (Rutter 1971). The Mesoamerican case is interesting, in that similar forms of the patio group had very different social compositions in Maya and Aztec contexts. In many Classic Maya cities, a patio group housed a single household, often an extended family. The buildings were specialized (typically, a kitchen, a sleeping building, and a shrine), and most households needed all of the building types. But in the Aztec sites I excavated in Morelos – such as Yautepec (Case Study 22) – the three or four structures around a patio were each inhabited by a separate household. I was able to determine this from both documents and archaeology;

the buildings were not specialized, and similar deposits of basic domestic trash were found behind each building (Smith 2016a).

(3) The walled compound is a larger unit consisting of several dwellings and other structures enclosed within a peripheral wall. These were quite common in early cities around the world, perhaps the dominant form of premodern urban housing. Compounds in Precolonial African cities had considerable open space within the walls (Hakim and Ahmed 2006; Tipple et al. 1994), whereas the dwellings in Inka (Gasparini and Margolies 1980) or imperial Chinese (Xu and Yang 2009) urban compounds were more closely packed (Figure 7.4). In Precolonial Bali, walled compounds varied in size and layout, based on family size and structure (nuclear versus extended), although the buildings conformed to a basic inventory (residences, kitchens, storage bins, and shrines); this suite of building types was also repeated on a larger scale in the royal palace (Geertz and Geertz 1975:47–52).

(4) Contiguous houses describes dense urban arrangements where houses abut one another, whether formally planned (like Olynthus), or unplanned and irregular. These were common in dense cities and villages throughout the Old World, from Ur (Figure 8.3) to medieval towns. One of the few cases in the Preolumbian New World is found in the coastal city of Chan Chan (Moseley and Mackey 1974). Population density was a major difference between cities in the Old and New World (Table 3.2), and few New World cities were sufficiently dense to have this kind of crowded contiguous housing. A common form of contiguous housing in cities in warm climates is the courtyard house, where rooms are arranged around a central courtyard, open to the sky; these are often called "Mediterranean-style" houses. They were common in ancient Mesopotamian cities, as well as cities of Greek, Roman, and other Mediterranean urban traditions (Nevett 2010; Petruccioli 2006).

(5) The apartment building is a building with a single entrance that contains several dwellings. These were built to house the immigrant poor in dense and rapidly growing cities, as in the Roman and Ottoman urban traditions, but otherwise rare in the ancient world. Roman apartment buildings are known as *insulae* (McKay 1975; Storey 2002). These were large, multi-storied structures in the center of dense Roman cities. Housing historian James Ford begins his historical survey of slums and tenements with the Roman insula. He suggests, "Rome in the days of the Empire suffered a crowding together of high tenement houses under conditions much more dangerous to health and safety than New York City has ever witnessed" (Ford 1936:17). The city of Teotihuacan (see Case Study 26) stands out as unusual, in that its apartment buildings for commoners were well-built and luxurious, with large comfortable dwellings; these present a stark contrast to the crowded tenements in Roman and Ottoman cities.

MAKING A LIVING

The quantity and diversity of urban occupations are some of the major distinctions between what I have called political cities and economic cities (Smith and Lobo 2019); see also Chapters 4 and 5. In premodern economic cities – that is, cities where economic activities and functions are more important than political or administrative activities and functions – there were many urban occupational specialists, marking an enormous contrast with smaller settlements and rural areas (Hanson et al. 2017). But in political cities – the reverse pattern to economic cities, and more common in the ancient New World than the Old World – there seem to have been fewer different occupations in cities, and fewer contrasts with smaller settlements. I use the phrase "seem to have been" because we lack systematic data on this topic (see further discussion later in this chapter).

Shops and Crafts

Two features of premodern urban occupations stand out. There were many small-scale specialists in crafts and commerce, and most of them plied their trade from their houses. This is an important domain of grassroots activity. In the terminology used in Chapter 5, most craft production work was done at the level of "Household Industry" (production for sale, carried out within the household). Urban bakeries provide an example. In the transition from village society to the city, it became difficult for individual households to have the space for a baking oven. As bakeries sprung up it became easier for households to purchase their bread rather than trying to bake it themselves. Figure 7.5 shows two views of bakeries at Pompeii. On the left is the ruin of a bakery, with parts of the large grain mills still intact; on the right is an image of a bakery from a mural painting at the site. Carbonized loaves of bread have been recovered at Pompeii, identical to those shown in the painting. Another Roman example is the relief of a butcher shown in Figure 5.1.

Craft production at home – household industry – was the norm in most premodern cities around the world, from Mesoamerica (Hirth 2009; Manzanilla and Hirth 2011) to Classical Greece (Cahill 2005). In commercial economies, petty craft producers sold their products in small shops or marketplaces (Amaroui 2020). The shops at Olynthus (discussed previously) are notable for the good preservation and analysis of both architecture and artifacts, but the convergence of house-workshop-shop was quite common (see Case Study 19, Jerash). In European Medieval towns, most people worked from their homes: "Throughout the period up to the later eighteenth century, the household-based workshop was the commonest unit of production" (Keene 1990); see also Dyer (2002:209). One implication of this pattern is that the

7.5. Bakeries at Pompeii. (A) Drawing of an excavated bakery; Gusman (1900:241);
(B) Image from a mural painting; Gusman (1900:243). Both public domain.

practice of job commuting – daily movements from one settlement to another for work, or between sectors of large cities – was quite rare prior to the Industrial Revolution.

Urban Occupations and Urban Life

It is almost a truism that premodern cities were the setting for a greater number and diversity of occupations than their smaller counterparts, but hard data are rare. For medieval European towns, Dyer notes, "The number of crafts increased with the size of the town, so that we know of 175 occupations practiced in London, but no more than twenty in a small market town" (Dyer 2002:202). A quick survey of works in economic history that list the number of occupations in various ancient societies and cities (Table 7.1) shows great variation in the numbers, much of which must be due to variation in the nature of the sources and in the decisions made by modern authors.

Nevertheless, in settings with data on both rural and urban (or large and small city) contexts, the larger urban center – not surprisingly – had more occupations. One would expect the number of occupations to vary with the population and level of commercialization of a city, a relationship that has been confirmed for the Roman Empire. A total of some 700 occupations have been documented for the entire empire (Hanson et al. 2017; Wilson and Flohr 2016), and the number of formal associations of traders and crafters goes up with city size (Hanson et al. 2017). Of the various capital cities in Table 7.1, the two with the smallest number of occupations (Tenochtitlan and

TABLE 7.1 *The number of occupations (jobs) in selected settlements*

Context	# occupations	Type of evidence	Source
Large city–small city comparisons:			
London (medieval)	175	Documents	Dyer 2002: 202
Small market town	20	Documents	Dyer 2002: 202
Rome	40	Inscriptions	Joshel 1992: appendix II
Cilicia (province)	18	Inscriptions	Varinlioglu 2012: 177
Tenochtitlan	25	Documents	Smith 2012: 95
Huexotzinco	17	Documents	Smith 2012: 95
Other contexts:			
Amarna	27	Documents	Shaw 2004: 20
Athens	172	Documents	Harris 2002: 98–99
Medieval Islamic	1,018	Documents	Shatzmiller 1994: passim

Amarna) have economies that were considerably less commercialized than the other cities in the table. Beyond this, it is difficult to draw conclusions from these data.

Urban Agriculture: Farmers in the City

Although writers on farming within cities today like to portray urban agriculture as a new practice (Redwood 2008), in fact urbanites were farming within the city limits long before modern times (Goodson 2021). This is clearest in low-density tropical cities, such as Angkor (Hawken 2013), or Maya cities, where chemical analyses of soils reveal traces of past agricultural activity (Isendahl 2012). Many walled high-density cities – from Chang'an to Constantinople – include designated farmland within the city walls, for both regular food supply and for emergency use in case of siege (Barthel and Isendahl 2013). Evidence for "rural" activities such as crop production and animal raising have been found in many premodern cities, including the Amarna workers compound (Case Study 13), Pompeii (Day 1932), Tenochtitlan (Smith 2012a:74–77), and many Medieval towns (Heitzmann 2011); see Stark (2014).

In these cases, it may be difficult to determine whether urban plots were farmed by full-time farmers, or maintained by households whose primary economic activity was elsewhere. In a different pattern, farmers of rural fields lived in town and walked out to their fields. This was certainly the case for the nucleated villages known as agrotowns (Chapter 1). But this was also the case in many of the ancient cities of the New World. The numbers of people practicing specialized (non-agricultural) occupations in Aztec or Inka cities were far lower than the numbers of urban residents in these cities, leading to the conclusion that many urbanites must have farmed outside the city. Even in the large, planned metropolis of Teotihuacan, many or most residents walked out to rural fields to grow the food required by the city's 100,000 residents.

NEIGHBORHOODS

One of the big advantages cities hold for their residents – large cities, in particular – is that, in comparison with smaller settlements, they have more opportunities, more goods and services, and more potential social interactions that can have positive outcomes. The settlement scaling research described in Chapter 3 shows that in cities ancient and modern, people do take advantage of the greater intensity of energized crowding as cities grow larger. On the other hand, the increased number of people and the increased density have negative consequences in terms of crime, poverty, disease, and other outcomes of interaction stress. People in cities throughout history have come up with the same solution for urban crowds and the enlarged scale of life in cities: the neighborhood.

Neighborhood and Community

Neighborhood organization is one of the few universals of urban life around the world and through history (McKnight 2013; Smith 2010a); in fact, neighborhoods are even present in many non-urban, tribal settlements (Tuzin 2001:72–75). One way to think about neighborhoods is to consider them villages within the city. That is, people have found ways of recreating the small scale and the slow pace of village live, but within an urban settlement. Indeed, here are the observations of London neighborhoods made by Mark Twain on his visit to the city in 1896. Outside of the financial center of London ("the city"),

> the rest of London is not a city. It is fifty villages massed solidly together over a vast stretch of territory. Each village has its own name and its own government. Its ways are village ways, and the great body of its inhabitants are just villagers, and have the simple, honest, untraveled, unworldly look of villagers. Its shops are village shops; little cramped places where you can buy an anvil or paper of pins, or anything between . . . . [The shopowner] is not brusque and fussy and unpleasant, like a city person, but takes the simple and kindly interest of a villager in the matter, and will discuss it as long as you please. They have no hateful city ways, and indeed no ways that suggest that they have ever lived in a city. (Twain 2010:108)

While Twain's depiction is certainly idealized and romanticized, the image of the "urban village" was a common one in social science in the mid-twentieth century. Sociologist Herbert J. Gans (1962), for example, noted the following village-like traits in an Italian neighborhood in Boston: an active street life, most people knew one another, and life was lived on a smaller scale than in most areas of cities and suburbs. Although it is now clear that the metaphor of the urban village does not apply to inner city neighborhoods in the United States today (Sampson 2012), it remains a useful concept for understanding neighborhoods in premodern cities.

A more precise way to describe premodern neighborhoods is to say that they are social communities. In Chapter 3 I show that community formation – in the form of neighborhoods – is one of the three major outcomes of the process of energized crowding in cities. I follow economists Sam Bowles and Herbert Gintis (Bowles and Gintis 2002: F420) in defining the community as a form of grassroots organization as follows:

> By community we mean a group of people who interact directly, frequently and in multi-faceted ways. People who work together are usually communities in this sense, as are some neighbourhoods, groups of friends, professional and business networks, gangs, and sports leagues. The list suggests that connection, not affection, is the defining characteristic of a community. Whether one is born into a community or one entered by choice, there are normally significant costs to moving from one to another. (Bowles and Gintis 2002:F420)

Urban planners view social interactions – with friends, neighbors, and strangers – not only as factors that generate community, but as creating *successful* cities and towns. This is because social interaction – particularly in or near neighborhood physical facilities like parks, plazas, and pedestrian-friendly streets – is a key dimension of social cohesion in cities today (Jacobs 1961). Planners know that stable neighborhoods facilitate social interaction, which promotes social cohesion and integration (Brower 2011; Kisar Koramaz 2014), an observation that goes back to Emile Durkheim (Chapter 2). These insights have been incorporated into the principles of the New Urbanism movement within the planning profession. New Urbanist thinkers stress the importance of density for generating social cohesion and successful communities: "To new urbanists, the ability of physical design characteristics . . . to improve social interaction and therefore sense of community is indisputable. Putting people closer together, getting them out on the streets and mingling in shopping areas close to their places of residence seem intuitively obvious methods for gaining resident cohesion" (Talen 1999:1364). These insights are the basis for community-building activities in cities today (McKnight 2013; McKnight and Block

2010). In efforts to promote civic participation, getting people out of their homes and talking to their neighbors (i.e., interacting) is a key process.

The ability of cohesive communities to act – effectively and with positive outcomes – lies at the heart of the work of political economist and Nobel laureate, Elinor Ostrom (1990, 2005). One of her basic findings is that local communities can manage common-pool resources, such as forests or fisheries, more successfully and sustainably than either states (government ownership) or markets (privatization). For Ostrom, one of the key attributes that allows communities to be successful is the prominence of face-to-face communication, which promotes trust, reputation, and reciprocity.

Neighborhood Creation: Institutional and Generative Pathways

Energized crowding is one of the main forces that stimulate the desire of urban residents to live their life on a smaller scale than the entire city. Generative processes have led to the formation of neighborhoods in just about all settlements of any size throughout history (Smith 2010a), including the temporary camps and practical machine sites discussed in Chapters 3 and 4 (Smith et al. 2015). There are two basic forms of premodern neighborhood, corresponding to the way they were created. Most common are zones of irregular form, created by generative processes (Figure 7.6, A). People living near one another interact more frequently with one another than they do with people in other parts of the city, and this interaction leads to both the informal processes and the formal institutions (markets, shops, shrines) that constitute a neighborhood.

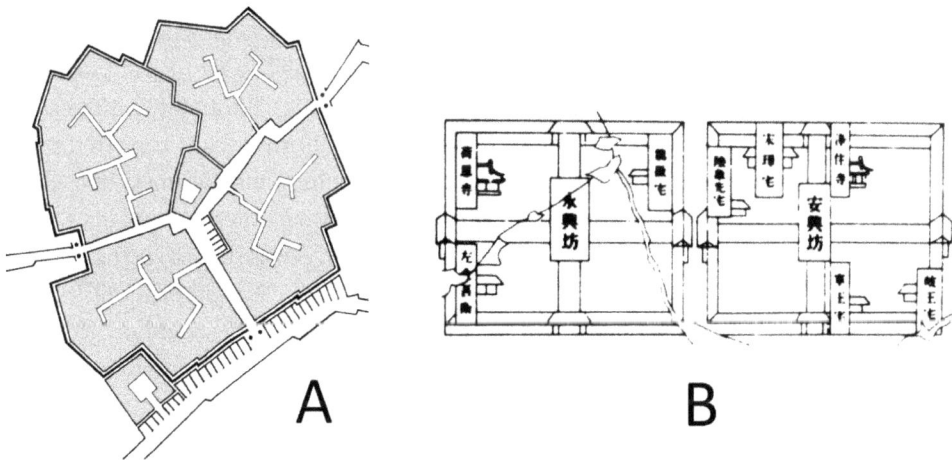

7.6. Two types of neighborhoods. (A) Idealized plan of neighborhoods in Islamic cities, formed by generative processes; (B) Chang'an wards, as depicted in a stone map from 1080 CE, formed by top-down institutional processes. (A) Bianca (2000:30); reproduced with permission. (B) Modified after Steinhardt (1990:103).

Less commonly (for past cities), authorities who design and build a city create neighborhoods from the start, as in Chang'an (Figure 7.6, B).

Neighborhoods created by generative processes can be difficult to identify archaeologically. In cities of low and intermediate density, archaeologists use spatial clustering methods to identify clusters of residences that likely constituted a neighborhood (Smith 2011a; Smith and Novic 2012). We can infer the presence of generative neighborhoods in cities such as Mohenjo-daro (Figure 3.3), Cahokia (Figure 4.1), or Shanga (Figure 4.5). Housing in pre-modern generative neighborhoods was likely built by the residents, much like so-called slum housing in the informal neighborhoods surrounding many cities in the developing world today (Kellett and Napier 1995; Turner 1991; Ward 1973). This is a major reason for the unplanned look of the layouts of generative neighborhoods (Figure 7.6, A).

The planners of Chang'an (Figure 4.17), on the other hand, almost surely had neighborhood structure in mind when they laid out the city. The *Guanzi*, a political-philosophical text attributed to the Tang period (the height of Chang'an), extols the virtues of having different categories of people live in separate quarters:

> The scholar-official, the peasant, the draftsman and the merchant . . .
> should not mix with one another, for it would inevitably lead to conflict
> and divergence of opinions and thus complicate things unnecessarily . . .
> Let the scholar-official reside near school areas, the peasants near fields,
> the craftsmen in the construction workshops near the officials' palace, and
> the merchants in the *shih* [commercial wards]. (*Guanzi*, quoted in Kostof
> 1992:102)

Interestingly, this sentiment of separating groups by neighborhood is also expressed in Plato's *Republic*, where it is advised to keep the rich and poor neighborhoods of cities separate (Marcuse 2002:11). The reorganization of the settlement of the Burning Man festival (Chapter 3) illustrates the transition from generative to planned and instituted neighborhoods, as triggered by an increase in population size, density, and the resulting institutional changes.

Once neighborhoods existed, the nature of their internal dynamics – the balance between top-down and generative forces – was shaped strongly by the nature of the dominant political regime (Chapter 4). Neighborhoods in cities with an autocratic central regime typically received little attention from the authorities; they were offered fewer public goods, and there was a very low level of intrusion by the state into neighborhood affairs. In Ottoman cities, for example, neighborhoods tended to form around end segments of the irregular street pattern (Figure 7.6). Because the regime provided few resources for security or control, residents took it upon themselves to build walls and gates to close off the neighborhood against intruders. By contrast, neighborhoods in cities under more collective regimes not only received more public goods, but they also showed the presence of officials and central institutions within the neighborhood (Blanton and Fargher 2008); see Chapter 4.

Janet Abu-Lughod's (1987) analysis of neighborhoods in Islamic cities illustrates these two patterns as they alternated through time; her discussion of periods with a strong power corresponds to periods of more collective rule, and her discussion of periods of unrest corresponds to intervals of more autocratic rule.

> Historically, in Arabo-Islamic cities, the neighborhood has been in dialectical process with the external society. When central power was strong and when the city-wide hierarchical structure was working smoothly, agents of the central administration operated within the neighborhoods to provide information to the center and ensure conformance with central directives. This was certainly the case with the *sheikh* of the *hara* in Cairo at certain points, when he was essentially an informer for the police as well as for the *muhtasib* (inspector of morals). He acted, in his capacity as real estate expert, to "steer" or supervise who should have access to vacant dwelling units in the quarter. Sometimes, the neighborhood was an administrative subset of the state.
>
> More often, however, the quarter played the opposite role, that of a defended neighborhood, particularly when chaos reigned. One reads, in the historical accounts, of civil strife / invasions / street battles, the recurring phrase, "and people closed the gates to their *harat*." Alternatively, to gain control over the city, conquerors always had to destroy the gates to the *harat*, as Napoleon's forces did when they invaded Cairo. (Abu-Lughod 1987:171)

Abu-Lughod also singled out the persistence of neighborhoods in these cities. For her, a striking feature of the Middle Eastern city "is its subdivision into smaller quarters whose approximate boundaries remain relatively constant over time and whose names continue to be employed as important referential terms, even when they do not appear on modern markers of street names, etc." (Abu-Lughod 1987:163). The generative nature of neighborhood creation and maintenance is one reason for the remarkable persistence of neighborhoods through time in many parts of the world (Behar 2003:10; Dempsey et al. 2011; Lin 2015).

Neighborhood Clustering

The clustering of social groups into neighborhoods – whether ethnic groups, social classes, or occupational groups – was quite common in premodern cities, but scholars have yet to disentangle crucial questions of causality. Why do some cities have neighborhoods sharply divided by race and class, while others have mixed neighborhoods? Although the causes of segregated and divided neighborhoods today are becoming better understood with ongoing research (Marcuse and van Kempen 2002; Massey and Denton 1993; Nightingale 2012; Sampson 2009), such understanding is still lacking for the premodern world. One survey that covered both modern and ancient cities (York et al. 2011) identified fifteen different drivers that create social clustering. These include both institutional and structural factors (commercialization, state policies) and generative processes (mutual support and chain migration).

Ethnic neighborhoods provide a good example. These are common, but by no means universal, in premodern cities (Albrecht 2020; Rattray 1993; York et al. 2011). One of the primary mechanisms that accounts for the growth of ethnic neighborhoods is well known: chain migration (Tilly 2000). This is the process by which new migrants to a city tend to settle with relatives or people known from their village, region, or ethnic group. Urban residents provide information, aid, and encouragement to new migrants from their group. Residents of ethnic neighborhoods often maintain ties to their place of origin and make an effort to preserve distinctive customs and practices. Over time, the mechanisms of chain migration create spatial clusters – neighborhoods – of residents that share traits of ethnicity and/or origin.

Whereas the importance of chain migration in creating and maintaining ethnic neighborhoods is widely acknowledged, scholars remain uncertain why this is an important feature in some cases but of little importance in others. One clue comes from the work of anthropologist Ralph Grillo on "plural cities" through history. These are cities whose groups of people "with varying degrees of consciousness and consequence believe, or are led to believe, that they are different from each other in lifestyle, language, religion, historic identity, and so on" (Grillo 2000:958). Grillo organizes his discussion around three historical types of cities: preindustrial, colonial, and modern capitalist. He found that governmental authorities in preindustrial cities did not worry much about ethnicity; they cared more about extracting taxes and corvée labor from their subjects. As a result, any ethnic clustering was created almost entirely by generative processes. In colonial cities, on the other hand, authorities were highly concerned with racial and ethnic differences, and invested great effort in designing cities that kept European elites separated from natives (Stanley 2012). Many cities today are marked by strong segregation that originated through a complex mixture of generative processes, laws, and other institutional factors (Massey 2016; Massey and Denton 1993; Sampson 2009).

The situation of neighborhoods specialized by economic occupation is similar to that for ethnic clustering: there are many cases of occupation-based neighborhoods in premodern cities (Béal and Goyon 2002; Manzanilla and

Chapdelaine 2009; Smail 2000), but an explanation for why this is common in some cities and not others, or in some urban traditions but not others, is lacking. A few functional forces are common cross-culturally. For example, crafts that produce noxious waste and pollution – such as metallurgy, ceramic production, and slaughterhouses – are more likely to be located at the edges of cities. But beyond this, scholars still cannot say why craft quarters were common in some cities and in some urban traditions, but uncommon in others.

POVERTY, PROSPERITY, AND ANCIENT URBAN LIFE

When we look at how the institutions of social classes and the distribution of wealth (Chapter 7) impact households and the lives of people in cities, we enter the realm of quality of life. Terms like *quality of life*, *poverty*, and *prosperity* have only been used sparingly by archaeologists and ancient historians, primarily in studies of classical Greece and Rome (Atkins and Osborne 2006; Bintliff 2014; Ober 2015) Some historians have claimed that poverty and pauperism were widespread and serious in medieval cities (Lis and Soly 1979), and one study reports that beggars and other very poor people composed some 13 percent of the urban population of European cities in the fifteenth to seventeenth centuries (Cipolla 1993:13). By contrast, fewer than 4 percent of all households at Teotihuacan were of the lowest status or wealth level: those living in substandard housing (Smith et al. 2019). Is this comparison valid? Or are the data so different as to make any conclusion suspect?

Concepts and methods for studying prosperity, poverty, and quality of life are crucial for understanding variation in urban life in the world today (Vogel et al. 2021), and they have the potential to illuminate at least two aspects of early cities: urban life in general, and variation in the sustainability and persistence of cities (Dempsey et al. 2011; Matson et al. 2016). Societies like those of the early Roman Empire and Teotihuacan appear to have been highly prosperous, creating a high quality of life for many residents. Can archaeologists pursue this topic with rigor?

Quality of Life in Premodern Cities

While there are many definitions of quality of life (QOL; Phillips 2006), the most productive approach for the distant past views QOL as a combination of two elements: standard of living, and capabilities. *Standard of living* describes the basic economic resources, or wealth, of a household, in relation to other households in a community or a society. A household's standard of living comes about through the intersection of the household's activities with the social conditions and institutions. It can be measured archaeologically through things like house size, amount of farmland, or possession of valuable goods

(Smith 1987; Walsh 1988). Thus the size of a house (this chapter) is a measure of the standard of living of the individual households within a community or a society.

Capabilities, the second component of QOL, was introduced by economist Amartya Sen (1999) to describe the non-economic component of the quality of life. As described by Stiglitz, Sen, and Fitoussi, the capabilities approach

> conceives a person's life as a combination of various 'doings and beings' (functionings) and of his or her freedom to choose among these functionings (capabilities). Some of these capabilities may be quite elementary, such as being adequately nourished and escaping premature mortality, while others may be more complex, such has having the literacy required to participate actively in political life. (Stiglitz et al. 2010:62–63)

Sen's approach has been highly influential, particularly in the field of development economics. For example, the United Nations uses income to measure standard of living, and education and longevity as markers of capabilities (McGillivray and White 2006).

Roman economic historian Willem Jongman claims that QOL is *the* major question that economic historians seek to answer about the past: "The most fundamental question for an economic historian is a very simple one: how successful was the economy in meeting people's demands when the means to do so were scarce? How prosperous and happy were people, and how and why did the economy succeed or fail in this respect?" (Jongman 2014:31). This sentiment applies not just for whole economies in the past, but for cities as well. We would like to know whether people in some cities were more prosperous than people in other cities, or whether poverty gripped some cities more strongly than others. Is it true that the economy of the Roman Empire improved the QOL of millions of subjects, making Roman cities rich and prosperous? While Romanists, and to a lesser extent Greek specialists, have made advances in addressing these questions (Hanson et al. 2017; Morris 2005; Ober 2015; Ward-Perkins 2006:chapter 6), they are difficult to answer for other ancient societies and cities. One promising development is that archaeologists are starting to operationalize Amartya Sen's capabilities concept for past societies.

Operationalizing Amartya Sen's Capabilities Approach

National-level statistics on income, education, and longevity – the basis for measuring Sen's capabilities in the developing world today – obviously will not work for the premodern world because of the rarity of this kind of data. For the Aztec sites I excavated in Mexico, I worked out ways of operationalizing QOL with the data I had at hand (Smith 2016a; M. E. Smith 2019c). This scheme addresses QOL on two scales: the household and the community (Table 7.2).

TABLE 7.2 *Quality of life ("QOL") measures for Aztec sites*

Component	Indices
QOL at the household level:	
Wealth	Standard of living
Capabilities	Diversity of possessions
	External social networks:
	• Exchange systems
	• Style networks
Prosperity at the community level:	
Wealth	Sum of household wealth
Capabilities	Collective construction projects
	Stability of residence
	Population growth
	Persistence of settlement
	Resilience to external shocks

Note: From Smith (2016).

I have discussed the wealth component of QOL earlier in this chapter; here, I concentrate on the capabilities component.

I used two kinds of measures for the capabilities of households and household members. The *diversity of possessions* is based on the assumption that greater diversity within a category of material culture suggests more options or capabilities for a household. In the sites I excavated, this was particularly dramatic for objects used in domestic rituals. All houses had ceramic figurines, used in domestic ceremonies of curing and fertility (Smith 2002), and most houses had one or more additional kinds of ritual object, including two types of incense burner and quartz crystals. To conduct a domestic ceremony, women had the choice of several alternative ritual items, rather than being limited to only one. *Participation in external social networks* is a similar measure: it shows increased options for fulfilling basic needs and desires. This can be measured both by frequencies of imported goods, and by the presence of foreign styles in various domains of material culture.

At the community level, I used the term *prosperity* instead of QOL to avoid confusion with the household level. The wealth component of a community is just the sum (or average) of the wealth levels of individual households. For capabilities, I used the following measures: collective construction projects, whether of civic or private buildings; stability of residence; population growth; persistence (longevity) of settlement; and resilience to external shocks. My logic is that these markers signal that community residents had options or capabilities beyond the level of poor, subsistence farmers to pursue the kinds of life they preferred (for details, see M. E. Smith 2019c). A major reason they were able to do this was their participation in smallholder intensive agriculture (Netting 1993); see Chapter 5. This approach, based explicitly on the ideas of Amartya Sen (Sen 1999; Stiglitz et al. 2010), is now starting to be applied by archaeologists (Arponen et al. 2016; Hegmon

Case Study 26 Teotihuacan: Palaces for Everyone

When the Aztec peoples settled in central Mexico after their migration from Aztlan, they marveled at the ruins of huge pyramids arranged along an impressive avenue. They gave the place its name – Teotihuacan – and made it the setting for their myths of creation. It would not have looked all that different from its condition today (Figure 7.7). While much public and archaeological attention have been directed at the pyramids and their rich offerings (Shaer 2016; Sugiyama 2005), other contexts at Teotihuacan provide unique new insights into life in the city.

7.7. Air photo of Teotihuacan from 1965. Companía Mexicana de Aerofoto, used with permission.

Flourishing from the first through the sixth centuries CE, Teotihuacan was the largest city in the New World at that time (with a population of 100,000). It exhibited a level of urban planning not seen before or after in the New World (Smith 2017c). Insights on urban life come from two types of fieldwork at the site. First, the Teotihuacan Mapping Project created the iconic map of the site (Millon et al. 1973); see Figure 1.5. This map showed that the unique residential form of Teotihuacan – the apartment compound – was replicated over the entire extent of the site, with several thousand examples. That project also collected surface artifacts from all of these structures, a source of continuing insights on life and society in the ancient city (Millon and Altschul 2015; Robertson 2015). The second kind of fieldwork focused on urban life at Teotihuacan has been the excavation of these apartment compounds.

Life in Apartment Compounds. When the pioneering Mexican archaeologist Laurette Séjourné finished the first full excavation of an apartment compound (called Zacuala; Figure 7.8), she titled her report "A palace in the city of the Gods" (Séjourné 1959). She assumed that a well-constructed building with large and spacious rooms, open patios with drains, whose walls were covered with mural paintings of elaborate scenes, must be a palace. But as evidence came in from other excavations, it became clear that Zacuala was

Case Study 26 (cont.)

7.8. The Zacuala compound, a typical apartment compound at Teotihuacan.
Photograph by Michael E. Smith. The Pyramid of the Sun is visible in the background.

not anomalous. Most of the apartment compounds were just as luxurious. It may sound strange to say it, but the majority of the residents of ancient Teotihuacan lived in palaces! This signals an unprecedented level of wealth and prosperity for the residents of this city.

Nearly half of the interior space of the Zacuala apartment compound (Figure 7.8) is common space (the open courtyard in the middle and its surrounding rooms and platform). There are four dwellings, each with an average of 520 square meters of living space (not counting the common area). As shown in Table 6.1, the Teotihuacan average (which is smaller than the dwellings in Zacuala) is much larger than commoner dwellings in other Mesoamerican cities. The Teotihuacan Mapping Project also identified a series of fancier and more elaborate compounds that they called *high-status residences*. While these compounds are smaller overall, they housed fewer households than the regular compounds; their average dwelling size is 1,570 square meters per household (Smith et al. 2019). As shown in Table 6.1, Teotihuacan had a smaller elite-commoner difference than most Mesoamerican cities, largely because commoner dwellings were quite large.

Living quarters were arranged around a small central patio, open to the sky. The mural paintings that adorned most interior walls were luxurious in several respects. They were true fresco paintings, whose pigments were fused with lime-based cement, using a process very similar to that used by Michelangelo to paint the Sistine Chapel (Magaloni 2017). Production of the cement took considerable effort: limestone had to be quarried at a distant location, burned in an oven, and transported to Teotihuacan (Barba Pingarrón and Córdova Frunz 2010). The paintings were well executed in technique and style. In Renaissance Europe, fresco painting was mostly limited to churches and the residences of the wealthiest elites. At Teotihuacan, many or even most residents enjoyed such art in their homes. Also, most residents had ready access to several types of imported goods, including ceramic types and obsidian.

Comparative Insights. Archaeologists still do not have a clear understanding of the economic basis of the wealth and luxury of the residents of Teotihuacan. We know that Teotihuacan artisans produced tools of obsidian (and some other goods) and traded them throughout Mesoamerica, but

Case Study 26 (cont.)

it seems unlikely that this one industry could finance such a system of wealth and luxury at the site. It is tempting to relate this prosperity to the likely collective rule at Teotihuacan (Carballo 2020), although some archaeologists continue to promote a view of strong autocratic rulership in the city (Sugiyama 2022). But regardless of their specific economic and political contexts, the apartment compounds of Teotihuacan show that class differences were muted in this city, and that its commoners enjoyed a surprising level of prosperity.

Case Study 27 Odense: High-Definition Archaeology and Medieval Life

Another perspective on prosperity and the quality of urban life is provided by the medieval town of Odense in Denmark. Like most medieval European towns, the remains of early Odense lie buried under the modern city of the same name. Today the city is famous as the birthplace of Hans Christian Andersen, but its early history is now becoming known in some detail in part through what is called *high-definition archaeology*. This refers to the application of new methods that allow a higher analytical resolution for archaeological data. Techniques such as the chemical sourcing of artifacts, geophysical prospection, or accelerator methods of radiocarbon dating allow archaeologists to focus on more detailed and fine-grained aspects of artifacts and sites. Odense is one of the targets of a program of high-definition archaeology by the Centre for Urban Network Evolutions at Aarhus University in Denmark.

A map from 1593 (Figure 7.9) shows the town of Odense at the end of the medieval period. Ruins of a Viking ring-fort just outside the town (visible at the bottom of the map) provide evidence of activity in the late tenth century CE (see Figure 4.11 for another such ring-fort). This feature marks the start of a period of strategic importance for Odense within the Danish and German kingdoms (Runge and Henriksen 2018).

7.9. Map of Odense in 1593. Note the Viking ring-fort in the foreground. From the town atlas of Braun and Hogenberg, 1572–1617, volume 5, map 30; see van der Krogt (2008); Braun and Hogenberg (2008). Public domain.

Case Study 27 (cont.)

7.10. Medieval wood-stave bowl excavated in Odense. Photograph by Jens G. Aagaard, Odense City Museums. Reproduced with permission.

Life in an Early Medieval Town. In 2013–2014, the Odense City Museums undertook a rescue excavation in the middle of the city, uncovering deposits from the tenth through sixteenth centuries. The application of a variety of high-definition methods to the finds gives a picture of a prosperous town deeply engaged in early medieval northern European trade and information networks. A major growth of imports coincided with an increase in the size of northern European cargo ships after 1180. Most abundant was German stoneware, but ceramic objects were also imported from Belgium, France, and England; grinding stones from Norway; barrels from Germany, Poland, and Belgium; lead ingots from Wales; and whale bones and walrus tusk from Norway (Haase and Hammers 2021). Imported foods included figs and hops (Hammers 2018). High-definition methods were responsible for many of these identifications. For example, a new approach to mass spectrometry allows rapid analysis of many samples of faunal material (Brandt et al. 2018). This technique not only identified a walrus-tusk gaming piece, but it also showed that the leather of cattle, goats, and sheep were all used to make shoes.

Over one hundred wood stave vessels (Figure 7.10), whole or fragments, were recovered in the excavations. Technical analysis of the wood reveals that these were constructed from spruce, a species of tree not introduced into Denmark until the eighteenth century. Most likely made in Germany, the fluorescence of these vessels after 1300 coincided with three key developments. First was an expansion of trade by merchants of the Hanseatic League (Gaimster 2014), who likely brought the vessels to Denmark. Second was a switch from locally gathered bog myrtle to imported hops as a flavoring for beer in Denmark. The third development was the adoption of German and continental eating and drinking practices. The wood stave vessels were fine drinking vessels for wine or beer.

At some point in the life history of individual wood-stave vessels – most likely after they became worn or broken – their use underwent a radical change. Many of these items were recovered from latrines, where they were associated with artifacts used in personal hygiene: fragments of leather, sticks, and various kinds of bowls. The logical conclusion is that later in their life, wood-stave vessels were used as water containers for personal rinsing in urban latrines (Haase and Hammers 2021).

Comparative Insights. The high-definition methods applied to excavated remains from medieval Odense provide direct evidence for a wide variety of imported goods from throughout northern Europe and Scandinavia. The exotic origins and reconstructed uses of these goods – particularly items like the wood-stave vessels – point to a town of increasing prosperity as it was drawn into the commercial networks of the time. For archaeological reconstructions of ancient urban life, these results are only a start; new discoveries from high-definition methods are now coming at a faster rate, all over the world.

2016; Munson and Scholnick 2021; Vésteinsson et al. 2019). The previous two case studies, although not framed explicitly in terms of Sen's approach, are premodern cities where prosperity and quality of life were particularly high. Classic-period Teotihuacan and medieval Odense seem to show high levels of prosperity for their residents. As this approach to ancient households and communities is extended, it should become clear whether these were exceptions, or whether this was a more regular pattern in the past.

URBAN LIFE THROUGH THE AGES: INSTITUTIONS AND GENERATIVE PROCESSES

For much of the twentieth century, social scientists painted a negative view of urban life. They had a romantic view that life and society were better before the Industrial Revolution, and that modern changes led to the decline of traditional values and family bonds and the rise of anomie, crime, poverty, and a host of other negative consequences (Nisbet 1966). The migration of poor farmers into cities was singled out as a major source of social disintegration (Wirth 1938). Ethnographer Oscar Lewis was the first to point out the flaws of this viewpoint. In an article titled "Urbanization without Breakdown," Lewis (1952) described migrants to Mexico City, who maintained the same kind of family structure they had previously in their village of origin. Religion remained strong and crime was rare, and many practices and beliefs from their original village changed little. If twentieth-century cities in the United States were places of social breakdown, crime, and anomie, Lewis argued, this was not due to the urbanization process per se, but rather to wider institutional forces and conditions.[2]

The work of Oscar Lewis points to the importance of broad structural forces – particularly the nature of government and the overall economic system – in shaping urban life. These are the external political and economic forces depicted in my basic model (Figure 1.9). Population size and density were also important determinants of the nature of urban life. But when we look more closely at urban life itself, it is composed of the two interwoven realms of institutions and generative processes (Figure 6.1).

If one were to accept the claim of Thomas Hobbes that life without the state was a "war of all against all" (see Chapter 4), then government and its associated institutions, as described in Chapters 4 and the current chapter, should be

---

[2]   Oscar Lewis received an inordinate amount of poorly conceived criticism and bad publicity over the decades. His concept of the "culture of poverty" (Lewis 1960) was criticized strongly for many years for supposedly "blaming poverty on the poor" (Leacock 1971). But Lewis was a materialist – a Marxist – who attributed poverty to the operation of the capitalist economy. Harvey and Reed (1996) detail the distortions and biases that led to the public vilification of Lewis for supposedly promoting ideas that were, in fact, antithetical to his own views.

sufficient to explain the nature of urban life. But, as any student of anthropology knows, Hobbes was wrong (Widerquist and McCall 2017). Small-scale societies had – and have – innumerable ways to keep order and thrive in the absence of kings, states, and empires. The small scale of campsites and villages allows frequent interactions and monitoring of others. Families and households play major roles in keeping order. Disputes are settled in time-worn methods, from ridicule to shunning to arbitration among groups (Harris 1989; Taylor 1982). These are generative forces: people acting together, without institutional control, to create the lives and societies they desire. The grassroots actions of households and people in neighborhoods, as described in the present chapter, were a crucial part of life in premodern (and contemporary) cities. In Chapters 6 and 7, I have provided an answer to one of the major questions of urban life, as articulated by Alan Latham (2009): How do cities manage to generate order despite their size and heterogeneity? The short answer is, institutions and generative forces.

EIGHT

THE VALUE OF PREMODERN CITIES TODAY

THE PREMODERN CITIES AND SETTLEMENTS DISCUSSED IN THIS BOOK have value today in a variety of domains, both local and general. Locally, each settlement we document from the past – whether through archaeology or history – reveals something of the early inhabitants of an area. Any archaeological study of an ancient settlement begins with its specific context. We do fieldwork in order to learn something about *these* ruins in *this* location. For the archaeologist, the specific localized remains have scientific value of their own, and broader interpretations must be built on this foundation.

A local perspective on early settlements also has heritage value beyond archaeology. Residents of the area today may take an interest in the ancient history of *their* town or region. The Roman amphitheater in Paris is an example (Figure 8.1). Built in the first century CE, this arena held fifteen thousand spectators. It fell into ruin and its location was lost until rediscovered in the 1860s. A citizens group that included writer Victor Hugo petitioned municipal officials to preserve the structure. Excavations were done in the late nineteenth and early twentieth century. In the photo you can see the apartment buildings that cover part of the Roman structure. While this is a rather minor feature in a city full of notable historic buildings, the amphitheater provides a focal point in its neighborhood and serves as a reminder of the Roman occupation two thousand years ago.

Many ruins of ancient cities are not as fortunate as the Paris amphitheater; conditions in the modern world have damaged or destroyed many sites. I begin

8.1. Ruins of a Roman amphitheater in a residential area of Paris, France. Photograph by
Michael E. Smith.

the chapter by linking this topic to the question of the ownership of ruins.
I then turn to their scientific value. This entire book can be considered an
argument for the scientific value of early cities and settlements. They provide
information about their encompassing societies; they furnish facts to help build
a body of knowledge of early urban settlements; and they form a source of
insights for an understanding of broader patterns of urbanism in the past, the
present, and the future.

WHO OWNS THE PAST?

Visitors rarely pause to ask who owns an archaeological site. Most of the ruins
of early cities that have spectacular remains – and are tourist destinations – are
owned by a government at some level. Many such ruins were once privately
owned. In 1839, for example, explorer John Lloyd Stephens purchased the
Maya ruins of Copan for $50 (Stephens and Catherwood 1854), but today they
belong to the government of Honduras. If owned by a government, there is
usually a plan for the conservation and preservation of ruins. But less spectacular
remains – perhaps a scatter of potsherds and a few temple platforms in a rural
area – may be on private property, and not officially protected. When we
consider the objects and artifacts excavated from ancient urban sites, the
question of ownership takes on a different kind of importance. Stone reliefs

from Angkor, polychrome burial vessels from Tikal, and a host of other remains have been stolen and carried off as parts of an international market in illicit antiquities.

A Multitude of Laws and Practices

The question "Who owns the past?" has a variety of answers. Here are some categories of ownership of both sites and portable objects:

1. **Commercial, private ownership.** In the United States, and some other countries, archaeological remains belong to the owner of the land where they are located, unless there is special government protection and ownership. My house sits on former agricultural fields of the Hohokam culture in Arizona. If I were to uncover the remains of an ancient house or canal while digging in my yard, I am free to do what I like: preserve them, destroy them, or sell them. Many valuable objects from ancient urban sites are in private ownership; these may have been illegally obtained and/or illegally exported from the country of origin and/or illegally purchased. Such objects may or may not be available for study by scholars, and they are rarely seen by the public. This robs the objects of their ability to inform scholars and the public about their past context.

2. **National patrimony.** Some nations assert blanket ownership of all archaeological remains, whether found on private or public land. This is the case in Mexico. When Mexicans find remains, they must report them to the government (the National Anthropology and History Institute). Private collections are only permitted if they are registered with the Institute. One implication of this policy – for foreign archaeologists like me – is that we are not allowed to bring artifacts out of Mexico (except for small samples for technical analysis, which can be exported with a permit from the Institute). A broader implication is that many landowners worry about letting archaeologists onto their property. If we were to find an important site, the government could theoretically seize the land. Although this rarely happens, it does not prevent landowners from distrusting archaeologists. A slightly different situation exists in Denmark, where the government has control, but not always ownership, of archaeological sites and objects. When one encounters archaeological remains, one must notify the National Museum, which makes a decision about how to handle the finds.

3. **Government organizations.** While government agencies, universities, museums, and other organizations only occasionally own archaeological sites, they often curate major collections of artifacts from urban sites. These are often made available for study by researchers, and selected objects may be put on display for the public.

4. **Other public institutions.** Private universities, museums, and other organizations may also own objects from archaeological sites. Such organizations may be more restrictive in their access policy, and they are more likely than government institutions to deaccession (i.e., sell) collections to pay the bills or clear out storage space.

5. **Descendants of the ancient inhabitants.** In some settings, modern indigenous groups whose members are descended from the inhabitants of known sites are granted ownership of the artifacts and human remains – but rarely whole sites – of their ancestors. The US legislation known as NAGPRA (North American Graves Protection and Repatriation Act) requires museums and other institutions to deliver to Native American tribes those human remains and associated objects that came from the sites of their ancestors (Mihesuah 2000). The historical connections between remains and tribes today can be the subject of dispute and lawsuits.

This variation in the potential owners of archaeological sites and artifacts makes the question "Who owns the past?" a complex one. When we go beyond legal ownership to examine the stakeholders in local heritage remains, the arena grows even larger. Local communities, whether or not people are descendants of those who once lived at the site, often have a strong interest in nearby remains. Nation states often take an interest in the remains in their territory, regardless of legal ownership. And the advent of the category of "World Heritage Site," granted by the United Nations Educational and Scientific Organization, recognizes the interest of people around the world in heritage sites, regardless of their national location.

Looting and the Antiquities Trade: The Dark Side of Private Ownership

The ruins of many of the earliest cities – with rich remains of tombs and palaces – are located in nations that are relatively poor today. In the age of imperialism and colonialism, antiquities from these sites were carried off by European adventurers and early archaeologists for museums in the imperial capitals. Figure 8.2 shows a huge stone sculpture from Nineveh in Mesopotamia arriving at the British Museum in London in 1852. Numerous ancient urban sites have been damaged by looting in the past few centuries, but the looting of valuable goods from the ruins of ancient cities is nothing new.

When Leonard Woolley excavated the so-called death pits at Ur (royal tombs; see Case Study 28), he found that fourteen of the sixteen royal graves had been looted in antiquity. The remains had been disturbed long ago: valuable objects were missing, and Woolley identified ancient looters' tunnels (Woolley and Moorey 1982). Such ancient looting has been documented at urban sites from Mexico to Egypt to China. But today, looting of sites has

8.2. Ancient reliefs stolen from Nineveh arrive at the British Museum in 1852. *Illustrated London News*, February 28, 1852. Public domain.

become a big business, carried out by professional tomb robbers, poor peasant farmers, and organized crime syndicates, all aided and abetted by collectors of ancient art and the high-end art dealers of New York City, Tokyo, and London.

The contrast between the rich remains from ancient ruins and the current poverty and insecurity in those regions has led to simple collecting as well as deliberate looting. Such activities cover a wide range, from low-level collecting to full-time specialized looting as an occupation. At the low end of the scale, most peasant farmers in central Mexico have a shoebox full of ceramic figurines, spindle whorls, and obsidian blades, collected in agricultural fields over the years. Similarly, most farmers in the United States today have collections of arrowheads that have turned up on their land. One step up in intensity are recreational looters – people who destroy sites to find artifacts to bring home. At the other extreme, the rich tombs of Colombia – often full of gold objects – are targeted by professional tomb robbers called *huaqueros*. It has been estimated that more than fifty thousand huaqueros operate in the country today (Atwood 2004).

Looting and site destruction can be stimulated by war and political instability. The chaos and fighting that accompanied the US invasion of Iraq, for example, led directly to the looting of the Baghdad Museum and destructive digging in numerous Mesopotamian sites (Emberling and Hanson 2008; Stone 2008). But most of the commercially induced destruction of early urban sites occurs in remote jungles or deserts, in countries whose limited resources cannot protect the thousands of remote sites within their borders. Classic-period Maya sites have been particularly vulnerable; many are hidden away in the jungle, far from modern cities, and they yield extremely valuable objects. An intact Maya polychrome vase from a burial can sell for several tens of thousands of dollars on the international antiquities market, and a piece of a stone monument carved with hieroglyphs can fetch hundreds of thousands of dollars.

Archaeologist Ian Graham spent decades visiting remote Maya sites – often hiking through the jungle for days at a time – to photograph and draw the hieroglyphic inscriptions before they were stolen or damaged. He produced an extremely valuable series of publications that continues today (starting with Graham 1975). When he arrived with a small crew at the site of La Naya in 1971, the noise they made setting up camp alerted looters, who were in the process of plundering the site. Graham's guide was shot and killed by a looter, and the rest of his crew had to flee into the jungle to escape (Graham 2010:349–354). His autobiography – a fascinating read – is filled with stories of looting and its consequences. Most museums in the United States follow a UNESCO convention that defines ancient (foreign) objects that entered the United States after 1974 as stolen property. One museum displayed a newly acquired Maya monument, claiming to have the proper paperwork showing it had been in the United States since before that date. A Maya specialist, however, had photographed the monument in situ at a site in Guatemala only a year or two previously! Falsified paperwork is a real problem in the museum world.

Conditions are even worse in the commercial art world. Art dealers are far less diligent than museums in limiting their trade to legally obtained antiquities. Some wealthy art collectors have collections superior to those of most museums. This leads to dilemmas for scholars: Should we study these collections or not? Archaeologists like the late Michael Coe work with private collectors regularly, and study and publish their looted and stolen materials (Graham 2010:442–445). To them, the information value of these objects is just too high to ignore. Others, such as the late Robert Sharer, refused to have anything to do with private collectors or collections. When an archaeologist validates these collections, and publishes the objects, their commercial value can only increase. The resulting higher prices for illicit antiquities may in turn stimulate additional looting and site destruction.

Philosopher of science Alison Wylie (1996, 2002) has analyzed the ethical issues involved in the relationships between archaeologists and owners of private collections of looted objects. She finds that individual scholars make decisions about where to draw the line in reference to the trade-off between the new information that can be gleaned from materials in private collections, versus the increased damage to the archaeological record that may result from looting caused by higher prices for illicit antiquities. Should scholars have refused to use the Rosetta Stone just because it was looted? Should archaeologists bolster and support the illegal market in stolen antiquities just to record a few more Maya polychromes? These are some of the ethical issues involved at the interface between urban ruins, archaeologists, and the illicit international market for antiquities (Barker 2018; Brodie 2014; Tremain and Yates 2019).

SCIENTIFIC VALUE

This book is about the scientific value of premodern cities. As discussed in Chapter 1, I avoid the nonscientific and antiscientific strains of scholarship that infect much of archaeology today. My career-long goals – for excavating urban and rural sites in Mexico, for comparing them to other ancient cities, and for developing a comparative and transdisciplinary urban framework – are to develop a body of data and theory to understand premodern urbanism from a scientific perspective. In Chapter 1, I describe my views of science and archaeology as a science (Smith 2017b). One of the central components of this approach is comparison: the methods and procedures for rigorous comparative analysis.

Why Is a Comparative Perspective So Important?

I will suggest four kinds of answers to the question of why a comparative perspective is important (M. E. Smith 2018; Smith 2020a): discovery, generalization, causality, and broader professional benefits.

(1) Discovery. Two reasons to compare cities and urban systems aid in the discovery of new information and perspectives. First, one compares in order to better understand a given case. Archaeological remains are localized, consisting of individual buildings, sites or regions. Given the importance of analogy – a kind of comparison – for understanding the social implications of archaeological remains (Chapter 1), it is almost impossible to say anything interesting about a given site without some kind of comparison. All archaeologists use comparative data this way to illuminate their finds, whether or not they are interested in a generalizing approach. Not surprisingly, attention to explicit and systematic comparisons – including concern with sampling and other aspects of comparative methods – produces richer, stronger, and better archaeological interpretations of individual cases than hasty comparisons using a few ad hoc examples (Smith 2015). Second, comparison is valuable in order to identify new processes and patterns. A particular city or urban topic that one focuses on may, when compared to other examples, create insights into new patterns that can be evaluated with additional research.

(2) Generalization. Two aspects of generalization arise from comparisons. First, comparison allows a researcher to generalize about a phenomenon. The purpose of this book is to generalize about premodern cities. I use the term *generalize* not in its vernacular sense (an unwarranted inference from too few cases) but rather in its scientific definition (an inductive process that compares cases to draw conclusions about phenomena). I seek to generate knowledge about the variability and continuities in settlements around the world and through history. This would clearly be impossible without comparison. Second, comparison is required in order to distinguish the unique from the universal. As a Mesoamerican city, Teotihuacan was unique in a number of respects, including the extent of its orthogonal planning (Smith 2017c). Yet its inhabitants participated in a near-universal Mesoamerican cult based on specific gods of rain and storms (Carballo 2016). This knowledge of unique and universal features can only come from comparing Teotihuacan with other Mesoamerican settlements. Inadequate attention to comparison has led to many incorrect conclusions about premodern cities. For example, even the great historical sociologist Max Weber (1958) claimed falsely that the defensive wall was a universal feature of premodern cities (Chapter 4), a clear failure of his comparative method.

(3) Causality. Comparison is necessary in a historical science like archaeology in order to uncover causal dynamics. Causation in the human sciences is a complex issue, one that archaeologists have tended to ignore in recent decades. But some notion of causality — whether of traditional causal forces or systems models with feedback — is required for a scientific approach to premodern cities. Because of the difficulty of applying statistical models of causality to archaeological data, archaeologists must be satisfied with more informal causal models; my basic dynamic model (Figure 1.9) is an example. While I cannot demonstrate definitively that this model is correct (or incorrect), I believe that the findings presented in this book support the model. Whether one is using formal causal methods (Pearl and Mackenzie 2018), causal mechanisms (Bunge 2004; Demeulenaere 2011), a natural experiment model (Diamond and Robinson 2010), or an informal causal scheme (Blanton and Fargher 2008), comparative data — and rigorous comparative methods — are crucial if we are to understand how societies and cities worked in the past, and how they changed (Hoyer and Manning 2018). But before we can start talking about causal dynamics and the other advantages of comparative analysis, archaeologists need well-excavated remains to work from. Leonard Woolley's excavations at Ur in Mesopotamia stand as a major fieldwork project that was ahead of its time for urban archaeology.

(4) Professional benefits. Comparative analysis has a number of additional professional benefits for research on early cities and societies. First, it helps

counter the creeping recentism that affects most historical disciplines. *Recentism* refers to a trend that sees research and publication progressively ignoring early periods and concentrating increasingly on the very recent past; for example, medieval history has been replaced by modern history in many journals and books (Jones 2004; Sluyter 2005). A second benefit of comparison is that it promotes synthesis. In a number of scientific disciplines, efforts have been directed at the assembly of published data from many sources and promoting its re-analysis in order to draw new conclusions (Hackett and Parker 2016; Rodrigo et al. 2013). Archaeologists have only just begun to turn to formal synthesis (Altschul et al. 2017), and this is a trend with much potential for the future.

Case Study 28 Ur: Top-Down and Bottom-Up Forces in Early Mesopotamia

Ur is the best-known ancient city in Mesopotamia – well-known as a major capital in its heyday, and well-known today through excavations and tourist visits. Ur flourished from around 2900 to 1800 BCE, ruled by a series of dynasties. The site was extensively excavated by Leonard Woolley from 1922 to 1934. Although Woolley concentrated his efforts on the major civic architecture in Ur's epicenter, and on spectacular royal burials, he also cleared several residential areas (Woolley 1927–65; Woolley and Moorey 1982). The extensive records of his excavations reveal the operations of both top-down and bottom-up forces in the ancient city. Cuneiform texts provide historical and contextual details about the dynasties and society of Ur.

Shops, Temples, and Death Pits. Woolley's excavations made headlines around the world when he uncovered a series of royal graves with remarkable offerings. Dating early in the history of the city (the Early Dynastic III period, ca. 2600–2400 BCE), the kings and queens of the Ur city-state were buried in deep graves with rich offerings, including human retainers and objects of gold and fine stones (Zettler et al. 1998). Woolley located the sloping ramps used to convey the individuals and offerings down to the tomb. One richly ornamented female was identified in an inscription (on a cylinder seal) as Queen Puabi. In the press, the graves were called "death pits." Up to eighty human bodies were carefully arranged in rows, many with elaborate jewelry and costumes. Although the height of power and influence of Ur rulers would not occur for another three or four centuries, these graves show the wealth and opulence of rulers – both men and women – in the Early Dynastic period. The rich and elaborate tomb offerings are on display in the British Museum and at the University of Pennsylvania, the sponsors of Woolley's fieldwork.

Woolley also excavated the ziggurat and other buildings in an enclosed compound known as the *temenos* (a walled precinct containing civic and religious buildings). A ziggurat is a pyramid with a temple on its flat summit, very similar in form to Aztec and Mayan temple-pyramids. The ziggurat at Ur was built later than the royal burials, during the so-called Third Dynasty of Ur (ca. 2100–2000 BCE). King Ur-Nammu, famous for creating the earliest known written law code (Finkelstein 1968), began construction of the ziggurat, which was finished by his successor, Shulgi. With a height of over thirty meters, this was a monumental construction, designed to showcase royal power (Chapter 4).

While early archaeologists in the Near East typically focused on the monumental buildings and spectacular offerings from urban epicenters (Figure 8.2), Leonard Woolley was ahead of his time in devoting effort to excavating residential neighborhoods at Ur. He cleared several such areas, the largest of which is called Area AH. Extrapolating from Woolley's plans, architect Finn Barnow (2001:51) created

Case Study 28 (cont.)

a reconstruction drawing of Ur in the Isin-Larsa period, immediately following the Third Dynasty period (Figure 8.3). The pattern of twisting lanes and irregular, close-packed houses was later encountered in excavations at other southern Mesopotamian cities. Many of the houses at Ur had a small room opening onto the street, and Woolley interpreted these as shops (Woolley and Moorey 1982:202), following a logic similar to that applied to Olynthus (Case Study 25). He also excavated several craft workshops.[1]

Comparative Insights. Excavations at Ur have produced considerable scientific knowledge on a wide range of topics, from royal burials to household and neighborhood forms. Woolley's results are particularly noteworthy for highlighting both the top-down and bottom-up forces that shaped urban life in Ur.

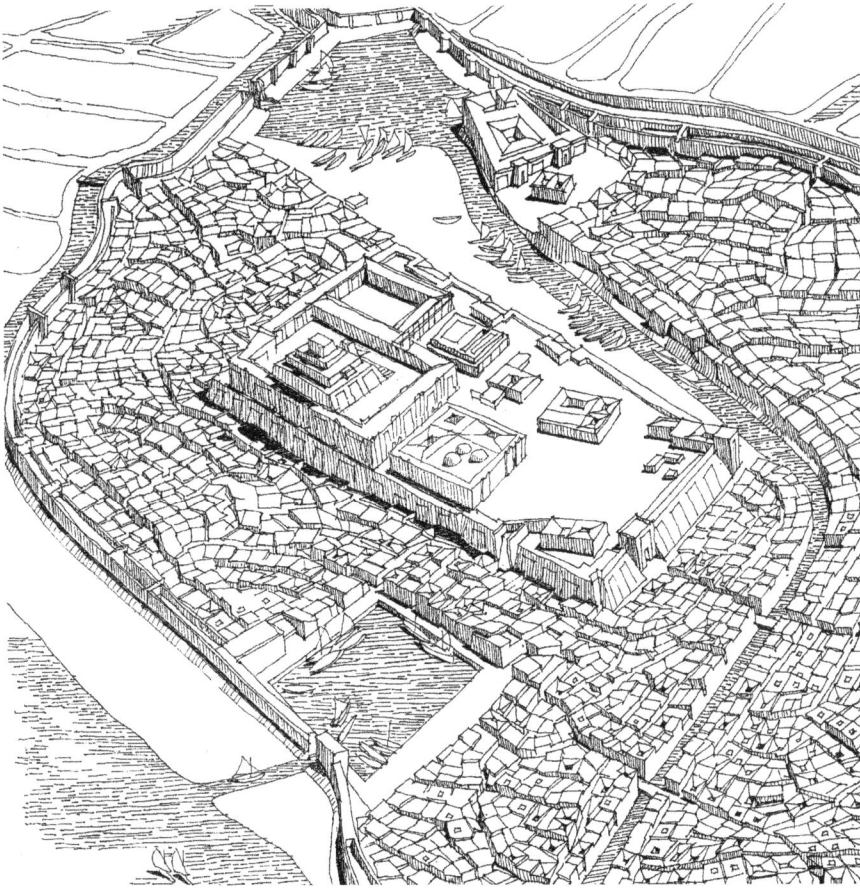

8.3. Reconstruction of Ur in the second millennium BCE. Source: Barnow (2001:51). Drawing by Claus Roloff, from the Cities and Modes of Production project. Reproduced with permission.

[1] Woolley's dig house at Ur was the model for the setting of Agatha Christie's mystery novel *Murder in Mesopotamia*. Christie married Woolley's field assistant at Ur, archaeologist Max Mallowan. She once remarked, "An archaeologist is the best husband a woman can have. The older she gets, the more interested he is in her."

Case Study 28 (cont.)

Their expression is shown clearly in Barnow's reconstructed city image (Figure 8.3) in the contrast between planned and monumental temenos and the irregular residential neighborhoods. Although Ur suffered from looting and destruction in the Iraq War, the site is now yielding new archaeological finds. Elizabeth Stone and Paul Zimansky (2016) are excavating at several locations in Ur, and one of their research goals is to illuminate the organization of neighborhoods at the site.

WHAT HAVE WE LEARNED?

The major conclusions of this book can be summarized under five categories as follows.

Definitional issues. My approach to premodern urbanism begins with a scientific perspective on concepts and definitions. Most basically, definitions of city or urban depend on one's goals and research questions (Chapter 1; thesis 1). The concepts of city and urban should not be reified (Chapter 1; thesis 2); in philosopher John Searle's terms, settlements are the brute facts of the archaeological record, and cities are the institutional facts. Scholarship is not advanced by proposing a single, best definition of urban, and then proving that one's settlement conforms to it. For many purposes, settlements are a more useful unit of study than are cities (Chapter 1; thesis 3); indeed urban settlements are not always permanent settlements (Chapter 4).

Energized crowding. Three major causal forces – population, economic processes, and political structures – shaped urban life on a large scale (Figure 1.9; Chapters 1, 3, and 5). Of these, I argue that population size and density are the most important (Chapters 2, 3). Energized crowding is the key process that connects population to urban life (Figure 2.1; Chapters 2, 3; thesis 5). The most important political factors that influence urban life are political status (city-state capitals versus imperial capitals versus administrative centers), and the collective versus autocratic nature of the relevant regime (Chapter 4).

The most important economic factors that influence urban life are the type of economy (command economies versus commercial economies) and the level of commercialization of the economy (Chapter 5). Urban life is shaped directly by both top-down and bottom-up forces (thesis 4). The major top-down (institutional) forces are the central institutions of the political and economic system, social inequality, the royal palace, and urban services (Chapters 6, 7). The major bottom-up (generative) forces are commercial forces, household and neighborhood dynamics, and the processes leading to prosperity or poverty (Chapters 6, 7).

Epicenter planning. The most widespread principle of planning in premodern cities around the world is a carefully planned and laid out urban epicenter with civic architecture, coupled with unplanned residential neighborhoods (Chapter 4). Premodern urban planning was always a political act. Cosmological models for planned layouts were influential in some urban traditions and absent in others (Chapters 4, 6).

Data and methods. Comparative analysis and quantitative data are essential to understanding the nature and functioning of premodern cities (Chapters 1, 3, 8). Semi-urban settlements help our understanding of premodern (and contemporary) cities (Chapters 3 and 4).

Ancient-modern comparisons. With proper attention to questions, methods, and concepts, useful comparisons can be made between premodern and contemporary cities (as discussed later in this chapter). The earliest cities are most similar to those today in processes related to energized crowding, and they differ in processes related to economic and political activities and functions (Chapters 4 and 5).

RESEARCH PRIORITIES

Based on the current status of knowledge and theory in the study of premodern urbanism, I suggest some important priorities for advancing the field within an overall social scientific perspective.

The Built Environment

Many of my suggestions for productive future research directions focus on the built environment;[2] I organize these under four categories: types of buildings, infrastructure, spatial patterns, and social significance.

Types of Buildings. To understand life in premodern cities, the most important type of building is the house. My typology of premodern urban house forms in Chapter 7 needs to be extended. House forms vary widely, both within and between cities and traditions. While I was able to point out some patterns –

---

[2] A more traditional approach to organizing a book like this would be to start with a chapter on the urban built environment; indeed, some books about early cities talk of little else than architecture and built environments (Gates 2011). My approach to premodern cities, in contrast, is grounded in Winston Churchill's observation (quoted in Chapter 4) that "we shape our buildings, and thereafter they shape us." This leads me to embed my discussion of buildings and spaces in chapters organized by social, political, and economic topics.

such as the role of density in structuring house form – much more comparative research is needed. Another type of building requiring more research is the royal palace. Apart from the role of the palace as a seat of power, its activities also structured urban life in a variety of ways (Chapter 6). Surprisingly, the only adequate comparative cross-cultural analysis of such palaces is an obscure book chapter (Sheehy 1996).

The specific forms and types of buildings and spaces vary tremendously among urban traditions, making this a difficult topic for comparative analysis. One comparative claim at a larger scale is Bruce Trigger's (1990:121) contrast between buildings in the early states and those in the Classical world: "The early civilizations provide few examples of elaborate public amenities, such as baths, stadia, gymnasia, libraries, schools, theatres, and aqueducts, which are found in the classical civilizations of Greece and Rome." Greg Woolf (2020) suggests that this flourishing of building types in Mediterranean cities derived from the spread of more collective regimes; it "was all about participation" (p. 308). This observation should be tested and extended with research in diverse areas.

Infrastructure. In spite of a growing recognition of the crucial influence of infrastructure on urban life and sustainability in the world today (Boone and Modarres 2006; Ramaswami et al. 2016), our understanding of premodern urban infrastructure remains quite poor. There are some good analyses of specific kinds of infrastructure at individual sites, from Roman streets (Poehler 2017) to water supply and sewage at Mohenjo-daro (Jansen 1989). Conceptual and comparative work by archaeologists, on the other hand, remains at a very simplistic level (e.g., Wilkinson 2019), although some recent advances can be listed (Fafinski 2021; Gabrielsen 2013; Stanley et al. 2012; Stark 2014). In Chapter 3, I note how quantitative measures of infrastructure scale with population in modern cities, a relationship that has now been identified for Roman cities (Hanson et al. 2019).

Given the importance of energized crowding in structuring urban life and society, we still lack a good understanding of the formal open spaces where people interacted in early cities. Such locations are part of a city's infrastructure (Ramaswami et al. 2016); in fact, they served as "social infrastructure" (Klinenberg 2018) for promoting interaction in past cities. Quantitative analyses (Hanson et al. 2019) are important, but we also need better information on just how such spaces were used (Norwood and Smith 2021; Ossa et al. 2017; Wouters et al. 2017) and how they fit into their ancient built environments.

Spatial Patterns. I discuss in Chapters 4 and 6 a very simple spatial model that fits many premodern cities: civic architecture in the center is carefully laid out following planning principles, whereas residential neighborhoods show little spatial planning at all (Smith 2007); clearly, Greek and Roman cities are outliers.[3] Spatial analysis of early cities is a topic where methodological advances are running far ahead of theory and comparative understanding. Geophysical prospection can sometimes uncover entire ancient urban plans when conditions are good (Benech 2007; Corsi and Vermeulen 2012), LiDAR methods have much unrealized potential for urban spatial analysis (Canuto et al. 2018; Chase 2016), and GIS-based techniques can readily create sophisticated spatial models of many phenomena.

But just what data – quantitative and qualitative – should we plot? High priorities would include analyses of variation in land use and density within cities using the spatial equilibrium concept (Klassen et al. 2021b). Can we identify categories of urban land use in the past? In well-studied ancient cities it should be possible to analyze some of the categories of land use as identified by Angel et al. (2016): open space, nonresidential areas, informally divided land, formally divided land, housing projects, and road space; see also Stanley et al. (2012). Until archaeologists can ask relevant questions – framed from appropriate comparative and theoretical perspectives – and code the appropriate data, GIS software will continue to produce attractive maps that teach us little about urban life in the past.

Social Significance of Architecture and Settlement. The obsession of postprocessualist archaeologists with high-level meanings of buildings and cities (e.g., Richards 1994) set archaeologists on an unproductive path that hindered advances in understanding the social significance of architecture and cities.[4] As Amos Rapoport and others have shown (Chapter 4), the culturally specific and idiosyncratic nature of high-level meanings makes them virtually impossible to reconstruct without texts. Middle-level meanings, on the other hand (the ways monumental architecture reflected power, identity, and memory in premodern cities), are now relatively well understood (Smith 2011b); see Chapter 4.

An exciting area of research relates the low-level meaning of buildings to social factors such as density and social complexity. In Roland Fletcher's (1995) model of settlement size, features like rectangular houses, subdivision of space into public and private zones, and the creation of divided lots or yards become necessary as settlements grow in size and density (Chapter 2). In an alternative – and less convincing – model, Susan Kent (1990) attributes these features to socio-political complexity, not demography. The next step is to devise codes

---

[3] The extensive archaeological discussion of spatial models derived from twentieth century urban sociology and geography – such as the concentric zoning models of Burgess and Sjoberg – has yielded few insights. We need new models, derived from current data and theory, not old models by sociologists who knew little about early cities.

[4] See Blanton (1995) for a critique of that volume.

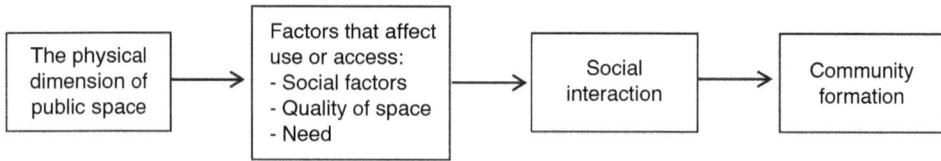

8.4. New Urbanist model relating the built environment to community formation. Diagram by Michael E. Smith, based on Talen (2000:348).

and measures to examine such features quantitatively in a sample of settlements. Lisa Nevett (2010:55) has suggested that houses in the Mediterranean Classical period had a larger number and variety of specialized rooms than in earlier settlements; this intriguing suggestion should be tested. A more general restatement of these questions asks precisely how built environments promote social interaction and community formation; the general view of the New Urbanists is shown in Figure 8.4 (see Chapter 7).

Drivers of Change

The causal diagram that lies at the center of this book – Figure 1.9 – shows my interpretation of drivers of change that create the conditions of urban life in premodern cities. This is an informal causal model because I am not yet able to operationalize the factors in a way that permits formal testing. This model derives from my understanding of the data presented throughout this book. The strong role of population size and density in structuring urban life – particularly as expressed in energized crowding – is demonstrated by the success of research on settlement scaling theory in predicting the quantitative attributes of premodern (and contemporary) cities (Lobo et al. 2020; M. E. Smith 2019a); see Chapter 3. The influence of political and economic forces in shaping urban life is almost a truism; this is something that nearly all treatments of early urban life show clearly (Hassett 2017; Lilley 2002; Sjoberg 1960). My contribution lies in documenting the diversity of political and economic forms in premodern cities, and in linking these forms to the institutional and generative forces that create and shape life in cities (Chapters 4–7).

All of these dynamic elements – particularly their interconnections – need additional research to advance our understanding of urban life in the distant past. We need to know precisely how cities embedded in premodern command economies differed from those in commercialized economies, or the level of impact that external conquest or trade had on urban life. Blanton and Fargher (2011, 2012) have made a start on this kind of question by examining how urban features in their sample of thirty premodern states relate to the autocratic versus collective nature of government regimes, but much more needs to be done. The separation of top-down from bottom-up forces within settlements is only in its infancy in archaeology (Furholt et al. 2020) and promises to be a growth area in the future.

Epistemology and Theory

The previously noted suggestions about research on built environments and drivers of change are close to worthless if pursued using a nonscientific epistemology. As discussed in Chapter 1, the postprocessual theoretical approach and its offshoots (Hodder 2012; Thomas 2015) produce urban research that is tightly focused on individual contexts, antithetical to formal comparative analysis or quantification, and lacking middle-range theory that allows archaeological observations to be transformed into reliable scientific data. Because the practitioners of this kind of archaeology look for inspiration in the realm of literary theory and the humanities – rather than the social sciences – they are often unaware of the larger epistemological and theoretical literature in the social sciences. That literature shows quite clearly the necessity of using a social scientific epistemology if scholars are to build reliable knowledge of social phenomena; several of my recent papers discuss these issues (Smith 2011b, 2015, 2017b, 2021b).

New data are necessary if the field of early urbanism is to advance, but data alone are not sufficient. As more archaeologists approach their research using a scientific epistemology, a variety of methods will contribute to this effort. Formal comparative approaches are paramount (M. E. Smith 2018; Smith and Peregrine 2012). Causality can be investigated through methods like natural experiments (Diamond and Robinson 2010) and process tracing (Bengtsson and Ruonavaara 2017; Mahoney 2012). And, finally, it is hard to see how research on early urbanism can get very far unless the insights, concepts, and data of a variety of disciplines are brought together into a rich, interdisciplinary perspective (Butzer 2008; Graff 2015).

PREMODERN CITIES INTO THE FUTURE

The scientific, comparative perspective I promote implies that early cities can be placed into the same framework as contemporary – and even future – cities. If so, then knowledge of early cities has value for understanding contemporary urbanization in three ways; I call these the urban trajectory argument, the sample size argument, and the laboratory argument. They are all part of a more general rationale for the value of the past for understanding the present: history matters. The following well-known quotations illustrate this point:

> "The farther back we look, the farther ahead we can see"
>
> —Winston Churchill, statesman

> "It is hard to know where you are going if you don't know where you have been"
>
> —Sandra Day O'Connor, former US Supreme Court justice

> "Those who cannot remember the past are condemned to repeat it."
>
> —George Santayana, philosopher

Of course, there are also pithy quotations expressing a contrary sentiment:

> "History is bunk!"
>
> —Henry Ford, industrialist

This is not the place to debate the philosophical and methodological issues surrounding the value of history today (Cohen and Mandler 2015; Guldi and Armitage 2014). Instead, I review the three arguments for the value of premodern cities to help understand urbanism today, and perhaps into the future. But first, just how can we put premodern and contemporary cities into a common framework in order to make comparisons or lessons even possible?

How Can We Connect Archaeological, Historical, and Contemporary Urban Research?

Rigorous comparisons between premodern and contemporary cities are difficult to accomplish, if only because of some basic differences between the two contexts. In comparison with cities today, premodern cities show too few examples, insufficient data about each, more prominent regional/cultural variation, and too many dubious interpretations. Contemporary cities, on the other hand, exhibit contrasting features: too many examples, too much data about each, too much emphasis on western or "W.E.I.R.D." societies,[5] and too many theories and models. I came to appreciate these contrasts while participating in transdisciplinary research projects that compared ancient and modern cities (Dennehy et al. 2016; Smith et al. 2021b; Stanley et al. 2016; York et al. 2011).

Notwithstanding these difficulties, two research strategies can help archaeologists bridge the gap between knowledge of past and present cities: (1) ask comparable social-scientific research questions, and (2) use comparable methods and concepts. Research questions like the following can be studied for both premodern and contemporary cities, and thus can serve as points of comparison and connection:

---

[5] The acronym W.E.I.R.D. stands for societies that are western, educated, industrialized, rich, and democratic. Originally devised as a critique of the bias of samples of people in psychology experiments (Henrich et al. 2010), this concept also highlights biases in scientific knowledge of cities today.

- How does population size relate to density?
- Why do some cities succeed while others fail?
- Why does the quality of life vary so greatly among (and within) cities?
- How do cities affect and respond to their hinterlands?
- What is the relationship between people and the urban built environment?

In contrast, some archaeologists ask research questions of premodern cities that have little correspondence to the modern world, limiting their value for comparison. For example, what is the religious meaning or symbolism of city layouts?

Many methods and concepts are applicable to both premodern and contemporary cities. These include the following:

- Demographic analysis: population size and density
- Methods for scaling urban variables against city size
- Spatial analysis (distributional studies, space syntax, urban morphology, etc.)
- Quantitative measures of inequality, such as the Gini index
- Political concepts (e.g., polity type, autocratic versus collective regimes, direct versus indirect control)
- Economic concepts (e.g., commercialization, division of labor, exchange)
- Social concepts (e.g., social class, inequality, neighborhoods, poverty, and prosperity)

If archaeologists and historians can ask questions that are comparable to those being asked of cities today, and if they can use similar or parallel methods and concepts, then three kinds of arguments can be made for the usefulness or relevance of premodern cities for research and policy work on cities today.

The Urban Trajectory Argument and Urban Sustainability

Archaeologists like to point out that one of our unique contributions to knowledge is the long-term perspective on change that the archaeological record provides (Kintigh et al. 2014; Perreault 2019). Research on contemporary cities operates on time scales of days to years, and the record of urban history typically has a resolution from years to decades (and, occasionally, centuries). Urban archaeology, on the other hand, operates on times scales from decades to millennia. This provides an opportunity for fresh insights on a whole variety of urban issues, from planning to quality of life. Here I concentrate on one such topic: urban sustainability. While there are many definitions of sustainability in the scholarly literature, most works on sustainability science converge on two prominent themes: persistence and quality of life. A sustainable society or city is one that persists through time while providing an adequate quality of life for its residents (Clark and Harley 2020; Kates et al. 2001; Matson et al. 2016; Tainter and Taylor 2014).

Nearly thirty years ago, ecological economists Robert Costanza and Bernard Patten stated, "The basic idea of sustainability is quite straightforward: a sustainable system is one which survives or persists" (Costanza and Patten 1995:193). Most scholars of contemporary urbanism have little idea how long cities will last into the future, and little interest in the history of past settlements (e.g., Ramaswami et al. 2018), although economists have begun looking at urban history for insights into cities today (Bosker et al. 2013; Glaeser 2021). Archaeologists have considerable data on settlement persistence in the past, but the data remain buried in reports and difficult to synthesize (Smith 2010b). In recent papers, my colleagues and I argue that the archaeological and historical record of past settlement persistence holds potential for illuminating issues of urban sustainability today (Crawford et al. n.d.; Smith et al. 2021b). If we can develop rigorous explanations for variation in settlement persistence – why did some settlements last longer than others? – then perhaps those factors can be singled out as drivers of sustainability today.

The second component of sustainability is quality of life. An extension of Amartya Sen's approach to quality of life (Chapter 7) to sustainability science identifies both standard of living and capabilities as building blocks of sustainability (Matson et al. 2016; Sampson 2017; Sen 2013; Simon et al. 2018). As archaeologists continue to develop methods for the analysis of quality of life in cities (Chapter 7), we will be better able to contribute to the broad field of sustainability science. Although archaeologists have made some suggestions about early urban sustainability (Barthel and Isendahl 2013; Woolf 2020:375), this field has yet to see much systematic research.

To give an example of one approach to settlement persistence, Figure 8.5 illustrates the persistence of urban sites in the Yautepec Valley of central Mexico, where my students and I carried out a survey in the 1990s (Smith 2006; Smith et al. 2021a). Each vertical bar is a settlement larger than thirteen hectares (the size of the smallest documented Aztec city-state capital in this region). A few patterns stand out. The earliest urban settlements – founded in the Late Formative period – were located adjacent to the largest and richest expanse of floodplain farmland along the Río Yautepec, and these settlements lasted for two millennia. By contrast, most of the Classic period towns and cities had a much shorter lifespan, corresponding to the interval during which this area was a province of the Teotihuacan empire (Smith and Montiel 2001). When the empire withdrew, the settlements were abandoned. Clearly both environmental and institutional (political) factors are needed to explain settlement longevity or persistence in this region. If archaeologists were to carry out this kind of study – comparative projects with much

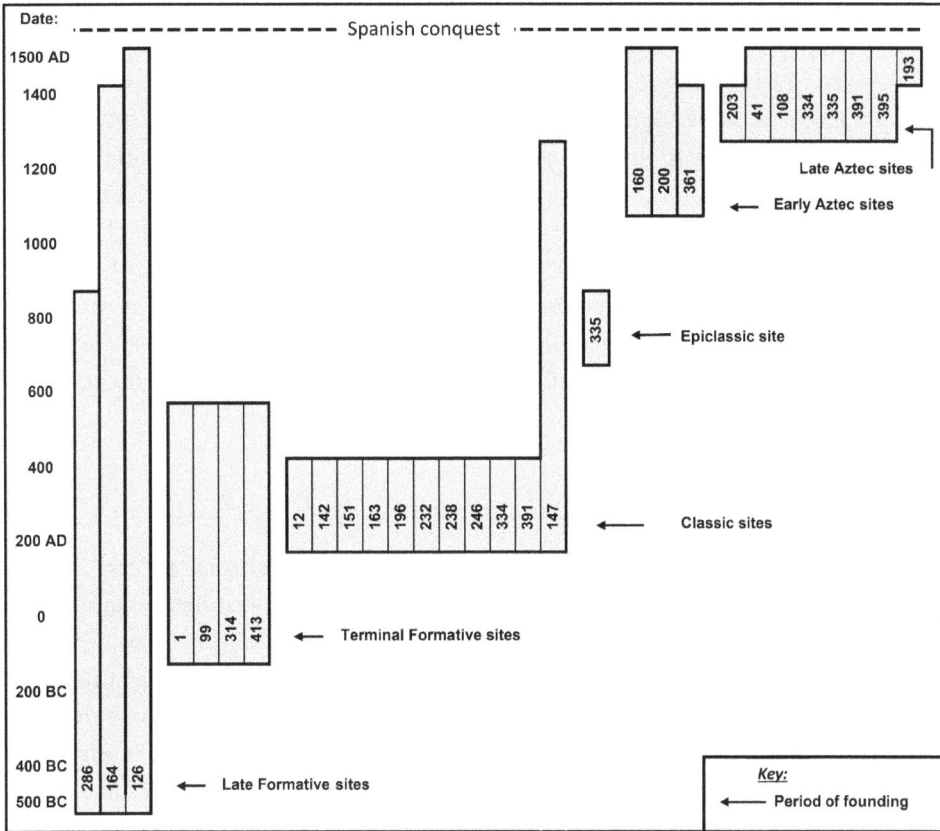

8.5. Persistence (longevity) of pre-Spanish urban settlements (cities and towns) in the Yautepec Valley, Mexico. Each vertical bar is a settlement larger than thirteen hectares, with its site identification number (see text for discussion). Graphic by Michael E. Smith.

greater detail and in many areas – we could gain systematic knowledge about the determinants of past urban sustainability, and these results will likely have relevance to conditions today. The data exist, but no one has done the analysis (Smith 2010b; Smith et al. 2021b).

The Sample Size Argument

The sample size argument states that scholars, planners, and officials can benefit from the larger sample of cases provided by premodern cities. If urban scholars are content to limit their consideration to cities today, then premodern cases have little to offer. On the other hand, if they are interested in general urban patterns that transcend contemporary cities in W.E.I.R.D. nations, then early cities provide a larger sample to examine homogeneity and diversity in a variety of realms. For example, "planning history" is now a discipline of its own (Hein 2017), one that is starting to take early cities seriously as sources of information and even inspiration (Grant 2001; Hakim 2007; Smith 2007; Smith and Hein 2017).

By opening up the domain of cities and urbanism to input from premodern cases, urban scholars can correct errors that have arisen from parochial views of the urban world. I have already discussed Max Weber's erroneous claim that all cities have defensive walls. Other false claims are that all cities have streets (Hillier 1996a), that urban sprawl occurs around all cities in all periods (Bruegmann 2005), that all cities have markets and commercial institutions (see Chapter 5), or even that cities must be permanent settlements (Wirth 1938); see Chapter 4.

The Laboratory Argument and Settlement Scaling

The laboratory argument suggests that premodern cities can serve as a kind of "laboratory" to test models and generalizations formulated for contemporary cities. A more general form of this argument was stated by some historians as follows: "The historical record is one 'laboratory' in which hypotheses developed by sociologists, economists, and even natural scientists can be explicitly tested" (Curtis et al. 2016:751). If early cities show the same patterns as contemporary cities, then a particular model or theory achieves a much greater level of generality. Settlement scaling, outlined in Chapter 3, is the most successful example. First, quantitative empirical regularities identified for systems of cities today were investigated for premodern cities and found to hold for a variety of cases. Next, an explanatory model devised for the modern systems (Bettencourt 2013) was examined and its terms proved applicable to the premodern world (Ortman et al. 2014, 2015), allowing it to be applied to early urban systems. The final step was to infer that the same (or very similar) social and economic dynamics generated the empirical patterns in both contemporary and ancient urban systems (Lobo et al. 2020; M. E. Smith 2019a). Alternatively, there are many models of cities today that are not appropriate for the ancient world because they rely on industrial technology (e.g., smart cities), the capitalist economy (e.g., the urban growth machine), or the legal institutions of modern nation-states (e.g., regulation through zoning laws).

A more diffuse and qualitative example is provided by neighborhoods. In the contemporary world, urban neighborhoods are both important to residents and scientifically crucial for understanding urban organization (Brower 2011; Forrest 2008; Sampson 2012). Is this just a feature of cities today, or does it signal something more general, perhaps a universal role for neighborhoods in urban settlements? Research by historians (Garrioch and Peel 2006) and archaeologists (Arnauld et al. 2012; Pacifico and Truex 2019; Smith 2010a) revealed the prevalence and social importance of neighborhoods in cities throughout the past (Chapter 7). Indeed, neighborhoods seem to be one of the very few urban universals.

In each of these two cases – settlement scaling and neighborhoods – cities of the premodern world served as "laboratories" for investigating the prevalence and nature of urban features first identified for contemporary cities. These cases provide some of the strongest evidence for the value of considering the urban world – past, present, and future – as a single domain. This does not mean that premodern cities are the same as cities today; rather, it means that there are some domains in which *all* cities share key features (e.g., neighborhoods) or properties (e.g., scaling regularities). These domains tend to involve settings and processes in which social interactions lead to energized crowding (M. E. Smith 2019a; Smith and Lobo 2019).

NEW LIFE FROM OLD RUINS

Case Study 29 Fyrkat: Viking Ring-Fort and Heritage Site

Fyrkat was one of the "Trelleborg type" circular fortresses built by King Harald Bluetooth in the late tenth century. It was similar to Aggersborg (Figure 4.11), although smaller. Whereas the fortified ring at Aggersborg has a diameter of 240 meters and contained 48 longhouses, Fyrkat's diameter is 120 meters and it contained 16 longhouses. The site was excavated in the 1950s by C. G. Schultz, and later O. Olsen, both of the Danish National Museum. Fyrkat is one of seven of these fortresses in Denmark and Sweden (Goodchild et al. 2017; Roesdahl 1987; Roesdahl et al. 2014).[6]

Reconstructed Viking Village. When my wife and I visited Fyrkat in 2018, we found the site has two parts. The first is the circular remains of the fortress itself, with the outlines of some of the longhouses marked on the ground. The second part of the site is the "Viking Center Fyrkat," a reconstructed Viking village and living museum that opened near the ruin in 1993. The village contains a full-size reconstruction of a longhouse (Figure 8.6), built with materials and methods that were available to the Viking builders of the site. The interior was furnished using authentic-looking materials, and a woman in Viking dress was spinning thread and answering questions on the Saturday morning we visited.

The Viking Center Fyrkat also includes a blacksmith shop, a barn, and other reconstructed buildings, as well as a modern structure with some exhibits and a closet full of Viking clothes that visitors can try on. We came across a reenactor tending a fire where some fish were being preserved by smoking. He was experimenting with two different ways of smoking the fish, and suggested we return in a few hours to sample the results. One of the outstanding features of the Viking Center Fyrkat is the accuracy of the reconstructions. The buildings were modeled very closely on the actual remains of the excavated village of Vorbasse (Hvass 1979), coupled with detailed, experiment-based knowledge of Viking-era construction methods and materials (Schmidt 1994).

---

[6] See my blog post "Viking Urban Planning," http://wideurbanworld.blogspot.com/2011/05/viking-urban-planning.html.

Case Study 29 (cont.)

8.6. Reconstructed Viking longhouse at Fyrkat, Denmark. Photograph by Malene Thyssen. Creative Commons Attribution–Share Alike 3.0 Unported license. Source: Wikimedia Commons.

8.7. Reenactment at the Moesgaard Viking Moot, Aarhus, Denmark, 2005. Photography by Tone. GNU Free Documentation License. Source: Wikimedia Commons (https://commons .wikimedia.org/wiki/File:Vikings_fight.JPG).

Case Study 29 (cont.)

The Viking Center Fyrkat is part of a series of places promoting Viking-related tourism in Denmark. Viking heritage tourism consists of "museums, heritage centres, theme parks, village reconstructions, and seasonal trading fairs or markets supplemented by the activities of Viking re-enactment of 'living history' societies" (Halewood and Hannam 2001:565). We visited several of these places, including the Viking Museum (remains of excavations, located in the basement of an office building in Aarhus) and the Lindhold Hoeje Viking burial ground and museum. A Viking market was in full swing at this site, with hundreds of tents set up for the weekend and thousands of visitors who came to witness re-enactments of daily life and swordfights, and to buy jewelry and other handcrafted items at stalls (Figure 8.7). Viking heritage sites in Denmark are very popular, with both Danes and foreign visitors like us.

Comparative Insights. Fyrkat and the other Viking heritage sites have two important messages for the study of premodern cities. First, they show how the remains of premodern semi-urban settlements and cities have become highly popular places for tourism today. Tourists are both entertained and educated as they experience a modern version of Viking life and society. Similar stories can be told about many of the archaeological sites that preserve early cities around the world. Furthermore, archaeological remains can be a powerful force for national identity today (Kohl and Fawcett 1995). While they can be used by governments for their own – sometimes nefarious – purposes (Fowler 1987), they also can be the focus of public education about the past. The second message is that heritage sites can bring the real science of archaeology and early urbanism into the public realm. For the Viking case, these findings and reconstructions help counter the misleading popular image of the Viking Age as a time of ceaseless violence and warfare. For premodern cities more generally, they vindicate and promote a scientific approach to research and public education.

The ruins of early cities are places of interest to people today. I have already explored some of the negative effects that arise when sites and artifacts are treated as private property with commercial value: their availability to scholars and the public alike is diminished, and the high price of looted objects can stimulate further looting and destruction. But when ancient urban sites are open to the public, they become important places for tourism, which has value in both the heritage and scientific realms. I illustrate this point with the reconstructed Viking site of Fyrkat in Denmark (Case Study 29).

The Poetry of Ruins

I close with an elegy about the ruins of the city of Chang'an, written in the year 292. The author's reaction to the remains is similar to the way many of us feel when we encounter the architectural ruins of an ancient settlement (Figure 8.8). The living city is no more, and the places that were once active and vibrant are now ruined and fragmentary, leaving only mute stones.

> Street wards are deserted and desolate;
> Town dwellings are sparsely scattered.
> The buildings and offices, stations and bureaus,
> Shops and markets, official storehouses,

8.8. Urban ruins at Umm ar-Rasas, Jordan. Photograph by Daniel Kirk. Public domain. Source: Wikipedia Commons (https://commons.wikimedia.org/wiki/File:Umm_Rasas_House_ruins.JPG).

> Are now concentrated on a single corner of the wall –
> Of a hundred, barely one survives . . .
>
> Great bells have fallen in the ruined temple;
> Bellframes have collapsed and suspend no more
> The forbidden chancellery has turned to thick grass
> (Knechtges and Xiao 2014), pp. 211, 212

For the author of these lines, the deserted ruins evoked a time when Chang'an had been a busy and important place. But Chang'an would grow again, to even greater heights. Within a few centuries, it would become the largest city in the world (Case Study 16), capital of an extensive empire. The rise of Chang'an from the dust is a metaphor for the role that premodern cities can play in the scientific study of cities and urbanism more generally. The ruined buildings and fragmentary pots and tools that are excavated by archaeologists may seem desolate today. But, with proper analysis – using a scientific approach – data can be extracted from these ruins to recreate many aspects of ancient urban life and to place premodern cities within a rich comparative framework that includes cities today and into the future.

APPENDIX A

SOURCES OF POPULATION AND COMMERCIALIZATION DATA FOR THE CASE STUDIES

This appendix describes the origins of the data on the case studies presented in Tables 3.2 (Population) and 5.3 (Commercialization). For the population estimates, I use a household size of five persons for cases where I cannot find a reliable local estimate. I should repeat the caveat mentioned in Chapter 3: This is not any kind of representative sample of premodern cities. The twenty-nine case studies were selected to illustrate specific points in the chapters of this book. While it is certainly valid to discuss the patterns exhibited by these data, this cannot be taken as a reasonable sample for further quantitative analysis.

1 TIKAL

Population. I use a new population estimate for Tikal as described in Dennehy et al. (n.d.). Based on the density categories of settlement at Maya cities published by Canuto et al. (2018), we estimate a population of 7,000 for an area of 1,127 hectares that comprises the urban core, urban, and periurban zones (rural and vacant areas are not included). This area is much smaller than traditional estimates, of which 12,000 hectares (120 square kilometers) is typical (Culbert 1991).

Commercialization. My commercialization score is taken from the project "Service Access in Premodern Cities"; for a discussion of coding procedures, see Smith et al. (2016). Arlen Chase (personal communication, October 2019) sees a more highly commercialized economy for Tikal, adding entrepreneurial merchants and wholesale infrastructure as commercial traits for this city, plus standardized weights and measures and a written accounting system as likely traits. I cannot find published documentation for these features, however.

2 ÇATALHÖYÜK

Population. I begin with the demographic estimates of Cessford (2005), which are evidently accepted by Ian Hodder (2016). These seem far too high, based both on the specific analysis of Bernardini and Schachner (2018), and on my own comparative knowledge of settlement densities. My population is an average of two figures. First, I take the midpoint of all of the minimal estimates of Cessford's calculations (1,750). Second, I increase the proportion of open space from Cessford's 25 to 30 percent to 50 percent, based on the suggestion of Bernardini and Schachner (2018), which yields a midpoint estimate of 3,833. My figure is the average of these two estimates.

Commercialization. Imported goods signal the only commercial institution at this early settlement.

3 PINCEVENT

Population. For the population of Level IV, I multiply four tent-hearth units (houses) by a family size of five persons, for a population of twenty. I measure the total site area (Julien 2003:107) at 1,216 square meters. The camp (settlement) area is approximately 60% of the total area, yielding an estimated settlement area of 730 square meters.

Commercialization. Imported goods signal the only commercial institution at this early settlement.

4 BEIDHA

Population. I use population and area figures from Birch-Chapman et al. (2017:15). They evaluate several alternative methods to estimate populations. My figures are midpoints of the population ranges from their preferred method of estimation, the "storage provisions" formula.

Commercialization. Imported goods signal the only commercial institution at this early settlement.

5 MOHENJO-DARO

Population. The urban population and area data are from Lahiri (1998). My neighborhood population figures are from the HR area, which covers 2.6 hectares. Based on the map of that area (Jansen 1993:38), I made my own rough estimate of seventy-two dwellings, and I used a household size of six persons, for a total of 432 persons in this neighborhood. For comparison, Lahiri (1998) estimates a population of 37,155 for Harappa, in an area of 194 hectares, for a density of 192.

Commercialization. Imports and standardized weights and measures are the only commercial institutions attested at this site (Kenoyer 1998).

6 SW PUEBLOS

Population. I use average figures from a sample of recent historic pueblos published by Dohm (1990).[1]

Commercialization. Imported goods signal the only commercial institution at these settlements.

7 BURNING MAN

Population. The 1996 population of the Burning Man settlement – eight thousand – is from a list of the annual population on Wikipedia. I measured the size of the settlement from a map of the settlement that year, downloaded from the "Burning Man" website (http://burningman.org). This map lacks an absolute scale bar, but gives the scale in units. I assume that the size of the posted map (11 × 17 inches) is the same as the original size, allowing calculation of the area.

Commercialization. Burning Man is not included in the commercialization analysis because it is an avowedly noncommercial settlement that nevertheless has important commercial elements (e.g., the admission charge), while being embedded in a highly commercialized modern economy.

---

[1] These figures are the means of the three variables, measured for ethnographic groups in the early twentieth century. Because of the nature of the distributions, the mean density (given here) differs from the mean population divided by the mean area.

8   ANGKOR

Population. I use the population estimate for Period 5 published in Klassen et al. (2021a:4). They list an area of 3,000 square kilometers for the city in each of the five periods, suggesting to me that the areal extent of the city is not yet well measured. For neighborhood population, I use data from Carter et al. (2018). The temple community of Ta Prohm contains houses and a large temple, all enclosed by a wall. The wall encloses 68.3 hectares. My population estimate is the midpoint of the low and high estimates of Carter et al. Klassen et al. (2021a:4) report a density of thirty-eight persons per hectare for the civic ceremonial center, a region that includes several of the temple communities discussed by Carter and others plus additional neighborhood units.

Commercialization. Commercialization scores are based on an in-person interview with Roland Fletcher in June 2018, at UrbNet, Aarhus University, Denmark.

9   PLAINS AGGREGATION SITES

Population. Although Banks and Snortland (1995) report an average of only forty tepees in a circular camp, Dorsey (1905:9) suggests the presence of up to a thousand families (tipis) in a large aggregation site. Based on data in Dorsey, Fraser (1968:20–21) suggests that the large camps were about one mile in diameter. This yields an area of 201 hectares for a large circular aggregation site. Moore (1987) reports an average number of 5.6 persons per tepee, yielding an estimate of 5,600 persons per large aggregation site.

Commercialization. Imported goods signal the only commercial institution at this early settlement.

10   CAHOKIA

Population. I use figures for the Edelhardt phase, the demographic maximum for the settlement; 12,700 persons in 1.8 square kilometers of "high-density occupation" around Cahokia (Benson et al. 2009:468). For comparison, Lawler (2011) reports that John Kelly estimates the maximal population between 10,000 and 20,000.

Commercialization. Imported goods signal the only commercial institution at this site.

11   SWAHILI CITY–STATE CAPITALS

Population. The figures in Table 3.1 are for Shanga, which covers 15 hectares (Horton 1996). There are 185 houses, which I multiply by a household size of 5 persons to yield a population estimate of 925 persons. This is a particularly small Swahili town, however. Perhaps more typical is Kilwa, approximately 100 hectares in size (Wynne-Jones 2007:372). Use of the density from Shanga would yield a population of 6,200 for Kilwa.

Commercialization. Commercialization scores are based on an in-person interview with Federica Sulas in June 2018, at UrbNet, Aarhus University, Denmark.

12   HUANUCO PAMPA

Population. Murra and Morris (1976:273) state, "But we can tentatively estimate the centre's housing capacity at between 12,000 and 15,000, based on a still tentative calculation of the dwelling space" Wikipedia gives an area of 200 hectares for the site.

Commercialization. Imported goods signal the only commercial institution at this settlement.

13   AMARNA WORKERS VILLAGE

Population. I consider this settlement to be a neighborhood of the larger city of Amarna. It covers an area of ca. 0.5 hectares (Kemp 2012:191). There are seventy-two houses, and I assume a household size of five persons. As a comparison to the very high density of this walled settlement, Amarna's North Suburb has 298 buildings (ca. 1,490 persons) in an area of ca. 30 hectares, which yields a neighborhood density of 50 persons/hectare.

Commercialization. Imported goods signal the only commercial institution at this early settlement.

14   THING SITES

Population. It is not yet possible to estimate the population or the settlement area of a Viking Thing site.

Commercialization. Commercialization scores are based on an in-person interview in June 2018 with Søren Sindbaek (at UrbNet, Aarhus University, Denmark) and follow-up conversations in 2021.

15   PERSEPOLIS

Population. I use my own educated guesswork, as follows. Aminzadeh and Samani (2006) show an area of approximately 120 hectares within the reconstructed city walls (my estimate). I assume that half of the total area is residential, with a density of 100/hectare, yielding a subtotal of 6,000 persons. I assume that the royal palace adds another 500 persons (for the royal family, servants, and others). Therefore, the total population is estimated at 6,500, for a density of 54/hectare.

Commercialization. I scored Persepolis for commercial institutions using three sources. Pirngruber (2017) indicates the presence of traits 2–4, 6, 9, 13, and 14; Van der Spek (2011) documents traits 7, 10, and 13; and Dandamayev (1996) documents trait 1 and scattered information on other traits.

16   CHANG'AN

Population. The areal extent is from Steinhardt (1990:94) and Heng (2014). A population of 1,000,000 is accepted by many specialists (Seo 1986; Xiong 2000:198). Heng's (2014) recalculations produce lower estimates for the total population (700,000) and a higher figure for area (88 square kilometers), but these do not seem any more secure than the standard estimates, which I use in Table 3.1.

Commercialization. My commercialization score is taken from the project "Service Access in Premodern Cities"; for a discussion of coding procedures, see Smith et al. (2016).

17   KNOSSOS

Population. Data are for the Neopalatial period, taken from Whitelaw (2004). I use the midpoints of his high and low estimates of settlement size (60 to 80 hectares) and population (14,000 to 18,000).

Commercialization. Imported goods and standardized weights and measures signal the only commercial institutions at this settlement.

18   OTUMBA

Population. Data are from Smith (2008:152).

Commercialization. Most of the six commercial institutions inferred for Otumba are very likely, based on knowledge of Aztec regional exchange systems and urbanism (Berdan 2014; Hirth 2016; Smith 2008), and the heavy economic activity revealed by archaeological fieldwork at the site (Charlton et al. 1991; Nichols 2013).

19   JERASH

Population. I use the figure of Rattenborg and Blanke (2017) of 85 hectares within the Roman-period walls, assuming a similar size for the Islamic period; see the map in Lepaon (2011). The population is estimated from a density constant – 169 persons/hectare – taken from three well-studied Roman cities (Jack Hanson, personal communication, fall 2018).

Commercialization. Commercialization scores are based on an in-person interview with Rubina Raja in June 2018, at UrbNet, Aarhus University, Denmark.

20   RIBE

Population. This is the estimate made by Søren Sindbaek (personal communication, July 2, 2018).

Commercialization. Commercialization scores are based on an in-person interview with Søren Sindbaek in June 2018, at UrbNet, Aarhus University, Denmark.

21   RHODES

Population. I use figures from Hansen (2006b) to estimate the Hellenistic size of the city. I use the area within the city walls (300 hectares) and the corresponding population (Hansen 2006b:appendix 4).

Commercialization. The high commercialization of Hellenistic Rhodes is shown by the diversity and intensity of commercial institutions, discussed by Gabrielsen (2005, 2011, 2013) and in other works (Berthold 1984; Lund 1999).

22   YAUTEPEC

Population. Aztec-period Yautepec covered an area of 209 hectares (Smith et al. 1994). My population figure is an average of a density-based archaeological estimate and an independent historical demographic estimate, both reported in Smith et al. (1994).

Commercialization. Most of the six commercial institutions inferred for Yautepec are very likely, based on knowledge of Aztec regional exchange systems and urbanism (Berdan 2014; Hirth 2016; Smith 2008), and the heavy economic activity revealed by archaeological fieldwork at the site (M. E. Smith 2019b).

23   ADO EKITI

Population. There a no published population figures for the city. I estimate population as follows. There are 1,816 houses within the city wall and 43 outside the wall in Ojo's maps of the city (Ojo 1966a, 1966b). Marris (1961:table 8) provides data on the size of households in a traditional Yoruba city, and I used his average size of 4.8 persons per household, yielding a subtotal of 9,000 persons. I added another 100 for the precolonial royal palace. The area was measured to include the total settlement area in Ojo's maps.

Commercialization. Calculation of my commercialization score began with the project "Service Access in Premodern Cities"; for a discussion of coding procedures, see Smith et al. (2016). Ado Ekiti scored only 1 in that project. I have consulted works not considered by the earlier project, particularly Adebayo (1994), which raises the score to 4.

24   POMPEII

Population. I use data from Hanson (2016).

Commercialization. Both of the Roman cities in the Service Access Project sample – Ostia and Empuries – have a commercialization score of 14. As a city with an active and diverse commercial economy, Pompeii likely had all 16 of the commercial traits (Flohr and Wilson 2016; Jongman 1988; Poehler et al. 2011).

25   OLYNTHUS

Population. I use population figures reported by Nevett et al. (2020: 21–23). They calculate areas and populations for three parts of the settlement: the North Hill, the South Hill, and the Lower City. I use the summed population estimate (4,004 persons) and area (80.5 hectares) for the entire town. I also calculate figures for the neighborhood excavated by Robinson in the North Hill zone. This area has 45 houses, for a population of 270 (assuming a household size of 6), in an area of 1.7 hectares, measured from Cahill (2001:figure 6). Not surprisingly, the neighborhood density is twice that of the overall settlement (and slightly higher than the North Hill density as calculated from Nevett et al. 2020).

Commercialization. Cahill (2001) documents traits 1–4, 6, 7, 10, and 14. Foreign merchants and wholesale markets, discussed for Classical Greece by Karayiannis (1992), are assumed to have been present in Olynthus. Lisa Nevett identified trait 5 (personal communication). She suggests that Athens shows evidence for traits 13 and 16, but I am hesitant to transfer these traits to Olynthus.

26   TEOTIHUACAN

Population. Data are from Smith et al. (2019).

Commercialization. Calculation of my commercialization score began with the project "Service Access in Premodern Cities"; for a discussion of coding procedures, see Smith et al. (2016). Teotihuacan scored 3 in that project. I have added one trait – entrepreneurial merchants – based on recent research on the level of imported goods from all parts of Mesoamerica (Hirth et al. 2020; Manzanilla et al. 2017).

27   ODENSE

Population. Kirstine Haase (personal communication, April 2019) provided data for Odense in 1672. The town covered 56 hectares, with a population of 3,800. In the Viking period the size was 29 hectares. Assuming rapid growth in the thirteenth and seventeenth centuries, I reduced the 1672 figures by 30 percent to estimate the town's size in the medieval period. See also Haase (2019).

Commercialization. Commercialization scores are based on an in-person interview with Kirstine Haase in June 2018, at UrbNet, Aarhus University, Denmark.

28   UR

Population. Woolley's (1934:1) estimate from 1934 – 500,000 people over an area of 4 square miles – seems far too high (this would yield a density of 482/hectare). In Woolley's map, the walled city covers ca. 96 hectares (Zettler et al. 1998:8). I cannot find a population estimate other than Woolley's 1934 guess, so I estimate population using a density constant. The mean density for three Mesopotamian cities in Yoffee's (2005:43) list of ancient cities is 125 persons/hectare. This is well within the range of densities used by Wilkinson (1994:503) for northern Mesopotamian cities; he uses three density levels, 100, 150, and 200 persons/hectare. A density constant of 125 persons/hectare yields a population of 12,000.

Commercialization. I have scored Ur (Old Babylonian and Isin-Larsa periods) rather informally, based on the following sources: Steinkeller (2015), Hudson and Levine (1996, 1999), and Woolley and Moorey (1982).

29   FYRKAT

Population. The ring-fort is 240 meters in diameter, with an area of 1.13 hectares. It had 12 longhouses. I found two estimates for the average population of a Viking longhouse: 10 to 20 people (Short 2019) and 10 to 13 people (Wolf 2004:8); I used 13 persons to calculate a population of 156 for the settlement.

Commercialization. Commercialization scores are based on an in-person interview in June 2018, with Søren Sindbaek (at UrbNet, Aarhus University, Denmark), and follow-up conversations in 2021.

APPENDIX B

SOURCES OF GOVERNANCE DATA IN TABLE 4.1

The data in Table 4.1, "Scale of Governance for Selected Premodern Cities," were generated by the research project "Service Access in Premodern Cities" (https://shesc.asu.edu/research/projects/cities-through-ages-service-access-premodern-cities). That project analyzed twenty-three premodern cities, documented by historical sources and/or archaeological data, to examine inequality in neighborhood access to urban services. We scored each city on a number of contextual dimensions, including size, urban functions, governance, civic associations, commercialization, and class mobility. Our coding methods are described in Smith et al. (2016). For each dimension, cities were scored for several variables, taking scores of either 0 and 1, or 0, 0.5, and 1.

The governance scale is shown in Table Appendix 1. Variables with data present are scored as 0 or 1. Variables 3.4 and 3.5 are treated as a composite variable with an "OR" relationship. That is, the highest value is taken from the scores for those two variables. The raw scores range from 0 to 7. These were converted to a percentage scale that expresses the score as a percent of the maximum total of the non-missing variables. Those scores, which range from 0 to 100, are shown in the table. As explained in Smith et al. (2016), each city was coded independently by three coders. Their agreement was monitored using inter-coder reliability methods. The three coders then met and produced a consensus score.

This dimension is based on the concept of governance as presented by Blanton and Fargher (2008), a scale that runs from collective to autocratic. It differs in that we are coding cities, not polities. The variables were selected from a longer list of variables that were initially tested. They are designed to be measurable for both archaeological and historical data. Variable 3.6, governance mode, refers to the inferred mode of governance of the entire polity. The publication on our coding (Smith et al. 2016) explains our methods in greater detail.

TABLE APPENDIX 1 *Coding scale for governance*

Variable	Scores
3.1. Tax revenue source	(0) Mainly outside the polity; (1) Inside the polity
3.3. Tax revenue distribution	(0) Held by ruler; (0.5) Held by ruler and elites; (1) Redistributed among populace
3.4. Material culture of ruler(s) and elites	Contrast betw/ ruler(s) & elites in residence size/burial treatment: (0) Big contrast; (1) Modest or no contrast
3.5. Public commemoration (images or texts) of ruler(s) and elites	(0) Commemorate the ruler alone; (0.5) Commem. ruler and other elites; (1) No commemoration of individuals

(continued)

TABLE APPENDIX 1 *(continued)*

Variable	Scores
3.6. Governance mode	(0) Autocratic rule; (0.5) Partially collective; (1) Strongly collective
3.7. Neighborhood autonomy	Degree to which central city government regulates or administers neighborhoods: (0) None; (0.5) Moderately; (1) Strongly
3.8 Central planning of neighborhoods	Degree of top-down planning in neighborhood layouts. Coding: (0) Strong central planning; (0.5) Some central planning; (1) No central planning
3.9. Pathways to power	Avenues to power: religious/ritual, wealth-based, lineage-based, governmental, etc. Coding: (0) Only one avenue to power; (1) Multiple avenues to power
3.11. Civil code	Are there laws or a civil code enforced by government distinct from societal norms or religious laws? No (0); Yes (1)

REFERENCES

Abbott, Andrew 2004 *Methods of Discovery: Heuristics for the Social Sciences.* Norton, New York.

Abbott, Walter F. 1974 Moscow in 1897 as a Preindustrial City: A Test of the Inverse Burgess Zonal Hypothesis. *American Sociological Review* 39: 542–550.

Abend, Gabriel 2008 The Meaning of "Theory." *Sociological Theory* 26: 173–199.

Abercrombie, Nicholas, Stephen Hills, and Bryan S. Turner 1980 *The Dominant Ideology Thesis.* George Allen and Unwin, London.

Abu-Lughod, Janet L. 1987 The Islamic City: Historic Myth, Islamic Essence, and Contemporary Relevance. *International Journal of Middle Eastern Studies* 19: 155–176.

1989 *Before European Hegemony: The World System, A.D. 1250–1350.* Oxford University Press, New York.

Acemoglu, Daron 2009 *Introduction to Modern Economic Growth.* Princeton University Press, Princeton, NJ.

Acemoglu, Daron, and James A. Robinson 2012 *Why Nations Fail: The Origins of Power, Prosperity, and Poverty.* Profile Books, New York.

2019 *The Narrow Corridor: States, Societies, and the Fate of Liberty.* Penguin, New York.

Acuto, Michele, Susan Parnell, and Karen C. Seto 2018 Building a Global Urban Science. *Nature Sustainability* 1 (1): 2–4.

Adamic, Lada 2011 Unzipping Zipf's Law. *Nature* 474: 164–165.

Adams, Robert McC. 1966 *The Evolution of Urban Society: Early Mesopotamia and Prehispanic Mexico.* Aldine, Chicago.

Adebayo, Akanmu G. 1994 Money, Credit, and Banking in Precolonial Africa: The Yoruba Experience. *Anthropos* 89: 379–400.

Ades, Alberto F., and Edward L. Glaeser 1995 Trade and Circuses: Explaining Urban Giants. *Quarterly Journal of Economics* 110: 195–227.

Adler, Michael A. (ed.) 1996 *The Prehistoric Pueblo World, A.D. 1150–1350.* University of Arizona Press, Tucson.

Adler, Michael A., and Richard H. Wilshusen 1990 Large-Scale Integrative Facilities in Tribal Societies: Cross-Cultural and Southwestern United States Examples. *World Archaeology* 22: 133–146.

Agier, Michel 2011 *Managing the Undesirables: Refugee Camps and Humanitarian Government.* Polity, Oxford.

Albrecht, Ryan R. 2020 An Immigrant Neighbourhood in Ancient Rome. *Urban History* 47: 2–22.

Alexander, Christopher 1979 *The Timeless Way of Building.* Oxford University Press, New York.

Alexander, Christopher, Sara Ishikawa, and Murray Silverstein 1977 *A Pattern Language: Towns, Buildings, Construction.* Oxford University Press, New York.

Algaze, Guillermo 2018 Entropic Cities: The Paradox of Urbanism in Ancient Mesopotamia. *Current Anthropology* 59 (1): 23–54.

Altaweel, Mark 2015 Settlement Dynamics and Hierarchy from Agent Decision-Making: A Method Derived from Entropy Maximization. *Journal of Archaeological Method and Theory* 22: 1122–1150.

Altschul, Jeffrey H., Keith W. Kintigh, Terry H. Klein et al. 2017 Opinion: Fostering Synthesis in Archaeology to Advance Science and Benefit Society. *Proceedings of the National Academy of Sciences* 114 (42): 10999–11002.

Amaroui, Toutia 2020 The Archaeology of Urban Workshops in the Roman Maghreb. In *Urban Space and Urban History in the Roman World*, edited by Miko Flohr, pp. 221–240. Routledge, New York.

Aminzadeh, Behnaz, and Firuzeh Samani 2006 Identifying the Boundaries of the Historical Site of Persepolis Using Remote Sensing. *Remote Sensing of Environment* 102 (1–2): 52–62.

Angel, Shlomo, Patrick Lamson-Hall, and Zeltia Gonzalez Blanco 2021 Anatomy of Density: Measurable Factors that Constitute Urban Density. *Buildings and Cities* 2 (1): 264–282.

Angel, Shlomo, Patrick Lamson-Hall, Madrid Manuel et al. 2016 *Atlas of Urban Expansion: 2016 Edition Volume 2: Blocks and Roads*. New York University, Urban Expansion Program, New York. www.lincolninst.edu/publications/other/atlas-urban-expansion-2016-edition-0.

Angel, Shlomo, Patrick Lamson-Hall, Sharad Shingade, Suman Kumar, and Zetina Bonzález Blanco 2020 Anatomy of Density I: Measurable Factors That Together Constitute Urban Density. Working paper. New York University, Marron Institute of Urban Management, New York. https://marroninstitute.nyu.edu/uploads/content/Anatomy_of_Density_I_11_August_2020.pdf.

Arnauld, Marie Charlotte, Linda R. Manzanilla, and Michael E. Smith (eds.) 2012 *The Neighborhood as a Social and Spatial Unit in Mesoamerican Cities*. University of Arizona Press, Tucson.

Arnold, Dean E. 1985 *Ceramic Theory and Cultural Processes*. Cambridge University Press, New York.

Arponen, V. P. J., Johannes Müller, Robert Hofmann et al. 2016 Using the Capability Approach to Conceptualise Inequality in Archaeology: The Case of the Late Neolithic Bosnian Site Okolište c. 5200–4600 BCE. *Journal of Archaeological Method and Theory* 23 (2): 541–560.

Arrow, Kenneth J. 1962 The Economic Implications of Learning-By-Doing. *The Review of Economic Studies* 29: 155–173.

Arthur, W. Brian 1996 Increasing Returns and the New World of Business. *Harvard Business Review* 74 (4): 100–109.

Artursson, Magnus, Timothy Earle, and James Brown 2016 The Construction of Monumental Landscapes in Low-Density Societies: New Evidence from the Early Neolithic of Southern Scandinavia (4000–3300 BC) in Comparative Perspective. *Journal of Anthropological Archaeology* 41: 1–18.

Ashmore, Wendy 2015 Lived Experiences of Space, Time and Cosmovision. *Cambridge Archaeological Journal* 25 (1): 293–297.

Aston, Michael 1984 The Towns of Somerset. In *Anglo-Saxon Towns in Southern England*, edited by Jeremy Haslam, pp. 167–201. Phillimore, Chichester.

Atkins, Margaret, and Robin Osborne (eds.) 2006 *Poverty in the Roman World*. Cambridge University Press, New York.

Atwood, Christopher P. 2015 Imperial Itinerance and Mobilty Pastoralism: The State and Mobility in Medieval Inner Asia. *Inner Asia* 17: 293–349.

Atwood, Roger 2004 *Stealing History: Tomb Raiders, Smugglers, and the Looting of the Ancient World*. St. Martin's Press, New York.

Avery-Quinn, Samuel 2017 Cities of Zion: Methodist Camp Meeting Associations and Vernacular Town Planning. *Journal of Planning History* 17 (1): 42–66.

2019 *Cities of Zion: The Holiness Movement and Methodist Camp Meeting Towns in America*. Lexington Books, Lanham, MD.

Ayala, Francisco J. 1968 Biology as an Autonomous Science. *American Scientist* 56 (3): 207–221.

Bairoch, Paul 1988 *Cities and Economic Development: From the Dawn of History to the Present*. Translated by Christopher Braider. University of Chicago Press, Chicago.

Baker, John, and Stuart Brookes 2015 Identifying Outdoor Assembly Sites in Early Medieval England. *Journal of Field Archaeology* 40 (1): 3–21.

Balter, Michael 2005 *The Goddess and the Bull: Çatalhöyük, An Archaeological Journey to the Dawn of Civilization*. Free Press, New York.

Bandy, Matthew S. 2004 Fissioning, Scalar Stress, and Social Evolution in Early Village Societies. *American Anthropologist* 106: 322–333.

Bang, Peter F. 2009 Labor: Free and Unfree. In *A Companion to Ancient History*, edited by Andrew Erskine, pp. 447–462. Wiley-Blackwell, Malden, MA.

2016 Beyond Capitalism: Conceptualising Ancient Trade Through Friction, World Historical Context and Bazaars. In *Dynamics of Production in the Ancient Near East, 1300–500 BC*, edited by Juan Carlos Moreno García, pp. 75–89. Oxbow, Oxford.

Bangert, Susanne 2010 The Archaeology of Pilgrimage: Abu Mina and Beyond. In *Religious Diversity in Late Antiquity*, edited by David Gwynn and Susanne Bangert, pp. 293–327. Late Antique Archaeology, vol. 6. Brill, Leiden.

Banks, Kimball M., and J. Signe Snortland 1995 Every Picture Tells a Story: Historic Images, Tipi Camps, and Archaeology. *Plains Anthropologist* 40 (152): 125–144.

Bar-Yosef, Ofer 1998 The Natufian Culture in the Levant, Threshold to the Origins of Agriculture. *Evolutionary Anthropology* 6 (5): 159–177.

Barba Pingarrón, Luis A., and José Luis Córdova Frunz 2010 *Materiales y energía en la arquitectura de Teotihuacan*. Instituto de Investigaciones Antropológicas, Universidad Nacional Autónoma de México, Mexico City.

Barford, Gry, Ian C. Freestone, Achim Lichtenberger, and Rubina Raja 2018 Geochemistry of Byzantine and early Islamic Glass from Jerash, Jordan: Typology, Recycling, and Provenance. *Geoarchaeology* 33 (6): 623–640.

Barker, Alex W. 2018 Looting, the Antiquities Trade, and Competing Valuations of the Past. *Annual Review of Anthropology* 47: 455–474.

Barnow, Finn 2001 *The City of the Divine King: Urban Systems and Urban Architecture in Egypt, Mesopotamia, Indus, India, Nepal and China*. An Outline of the History of Urban Development, vol. 1. Royal Danish Academy of Fine Arts, School of Architecture Publishers, Copenhagen.

Barthel, Stephan, and Christian Isendahl 2013 Urban Gardens, Agriculture, and Water Management: Sources of Resilience for Long-Term Food Security in Cities. *Ecological Economics* 86: 224–234.

Batty, Michael 2013 *The New Science of Cities*. MIT Press, Cambridge.

Béal, Jean-Claude, and Jean-Claude Goyon (eds.) 2002 *Les Artisans dans la Ville Antique*. Collection Archeologie et Histoire de l'Antiquité, vol. 6. Université Lumière-Lyon 2, Lyon.

Beard, Mary 2008 *The Fires of Vesuvius: Pompeii Lost and Found*. Belknap Press (Harvard University), Cambridge.

Beaudry, Paul 2008 Growth and Learning-by-Doing. In *The New Palgrave Dictionary of Economics: Economic Growth*, edited by Steven N. Durlauf and Lawrence E. Blume, pp. 125–126. 2nd ed. Palgrave Macmillan, Basingstoke. www.dictionaryofeconomics.com/extract?id=pde2008_G000181.

Beck, Robin A., Jr. 2009 On Delusions. *Native South* 2: 111–120.

Becker, Gary S., and Kevin M. Murphy 1994 The Division of Labor, Coordination Costs, and Knowledge. In *Human Capital: A Theoretical and Empirical Analysis with Special Reference to Education*, pp. 299–322. 3rd ed. University of Chicago Press, Chicago.

Behar, Cem 2003 *A Neighborhood in Ottoman Istanbul: Fruit Vendors and Civil Servants in the Kasap Ilyas Mahalle*. State University of New York Press, Albany, NY.

Bell, Peter 1984 *Timber and Iron: Houses in North Queensland Mining Settlements, 1861–1920*. University of Queensland Press, Queensland.

Benech, Christophe 2007 New Approach to the Study of City Planning and Domestic Dwellings in the Ancient Near East. *Archaeological Prospection* 14: 87–103.

Bengtsson, Bo, and Hannu Ruonavaara 2017 Comparative Process Tracing: Making

Historical Comparison Structured and Focused. *Philosophy of the Social Sciences* 47 (1): 44–66.

Bennet, John 1985 The Structure of the Linear B Administration at Knossos. *American Journal of Archaeology* 89 (2): 231–249.

Benson, Larry V., Timothy R. Pauketat, and Edward R. Cook 2009 Cahokia's Boom and Bust in the Context of Climate Change. *American Antiquity* 74: 467–483.

Berdan, Frances F. 2014 *Aztec Archaeology and Ethnohistory*. Cambridge University Press, New York.

Berg, Nate 2010 Mobile Nation: A Motorhome Metropolis Blooms Each Year in the Arizona Desert. *High Country News*, March 15, 2010: 12–17. www.hcn.org/articles/issues/42.5/mobile-nation.

   2011 Essay: Burning Man and the Metropolis. *Design Observer Group*, January 10, 2011: (posted online). http://places.designobserver.com/entry.html?entry=23848.

Bernardini, Wesley, and Gregson Schachner 2018 Comparing Near Eastern Neolithic Megasites and Southwestern Pueblos: Population Size, Exceptionalism and Historical Trajectories. *Cambridge Archaeological Journal* 8 (4): 647–663.

Bernhardt, John W. 1993 *Itinerant Kingship and Royal Monasteries in Early Medieval Germany, 936–1075*. Cambridge University Press, New York.

Berrey, C. Adam, Robert D. Drennan, and Christian E. Peterson 2021 Local Economies and Household Spacing in Early Chiefdom Communities. *PLoS One* 16 (5): e0252532.

Berry, Joanne 2007 *The Complete Pompeii*. Thames and Hudson, New York.

Berthold, Richard M. 1984 *Rhodes in the Hellenistic Age*. Cornell University Press, Ithaca.

Betsinger, Tracy K., and Sharon N. DeWitte 2021 Toward a Bioarchaeology of Urbanization: Demography, Health, and Behavior in Cities in the Past. *American Journal of Physical Anthropology*.

Bettencourt, Luís M. A. 2013 The Origins of Scaling in Cities. *Science* 340: 1438–1441.

   2014 The Uses of Big Data in Cities. *Big Data* 2 (1): 12–22.

   2021 *Introduction to Urban Science: Evidence and Theory of Cities as Complex Systems*. MIT Press, Cambridge.

Bettencourt, Luís M. A., and José Lobo 2019 Quantitative Methods for the Comparative Analysis of Cities in History. *Frontiers in Digital Humanities*, 6 (Special issue: *Where Do Cities Come From and Where Are They Going To? Modelling Past and Present Agglomerations to Understand Urban Ways of Life*): Article 17. www.frontiersin.org/articles/10.3389/fdigh.2019.00017/full.

Bettencourt, Luís M. A., José Lobo, Dirk Helbing, Christian Kühnert, and Geoffrey B. West 2007 Growth, Innovation, Scaling, and the Pace of Life in Cities. *Proceedings of the National Academy of Sciences* 104: 7301–7306.

Bettencourt, Luís M. A., José Lobo, Deborah Strumsky, and Geoffrey B. West 2010 Urban Scaling and Its Deviations: Revealing the Structure of Wealth, Innovation and Crime Across Cities. *PLoS One* 5 (11): 1–9.

Bianca, Stefano 2000 *Urban Form in the Arab World*. Thames and Hudson, New York.

Binford, Lewis R. 1978 *Nunamiut Ethnoarchaeology*. Academic Press, New York.

   1980 Willow Smoke and Dog's Tails: Hunter-Gatherer Settlement Systems and Archaeological Site Formation. *American Antiquity* 45: 4–20.

   1983 *In Pursuit of the Past: Decoding the Archaeological Record*. Thames and Hudson, New York.

Binford, Lewis R., and W. J. Chasko, Jr. 1976 Nunamiut Demographic History: A Provocative Case. In *Demographic Anthropology: Quantitative Approaches*, edited by Ezra B. W. Zubrow, pp. 63–143. SAA, Washington, DC.

Bintliff, John 1999 Settlement and Territory. In *Companion Encyclopedia of Archaeology*, edited by Graeme Barker, pp. 505–545, vol. 1. Routledge, London.

2014 Prosperity, Sustainability, and Poverty in the Late Antique World: Mediterranean Case Studies. In *Production and Prosperity in the Theodosian period*, edited by Ine Jacobs, pp. 319–326. Peeters, Leuven.

Birch-Chapman, Shannon, Emma Jenkins, Fiona Coward, and Mark Maltby 2017 Estimating Population Size, Density and Dynamics of Pre-Pottery Neolithic Villages in the Central and Southern Levant: An Analysis of Beidha, Southern Jordan. *Levant* 49: 1–23.

Birch, Jennifer (ed.) 2013 *From Prehistoric Villages to Cities: Settlement Aggregation and Community Transformation*. Routledge, New York.

Birch, Jennifer, and Ronald F. Williamson 2013 Organizational Complexity in Ancestral Wendat Communities. In *From Prehistoric Villages to Cities: Settlement Aggregation and Community Transformation*, edited by Jennifer Birch, pp. 153–178. Routledge, New York.

Bittner, Egon 1965 The Concept of Organization. *Social Research* 32 (3): 239–255.

Blackman, David, P. Knoblauch, and A. Yiannikouri 1996 Die Schiffshäuser am Mandrakihafen in Rhodos. *Archäologischer Anzeiger* 1996: 371–426.

Blair, John 2018 *Building Anglo-Saxon England*. Princeton University Press, Princeton, NJ.

Blake, Michael 2015 *Maize for the Gods: Unearthing the 9,000-Year History of Corn*. University of California Press, Berkeley.

Blake, Stephen P. 1991 *Shahjahanabad: The Sovereign City in Mughal India, 1639–1739*. Cambridge University Press, New York.

Blanton, Richard E. 1976 Anthropological Studies of Cities. *Annual Review of Anthropology* 5: 249–264.

1982 Urban Beginnings: A View from Anthropological Archaeology. *Journal of Urban History* 8: 427–446.

1989 Continuity and Change in Public Architecture: Periods I Through V of the Valley of Oaxaca, Mexico. In *Monte Albán's Hinterland, Part II: Prehispanic Settlement Patterns in Tlacolula, Etla, and Ocotlan, the Valley of Oaxaca, Mexico*, edited by Stephen A. Kowalewski, Gary M. Feinman, Laura Finsten, Richard E. Blanton, and Linda M. Nicholas, pp. 409–447. Memoirs, vol. 23. Museum of Anthropology, University of Michigan, Ann Arbor.

1995 A Functionalist Paradigm for Architectural Analysis: Review of *Architecture and Order*, edited by Michael Parker Pearson and Colin Richards. *Cambridge Archaeological Journal* 5: 303–305.

Blanton, Richard E., and Lane F. Fargher 2008 *Collective Action in the Formation of Pre-Modern States*. Springer, New York.

2011 The Collective Logic of Pre-Modern Cities. *World Archaeology* 43 (3): 505–522.

2012 Neighborhoods and the Civic Constitutions of Pre-Modern Cities as Seen from the Perspective of Collective Action. In *The Neighborhood as a Social and Spatial Unit in Mesoamerican Cities*, edited by Marie Charlotte Arnauld, Linda R. Manzanilla, and Michael E. Smith, pp. 27–52. University of Arizona Press, Tucson.

Blanton, Richard E., Gary M. Feinman, Stephen A. Kowalewski, and Peter N. Peregrine 1996 A Dual-Processual Theory for the Evolution of Mesoamerican Civilization. *Current Anthropology* 37: 1–14.

Blanton, Richard E., with Lane Fargher 2016 *How Humans Cooperate: Confronting the Challenges of Collective Action*. University Press of Colorado, Boulder.

Blei, David M., and Padhraic Smyth 2017 Science and Data Science. *Proceedings of the National Academy of Sciences* 114 (33): 8689–8692.

Bloch, Marc 1961 *Feudal Society*. 2 vols. University of Chicago Press, Chicago.

Blok, Anton 1969 South Italian Agro-Towns. *Comparative Studies in Society and History* 11 (2): 121–135.

Blokland, Talja 2017 *Community as Urban Practice*. Polity, Oxford.

Boas, Franz 1925 *Contributions to the Ethnology of the Kwakiutl*. Contributions to Anthropology, vol. 3. Columbia University, New York.

Bocquet-Appel, Jean-Pierre 2011 The Agricultural Demographic Transition During and After the Agriculture Inventions. *Current Anthropology* 52 (S4): S497–S510.

Bocquet-Appel, Jean-Pierre, and Ofer Bar-Yosef (eds.) 2008 *The Neolithic Demographic Transition and its Consequences*. Springer, New York.

Bodley, John H. 2003 *The Power of Scale: A Global History Approach*. M. E. Sharpe, Armonk, NY.

Boehm, Christopher 2012 Ancestral Hierarchy and Conflict. *Science* 336: 844–847.

Bondarenko, Dmitri M., Stephen A. Kowalewski, and David A. Small (eds.) 2020 *The Evolution of Social Institutions*. Springer, New York.

Boone, Christopher G., and Ali Modarres 2006 *City and Environment*. Temple University Press, Philadelphia.

Booth, David 1998 Corvée. In *Macmillan Encyclopedia of World Slavery*, edited by Paul Finkelman and Joseph C. Miller, pp. 464–466, vol. 2. Macmillan, New York.

Borck, Lewis, and Matthew C. Sanger 2017 An Introduction to Anarchism in Archaeology. *The SAA Archaeological Record* 17 (1): 9–16.

Boserup, Ester 1965 *The Conditions of Agricultural Growth: The Economics of Agrarian Change Under Population Pressure*. Aldine, Chicago.

Bosker, Maarten, Eltjo Buringh, and Jan Luiten van Zanden 2013 From Baghdad to London: The Dynamics of Urban Growth in Europe and the Arab World, 800–1800. *The Review of Economics and Statistics* 95 (4): 1418–1437.

Bottomore, Tom 1965 *Elites and Society*. Basic Books, New York.

Bowles, Samuel 2004 *Microeconomics: Behavior, Institutions, and Evolution*. Princeton University Press, Princeton.

Bowles, Samuel, and Jung-Kyoo Choi 2013 Coevolution of Farming and Private Property During the Early Holocene. *Proceedings of the National Academy of Sciences* 110: 8830–8835.

2019 The Neolithic Agricultural Revolution and the Origins of Private Property. *Journal of Political Economy* 127 (5): 2186–2228.

Bowles, Samuel, and Herbert Gintis 2002 Social Capital and Community Governance. *The Economic Journal* 112 (483): F419–F436.

Bowles, Samuel, Alan Kirman, and Ravioj Sethi 2017 Retrospectives: Friedrich Hayek and the Market Algorithm. *Journal of Economic Perspectives* 31 (3): 215–230.

Bowser, Brenda J., and María N. Zedeño (eds.) 2009 *The Archaeology of Meaningful Places*. University of Utah Press, Salt Lake City.

Boyd, Brian 2006 On "Sedentism" in the Later Epipalaeolithic (Natufian) Levant. *World Archaeology* 38 (2): 164–178.

Brandt, Luise Ørsted, Kirstine Haase, and Matthew J. Collins 2018 Species Identification Using ZooMS, with Reference to the Exploitation of Animal Resources in the Medieval Town of Odense. *Danish Journal of Archaeology*: published online.

Braudel, Fernand 1981 *The Structures of Everyday Life*. Translated by Sian Reynolds. Civilization and Capitalism, 15th–18th Century, vol. 1. Harper and Row, New York.

Braun, Georg, and Franz Hogenbert 2008 *Cities of the World / Civitates Orbis Terrarum*. Taschen, New York.

Brodie, Neil 2014 The Internet Market in Pre-Columbian Antiquities. In *Cultural Property Crime: An Overview and Analysis of Contemporary Perspectives and Trends*, edited by Joris Kila and Marc Balcells, pp. 235–262. Brill, Leiden.

Brower, Sidney N. 2011 *Neighbors and Neighborhoods: Elements of Successful Community Design*. APA Planners Press, Chicago.

Brown, Ann Cynthia 1983 *Arthur Evans and the Palace of Minos*. Ashmolean Museum, University of Oxford, Oxford.

Brown, Burton McC. 1987 Population Estimation from Floor Area: A Restudy of "Naroll's Constant." *Behavior Science Research* 21: 1–49.

Brown, Donald E. 1988 *Hierarchy, History, and Human Nature: The Social Origins of Historical Consciousness.* University of Arizona Press, Tucson.

Brown, Hannah, Helen Goodchild, and Søren M. Sindbaek 2014 Making Place for a Viking Fortress: An Archaeological and Geophysical Reassessment of Aggersborg, Denmark. *Internet Archaeology* 36: 1–30. http://intarch.ac.uk/journal/issue36/brown_toc.html.

Brubaker, Rogers, and Frederick Cooper 2000 Beyond "Identity." *Theory and Society* 29: 1–47.

Bruder, Jessica 2017 *Nomadland: Surviving America in the Twenty-First Century.* Norton, New York.

Bruegmann, Robert 2005 *Sprawl: A Compact History.* University of Chicago Press, Chicago.

Brughmans, Tom, and Jeroen Poblome 2016 Roman Bazaar or Market Economy? Explaining Tableware Distributions through Computational Modeling. *Antiquity* 90: 393–408.

Brumfiel, Elizabeth M. 1998 Huitzilopochtli's Conquest: Aztec Ideology in the Archaeological Record. *Cambridge Archaeological Journal* 8: 3–14.

Bunge, Mario 1993 Realism and Antirealism in Social Science. *Theory and Decision* 35: 207–235.

2004 How Does It Work?: The Search for Explanatory Mechanisms. *Philosophy of the Social Sciences* 34 (2): 182–210.

Burton, Jeffery F., Mary M. Farrell, Florence B. Lord, and Richard W. Lord 2002 *Confinement and Ethnicity: An Overview of World War II Japanese American Relocation Sites.* University of Washington Press, Seattle.

Butzer, Karl W. 2008 Other Perspectives on Urbanism: Beyond the Disciplinary Boundaries. In *The Ancient City: New Perspectives on Urbanism in the Old and New World*, edited by Joyce Marcus and Jeremy Sabloff, pp. 77–94. SAR Press, Santa Fe.

Byrd, Brian F. 1994 Public and Private, Domestic and Corporate: The Emergence of the Southwest Asian Village. *American Antiquity* 59 (4): 639–666.

2005 *Early Village Life at Beidha, Jordan: Neolithic Spatial Organization and Vernacular Architecture: The Excavations of Mrs. Diana Kirkbride-Helbæk.* British Academy Monographs in Archaeology. Oxford University Press, Oxford.

Cahill, Nicholas 2001 *Household and City Organization at Olynthus.* Yale University Press, New Haven.

2005 Household Industry in Greece and Anatolia. In *Ancient Greek Houses and Households: Chronological, Regional, and Social Diversity*, edited by Bradley A. Ault and Lisa C. Nevett, pp. 54–66. University of Pennsylvania Press, Philadelphia.

Calhoun, Craig (ed.) 2010 *Robert K. Merton: Sociology of Science and Sociological Explanation.* Columbia University Press, New York.

Campoli, Julie, and Alex S. MacLean 2007 *Visualizing Density.* Lincoln Institute of Land Policy, Cambridge, MA.

Canuto, Marcello A., Francisco Estrada-Belli, Thomas G. Garrison et al. 2018 Ancient Lowland Maya Complexity as Revealed by Airborne Laser Scanning of Northern Guatemala. *Science* 361 (6409): online.

Carballo, David M. (ed.) 2013 *Cooperation and Collective Action: Archaeological Perspectives.* University Press of Colorado, Boulder.

2016 *Urbanization and Religion in Ancient Central Mexico.* Oxford University Press, New York.

2020 Power, Politics, and Governance at Teotihuacan. In *Teotihuacan: The World Beyond the City*, edited by Kenneth G. Hirth, David M. Carballo, and Barbara Arroyo, pp. 57–96. Dumbarton Oaks, Washington, DC.

Carballo, David M., and Gary M. Feinman 2016 Cooperation, Collective Action, and the Archeology of Large-Scale Societies. *Evolutionary Anthropology* 25 (6): 288–296.

Carballo, David M., Paul Roscoe, and Gary M. Feinman 2014 Cooperation and Collective Action in the Cultural Evolution of Complex Societies. *Journal of Archaeological Method and Theory* 21: 98–133.

Carneiro, Robert L. 1962 Scale Analysis as an Instrument for the Study of Cultural Evolution. *Southwestern Journal of Anthropology* 18: 149–169.

1987 Village Splitting as a Function of Population Size. In *Themes in Ethnology and Culture History: Essays in Honor of David F. Aberle*, edited by Leland Donald, pp. 94–124. Folklore Institute, Archana Publications, Meerut, India.

2010 Pauketat's *Chiefdoms and Other Archaeological Delusions:* A Challenge to Social Evolution. *Social Evolution and History* 9 (1): 135–165.

Carr, Robert F., and J. E. Hazard 1961 *Map of the Ruins of Tikal, El Peten, Guatemala*. Tikal Report, vol. 11. University of Pennsylvania, University Museum, Pennsylvania.

Carter, Alison, Heng Piphal, Miriam T. Stark, Chhay Rachna, and Damian Evans 2018 Urbanism and Residential Patterning in Angkor. *Journal of Field Archaeology* 43 (6): 492–506.

Cesaretti, Rudolf 2016 *Regional Settlement Demography: Integrating Controlled Analogues into Archaeological Population Modeling*. MA Paper, Department of Arizona State University.

Cesaretti, Rudolf, Luís M. A. Bettencourt, José Lobo, Scott G. Ortman, and Michael E. Smith 2016 Population-Area Relationship in Medieval European Cities. *PLoS One* 11 (10): e162678. http://journals.plos.org/plosone/article?id=10.1371/journal.pone.0162678.

Cesaretti, Rudolf, José Lobo, Luís M. A. Bettencourt, and Michael E. Smith 2020 Increasing Returns to Scale in the Towns of Early Tudor England. *Historical Methods: A Journal of Quantitative and Interdisciplinary History* 53 (3): 147–165. www.tandfonline.com/eprint/KJRFNDI

P4RM6HPKKCGE9/full?target=10.1080/01615440.2020.1722775.

Cessford, Craig 2005 Estimating the Neolithic population of Çatalhöyük. In *Inhabiting Çatalhöyük; Reports from the 1995–99 Seasons*, edited by Ian Hodder, pp. 323–326. Çatalhöyük Research Project, vol. 4. McDonald Institute for Archaeological Research, Cambridge.

Chang, Kwang-Chih 1968 Toward a Science of Prehistoric Society. In *Settlement Archaeology*, edited by Kwang-Chih Chang, pp. 1–9. Yale University Press, New Haven.

Chapman, John, and Bisserka Gaydarska 2016a From Domestic Households to Mega-Structures: Proto-Urbanism? In *Trypillia Mega-Sites and European Prehistory, 4100–3400 BCE*, edited by Johannes Müller, Knut Rassmann, and Mykhailo Videiko, pp. 289–299. Routledge, New York.

2016b Low-Density Urbanism: The Case of the Trypillia Group of Ukraine. In *Eurasia at the Dawn of History: Urbanization and Social Change*, edited by Dirk Krausse and Manuel Fernández-Götz, pp. 81–105. Cambridge University Press, New York.

Chapman, Robert, and Alison Wylie 2016 *Evidential Reasoning in Archaeology*. Bloomsbury Press, New York.

Charlton, Thomas H., Deborah L. Nichols, and Cynthia L. Otis Charlton 1991 Aztec Craft Production and Specialization: Archaeological Evidence from the City-State of Otumba, Mexico. *World Archaeology* 23: 98–114.

2000 Otumba and Its Neighbors: Ex Oriente Lux. *Ancient Mesoamerica* 11: 247–266.

Chase, Adrian S. Z. 2016 Districting and Urban Services at Caracol, Belize: Intra-Site Boundaries in an Evolving Maya Cityscape. *Research Reports in Belizean Archaeology* 13: 15–28.

2017 Residential Inequality among the Ancient Maya: Operationalizing Household Architectural Volume at Caracol, Belize. *Research Reports in Belizean Archaeology* 14: 31–39.

2019 Water Management among the Ancient Maya: Degrees of Latitude. *Research Reports in Belizean Archaeology* 16: 101–109.

Chase, Arlen F., and Diane Z. Chase 2016 The Ancient Maya City: Anthropogenic Landscapes, Settlement Archaeology, and Caracol, Belize. *Research Reports in Belizean Archaeology* 13: 3–14.

Chase, Arlen F., and Diane Z. Chase 2016 Urbanism and Anthropogenic Landscapes. *Annual Review of Anthropology* 45: 361–376.

Chase, Diane Z., Arlen F. Chase, and William A. Haviland 1990 The Classic Maya City: Reconsidering the "Mesoamerican Urban Tradition." *American Anthropologist* 92: 499–506.

Chen, Katherine K. 2009 *Enabling Creative Chaos: The Organization Behind the Burning Man Event.* University of Chicago Press, Chicago.

Childe, V. Gordon 1936 *Man Makes Himself.* Watts and Co., London.
    1950 The Urban Revolution. *Town Planning Review* 21: 3–17.

Chirikure, Shadreck, Thomas Moultrie, Foreman Bandama, Collett Dandara, and Munyaradzi Manyanga 2017 *What Was the Population of Great Zimbabwe (CE 1000 – 1800)?* PLOS One 12 (6): e0178335.

Chittick, H. Neville 1974 *Kilwa: An Islamic Trading City on the East African Coast.* 2 vols. Memoir, vol. 5. British Institute in Eastern Africa, Nairobi.

Christakis, Kostandinos S. 2008 *The Politics of Storage: Storage and Sociopolitical Complexity in Neopalatial Crete,* vol. 25. Institute for Aegean Prehistory, Athens.

Christakis, Kostandinos S. 2011 Redistribution in Aegean Palatial Societies. Redistribution and Political Economies in Bronze Age Crete. *American Journal of Archaeology* 115 (2): 197–205.

Christaller, Walter 1966 *Central Places in Southern Germany.* Translated by Carlisle W. Baskin. Prentice Hall, Englewood Cliffs.

Christie, Jan Wisseman 1991 States without Cities: Demographic Trends in Early Java. *Indonesia* 52: 23–40.

Christophersen, Axel 2015 Performing Towns: Steps Towards an Understanding of Medieval Urban Communities as Social Practice. *Archaeological Dialogues* 22 (2): 109–132.

Cipolla, Carlo M. 1993 *Before the Industrial Revolution: European Society and Economy, 1000–1700.* 3rd ed. Norton, New York.

Clark, Gregory 2007 *A Farewell to Alms: A Brief Economic History of the World.* Princeton University Press, Princeton.

Clark, William C., and Alicia G. Harley 2020 Sustainability Science: Toward a Synthesis. *Annual Review of Environment and Resources* 45: 331–386.

Coe, Michael D. 2003 *Angkor and the Khmer Civilization.* Thames and Hudson, New York.

Coe, William R. 1967 *Tikal: A Handbook of the Ancient Maya Ruins.* University Museum, University of Pennsylvania, Philadelphia.

Cohen, Deborah, and Peter Mandler 2015 The History Manifesto: A Critique. *The American Historical Review* 120 (2): 530–542.

Colclough, Nevill 2010 Variation and Change in Land Use and Settlement Patterns in South Italy: Ascoli Satriano 1700–1990. The Making of a Southern Agro-Town. *History and Anthropology* 21 (1): 1–17.

Collins, Randall 1988 *Theoretical Sociology.* Harcourt, Brace, Jovanovich, New York.

Congress for the New Urbanism 1996 *Charter of the New Urbanism,* Congress for the New Urbanism. www.cnu.org/charter.

Connah, Graham 2000 African City Walls: A Neglected Source? In *Africa's Urban Past,* edited by David M. Anderson and Richard Rathbone, pp. 36–51. Heinemann, Portsmouth, NH.

Copi, Irving M. 1982 *Introduction to Logic.* 6th ed. Macmillan, New York.

Corsellis, Tom, and Antonella Vitale 2005 *Transitional Settlement: Displaced Populations.* Oxfam, Cambridge, UK.

Corsi, Cristina, and Frank Vermeulen (eds.) 2012 *Ammaia I: The Survey. A Romano-Lusitanian Townscape Revealed.* Archaeological Reports of Ghent University, vol. 8. Academia Press, Ghent.

Costanza, Robert, and Bernard C. Patten 1995 Defining and Predicting Sustainability. *Ecological Economics* 15: 193–196.

Costin, Cathy Lynne 1991 Craft Specialization: Issues in Defining, Documenting, and Explaining the Organization of Production. *Advances in Archaeological Method and Theory* 3: 1–56.

Counts, Dorothy A., and David R. Counts 1996 *Over the Next Hill: An Ethnography of RVing Seniors in North America.* Broadview, Peterborough, Ontario.

Coward, Fiona, and Robin I. M. Dunbar 2014 Communities on the Edge of Civilization. In *Lucy to Language: The Benchmark Papers*, edited by Robin I. M. Dunbar, Clive Gamble, and John A. J. Gowlett, pp. 380–408. Oxford University Press, New York.

Cowgill, George L. 1975 On Causes and Consequences of Ancient and Modern Population Changes. *American Anthropologist* 77: 505–525.

2003 Teotihuacan: Cosmic Glories and Mundane Needs. In *The Social Construction of Ancient Cities*, edited by Monica L. Smith, pp. 37–55. Smithsonian Institution Press, Washington, DC.

2004 Origins and Development of Urbanism: Archaeological Approaches. *Annual Review of Anthropology* 33: 525–549.

Craig, Oliver E., Lisa-Marie Shillito, Umberto Albarella et al. 2015 Feeding Stonehenge: Cuisine and Consumption at the Late Neolithic Site of Durrington Walls. *Antiquity* 89 (347): 1096–1109.

Crawford, Katherine A., Angela Huster, Matthew Peeples et al. n.d. A Systematic Approach for Studying the Persistence of Settlements in the Past. *Antiquity* (in press).

Crawford, Margaret 1995 *Building the Workingman's Paradise: The Design of American Company Towns.* Verso, London.

Croix, Sarah 2015a Permanency in Early Medieval Emporia: Reassessing Ribe. *European Journal of Archaeology* 18 (3): 497–523.

2015b The Vikings, Victims of their Own Success? A Selective View on Viking Research and its Dissemination. *Danish Journal of Archaeology* 4: 82096.

Croix, Sarah, Michael Neiß, and Søren M. Sindbaek 2019 The Réseau Opératoire of Urbanization: Craft Collaborations and Organization in an Early Medieval Workshop in Ribe, Denmark. *Cambridge Archaeological Journal* 29(2): 345–364.

Cronk, Lee, and Beth L. Leech 2013 *Meeting at Grand Central: Understanding the Social and Evolutionary Roots of Cooperation.* Princeton University Press, Princeton, NJ.

Cruikshank, Justin 2012 Positioning Positivism, Critical Realism and Social Constructionism in the Health Sciences: A Philosophical Orientation. *Nursing Inquiry* 19 (1): 71–82.

Culbert, T. Patrick 1991 Polities in the Northeast Peten, Guatemala. In *Classic Maya Political History: Hieroglyphic and Archaeological Evidence*, edited by T. Patrick Culbert, pp. 128–146. Cambridge University Press, New York.

Culbert, T. Patrick, and Don S. Rice (eds.) 1990 *Precolombian Population History in the Maya Lowlands.* University of New Mexico Press, Albuquerque.

Curtis, Daniel R. 2013 Is There an "Agro-Town" Model for Southern Italy? Exploring the Diverse Roots and Development of the Agro-Town Structure through a Comparative Case Study in Apulia. *Continuity and Change* 28 (3): 377–419.

Curtis, Daniel R., Bas van Bavel, and Tim Soens 2016 History and the Social Sciences: Shock Therapy with Medieval Economic History as the Patient. *Social Science History* 40 (4): 751–774.

Cutting, Marion 2006 More Than One Way to Study a Building: Approaches to Prehistoric Household and Settlement Space. *Oxford Journal of Archaeology* 25: 225–246.

Dalziel, Paul, Caroline Saunders, and Joe Saunders 2018 *Wellbeing Economics: The Capabilities Approach to Prosperity.* Palgrave, London.

Dandamayev, Muhammed 1996 An Age of Privatization in Ancient Mesopotamia. In *Privatization in the Ancient Near East and Classical World*, edited by Michael Hudson and Baruch A. Levine, pp. 197–222. Peabody Museum Bulletin, vol. 5. Peabody Museum of Archaeology and Ethnology, Harvard University, Cambridge.

David, A. Rosalie 1986 *The Pyramid Builders of Ancient Egypt: A Modern Investigation of Pharaoh's Workforce*. Routledge, New York.

David, Nicholas, and Carol Kramer 2001 *Ethnoarchaeology in Action*. Cambridge University Press, New York.

Davis, Kingsley 1968 The Urbanization of the Human Population. *Scientific American* 213 (3): 3–16.

Day, John 1932 Agriculture in the Life of Pompeii. *Yale Classical Studies* 3: 165–208.

De la Llata, Silvano 2016 Open-Ended Urbanisms: Space-Making Processes in the Protest Encampment of the Indignados Movement in Barcelona. *Urban Design International* 21 (2): 113–130.

De la Pradelle, Michèle 2015 *Market Day in Provence*. University of Chicago Press, Chicago.

De Ligt, Luuk 1993 *Fairs and Markets in the Roman Empire: Economic and Social Aspects of Periodic Trade in a Pre-Industrial Society*. Gieben, Amsterdam.

De Ligt, Luuk, and John Bintliff (eds.) 2020 *Regional Urban Systems in the Roman World, 150 BCE–250 CE*. Brill, Leiden.

de Long, J. Bradford, and Andrei Shleifer 1993 Princes and Merchants: European City Growth before the Industrial Revolution. *Journal of Law and Economics* 36: 671–702.

de Ruiter, Jan, Gavin Weson, and Stephen M. Lyon 2011 Dunbar's Number: Group Size and Brain Physiology in Humans Reexamined. *American Anthropologist* 113: 557–568.

de Vries, Jan 1984 *European Urbanization 1500–1800*. Harvard University Press, Cambridge.

1990 Problems in the Measurement, Description, and Analysis of Historical Urbanization. In *Urbanization in History:* *A Process of Dynamic Interactions*, edited by Ad van der Woude, Akira Hayami, and Jan de Vries, pp. 43–60. Clarendon Press, Oxford.

Dearborn, Lynne M., and Abbilynne Harmon 2012 Hoovervilles. In *The Encyclopedia of Housing*, edited by Andrew T. Carswell, pp. 301–303. 2nd ed. Sage, New York.

DeMarrais, Elizabeth, Luis Jaime Castillo, and Timothy Earle 1996 Ideology, Materialization, and Power Strategies. *Current Anthropology* 37: 15–31.

Demeulenaere, Pierre (ed.) 2011 *Analytical Sociology and Social Mechanisms*. Cambridge University Press, New York.

Demographia 2017 *Definition of Urban Terms: Demographia World Urban Areas*. Wendell Cox Consultancy, Belleville, IL. http://demographia.com/db-define.pdf.

Dempsey, Nicola, Glen Bramley, Sinéad Power, and Caroline Brown 2011 The Social Dimension of Sustainable Development: Defining Urban Social Sustainability. *Sustainable Development* 19: 289–300.

Dennehy, Timothy, Michael E. Smith, and Dean Blumenfeld n.d. High-Definition Spatial and Social Analysis at the Maya City of Tikal. In *High-Definition Approaches to the Archaeology of Urbanism*, edited by Thomas Birch, Michael Blömer, and Federica Sulas (book in preparation). Routledge, New York.

Dennehy, Timothy, Benjamin W. Stanley, and Michael E. Smith 2016 Social Inequality and Access to Services in Premodern Cities. In *Archaeology of the Human Experience*, edited by Michelle Hegmon, pp. 143–160. Archaeological Papers, vol. 27. American Anthropological Association, Washington, DC.

Desmond, Matthew 2016 *Evicted: Poverty and Profit in the American City*. Broadway Books, New York.

Diachenko, Aleksandr, and Francesco Menotti 2017 Proto-Cities or Non-Proto-Cities? On the Nature of Cucuteni–Trypillia Mega-Sites. *Journal of World Prehistory* 30 (3): 207–219.

Diamond, Jared, and James A. Robinson (eds.) 2010 *Natural Experiments of History*. Harvard University Press, Cambridge.

Diehl, Michael W. 1992 Architecture as a Material Correlate of Mobility Strategies: Some Implications for Archaeological Interpretation. *Behavior Science Research* 26: 1–35.

Dietrich, Oliver, Manfred Heun, Jens Notroff, Klaus Schmidt, and Martin Zarnkow 2012 The Role of Cult and Feasting in the Emergence of Neolithic Communities: New Evidence from Göbekli Tepe, South-Eastern Turkey. *Antiquity* 86: 674–695.

Dinius, Oliver J., and Angela Vergara (eds.) 2011 *Company Towns in the Americas: Landscape, Power, and Working-Class Communities*. University of Georgia Press, Athens.

Dohm, Karen M. 1990 Effect of Population Nucleation on House Size for Pueblos in the American Southwest. *Journal of Anthropological Archaeology* 9: 201–239.

Dorsey, George A. 1905 *The Cheyenne*. Anthropological Series, vol. 9 (2). Field Columbian Museum, Chicago.

Douglas, Mary 2013 Institutions: Problems of Theory. In *Cultures and Crises: Understanding Risk and Resolution*, edited by Richard Fardon, pp. 36–52. Sage, Los Angeles.

Dovey, Kim, and Elek Pafka 2014 The Urban Density Assemblage: Modelling Multiple Measures. *Urban Design International* 19: 66–76.

Drennan, Robert D., C. Adam Berrey, and Christian E. Peterson 2015 *Regional Settlement Demography in Archaeology*. Eliot Werner Publications, Bristol, CT.

Drennan, Robert D., and Christian E. Peterson 2004 Comparing Archaeological Settlement Systems with Rank-Size Graphs: A Measure of Shape and Statistical Confidence. *Journal of Archaeological Science* 31: 533–549.

2006 Patterned Variation in Prehistoric Chiefdoms. *Proceedings of the National Academy of Sciences* 103: 3960–3967.

2012 Challenges for Comparative Study of Early Complex Societies. In *The Comparative Archaeology of Complex Societies*, edited by Michael E. Smith, pp. 62–87. Cambridge University Press, New York.

du Gay, Paul 2012 Leviathan Calling: Some Notes on Sociological Anti-Statism and Its Consequences. *Journal of Sociology* 48 (4): 397–409.

Dunbar, Robin I. M. 2010 *How Many Friends Does One Person Need? Dunbar's Number and Other Evolutionary Quirks*. Harvard University Press, Cambridge, MA.

2011 Constraints on the Evolution of Social Institutions and their Implications for Information Flow. *Journal of Institutional Economics* 7: 345–371.

Dungan, Katherine A., and Matthew A. Peeples 2018 Public Architecture as Performance Space in the Prehispanic Central Southwest. *Journal of Anthropological Archaeology* 50: 12–26.

Duranton, Gilles, and Diego Puga 2004 Micro-Foundation of Urban Agglomeration Economies. In *Handbook of Regional and Urban Economics*, edited by J. Vernon Henderson and Jacques-François Thisse, pp. 2064–2117, vol. 4. Elsevier, Amsterdam.

Durkheim, Emile 1947 *The Elementary Forms of the Religious Life*. Free Press, Glencoe, IL.

2014 *The Division of Labor in Society (orig. pub. 1893)*. Simon and Schuster, New York.

Dyer, Christopher 2002 *Making a Living in the Middle Ages: The People of Britain, 850–1520*. Yale University Press, New Haven.

Dyson-Hudson, Rada, and Eric Alden Smith 1978 Human Territoriality: An Ecological Reassessment. *American Anthropologist* 80: 21–41.

Eagleton, Terry 1991 *Ideology: An Introduction*. Verso, New York.

Earle, Timothy 1997 *How Chiefs Come to Power: The Political Economy in Prehistory*. Stanford University Press, Stanford.

2002 *Bronze Age Economics: The Beginnings of Political Economies*. Westview Press, Boulder, CO.

2011 Redistribution in Aegean Palatial Societies. Redistribution and the Political Economy: The Evolution of an Idea. *American Journal of Archaeology* 115: 237–244.

2021 *A Primer on Chiefs and Chiefdoms*. Eliot Werner Publications.

Early, Daniel K. 1992 The Renaissance of Amaranth. In *Chilies to Chocolate: Food the Americas Gave the World*, edited by Nelson Foster and Linda S. Cordell, pp. 15–34. University of Arizona Press, Tucson.

Easterly, William 2008 Institutions: Top Down or Bottom Up? *American Economic Review* 98 (2): 95–99.

Edwards, Catharine, and Greg Woolf 2002 Cosmopolis: Rome as a World City. In *Rome the Cosmopolis*, edited by Catharine Edwards and Greg Woolf, pp. 1–20. Cambridge University Press, New York.

Egerer, Monika, Dagmar Haase, Timon McPhearson et al. 2021 Urban Change as an Untapped Opportunity for Climate Adaptation. *npj Urban Sustainability* 1 (1): 1–9.

Ehlers, Caspar 2015 Between Marklo and Merseburg: Assemblies and Their Sites in Saxony from the Beginning of Christianization to the Time of the Ottonian Kings. *Journal of the North Atlantic* 8: 134–140.

Eisenstadt, S. N. 1963 *The Political Systems of Empires*. The Free Press, New York.

Ek, Jerald D. 2020 The Inertia of Old Ideas: A Historical Overview of Theoretical and Methodological Challenges in the Study of Classic Maya Political Organization. *Journal of Archaeological Research* 28 (2).

Elster, Jon 1989 *Nuts and Bolts for the Social Sciences*. Cambridge University Press, New York.

Emberling, Geoff, and Katharyn Hanson (eds.) 2008 *Catastrophe! The Looting and Destruction of Iraq's Past*. Oriental Institute Museum Publications, vol. 28. Oriental Institute of the University of Chicago, Chicago.

Emerson, Thomas E. 1997 *Cahokia and the Archaeology of Power*. University of Alabama Press, Tuscaloosa.

Enloe, James G. 2003 Food Sharing Past and Present: Archaeological Evidence for Economic and Social Interactions. *Before Farming: The Archaeology and Anthropology of Hunter-Gatherers* 1 (1): 1–23.

Epstein, Joshua M. 2007 *Generative Social Science: Studies in Agent-Based Computational Modeling*. Princeton University Press, Princeton, NJ.

Erdkamp, Paul 2008 Mobility and Migration in Italy in the Second Century BC. In *People, Land and Politics: Demographic Developments and the Transformation of Roman Italy 300 BC–AD 14*, edited by Luuk de Ligt and Simon Northwood, pp. 417–449. Brill, Leiden.

Erdkamp, Paul 2016 Economic Growth in the Roman Mediterranean World: An Early Good-Bye to Malthus? *Explorations in Economic History* 60: 1–20.

Ericson, Richard E. 2008 Command Economy. In *The New Palgrave Dictionary of Economics*, edited by Steven N. Durlauf and Lawrence Blume, pp. 1–11. 2nd ed., vol. 2. Palgrave Macmillan, Basingstoke, UK.

Eriksson, Lina 2011 *Rational Choice Theory: Potential and Limits*. Palgrave Macmillan, New York.

Evans, Damian, Christophe Pottier, Roland Fletcher et al. 2007 A Comprehensive Archaeological Map of the World's Largest Preindustrial Settlement Complex at Angkor, Cambodia. *Proceedings of the National Academy of Sciences* 104: 14277–14282.

Evans, Gary W. 2001 Crowding and Other Environmental Stressors. In *International Encyclopedia of the Social and Behavioral Sciences*, edited by Neil J. Smelser and Paul B. Baltes, pp. 3018–3022. Elsevier, New York.

Fafinski, Mateusz 2021 *Roman Infrastructure in Early Medieval Britain: The Adaptations of the Past in Text and Stone*. Amsterdam University Press, Amsterdam.

Fairs, Marcus 2015 Burning Man "Needed an Urban Design Because It's a City" says Founder Larry Harvey. *Dezeen* (25 August 2015). www.dezeen.com/ 2015/08/25/burning-man-needed-urban-design-because-its-a-city-says-founder-larry-harvey/.

Falah, Ghazi 1985 The Spatial Pattern of Bedouin Sedentarization in Israel. *GeoJournal* 11: 361–368.

Fargher, Lane F., Richard E. Blanton, and Ricardo R. Antorcha-Pedemonte 2019 The Archaeology of Intermediate-Scale Socio-Spatial Units in Urban Landscapes. In *Excavating Neighborhoods: A Cross-Cultural Exploration*, edited by David Pacifico and Lise A. Truex, pp. 159–179. Archaeological Papers, vol. 30. American Anthropological Association, Washington, DC.

Fargher, Lane F., Verenice Y. Heredia Expinoza, and Richard E. Blanton 2011 Alternative Pathways to Power in Late Postclassic Highland Mesoamerica. *Journal of Anthropological Archaeology* 30: 306–326.

Feather, Arwen L. 1996 Circular or Rectangular Ground Plans: Some Costs and Benefits. *Nebraska Anthropologist* 13 (1): 57–66.

Feinman, Gary M. 2011 Size, Complexity, and Organizational Variation: A Comparative Approach. *Cross-Cultural Research* 45 (1): 37–58.

Feinman, Gary M., and David M. Carballo 2018 Collaborative and Competitive Strategies in the Variability and Resiliency of Large-Scale Societies in Mesoamerica. *Economic Anthropology* 5: 7–19.

Feinman, Gary M., and Christopher P. Garraty 2010 Preindustrial Markets and Marketing: Archaeological Perspectives. *Annual Review of Anthropology* 39. 167–191.

Feinman, Gary M., and Joyce Marcus (eds.) 1998 *Archaic States*. School of American Research Press, Santa Fe, NM.

Feinman, Gary M., and Linda M. Nicholas (eds.) 2004 *Archaeological Perspectives on Political Economies*. University of Utah Press, Salt Lake City.

Fernández-Götz, Manuel A. 2018 Urbanization in Iron Age Europe: Trajectories, Patterns and Social Dynamics. *Journal of Archaeological Research* 26 (2): 117–162.

Feveile, Claus 2012 Ribe: Emporia and Town in the 8th and 9th Century. In *From One Sea to Another: Trading Places in the European and Mediterranean Early Middle Ages*, edited by Sauro Gelichi and Richard Hodges, pp. 111–122. Brepols, Turnhout.

Fichtl, Stephan 2005 *La ville celtique: Les oppida de 150 avant J.-C. à 15 après J.-C.* Revised ed. Errance, Paris.

Finkelstein, Jacob J. 1968 The Laws of Ur-Nammu. *Journal of Cuneiform Studies* 22 (3–4): 66–82.

Finlayson, Bill 2013 Imposing the Neolithic on the Past. *Levant* 45 (2): 133–148.

Fisher, Kevin D., and Andy Creekmore (eds.) 2014 *Making Ancient Cities: Space and Place in Early Urban Societies*. University Press of Colorado, Boulder.

Fiske, Alan P. 1991 *Structures of Social Life: The Four Elementary Forms of Human Relations: Communal Sharing, Authority Ranking, Equality Matching, Market Pricing*. The Free Press, New York.

Flannery, Kent V. (ed.) 1976 *The Early Mesoamerican Village*. Academic Press, New York.

— 2002 The Origins of the Village Revisited: From Nuclear to Extended Households. *American Antiquity* 67: 417–433.

Flannery, Kent V., and Joyce Marcus 1993 Cognitive Archaeology. *Cambridge Archaeological Journal* 3: 260–270.

— 2012 *The Creation of Inequality: How Our Prehistoric Ancestors Set the Stage for Monarchy, Slavery, and Empire*. Harvard University Press, Cambridge, MA.

Fleetwood, Steve 2008 Institutions and Social Structures. *Journal for the Theory of Social Behaviour* 38 (3): 241–265.

Fletcher, Roland 1991 Very Large Mobile Communities: Interaction Stress and Residential Dispersal. In *Ethnoarchaeological Approaches to Mobile Campsites: Hunter-Gatherer and Pastoralist Case Studies*, edited by Clive Gamble and William A. Boismer, pp. 395–420. Prehistory Press, Ann Arbor.

1995 *The Limits of Settlement Growth: A Theoretical Outline.* Cambridge University Press, New York.

2009 Low-Density, Agrarian-Based Urbanism: A Comparative View. *Insights (University of Durham)* 2: article 4. www.dur.ac.uk/ias/insights/volume2/article4/.

2012 Low-Density, Agrarian-Based Urbanism: Scale, Power and Ecology. In *The Comparative Archaeology of Complex Societies*, edited by Michael E. Smith, pp. 285–320. Cambridge University Press, New York.

2019 Trajectories to Low-Density Settlements Past and Present: Paradox and Outcomes. *Frontiers in Digital Humanities* 6 (14): Special issue: *Where do Cities Come From and Where Are They Going To? Modelling Past and Present Agglomerations to Understand Urban Ways of Life.* www.frontiersin.org/article/10.3389/fdigh.2019.00014.

Flohr, Miko, and Andrew Wilson (eds.) 2016 *Quantifying Pompeii: Population, Inequality and the Urban Economy.* Oxford University Press, New York.

Ford, James 1936 *Slums and Housing.* 2 vols. Harvard University Press, Cambridge, MA.

Forrest, Ray 2008 Who Cares about Neighbourhoods? *International Social Science Journal* 59: 129–141.

Foster, George M. 1967 Introduction: What Is a Peasant? In *Peasant Society: A Reader*, edited by Jack M. Potter, May N Díaz, and George M. Foster, pp. 2–14. Little, Brown, Boston.

Fowler, Don D. 1987 Uses of the Past: Archaeology in the Service of the State. *American Antiquity* 52: 229–248.

Fox, Richard G. 1977 *Urban Anthropology: Cities in their Cultural Settings.* Prentice Hall, Englewood Cliffs.

Fraser, Douglas 1968 *Village Planning in the Primitive World.* George Braziller, New York.

Freeman, Jacob, Erick Robinson, Noelle G. Beckman, Darcy Bird, Jacopo A. Baggio, and John M. Anderies 2020 The Global Ecology of Human Population Density and Interpreting Changes in Paleo-Population Density. *Journal of Archaeological Science* 120: 105168.

Freidson, Eliot 1976 The Division of Labor as Social Interaction. *Social Problems* 23 (3): 304–313.

French, Charles, Rob Scaife, Michael J. Allen et al. 2012 Durrington Walls to West Amesbury by Way of Stonehenge: A Major Transformation of the Holocene Landscape. *The Antiquaries Journal* 92: 1–36.

Furholt, Martin, Colin Grier, Matthew Spriggs, and Timothy Earle 2020 Political Economy in the Archaeology of Emergent Complexity: A Synthesis of Bottom-Up and Top-Down Approaches. *Journal of Archaeological Method and Theory* 27 (2): 157–191.

Gabrielsen, Vincent 2005 Banking and Credit Operations in Hellenistic Times. In *Making, Moving and Managing: the New World of Ancient Economies, 323–31 BC*, edited by Zofia Archibald, John K. Davies, and Vincent Gabrielsen, pp. 136–164. Oxbow, Oxford.

2011 Profitable Partnerships: Monopolies, Traders, Kings, and Cities. In *The Economies of Hellenistic Societies, Third to First Centuries, BC*, edited by Zofia Archibald, John K. Davies, and Vincent Gabrielsen, pp. 216–250. Oxford University Press, New York.

2013 Rhodes and the Ptolemaic Kingdom: The Commercial Infrastructure. In *The Ptolemies, the Sea and the Nile: Studies in Waterborne Power*, edited by Kostas Buraselis, Mary Stefanou, and Dorothy J. Thompson, pp. 66–81. Cambridge University Press, New York.

Gaimster, David 2014 The Hanseatic Cultural Signature: Exploring Globalization on the

Micro-Scale in Late Medieval Northern Europe. *European Journal of Archaeology* 17 (1): 60–81.

Galley, Chris 1995 A Model of Early Modern Urban Demography. *Economic History Review* 48: 448–469.

Gans, Herbert J. 1962 *The Urban Villagers: Group and Class in the Life of Italian-Americans*. The Free Press, New York.

Garner, John S. (ed.) 1992 *The Company Town: Architecture and Society in the Early Industrial Age* Oxford University Press, New York.

Garrioch, David, and Mark Peel 2006 Introduction: The Social History of Urban Neighborhoods. *Journal of Urban History* 32: 663–676.

Gasparini, Graziano, and Luise Margolies 1980 *Inca Architecture*. Translated by Patricia J. Lyon. Indiana University Press, Bloomington.

Gates, Charles 2011 *Ancient Cities: The Archaeology of Urban Life in the Ancient Near East and Egypt, Greece, and Rome*. 2nd ed. Routledge, New York.

Gaydarska, Bisserka, Marco Nebbia, and John Chapman 2020 Trypillia Megasites in Context: Independent Urban Development in Chalcolithic Eastern Europe. *Cambridge Archaeological Journal* 30 (1): 97–121.

Geertz, Clifford 1977 Centers, Kings, and Charisma: Reflections on the Symbolics of Power. In *Local Knowledge: Further Essays in Interpretive Anthropology*, edited by Clifford Geertz, pp. 121–146. University of Chicago Press, Chicago.

1980 *Negara: The Theatre State in Nineteenth Century Bali*. Princeton University Press, Princeton.

Geertz, Hildred, and Clifford Geertz 1975 *Kinship in Bali*. University of Chicago Press, Chicago.

Gerring, John 2007 *Case Study Research: Principles and Practices*. Cambridge University Press, New York.

Gerring, John, Daniel Ziblatt, Johan van Gorp, and Julián Arévalo 2011 An Institutional Theory of Direct and Indirect Rule. *World Politics* 63 (3): 377–433.

Gerster, Georg 2005 *The Past from Above: Aerial Photographs of Archaeological Sites*. J. Paul Getty Museum, Los Angeles.

Giddens, Anthony 1984 *The Constitution of Society: Outline of the Theory of Structuration*. University of California Press, Berkeley.

Gilliland, Bridgette 2011 *Planned Neighborhoods in Pre-Modern Egyptian Cities: A Comparison of Workers Villages*. Senior Honors Thesis, Department of Anthropology, Arizona State University.

Gintis, Herbert 2006 The Foundations of Behavior: The Beliefs, Preferences, and Constraints Model. *Biological Theory* 1 (2): 123–127.

Gintis, Herbert, Samuel Bowles, Robert T. Boyd, and Ernst Fehr (eds.) 2005 *Moral Sentiments and Material Interests: The Foundations of Cooperation in Economic Life*. MIT Press, Cambridge, MA.

Glaeser, Edward L. 2011 *The Triumph of the City: How Our Greatest Invention Makes Us Richer, Smarter, Greener, Healthier, and Happier*. Penguin, New York.

2021 Urban Resilience. *Urban Studies* 59 (1): 3–35. https://doi.org/10.1177/004209802 11052230.

Glaeser, Edward L., and David M. Cutler 2021 *Survival of the City: Living and Thriving in an Age of Isolation*. Penguin Press, New York.

Glaeser, Edward L., Bruce I. Sacerdote, and Jose A. Scheinkman 2003 The Social Multiplier. *Journal of the European Economic Association* 1: 345–353.

Gleeson, Patrick 2015 Kingdoms, Communities, and Óenaig: Irish Assembly Practices in Their Northwest European Context. *Journal of the North Atlantic* 8: 33–51.

Goldstone, Jack A. 2002 Efflorescences and Economic Growth in World History: Rethinking the Rise of the West and the British Industrial Revolution. *Journal of World History* 13: 323–389.

2017 Demographic Structural Theory: 25 Years On. *Cliodynamics* 8 (2): 85–112.

González-Val, Rafael, Luis Lanaspa, and Fernando Sanz-Gracia 2014 New Evidence on Gibrat's Law for Cities. *Urban Studies* 51 (1): 93–115.

Goodchild, Helen, Nanna Holm, and Søren M. Sindbaek 2017 Borgring: The Discovery of a Viking Age Ring Fortress. *Antiquity* 91: 1027–1042.

Goodson, Caroline 2021 *Cultivating the City in Early Medieval Italy*. Cambridge University Press, New York.

Gorham, Barlow Weed 1854 *Camp Meeting Manual: A Practical Book for the Camp Ground*. H. V. Degen, Boston.

Graeber, David 2011 *Debt: The First 5,000 Years*. Melville House, New York.

Graeber, David, and David Wengrow 2021 *The Dawn of Everything: A New History of Humanity*. Allen Lane, London.

Graff, Harvey J. 2015 *Undisciplining Knowledge: Interdisciplinarity in the Twentieth Century*. Johns Hopkins University Press, Baltimore.

Graham, Elizabeth 1999 Stone Cities, Green Cities. In *Complex Polities in the Ancient Tropical World*, edited by Elisabeth A. Bacus and Lisa J. Lucero, pp. 185–194. Archeological Papers, vol. 9. American Anthropological Association, Washington, DC.

Graham, Elizabeth, and Christian Isendahl 2018 Neotropical Cities as Agro-Urban Landscapes: Revisiting "Low-Density, Agrarian-Based Urbanism." In *The Resilience of Heritage: Cultivating a Future of the Past, Essays in Honour of Professor Paul J. J. Sinclair*, edited by Annelli Ekblom, Christian Isendahl, and Karl-Johan Lindholm, pp. 165–182. Uppsala University, Uppsala.

Graham, Ian 1975 *Corpus of Maya Hieroglyphic Inscriptions, Volume 1: Introduction*. Peabody Museum of Archaeology and Ethnology, Harvard University, Cambridge, MA.

2010 *The Road to Ruins*. University of New Mexico Press, Albuquerque.

Grant, Jill L. 2001 The Dark Side of the Grid: Power and Urban Design. *Planning Perspectives* 16: 219–241.

2018 The Dark Side of the Grid Revisited: Power and Urban Design. In *Gridded Worlds: An Urban Anthology*, edited by Reuben S. Rose-Redwood and Liora Bigeon, pp. 75–99. Springer, New York.

Greif, Avner 2006 *Institutions and the Path to the Modern Economy: Lessons from Medieval Trade*. Cambridge University Press, New York.

Grier, C., J. Kim, and J. Uchiyama (eds.) 2006 *Beyond Affluent Foragers: Rethinking Hunter-Gatherer Complexity*. Oxbow, Oxford.

Grillo, Ralph D. 2000 Plural Cities in Comparative Perspective. *Ethnic and Racial Studies* 23: 957–981.

Grinin, Leonid E., and Andrey V. Korotayev 2011 Chiefdoms and Their Analogues: Alternatives of Social Evolution at the Societal Level of Medium Cultural Complexity. *Social Evolution and History* 10 (1): 276–335.

Grube, Nikolai 2000 The City-States of the Maya. In *A Comparative Study of Thirty City-State Cultures*, edited by Mogens Herman Hansen, pp. 547–566. The Royal Danish Academy of Sciences and Letters, Copenhagen.

Guldi, Jo, and David Armitage 2014 *The History Manifesto*. Cambridge University Press, New York.

Gusman, Pierre 1900 *Pompei: The City, Its Life and Art*. Heinemann, London.

Gyucha, Attila (ed.) 2019 *Coming Together: Comparative Approaches to Population Aggregation and Early Urbanization*. State University of New York Press, Albany.

Haase, Kirstine 2019 *An Urban Way of Life: Social Practices, Networks, and Identities in Odense, c. 1000–1500 AD*. PhD dissertation, Aarhus University.

Haase, Kirstine, and Neeke M. Hammers 2021 Tracing the Trigger of Social Change in the Medieval Town through Imported Food, Objects, and Their Biographies. *Journal of Urban Archaeology* 3: 13–28.

Haber, Stephen 1999 Anything Goes: Mexico's "New" Cultural History. *Hispanic American Historical Review* 79: 309–330.

Hackett, Edward J., and John N. Parker 2016 From Salomon's House to Synthesis Centers. In *Innovation in Science and Organizational Renewal*, edited by Thomas Heinze and Richard Münch, pp. 53–87. Palgrave Macmillan, London.

Haggett, Peter, and Richard J. Chorley 1969 *Network Analysis in Geography*. St. Martin's Press, New York.

Hailey, Charlie 2008 *Campsite: Architectures of Duration and Place*. Louisiana State University Press, Baton Rouge.

2009 *Camps: A Guide to 21st Century Space*. MIT Press, Cambridge.

Håkansson, N. Thomas, and Mats Widgren (eds.) 2014 *Landesque Capital: The Historical Ecology of Enduring Landscape Modifications*. Left Coast Press, Walnut Creek.

Hakim, Besim S. 1986 *Arab-Islamic Cities: Building and Planning Principles*. Routledge, London.

2007 Generative Processes for Revitalizing Historic Towns or Heritage Districts. *Urban Design International* 12: 87–99.

2008 Mediterranean Urban and Building Codes: Origins, Content, Impact, and Lessons. *Urban Design International* 13: 21–40.

2014 *Mediterranean Urbanism: Historic Urban Building Rules and Processes*. Springer, New York.

Hakim, Besim S., and Zubair Ahmed 2006 Rules for the Built Environment in 19th Century Northern Nigeria. *Journal of Architectural and Planning Research* 23 (1): 1–26.

Halewood, Chris, and Kevin Hannam 2001 Viking Heritage Tourism: Authenticity and Commodification. *Annals of Tourism Research* 28 (3): 565–580.

Hall, Edward T. 1966 *The Hidden Dimension*. Anchor Books, New York.

Hallock, Richard T. 1969 *Persepolis Fortification Tablets*. Publications, vol. 92. Oriental Institute, University of Chicago, Chicago.

Halperin, Christina T. 2009 Figurines as Bearers of and Burdens in Late Classic Maya State Politics. In *Mesoamerican Figurines: Small-Scale Indices of Large-Scale Social Phenomena*, edited by Christina T. Halperin, Katherine A. Faust, Rhonda Taube, and Aurore Giguet, pp. 378–403. University Press of Florida, Gainesville.

Hammers, Neeke M. 2018 Trade, Import and Urban Development: An Archaeobotanical Approach to Economic Change in Medieval Denmark. In *Urban Network Evolutions: Towards a High-Definition Archaeology*, edited by Rubina Raja and Søren Sindbaek, pp. 229–234. Centre for Urban Network Evolutions, Aarhus University, Aarhus.

Hansen, Mogens Herman (ed.) 2000a *A Comparative Study of Thirty City-State Cultures*. The Royal Danish Academy of Sciences and Letters, Copenhagen.

2000b Conclusion: The Impact of City-State Cultures on World History. In *A Comparative Study of Thirty City-State Cultures*, edited by Mogens Herman Hansen, pp. 597–623. The Royal Danish Academy of Sciences and Letters, Copenhagen.

2000c Introduction: The Concepts of City-State and City-State Culture. In *A Comparative Study of Thirty City-State Cultures*, edited by Mogens Herman Hansen, pp. 11–34. The Royal Danish Academy of Sciences and Letters, Copenhagen.

2006a *Polis: An Introduction to the Ancient Greek City-State*. Oxford University Press, Oxford.

2006b *The Shotgun Method: The Demography of the Ancient Greek City-State Culture*. Fordyce W. Mitchel Memorial Lecture Series. University of Missouri Press, Columbia.

2008 Analyzing Cities. In *The Ancient City: New Perspectives on Urbanism in the Old and New World*, edited by Joyce Marcus and Jeremy Sabloff, pp. 67–76. SAR Press, Santa Fe.

Hanson, John W. 2016 *An Urban Geography of the Roman World, 100 BC to AD 300*. Roman Archaeology, vol. 18. Archaeopress, Oxford.

Hanson, John W., and Scott G. Ortman 2017 A Systematic Method for Estimating the

Populations of Greek and Roman Settlements. *Journal of Roman Archaeology* 30: 301–324.

Hanson, John W., Scott G. Ortman, Luís M. A. Bettencourt, and Liam C. Mazur 2019 Urban Form, Infrastructure and Spatial Organisation in the Roman Empire. *Antiquity* 93 (369): 702–718.

Hanson, John W., Scott G. Ortman, and José Lobo 2017 Urbanism and the Division of Labour in the Roman Empire. *Journal of the Royal Society Interface* 14 (136): online.

Hardoy, Jorge E. 1982 The Building of Latin American Cities. In *Urbanisation in Contemporary Latin America: Critical Approaches to the Analysis of Urban Issues*, edited by Alan G. Gilbert, pp. 19–34. Wiley, London.

Hare, Timothy S. 2004 Using Measures of Cost Distance in the Estimation of Polity Boundaries in the Postclassic Yautepec Valley, Mexico. *Journal of Archaeological Science* 31: 799–814.

Harris, Edward M. 2002 Workshop, Marketplace and Household: The Nature of Technical Specialization in Classical Athens and Its Influence on Economy and Society. In *Money, Labour and Land in Ancient Greece: Approaches to the Economies of Ancient Greece*, edited by Paul Cartledge, Edward E. Cohen, and Lin Foxhall, pp. 67–99. Routledge, New York.

Harris, Marvin 1989 Life without Chiefs. *New Age Journal* Nov/Dec: 42–45, 205–209.

Harris, Richard, and Michael E. Smith 2011 The History in Urban Studies: A Comment. *Journal of Urban Affairs* 33 (1): 99–105.

Harvey, David L., and Michael H. Reed 1996 The Culture of Poverty: An Ideological Analysis. *Sociological Perspectives* 39: 465–495.

Harvey, Larry 2010 Welcome to Metropole: The Study of a City. *Burning Man Journal*. https://journal.burningman.org/2010/04/black-rock-city/building-brc/welcome-to-metropol-the-story-of-a-city/.

Hassan, Fekri A. 1981 *Demographic Archaeology*. Academic Press, New York.

Hassett, Brenna 2017 *Built on Bones: 15,000 Years of Urban Life and Death*. Bloomsbury, London.

Hawken, Scott 2013 Designs of Kings and Farmers: Landscape Systems of the Greater Angkor Urban Complex. *Asian Perspectives* 52 (2): 347–367.

Hayden, Brian, and Aubrey Cannon 1984 *The Structure of Material Systems: Ethnoarchaeology in the Maya Highlands*. Papers, vol. 3. Society for American Archaeology, Washington, DC.

Hayek, Friedrich A. 1944 *The Road to Serfdom*. University of Chicago Press, Chicago.

Healy, Kieran 2017 F★★k Nuance. *Sociological Theory* 35 (2): 118–127.

Heckenberger, Michael J., J. Christian Russell, Carlos Fausto et al. 2008 Pre-Columbian Urbanism, Anthropogenic Landscapes, and the Future of the Amazon. *Science* 321: 1214–1217.

Hegmon, Michelle 1989 Social Integration and Architecture. In *The Architecture of Social Integration in Prehistoric Pueblos*, edited by William D. Lipe and Michelle Hegmon, pp. 5–14. Occasional Papers, vol. 1. Crow Canyon Archaeological Center.

2016 *Archaeology of the Human Experience*. Archaeological Papers, vol. 27. American Anthropological Association, Washington, DC.

Hein, Carola (ed.) 2017 *Routledge Handbook of Planning History*. Routledge, New York.

Heitzmann, Birte 2011 Rural Economies in Urban Situations: Production, Processing and Storage of Food. In *Processing, Storage, Distribution of Food: Food in the Medieval Rural Environment*, edited by Jan Klápště and Petr Sommer, pp. 321–333. Ruralia, vol. 8. Brepols, Turnhout, Belgium.

Heng, Chye Kiang 1999 *Cities of Aristocrats and Bureaucrats: The Development of Medieval Chinese Cityscapes*. University of Hawai'i Press, Honolulu.

2014 Visualizing Everyday Life in the City: A Categorization System for Residential

Wards in Tang Chang'an. *Journal of the Society of Architectural Historians* 73 (1): 91–117.

Henrich, Joseph 2016 *The Secret of Our Success: How Culture Is Driving Human Evolution, Domesticating Our Species and Making Us Smarter.* Princeton University Press, Princeton.

Henrich, Joseph, Steven J. Heine, and Ara Norenzayan 2010 Most People Are Not WEIRD. *Nature* 466: 29.

Hicks, Frederic 1999 The Middle Class in Ancient Central Mexico. *Journal of Anthropological Research* 55: 409–427.

Hill, David 1988 Towns as Structures and Functioning Communities through Time: The Development of Central Places from 600 to 1066. In *Anglo-Saxon Settlements*, edited by Della Hooke, pp. 197–212. Basil Blackwell, Oxford.

Hill, David, and Robert Cowie (eds.) 2001 *Wics: The Early Medieval Trading Centres of Northern Europe.* Sheffield Archaeological Monographs, vol. 14. Sheffield Academic Press, Sheffield.

Hill, James N. 1970 *Broken K Pueblo: Prehistoric Social Organization in the American Southwest.* Anthropological Papers, vol. 18. University of Arizona Press, Tucson.

Hillier, Bill 1996a Cities as Movement Economies. *Urban Design International* 1 (1): 41–60.

1996b *Space Is the Machine: A Configurational Approach to Architecture.* Cambridge University Press, New York.

Hines, Sara N. 2015 *Cottage Communities – The American Camp Meeting Movement: A Study in Lean Urbanism.* Hines Art Press, Lowell, MA.

Hirth, Kenneth G. 2000 *Archaeological Research at Xochicalco. Volume 1, Ancient Urbanism at Xochicalco: The Evolution and Organization of a Pre-Hispanic Society.* University of Utah Press, Salt Lake City.

2009 *Housework: Craft Production and Domestic Economy in Ancient Mesoamerica.* Archeological Papers, vol. 19. American Anthropological Association, Washington, DC.

2016 *The Aztec Economic World: Merchants and Markets in Ancient Mesoamerica.* Cambridge University Press, New York.

2020 *The Organization of Ancient Economies: A Global Perspective.* Cambridge University Press, New York.

Hirth, Kenneth G., David M. Carballo, and Barbara Arroyo (eds.) 2020 *Teotihuacan: The World beyond the City.* Dumbarton Oaks, Washington, DC.

Historic England 2018 *Medieval Settlements: Introduction to Heritage Assets.* Historic England, London.

Hodder, Ian 2006 *The Leopard's Tale: Revealing the Mysteries of Çatalhöyük.* Thames and Hudson, New York.

2007 Çatalhöyük in the Context of the Middle Eastern Neolithic. *Annual Review of Anthropology* 36: 105–120.

2012 Introduction: Contemporary Theoretical Debate in Archaeology. In *Archaeological Theory Today*, edited by Ian Hodder, pp. 1–14. 2nd ed. Polity Press, Oxford.

2016 More on History Houses at Çatalhöyük: A Response to Carleton et al. *Journal of Archaeological Science* 67: 1–6.

Hodgson, Geoffrey M. 2006 What Are Institutions? *Journal of Economic Issues* 40 (1): 1–25.

2007 Institutions and Individuals: Interaction and Evolution. *Organization Studies* 28 (1): 95–116.

Hofmann, Robert, Johannes Müller, Liudmyla Shatilo et al. 2019 Governing Tripolye: Integrative Architecture in Tripolye Settlements. *PLoS One* 14 (9): e0222243.

Holland-Lulewicz, Jacob, Megan Anne Conger, Jennifer Birch, Stephen A. Kowalewski, and Travis W. Jones 2020 An Institutional Approach for Archaeology. *Journal of Anthropological Archaeology* 58: 101163.

Horton, Mark 1996 *Shanga: The Archaeology of a Muslim Trading Community on the Coast of East Africa.* Memoir, vol. 14. British Institute in Eastern Africa, Nairobi.

Horvath, Ronald J. 1969 The Wandering Capitals of Ethiopia. *Journal of African History* 10: 205–219.

Hoyer, Daniel, and Joseph G Manning 2018 Empirical Regularities across Time, Space, and Culture: A Critical Review of Comparative Methods in Ancient Historical Research. *Historia* 67 (2): 160–190.

Hu, Di 2013 Approaches to the Archaeology of Ethnogenesis: Past and Emergent Perspectives. *Journal of Archaeological Research* 21 (4): 371–402.

Hudson, Michael, and Baruch A. Levine (eds.) 1996 *Privatization in the Ancient Near East and Classical World*. Peabody Museum Bulletin, vol. 5. Peabody Museum of Archaeology and Ethnology, Harvard University, Cambridge.

1999 *Urbanization and Land Ownership in the Ancient Near East*. Peabody Museum Bulletin, vol. 7. Peabody Museum of Archaeology and Ethnology, Harvard University, Cambridge.

Huff, Toby E. 2013 Why Some Nations Succeed (review of *Why Nations Fail*, by Acemoglu and Robinson). *Contemporary Sociology* 42 (1): 55–59.

Huster, Angela C. 2019 Looming Deficits: Textile Production Specialization in Postclassic Mesoamerica. *Latin American Antiquity* 30 (4): 780–797.

Hvass, Steen 1979 Vorbasse – the Viking-age Settlement at Vorbasse, Central Jutland. *Acta Archaeologica* 50: 137–172.

Hyslop, John 1984 *The Inka Road System*. Academic Press, New York.

1990 *Inka Settlement Planning*. University of Texas Press, Austin.

Inomata, Takeshi, and Kazuo Aoyama 1996 Central-Place Analyses in the La Entrada Region, Honduras: Implications for Understanding the Classic Maya Political and Economic Systems. *Latin American Antiquity* 7: 291–312.

Iseminger, William 2010 *Cahokia Mounds: America's First City*. The History Press, New York.

Isendahl, Christian 2012 Agro-Urban Landscapes: The Example of Maya Lowland Cities. *Antiquity* 86: 1112–1125.

Jackson, Tim 2009 *Prosperity without Growth: Economics for a Finite Planet*. Earthscan, London.

Jacobs, Jane 1961 *The Death and Life of Great American Cities*. Random House, New York.

1969 *The Economy of Cities*. Vintage Books, New York.

1984 *Cities and the Wealth of Nations*. Random House, New York.

Jansen, Michael R. N. 1989 Water Supply and Sewage Disposal at Mojenjo-Daro. *World Archaeology* 21: 177–192.

1993 Mohenjo-daro: Type Site of the Earliest Urbanization Process in South Asia. In *Urban Form and Meaning in South Asia: The Shaping of Cities from Prehistoric to Precolonial Times*, edited by Howard Spodek and Doris Meth Srinivasan, pp. 35–51. Studies in the History of Art, Center for Advanced Study in the Visual Arts, Symposium Papers XV, vol. 31. National Gallery of Art, Washington, DC.

2010 Architectural Measurements in the Indus Cities: The Case Study of Mohenjo-Daro. In *The Archaeology of Measurement: Comprehending Heaven, Earth and Time in Ancient Societies*, edited by Iain Morley and Colin Renfrew, pp. 125–129. Cambridge University Press, New York.

Jedwab, Remi, and Dietrich Vollrath 2015 Urbanization without Growth in Historical Perspective. *Explorations in Economic History* 58: 1–21.

Jefferson, Mark 1939 The Law of the Primate City. *Geographical Review* 29: 226–232.

Jennings, Justin 2016 *Killing Civilization: A Reassessment of Early Urbanism and Its Consequences*. University of New Mexico Press, Albuquerque.

Jennings, Justin, and Timothy Earle 2016 Urbanization, State Formation, and Cooperation: A Reappraisal. *Current Anthropology* 57 (5): 474–493.

Joffe, Alexander H. 1998 Disembedded Capitals in Western Asian Perspective. *Comparative Studies in Society and History* 40: 549–580.

Joffe, Michael 2017 Evidence and the Micro-Foundations of Economic Growth. *Economics and Business Review* 3 (3): 52–79.

Johnson, Allen W., and Timothy K. Earle 2000 *The Evolution of Human Societies: From Foraging Group to Agrarian State*. 2nd ed. Stanford University Press, Stanford.

Johnson, Gregory A. 1981 Monitoring Complex System Integration and Boundary Phenomena with Settlement Size Data. In *Archaeological Approaches to the Study of Complexity*, edited by Sander van der Leeuw, pp. 144–189. Universiteit van Amsterdam, Amsterdam.

Johnson, Paul, and Martin Millett (eds.) 2012 *Archaeological Survey and the City*. Oxbow Books, Oxford.

Johnston, Katrina 2011 Public Space and Protest: An Ethnographic Analysis of Alpha and Beta Camps at Occupy Portland. Unpublished paper.

Jones, Eric L. 2000 *Growth Recurring: Economic Change in World History*, rev. ed. University of Michigan Press, Ann Arbor.

Jones, Rhys 2004 What Time Human Geography? *Progress in Human Geography* 28: 287–304.

Jongman, Willem M. 1988 *The Economy and Society of Pompeii*. J. C. Geiben, Amsterdam.

2012 Roman Economic Change and the Antonine Plague: Endogenous, Exogenous, or What? In *L'Impatto della "Peste Antonina,"* edited by Elio Lo Cascio, pp. 253–263. Edipuglia, Bari.

2014 Why Modern Economic Theory Applies, Even to the Distant Roman Past. In *TRAC 2013: Proceedings of the Twenty-Third Annual Theoretical Roman Archaeology Conference, London 2013*, edited by Hannah Platts, John Pearce, Caroline Barron, Jason Lundock, and Justin Yoo, pp. 27–36. Oxbow Books, Oxford.

Jongsma, Tina, and Haskel J. Greenfield 2003 The Household Cluster Concept in Archaeology: A Brief Review. In *Early Symbolic Systems for Communication in Southeast Europe, Volume 1*, edited by Lolita Nikolova, pp. 21–24. BAR International Series, vol. S1139. Archaeopress, Oxford.

Jørgensen, Anne Nørgård, Lars Jørgensen, and Lone Gebauer Thomsen 2011 Assembly Sites for Cult, Markets, Jurisdiction and Social Relations. Historic-Ethnological Analogy between North Scandinavian Church Towns, Old Norse Assembly Sites and Pit House Sites of the Late Iron Age and Viking Period. In *Archäologie in Schleswig*, edited by Linda Boye, Per Ethelberg, Lene Heidemann Lutz, Pernille Kruse, and Anne Birgitte Sørensen, pp. 95–112. Museum Sønderjylland, Gram, Denmark.

Jørgensen, Dolly 2008 Cooperative Sanitation: Managing Streets and Gutters in Late Medieval England and Scandinavia. *Technology and Culture* 49 (3): 547–567.

Joshel, Sandra R. 1992 *Work, Identity, and Legal Status at Rome: A Study of the Occupational Inscriptions*. University of Oklahoma Press, Norman.

Joyce, Arthur A. 2009 Theorizing Urbanism in Ancient Mesoamerica. *Ancient Mesoamerica* 20: 189–196.

Joyce, Rosemary A. 1991 *Cerro Palenque: Power and Identity on the Maya Periphery*. University of Texas Press, Austin.

Julien, Michèle 2003 A Magdalenien Base Camp at Pincevent (France). In *Perceived Landscapes and Built Environments: The Cultural Geography of Late Paleolithic Eurasia*, edited by Sergei A. Vasil'ev, Olga Soffer, and Janusz Krzysztof Kozlowski, pp. 105–111. BAR International Series, vol. 1122. Archaeopress, Oxford.

Kagan, Jerome 2009 *The Three Cultures: Natural Sciences, Social Sciences, and the Humanities in the 21st Century*. Cambridge University Press, New York.

Kamp-Whittaker, April, and Bonnie J. Clark 2019 Social Networks and the Development of Neighborhood Identities in Amache, a WWII Japanese American Internment Camp. In *Excavating Neighborhoods: A Cross-Cultural Exploration,* edited by David Pacifico and Lise A. Truex, pp. 148–158. Archaeological Papers, vol. 30. American Anthropological Association, Washington, DC.

Karayiannis, Anastassios D. 1992 Entrepreneurship in Classical Greek Literature. *The South African Journal of Economics* 60 (1): 67–93.

Kates, Robert W. et al. 2001 Sustainability Science. *Science* 292: 641–642.

Keene, Derek 1990 Continuity and Development in Urban Trades: Problems of Concepts and the Evidence. In *Work in Towns: 850–1850*, edited by Penelope J. Corfield and Derek Keene, pp. 1–16, vol. Leicester University Press, Leicester.

Kehoe, Alice B. 1981 *North American Indians: A Comprehensive Account*. Prentice Hall, Englewood Cliffs.

Kellett, Peter, and Mark Napier 1995 Squatter Architecture? A Critical Examination of Vernacular Theory and Spontaneous Settlement with Reference to South America and South Africa. *Traditional Dwellings and Settlements Review* 6 (2): 7–24.

Kelly, Morgan 1997 The Dynamics of Smithian Growth. *The Quarterly Journal of Economics* 112 (3): 939–964.

Kelly, Robert L. 2011 Why Did Binford's Middle-Range Program Outcompete Schifer's Formation Process Program? *Journal of Archaeological Method and Theory* 18: 284–290.

2013 *The Lifeways of Hunter-Gatherers: The Foraging Spectrum*. Cambridge University Press, New York.

Kemp, Barry J. 1977 The Early Development of Towns in Egypt. *Antiquity* 51: 185–200.

1987 The Amarna Workmen's Village in Retrospect. *The Journal of Egyptian Archaeology* 73: 21–50.

2006 *Ancient Egypt: Anatomy of a Civilization*. 2nd ed. Routledge, New York.

2012 *The City of Akhenaten and Nefertiti: Amarna and Its People*. Thames and Hudson, New York.

Kennedy, Daniel P. and Ralph Adolphs 2011 Social Neuroscience: Stress and the City. *Nature* 474: 452–453.

Kenoyer, J. Mark 1998 *Ancient Cities of the Indus Valley Civilization*. Oxford University Press, Karachi and New York.

2012 Households and Neighborhoods of the Indus Tradition: An Overview. In *New Perspectives on Household Archaeology*, edited by Bradley J. Parker and Catherine P. Foster, pp. 373–406. Eisenbrauns, Winona Lake, IN.

Kent, Susan 1990 A Cross-Cultural Study of Segmentation, Architecture, and the Use of Space. In *Domestic Architecture and the Use of Space: An Interdisciplinary Cross-Cultural Study*, edited by Susan Kent, pp. 127–152. Cambridge University Press, New York.

Kertzer, David I. 1988 *Ritual, Politics, and Power*. Yale University Press, New Haven.

Kidder, Alfred V. 1958 *Pecos, New Mexico: Archaeological Notes*. Phillips Academy, Andover, MA.

Killinger, John Eric 2010 Communitas. In *Encyclopedia of Psychology and Religion*, edited by David A. Leeming, Kathryn Madden, and Stanton Marlan, pp. 162–164. Springer, Boston.

Kintigh, Keith W., Jeffrey H. Altschul, Mary C. Beaudry et al. 2014 Grand Challenges for Archaeology. *Proceedings of the National Academy of Sciences* 122: 879–880.

Kirch, Patrick V. 1994 *The Wet and the Dry: Irrigation and Agricultural Intensification in Polynesia*. University of Chicago Press, Chicago.

Kisar Koramaz, Elif 2014 The Spatial Context of Social Integration. *Social Indicators Research* 119 (1): 49–71.

Kiser, Edgar, and Justin Baer 2005 The Bureaucratization of States: Toward an Analytical Weberianism. In *Remaking Modernity: Politics, History, and Sociology*, edited by Julia Adams, Elizabeth S. Clemens, and Ann Shola Orloff, pp. 225–248. Duke University Press, Durham.

Klassen, Sarah, Alison K. Carter, Damian H. Evans et al. 2021a Diachronic Modeling of the Population within the Medieval Greater Angkor Region Settlement Complex. *Science Advances* 7 (19): eabf8441.

Klassen, Sarah, and Damian Evans 2020 Top-Down and Bottom-Up Water Management: A Diachronic Model of Changing Water Management Strategies at Angkor, Cambodia. *Journal of Anthropological Archaeology* 58: 101166.

Klassen, Sarah, Scott Ortman, José Lobo, and Damian H. Evans 2021b Provisioning an Early City: Spatial Equilibrium in the Agricultural Economy at Angkor, Cambodia. *Journal of Archaeological Method and Theory* 29: 763–794.

Kline, Michelle A., and Robert Boyd 2010 Population Size Predicts Technological Complexity in Oceania. *Proceedings of the Royal Society B: Biological Sciences* 277: 2559–2564.

Klinenberg, Eric 2018 *Palaces for the People: How Social Infrastructure Can Help Fight Inequality, Polarization, and the Decline of Civic Life*. Crown, New York.

Knechtges, David R., and Tong Xiao 2014 *Wen Xuan or Selections of Refined Literature, Volume I: Rhapsodies on Metropolises and Capitals*. Princeton University Press, Princeton.

Kohl, Philip L., and Clare Fawcett (eds.) 1995 *Nationalism, Politics, and the Practice of Archaeology*. Cambridge University Press, Cambridge.

Kohler, Timothy A., and Michael E. Smith (eds.) 2018 *Ten Thousand Years of Inequality: The Archaeology of Wealth Differences*. University of Arizona Press, Tucson.

Kohler, Timothy A., Michael E. Smith, Amy Bogaard et al. 2017 Greater Post-Neolithic Wealth Disparities in Eurasia than in North and Mesoamerica. *Nature* 551: 619–622.

Kohler, Timothy A., Michael E. Smith, Amy Bogaard et al. 2018 Deep Inequality: Summary and Conclusions. In *Ten Thousand Years of Inequality: The Archaeology of Wealth Differences*, edited by Timothy Kohler and Michael E. Smith, pp. 289–317. University of Arizona Press, Tucson.

Kosso, Peter 2009 The Large-Scale Structure of Scientific Method. *Science and Education* 18 (1): 33–42.

Kostof, Spiro 1991 *The City Shaped: Urban Patterns and Meanings through History*. Bullfinch, Boston.

— 1992 *The City Assembled: The Elements of Urban Form through History*. Bullfinch, Boston.

Kotkin, Joel 2006 *The City: A Global History*. Modern Library, New York.

Krapf-Askari, Eva 1969 *Yoruba Towns and Cities: An Enquiry into the Nature of Urban Social Phenomena*. Oxford University Press, London.

Kristensen, Troels Myrup and Wiebke Friese (eds.) 2017 *Excavating Pilgrimage: Archaeological Approaches to Sacred Travel and Movement in the Ancient World*. Routledge, New York.

Kristiansen, Kristian 2014 Towards a New Paradigm? *Current Swedish Archaeology* 22: 11–34.

Krugman, Paul 1991 Increasing Returns and Economic Geography. *Journal of Political Economy* 99: 483–499.

Kuijt, Ian (ed.) 2000 *Life in Neolithic Farming Communities: Social Organization, Identity, and Differentiation*. Kluwer, New York.

— 2011 Home Is Where We Keep Our Food: The Origins of Agriculture and Late Pre-Pottery Neolithic Food Storage. *Paleorient* 37: 137–152.

Kuran, Timur 2001 The Provision of Public Goods under Islamic Law: Origins, Impact, and Limitations of the Waqf System. *Law and Society Review* 35 (4): 841–897.

Kurtz, Donald V. 1978 The Legitimation of the Aztec State. In *The Early State*, edited by Henri Claessen and Peter Skalnik, pp. 169–189. Mouton, The Hague.

Kusimba, Chapurukha M., Nam C. Kim, and Sibel B. Kusimba 2017 Trade and State

Formation in Ancient East African Coast and Southern Zambezia. In *Feast, Famine or Fighting?: Multiple Pathways to Social Complexity* edited by Richard J. Chacon and Rubén G. Mendoza, pp. 61–89. Springer, New York.

Kusmer, Kenneth L. 2002 *Down and Out, On the Road: The Homeless in American History.* Oxford University Press, New York.

Laborde, Sarah, Aboukar Mahamat, and Mark Moritz 2018 The Interplay of Top-Down Planning and Adaptive Self-Organization in an African Floodplain. *Human Ecology*: 1–12.

Lahiri, Nayanjot 1998 South Asian Demographic Archaeology and Harappan Population Estimates: A Brief Reassessment. *The Indian Economic and Social History Review* 35 (1): 1–22.

Láng, Orsolya 2016 Industry and Commerce in the City of Aquincum. In *Urban Craftsmen and Traders in the Roman World*, edited by Andrew Wilson and Miko Flohr, pp. 352–376. Oxford University Press, New York.

Lansing, J. Stephen 1991 *Priests and Programmers: Technologies of Power in the Engineered Landscape of Bali.* Princeton University Press, Princeton.

Latham, Alan 2009 Urban Life. In *Encyclopedia of Urban Studies*, edited by Ray Hutchison, pp. 891–894. Sage, New York.

Laurence, Ray 2007 *Roman Pompeii: Space and Society.* 2nd ed. Routledge, London.

Lawler, Andrew 2011 America's Lost City. *Science* 334: 1618–1623.

Lawrence, Dan, and T. J. Wilkinson 2015 Hubs and Upstarts: Pathways to Urbanism in the Northern Fertile Crescent. *Antiquity* 89: 328–344.

Layton, Robert, Sean O'Hara, and Alan Bilsborough 2012 Antiquity and Social Functions of Multilevel Social Organization Among Human Hunter-Gatherers. *International Journal of Primatology* 33 (5): 1215–1245.

Leacock, Eleanor (ed.) 1971 *The Culture of Poverty: A Critique.* Simon and Schuster, New York.

Lebecq, Stéphane 2012 The New Wiks or Emporia and the Development of a Maritime Economy in the Northern Seas (7th–9th Centuries). In *From One Sea to Another: Trading Places in the European and Mediterranean Early Middle Ages*, edited by Sauro Gelichi and Richard Hodges, pp. 11–21. Brepols, Turnhout.

Leeds, Anthony 1979 Forms of Urban Integration: "Social Urbanization" in Comparative Perspective. *Urban Anthropology* 8: 227–247.

——— 1980 Towns and Villages in Society: Hierarchies of Order and Cause. In *Cities in a Larger Context*, edited by Thomas W. Collins, pp. 6–33. University of Georgia Press, Athens.

Legesse, Asmarom 1998 The Design of Community and Its Socioecological Consequences: Marsabit District, Kenya. In *Rural Settlement Structure and African Development*, edited by Marilyn Silberfein, pp. 229–247. Westview, Boulder.

Lenski, Gerhard E. 1966 *Power and Privilege: A Theory of Social Stratification.* McGraw-Hill, New York.

Lepaon, T. 2011 Un nouveau plan pour Jerash/Gerasa (Jordanie). *Annual of the Department of Antiquities of Jordan* 55: 409–422.

Leroi-Gourhan, André, and Michel N. Brézillon 1973 *Fouilles de Pincevent: essai d'analyse ethnographique d'un habitat magdalénien (La section 36).* 2 vols. Centre National de la Recherche Scientifique, Paris.

Lesko, Leonard H. (ed.) 1994 *Pharaoh's Workers: The Villagers of Deir el Medina.* Cornell University Press, Ithaca.

Lesure, Richard G., R. J. Sinensky, Gregson Schachner, Thomas A. Wake, and Katelyn J. Bishop 2021 Large-Scale Patterns in the Agricultural Demographic Transition of Mesoamerica and Southwestern North America. *American Antiquity* 86 (3): 593–612.

Letesson, Quentin, and Carl Knappett (eds.) 2017 *Minoan Architecture and Urbanism: New Perspectives on an Ancient Built Environment.* Oxford University Press, New York.

Levi, Margaret 1988 *Of Rule and Revenue.* University of California Press, Berkeley.

Lewis, Oscar 1952 Urbanization without Breakdown: A Case Study. *Scientific Monthly* 75: 31–41.

1960 The Culture of Poverty in Mexico City: Two Case Studies. *The Economic Weekly* 12 (23–25): 965–972.

Lichtenberger, Achim, and Rubina Raja 2015 New Archaeological Research in the Northwest Quarter of Jerash and Its Implications for the Urban Development of Roman Gerasa. *American Journal of Archaeology* 119 (4): 483–500.

2017 Mosaicists at Work: The Organisation of Mosaic Production in Early Islamic Jerash. *Antiquity* 91: 998–1010.

Lilley, Keith D. 2002 *Urban Life in the Middle Ages, 1000–1450.* Palgrave, New York.

Lin, Jeffrey 2015 The Puzzling Persistence of Place. *Business Review, Federal Reserve Bank of Philadelphia, Research Department* (second quarter): 1–8.

Lindenfors, Patrik, Andreas Wartel, and Johan Lind 2021 "Dunbar's Number" Deconstructed. *Biology Letters* 17 (5): 20210158.

Lindsay, Brendan C. 2012 *Murder State: California's Native American Genocide, 1846–1873.* University of Nebraska Press, Lincoln.

Lis, Catharina, and Hugo Soly 1979 *Poverty and Capitalism in Pre-Industrial Europe.* Humanities Press, Atlantic Highlands, NJ.

Little, Daniel 2010 *New Contributions to the Philosophy of History.* Springer, New York.

Liu, Li 2004 *The Chinese Neolithic: Trajectories to Early States.* Cambridge University Press, New York.

Ljungkvist, John, and Per Frölund 2015 Gamla Uppsala: The Emergence of a Centre and a Magnate Complex. *Journal of Archaeology and Ancient History* 16: 2–30.

Lloyd, Peter E., and Peter Dicken 1977 *Location in Space: A Theoretical Approach to Economic Geography.* 2nd ed. Harper and Row, New York.

Lo Cascio, Elio 2006 Did the Population of Imperial Rome Reproduce Itself? In *Urbanism in the Preindustrial World: Cross-Cultural Approaches*, edited by Glenn R. Storey, pp. 52–68. University of Alabama Press, Tuscaloosa.

Lobo, José, Marina Alberti, Melissa Allen-Dumas et al. 2021 A Convergence Research Perspective on Graduate Education for Sustainable Urban Systems Science. *npj Urban Sustainability* 1 (1): 39.

Lobo, José, Luís M. A. Bettencourt, Scott G. Ortman, and Michael E. Smith 2020 Settlement Scaling Theory: Bridging the Study of Ancient and Contemporary Urban Systems. *Urban Studies* 57 (4): 731–747.

Lobo, José, Todd Whitelaw, Luís M. A. Bettencourt, Polly Wiessner, Michael E. Smith, and Scott G. Ortman 2022 Scaling of Hunter Gatherer Camp Size Indicates a Major Transition in Human Sociality. *Current Anthropology* 63: 69–94.

Lockhart, James 1992 *The Nahuas after the Conquest: A Social and Cultural History of the Indians of Central Mexico, Sixteenth through Eighteenth Centuries.* Stanford University Press, Stanford.

Lohse, Jon C. 2007 Commoner Ritual, Commoner Ideology: (Sub)-Alternative Views of Social Complexity in Prehispanic Mesoamerica. In *Commoner Ritual, Commoner Ideology: Evidence from Households Across Mesoamerica*, edited by Nancy Gonlin and Jon C. Lohse, pp. 1–54. University Press of Colorado, Boulder.

Lowell, Julie C. 1996 Moieties in Prehistory: A Case Study from the Pueblo Southwest *Journal of Field Archaeology* 23: 77–90.

Lucas, Rex A. 1971 *Minetown, Milltown, Railtown: Life in Canadian Communities of Single Industry.* University of Toronto Press, Toronto.

Lucas, Robert E., Jr. 1988 On the Mechanics of Economic Development. *Journal of Monetary Economics* 229 (1): 3–42.

Lucero, Lisa J., Roland Fletcher, and Robin Coningham 2015 From "Collapse" to Urban Diaspora: The Transformation of

Low-Density, Dispersed Agrarian Urbanism. *Antiquity* 89: 1139–1154.

Lund, John 1999 Rhodian Amphorae in Rhodes and Alexandria as Evidence of Trade. In *Hellenistic Rhodes: Politics, Culture, and Society*, edited by Vincent Gabrielsen, Per Bilde, Troels Engberg-Petersen, Lise Hannetsad, and Jan Zahle, pp. 187–204. Studies in Hellenistic Civilization, vol. 9. Aarhus University Press, Aarhus.

    2011 Rhodian Transport Amphorae as a Source for Economic Ebbs and Flows in the Eastern Mediterranean in the Second Century BC. In *The Economies of Hellenistic Societies, Third to First Centuries BC*, edited by Zosia Archibald, John K. Davies, and Vincent Gabrielsen, pp. 280–295. Oxford University Press, New York.

Lustig, Terry, Sarah Klassen, Damian Evans, Robert French, and Ian Moffat 2018 Evidence for the Breakdown of an Angkorian Hydraulic System, and Its Historical Implications for Understanding the Khmer Empire. *Journal of Archaeological Science: Reports* 17: 195–211.

Lynch, Kevin 1981 *A Theory of Good City Form.* MIT Press, Cambridge.

MacGinnis, John 2003 A Corvée Gang from the Time of Cyrus. *Zeitschrift für Assyrologie* 93: 88–115.

Magaloni, Diana 2017 The Colors of Time: Teotihuacan Mural Painting Tradition. In *Teotihuacan: City of Water, City of Fire*, edited by Matthew H. Robb, pp. 174–179. Fine Arts Museums of San Francisco, De Young, and University of California Press, San Francisco.

Magnoni, Aline, Traci Ardren, Scott R. Hutson, and Bruce H. Dahlin 2014 The Production of Space and Identity at Classic-Period Chunchuil, Yucatan, Mexico. In *Making Ancient Cities: Space and Place in Early Urban Societies*, edited by Kevin D. Fisher and Andy Creekmore, pp. 145–180. University Press of Colorado, Boulder.

Maher, Lisa A., Tobias Richter, Danielle Macdonald, Matthew D. Jones, Louise Martin, and Jay T. Stock 2012 Twenty Thousand-Year-Old Huts at a Hunter-Gatherer Settlement in Eastern Jordan. *PloS One* 7 (2): e31447.

Mahoney, James 2012 The Logic of Process Tracing Tests in the Social Sciences. *Sociological Methods and Research* 41 (4): 570–597.

Makarewicz, Cheryl A., and Bill Finlayson 2018 Constructing Community in the Neolithic of Southern Jordan: Quotidian Practice in Communal Architecture. *PloS One* 13 (6): e0193712.

Makky, Ghazy Abdul Wahed 1978 *Mecca the Pilgrimage City: A Study of Pilgrim Accommodation.* Croom Helm for The Hajj Research Centre, King Abdul Aziz University, London.

Mann, Michael 1986 *The Sources of Social Power, Volume 1: A History of Power from the Beginning to A.D. 1760.* Cambridge University Press, New York.

Manzanilla, Linda R., Xim Bokhimi, Dolores Tenorio et al. 2017 Procedencia de la mica de Teotihuacan: control de los recursos suntuarios foráneos por las élites gobernantes. *Anales de Antropología* 51 (1): 23–38.

Manzanilla, Linda R., and Claude Chapdelaine (eds.) 2009 *Domestic Life in Prehispanic Capitals: A Study of Specialization, Hierarchy, and Ethnicity.* Memoirs, vol. 46. University of Michigan, Museum of Anthropology, Ann Arbor.

Manzanilla, Linda R., and Kenneth G. Hirth (eds.) 2011 *Producción artesanal y especializada en Mesoamérica: Áreas de actividad y procesos productivos.* Universidad Nacional Autónoma de México, Mexico City.

Marcus, Joyce 1983 On the Nature of the Mesoamerican City. In *Prehistoric Settlement Patterns: Essays in Honor of Gordon R. Willey*, edited by Evon Z. Vogt and Richard M. Leventhal, pp. 195–242. University of New Mexico Press, Albuquerque.

Marcus, Joyce, and Jeremy Sabloff (eds.) 2008 *The Ancient City: New Perspectives on Urbanism in the Old and New World.* SAR Press, Santa Fe.

Marcuse, Peter 2002 The Partitioned City in History. In *Of States and Cities: The Partitioning of Urban Space*, edited by Peter Marcuse and Ronald van Kempen, pp. 11–34. Oxford University Press, New York.

Marcuse, Peter, and Ronald van Kempen (eds.) 2002 *Of States and Cities: The Partitioning of Urban Space*. Oxford University Press, New York.

Marris, Peter 1961 *Family and Social Change in an African City*. Routledge and Kegan Paul, London.

Martin, Simon, and Nikolai Grube 2008 *Chronicle of the Maya Kings and Queens: Deciphering the Dynasties of the Ancient Maya*. 2nd ed. Thames and Hudson, New York.

Martinón-Torres, Marcos, and David Killick 2013 Archaeological Theories and Archaeological Sciences. In *Oxford Handbook of Archaeological Theory*, edited by Andrew Gardner, Mark Lake, and Ulrike Sommer. Oxford University Press (published online), New York.

Massey, Douglas S. 2016 Residential Segregation is the Linchpin of Racial Stratification. *City and Community* 15 (1): 4–7.

Massey, Douglas S., and Nancy A. Denton 1993 *American Apartheid: Segregation and the Making of the Underclass*. Harvard University Press, Cambridge, MA.

Matson, Pamela, William C. Clark, and Krister Andersson 2016 *Pursuing Sustainability: A Guide to the Science and Practice*. Princeton University Press, Princeton, NJ.

Mayer, Ernst E. 2014 *The Ancient Middle Classes: Urban Life and Aesthetics in the Roman Empire, 100 BCE–250 CE*. Harvard University Press, Cambridge.

Mayhew, Bruce H., and Robert L. Levinger 1977 Size and the Density of Interaction in Human Aggregates. *American Journal of Sociology* 82: 86–110.

Mayr, Ernst 1982 *The Growth of Biological Thought: Diversity, Evolution, and Inheritance*. Harvard University Press, Cambridge.

McCloskey, Dierdre 2010 *Bourgeois Dignity: Why Economics Can't Explain the Modern World*. University of Chicago Press, Chicago.

McEnroe, John C. 2010 *Architecture of Minoan Crete: Constructing Identity in the Aegean Bronze Age*. University of Texas Press, Austin.

McGillivray, Mark, and Howard White 2006 Measuring Development? The UNCP's Human Development Index. *Journal of International Development* 5: 183–192.

McGuire, Randall H., and Michael B. Schiffer 1983 A Theory of Architectural Design. *Journal of Anthropological Archaeology* 2: 277–303.

McKay, Alexander G. 1975 *Houses, Villas and Palaces in the Roman World*. Cornell University Press, Ithaca.

McKeown, Maeve 2019 The Natural Condition of Mankind. *European Journal of Political Theory* 18 (2): 281–292.

McKitterick, Rosamond 2011 A King on the Move: The Place of an Itinerant Court in Charlemagne's Government. In *Royal Courts in Dynastic States and Empires: A Global Perspective*, edited by Jeroen Duindam, Tülay Artan, and Metin Kunt, pp. 145–169. Brill, Leiden.

McKnight, John 2013 Neighborhood Necessities: Seven Functions That Only Effectively Organized Neighborhoods Can Provide. *National Civic Review* 102 (3): 22–24.

McKnight, John, and Peter Block 2010 *The Abundant Community: Awakening the Power of Families and Neighborhoods*. Berrett-Koehler, San Francisco.

McNeill, William H. 1979 Historical Patterns of Migration. *Current Anthropology* 20 (1): 95–102.

Mehaffy, Michael W. 2008 Generative Methods in Urban Design: A Progress Assessment. *Journal of Urbanism* 1: 57–75.

Meier, Richard L. 1962 *A Communications Theory of Urban Growth*. MIT Press, Cambridge.

Meir, Avinoam 1997 *As Nomadism Ends: The Israeli Bedouin of the Negev*. Westview, Boulder, CO.

Mellaart, James 1967 *Çatal Hüyük: A Neolithic Town in Anatolia.* McGraw-Hill, New York.

Merton, Robert K. 1968 *Social Theory and Social Structure.* 3rd ed. Free Press, New York.

Mesqui, Jean 1979 *Provins: La fortification d'une ville au Moyen Age.* Bibliothèque de la Société française d'archéologie. Droz, Geneva.

Mihesuah, Devon A. (ed.) 2000 *Repatriation Reader: Who Owns American Indian Remains?* University of Nebraska Press, Lincoln.

Milanovic, Branko 2011 *The Haves and the Have-Nots: A Brief and Idiosyncratic History of Global Inequality.* Basic Books, New York.

Milanovic, Branko, Peter H. Lindert, and Jeffrey G. Williamson 2011 Pre-Industrial Inequality. *The Economic Journal* 121: 255–272.

Miller, Heather M.-L. 2000 Reassessing the Urban Structure of Harappa: Evidence from Craft Production Distribution. In *South Asian Archaeology 1997*, edited by Marrizio Taddei and Giuseppe de Marco, 3 vols., pp. 77–100, vol. 1. Istituto Italiano per l'Africa e l'Oriente, Rome.

Millon, René, and Jeffrey H. Altschul 2015 The Making of the Map: The Origin and Lessons of the Teotihuacan Mapping Project. *Ancient Mesoamerica* 26 (1): 135–151.

Millon, René, R. Bruce Drewitt, and George L. Cowgill 1973 *Urbanization at Teotihuacan, Mexico, Volume 1: The Teotihuacan Map, Part 2: Maps.* University of Texas Press, Austin.

Milner, George R. 2005 *The Moundbuilders: Ancient Peoples of Eastern North America.* Thames and Hudson, New York.

Mintz, Sidney W. 1961 Pratik: Haitian Personal Economic Relationships. In *Proceedings of the 1961 Annual Spring Meeting of the American Ethnological Society*, edited by Viola E. Garfield, pp. 54–63. University of Washington Press, Seattle.

Mitchell, Melanie 2009 *Complexity: A Guided Tour.* Oxford University Press, New York.

Mitchell, Timothy 1991 The Limits of the State: Beyond Statist Approaches and Their Critics. *American Political Science Review* 85 (1): 77–96.

Moeller, Nadine 2016 *The Archaeology of Urbanism in Ancient Egypt: From the Predynastic Period to the End of the Middle Kingdom.* Cambridge University Press, New York.

Mogren, Mats 2013 The First Sparks and the Far Horizons: Stirring Up the Thinking on the Earliest Scandinavian Urbanization Processes – Again. *Lund Archaeological Review* 18: 73–88.

Moore, Jerry D. 1996 *Architecture and Power in the Ancient Andes: The Archaeology of Public Buildings.* Cambridge University Press, New York.

2012 *The Prehistory of Home.* University of California Press, Berkeley.

Moore, John H. 1987 *The Cheyenne Nation: A Social and Demographic History.* University of Nebraska Press, Lincoln.

Moroni, Stefano, Ward Rauws, and Stefano Cozzolino 2020 Forms of Self-Organization: Urban Complexity and Planning Implications. *Environment and Planning B: Urban Analytics and City Science* 47 (2): 220–234.

Morris, Craig 1972 State Settlements in Tawantinsuyu: A Strategy of Compulsory Urbanism. In *Contemporary Archaeology: A Guide to Theory and Contributions*, edited by Mark P. Leone, pp. 393–401. SIU Press, Carbondale.

Morris, Craig, R. Alan Covey, and Pat Stein 2011 *The Huánuco Pampa Archaeological Project, Volume 1: The Plaza and Palace Complex.* Anthropological Papers, vol. 96. American Museum of Natural History, New York.

Morris, Craig, and Donald Thompson 1985 *Huánuco Pampa: An Inca City and its Hinterland.* Thames and Hudson, New York.

Morris, Ian 2004 Economic Growth in Ancient Greece. *Journal of Institutional and Theoretical Economics* 160: 709–742.

2005 Archaeology, Standards of Living, and Greek Economic History. In *The Ancient Economy: Evidence and Models*, edited by J. G. Manning and Ian Morris, pp. 91–126. Stanford University Press, Stanford.

2013 *The Measure of Civilization: How Social Development Decides the Fate of Nations.* Princeton University Press, Princeton.

Morrison, Kathleen D. 1994 The Intensification of Production: Archaeological Approaches. *Journal of Archaeological Method and Theory* 1: 111–159.

Moseley, Michael E., and Carol J. Mackey 1974 *Twenty-Four Architectural Plans of Chan Chan, Peru: Structure and Form at the Capital of Chimor.* Peabody Museum Press, Cambridge.

Müller, Johannes 2013 Demographic Traces of Technological Innovation, Social Change and Mobility: From 1 to 8 Million Europeans (6000–2000 BCE). In *Environment and Subsistence: Forty Years after Janusz Kruk's Settlement Studies*, pp. 493–506. Mittel and Verlag Dr. Rudolf Habelt, Rzeszów and Bonn.

Muller, Jon 1997 *Mississippian Political Economy.* Plenum, New York.

Mulligan, Gordon F., Mark D. Partridge, and John I. Carruthers 2012 Central Place Theory and Its Reemergence in Regional Science. *Annals of Regional Science* 48 (2): 405–431.

Munson, Jessica, and Jonathan Scholnick 2021 Wealth and Well-Being in an Ancient Maya Community. *Journal of Archaeological Method and Theory* 29:1–30.

Murdock, George P. 1949 *Social Structure.* The Free Press, New York.

Murphey, Rhoads 1982 *The Scope of Geography.* 3rd ed. Methuen, New York.

Murra, John V., and Craig Morris 1976 Dynastic Oral Tradition, Administrative Records and Archaeology in the Andes. *World Archaeology* 7 (3): 269–279.

Nadeau, Robert 1998 Spontaneous Order. In *Handbook of Economic Methodology*, edited by John B. Davis, D. Wade Hands, and Uskali Maki, pp. 477–484. Edward Elgar, Northampton, MA.

Naroll, Raoul 1956 A Preliminary Index of Social Development. *American Anthropologist* 58 (4): 687–715.

1962 Floor Area and Settlement Population. *American Antiquity* 27: 587–589.

Neale, Walter C. 1971 Monetization, Commercialization, Market Orientation, and Market Dependence. In *Studies in Economic Anthropology*, edited by George Dalton, pp. 25–29. Anthropological Studies, vol. 7. American Anthropological Association, Washington, DC.

Netting, Robert McC. 1993 *Smallholders, Householders: Farm Families and the Ecology of Intensive, Sustainable Agriculture.* Stanford University Press, Stanford.

Netting, Robert McC., Richard R. Wilk, and Eric J. Arnould (eds.) 1984 *Households: Comparative and Historical Studies of the Domestic Group.* University of California Press, Berkeley.

Nevett, Lisa C. 2010 *Domestic Space in Classical Antiquity.* Cambridge University Press, New York.

Nevett, Lisa C., E. Bettina Tsigarida, Zosia H. Archibald et al. 2020 Constructing the "Urban Profile" of an Ancient Greek City: Evidence from the Olynthos Project. *The Annual of the British School at Athens*: 1–50.

Nichols, Deborah L. 2013 Merchants and Merchandise: The Archaeology of Aztec Commerce at Otumba, Mexico. In *Merchants, Markets, and Exchange in the Pre-Columbian World*, edited by Kenneth G. Hirth and Joanne Pillsbury, pp. 49–84. Dumbarton Oaks, Washington, DC.

Nichols, Deborah L., Frances F. Berdan, and Michael E. Smith (eds.) 2017 *Rethinking the Aztec Economy.* University of Arizona Press, Tucson.

Nichols, Deborah L., Mary Jane McLaughlin, and Maura Benton 2000 Production Intensification and Regional Specialization: Maguey Fibers and Textiles in the Aztec

City-State of Otumba. *Ancient Mesoamerica* 11: 267–292.

Nightingale, Carl H. 2012 *Segregation: A Global History of Divided Cities*. University of Chicago Press, Chicago.

Nisbet, Robert A. 1966 *The Sociological Tradition*. Basic Book, New York.

Noble, Ian R., and Saleemul Huq 2014 Adaptation: Needs and Options. In *Climate Change 2014 – Impacts, Adaptation and Vulnerability: Regional Aspects, Part A: Global and Sectoral Aspects. Contribution of Working Group II to the Fifth Assessment Report of the Intergovernmental Panel on Climate Change*, edited by Christopher B. Field and Vicente R. Barros, pp. 833–868. Cambridge University Press, New York.

North, Douglass C. 1981 *Structure and Change in Economic History*. Norton, New York.

    1990 *Institutions, Institutional Change and Economic Performance*. Cambridge University Press, New York.

North, Douglass C., John J. Wallis, and Barry R. Weingast 2009 *Violence and Social Orders: A Conceptual Framework for Interpreting Recorded Human History*. Cambridge University Press, New York.

Norwood, Alexandra, and Michael E. Smith 2021 Urban Open Space and Governance in Ancient Mesoamerica. *Journal of Archaeological Method and Theory*. Published online.

O'Brien, Daniel Tumminelli 2011 Sociality in the City: Using Biological Principles to Explore the Relationship between High Population Density and Social Behavior. In *Advances in Sociology Research*, edited by Jared A. Jaworski, pp. 203–216, vol. 8. Nova Science Publishers.

O'Flaherty, Brendan 2005 *City Economics*. Harvard University Press, Cambridge.

O'Sullivan, Arthur 2011 *Urban Economics*. 8th ed. McGraw-Hill, New York.

Ober, Josiah 2015 *The Rise and Fall of Classical Greece*. Princeton University Press, Princeton, NJ.

Ogilvie, Sheilagh 2007 Whatever Is, Is Right? Economic Institutions in Pre-Industrial Europe. *Economic History Review* 60: 649–684.

    2011 *Institutions and European Trade: Merchant Guilds, 1000–1800*. Cambridge University Press, New York.

    2019 *The European Guilds: An Economic Analysis*. Princeton University Press, Princeton, NJ.

    2021 Thinking Carefully about Inclusiveness: Evidence from European Guilds. *Journal of Institutional Economics* 17 (2): 185–200.

Ogilvie, Sheilagh, and A. W. Carus 2014 Institutions and Economic Growth in Historical Perspective. In *Handbook of Economic Growth*, edited by Philippe Aghion and Steven N. Durlauf, pp. 403–513, vol. 2B. Elsevier, Amsterdam.

Ohlrau, René 2020 *Maidanets'ke: Development and Decline of a Trypillia Mega-Site in Central Ukraine*. Sidestone Press, Leiden.

Ojo, G. J. Afolabi 1966a *Yoruba Culture: A Geographical Analysis*. University of Ife and University of London Press, Ife and London.

    1966b *Yoruba Palaces: A Study of Afins of Yorubaland*. University of London Press, London.

Oliver, Chad 1962 *Ecology and Cultural Continuity as Contributing Factors in the Social Organization of the Plains Indians*. University of California Press, Berkeley.

Olson, Jan Marie 2001 *Unequal Consumption: A Study of Domestic Wealth Differentials in Three Late Postclassic Mexican Communities*. PhD dissertation, Department of Anthropology, University at Albany, SUNY.

Olson, Jan Marie, and Michael E. Smith 2016 Material Expressions of Wealth and Social Class at Aztec-Period Sites in Morelos, Mexico. *Ancient Mesoamerica* 27 (1): 133–147.

Ortman, Scott G. 2012 *Winds from the North: Tewa Origins and Historical Anthropology*. University of Utah Press, Salt Lake City.

2016 Why All Archaeologists Should Care about and Do Population Estimates. In *Exploring Cause and Explanation: Historical Ecology, Demography, and Movement in the American Southwest*, edited by Cynthia L. Herhahn and Ann F. Ramenofsky, pp. 103–120. University Press of Colorado, Boulder.

Ortman, Scott G., Andrew H. F. Cabaniss, Jennie O. Sturm, and Luís M. A. Bettencourt 2014 The Pre-History of Urban Scaling. *PLoS One* 9 (2): e87902.

2015 Settlement Scaling and Increasing Returns in an Ancient Society. *Science Advances* 1 (1): e1400066.

Ortman, Scott G., and Grant D. Coffey 2017 Settlement Scaling in Middle-Range Societies. *American Antiquity* 82 (4): 662–682.

Ortman, Scott G., Kaitlyn E. Davis, José Lobo, Michael E. Smith, Luís M. A. Bettencourt, and Aaron Trumbo 2016 Settlement Scaling and Economic Change in the Central Andes. *Journal of Archaeological Science* 73: 94–106. http://bit.ly/2aHXpGk.

Ortman, Scott G., and José Lobo 2020 Smithian Growth in a Non-Industrial Society. *Science Advances* 6: eaba5694.

Ortman, Scott G., José Lobo, and Michael E. Smith 2020a Cities: Complexity, Theory, and History. *PLoS One* 15 (12): e0243621. https://journals.plos.org/plosone/article?id=10.1371/journal.pone.0243621.

Ortman, Scott G., Michael E. Smith, José Lobo, and Luís M. A. Bettencourt 2020b Why Archaeology Is Necessary for a Theory of Urbanization. *Journal of Urban Archaeology* 1: 151–167. www.brepolsonline.net/doi/epdf/10.1484/J.JUA.5.120914.

Ossa, Alanna, Michael E. Smith, and José Lobo 2017 The Size of Plazas in Mesoamerican Cities: A Quantitative Analysis and Social Interpretation. *Latin American Antiquity* 28 (4): 457–475.

Ostrom, Elinor 1990 *Governing the Commons: The Evolution of Institutions for Collective Action*. Cambridge University Press, New York.

2005 *Understanding Institutional Diversity*. Princeton University Press, Princeton.

Otis Charlton, Cynthia L. 1994 Plebians and Patricians: Contrasting Patterns of Production and Distribution in the Aztec Figurine and Lapidary Industries. In *Economies and Polities in the Aztec Realm*, edited by Mary G. Hodge and Michael E. Smith, pp. 195–219. Institute for Mesoamerican Studies, Albany.

Pacichelli, Giovanni Battista 1703 *Il Regno de Napoli in prospettiva diviso in dodeci provincie* ... Nella stamperia di Michele Luigi Mutio, Naples.

Pacifico, David, and Lise A. Truex (eds.) 2019 *Excavating Neighborhoods: A Cross-Cultural Exploration*. Archaeological Papers, vol. 30. American Anthropological Association, Washington, DC.

Page, Abigail E., Sylvain Viguier, Mark Dyble et al. 2016 Reproductive Trade-Offs in Extant Hunter-Gatherers Suggest Adaptive Mechanism for the Neolithic Expansion. *Proceedings of the National Academy of Sciences* 113 (17): 4694–4699.

Page, Max, and Timothy Mennell (eds.) 2011 *Reconsidering Jane Jacobs*. American Planning Association, Chicago.

Palka, Joel W. 2014 *Maya Pilgrimage to Ritual Landscapes: Insights from Archaeology, History, and Ethnography*. University of New Mexico Press, Albuquerque.

Parker Pearson, Michael, and Colin Richards (eds.) 1994 *Architecture and Order*. Routledge, London.

Parker, Simon 2004 *Urban Theory and the Urban Experience: Encountering the City*. Routledge, New York.

Parkinson, William A., Dimitri Nakassis, and Michael L. Galaty 2013 Crafts, Specialists, and Markets in Mycenaean Greece: Introduction. *American Journal of Archaeology* 117 (3): 413–422.

Parry, William J. 2001 Production and Exchange of Obsidian Tools in Late Aztec City-States. *Ancient Mesoamerica* 12: 101–112.

Pauketat, Timothy R. 1997 Specialization, Political Symbols, and the Crafty Elite of Cahokia. *Southeastern Archaeology* 16: 1–15.

2000 The Tragedy of the Commoners. In *Agency in Archaeology*, edited by Marcia-Anne Dobres and John E. Robb, pp. 113–129. Routledge, London.

2007 *Chiefdoms and Other Archaeological Delusions*. AltaMira, Walnut Creek.

2009 *Cahokia: Ancient America's Great City on the Mississippi*. Viking, New York.

Paynter, Robert, and Randall H. McGuire 1991 The Archaeology of Inequality: Material Culture, Domination and Resistance. In *The Archaeology of Inequality*, edited by Randall H. McGuire and Robert Paynter, pp. 1–27. Blackwell, Oxford.

Peacock, D. P. S. 1982 *Pottery in the Roman World: An Ethnoarchaeological Approach*. Longman, New York.

Pearl, Judea, and Dana Mackenzie 2018 *The Book of Why: The New Science of Cause and Effect*. Basic Books, New York.

Peel, J. D. Y. 1983 *Ijeshas and Nigerians: The Incorporation of a Yoruba Kingdom, 1890s–1970s*. Cambridge University Press, New York.

2000 Yoruba as a City-State Culture. In *A Comparative Study of Thirty City-State Cultures*, edited by Mogens Herman Hansen, pp. 507–518. The Royal Danish Academy of Sciences and Letters, Copenhagen.

Peeples, Matthew A. 2018 *Connected Communities: Networks, Identity, and Social Change in the Ancient Cibola World*. University of Arizona Press, Tucson.

Perreault, Charles 2019 *The Quality of the Archaeological Record*. University of Chicago Press, Chicago.

Persson, Karl Gunnar, and Paul Sharp 2015 *An Economic History of Europe: Knowledge, Institutions and Growth, 600 to the Present*. 2nd ed. Cambridge University Press, New York.

Pestell, Tim 2011 Markets, Emporia, Wics, and "Productive" Sites: Pre-Viking Trade Centres in Anglo-Saxon England. In *Oxford Handbook of Anglo-Saxon Archaeology*, edited by Helena Hamerow, David A. Hinton, and Sally Crawford, pp. 556–579. Oxford University Press, New York.

Peterson, Christian E., and Gideon Shelach 2010 The Evolution of Early Yangshao Period Village Organization in the Middle Reaches of Northern China's Yellow River Valley. In *Becoming Villagers: Comparing Early Village Societies*, edited by Matthew S. Bandy and Jake R. Fox, pp. 246–275. University of Arizona Press, Tucson.

Petruccioli, Atillio 2006 The Courtyard House: Typological Variations Over Space and Time. In *Courtyard Housing: Past, Present and Future*, edited by Brian Edwards, Magda Sibley, Mohamad Hakmi, and Peter Land, pp. 2–26. Taylor and Francis, New York.

Philippsen, Bente, Claus Feveile, Jesper Olsen, and Søren M. Sindbæk 2022 Single-Year Radiocarbon Dating Anchors Viking Age Trade Cycles in Time. *Nature* 601 (7893): 392–396.

Phillips, David 2006 *Quality of Life: Concept, Policy and Practice*. Routledge, New York.

Pijawka, K. David, and Martin A. Gromulat (eds.) 2012 *Understanding Sustainable Cities: Concepts, Cases, and Solutions*. Kendall Hunt, Dubuque.

Pirngruber, Reinhard 2017 *The Economy of Late Achaemenid and Seleucid Babylonia*. Cambridge University Press, New York.

Plog, Stephen 1997 *Ancient Peoples of the American Southwest*. Thames and Hudson, New York.

Poehler, Eric E. 2017 *The Traffic Systems of Pompeii*. Oxford University Press, New York.

Poehler, Eric E., and Benjamin M. Crowther 2018 Paving Pompeii: The Archaeology of Stone-Paved Streets. *American Journal of Archaeology* 122 (4): 579–609.

Poehler, Eric, M. Flohr, and K. Cole (eds.) 2011 *Pompeii: Art, Industry and Infrastructure*. Oxbow, Oxford.

Pojani, Dorina 2019 The Self-Built City: Theorizing Urban Design of Informal Settlements. *International Journal of Architectural Research* 13 (2): 294–313.

Polanyi, Karl, Conrad M. Arensburg, and Harry W. Pearson (eds.) 1957 *Trade and Market in the Early Empires.* Henry Regnery Co., Chicago.

Possehl, Gregory L. 1990 Revolution in the Urban Revolution: The Emergence of Indus Urbanization. *Annual Review of Anthropology* 19: 261–282.

Prak, Maarten 2018 *Citizens without Nations: Urban Citizenship in Europe and the World, c. 1000–1789.* Cambridge University Press, New York.

Pryor, Frederic L. 1977 *Origins of the Economy: A Comparative Study of Distribution in Primitive and Peasant Economies.* Academic Press, New York.

Pumain, Denise, Fabien Paulus, Céline Vacchiana-Marcuzzo, and José Lobo 2006 An Evolutionary Theory for Interpreting Urban Scaling Laws. *Cybergeo: European Journal of Geography* (article 343). http://cybergeo .revues.org/2519?lang=en.

Pumain, Denise, and Céline Rozenblat 2018 Introduction: A Global View of Urbanization. In *International and Transnational Perspectives on Urban Systems,* edited by Céline Rozenblat, Denise Pumain, and E. Velasquez, pp. ix–xviii. Springer, New York.

Ragin, Charles C., and Lisa M. Amoroso 2011 *Constructing Social Research: The Unity and Diversity of Method.* 2nd ed. Sage, Thousand Oaks, CA.

Raja, Rubina, and Søren M. Sindbaek (eds.) 2018 *Urban Network Evolutions: Towards a High-Definition Archaeology.* Aarhus University Press, Aarhus.

Ramaswami, Anu, Luís Bettencourt, Andres Clarens et al. 2018 *Sustainable Urban Systems: Articulating a Long-Term Convergence Research Agenda.* National Science Foundation, Sustainable Urban Systems Subcommittee, Washington DC. www.nsf.gov/ere/ere web/ac-ere/sustainable-urban-systems.pdf.

Ramaswami, Anu, Armistead G. Russell, Patricia J. Culligan, Karnamadakala Rahul Sharma, and Emani Kumar 2016 Meta-Principles for Developing Smart, Sustainable, and Healthy Cities. *Science* 352: 940–943.

Rao, Vijayendra 2008 Symbolic Public Goods and the Coordination of Collective Action: A Comparison of Local Development in India and Indonesia. In *The Contested Commons: Conversations between Economists and Anthropologists,* edited by Pranab Bardhan and Isha Ray, pp. 168–182. Blackwell, Oxford.

Rapoport, Amos 1969 *House Form and Culture.* Prentice Hall, New York.

1988 Levels of Meaning in the Built Environment. In *Cross-Cultural Perspectives in Non Verbal Communication,* edited by Fernando Poyatos, pp. 317–336. C. J. Hogrefe, Toronto.

1990a *The Meaning of the Built Environment: A Nonverbal Communication Approach.* Rev. ed. University of Arizona Press, Tucson.

1990b Systems of Activities and Systems of Settings. In *Domestic Architecture and the Use of Space: An Interdisciplinary Cross-Cultural Study,* edited by Susan Kent, pp. 9–20. Cambridge University Press, New York.

Rappaport, Roy A. 1968 *Pigs for the Ancestors: Ritual in the Ecology of New Guinea People.* Yale University Press, New Haven.

Rascovan, Nicolás, Karl-Göran Sjögren, Kristian Kristiansen, et al. 2019 Emergence and Spread of Basal Lineages of *Yersinia Pestis* during the Neolithic Decline. *Cell* 176 (1–2): 295–305, e10.

Rattenborg, Rune, and Louise Blanke 2017 Jarash in the Islamic Ages (c. 700–1200 CE): A Critical Review. *Levant* 49 (3): 312–332.

Rattray, Evelyn C. 1993 *The Oaxaca Barrio at Teotihuacan.* Monografías Mesoamericanas, vol. 1. Instituto de Estudios Avanzados, Universidad de las Américas, Puebla.

Rauh, Nicholas K. 1999 Rhodes, Rome, and the Eastern Mediterranean Wine Trade. In *Hellenistic Rhodes: Politics, Culture, and Society*, edited by Vincent Gabrielsen, Per Bilde, Troels Engberg-Petersen, Lise Hannetsad, and Jan Zahle, pp. 162–186. Studies in Hellenistic Civilization, vol. 9. Aarhus University Press, Aarhus.

Redfield, Robert 1941 *The Folk Culture of Yucatan*. University of Chicago Press, Chicago.

Redwood, Mark (ed.) 2008 *Agriculture in Urban Planning: Generating Livelihoods and Food Security*. Earthscan, London.

Renfrew, Colin 1975 Trade as Action at a Distance: Questions of Integration and Communication. In *Ancient Civilization and Trade*, edited by Jeremy A. Sabloff and C. C. Lamberg-Karlovsky, pp. 3–59. University of New Mexico Press, Albuquerque.

Renfrew, Colin, and Eric V. Level 1979 Exploring Dominance: Predicting Polities from Centers. In *Transformations: Mathematical Approaches to Culture Change*, edited by Colin Renfrew and Kenneth L. Cooke, pp. 145–167. Academic Press, New York.

Revi, Aromar, David E. Satterthwaite, Fernando Aragón-Durand et al. 2014 Urban Areas. In *Climate Change 2014 – Impacts, Adaptation and Vulnerability: Regional Aspects, Part A: Global and Sectoral Aspects. Contribution of Working Group II to the Fifth Assessment Report of the Intergovernmental Panel on Climate Change*, edited by Christopher B. Field and Vicente R. Barros, pp. 535–612. Cambridge University Press, New York.

Richardson, Gary 2003 Guilds, Laws, and Markets for Manufactured Merchandise in Late-Medieval England. *Explorations in Economic History* 41 (1): 1–25.

Roach, Levi 2011 Hosting the King: Hospitality and the Royal Iter in Tenth-Century England. *Journal of Medieval History* 37 (1): 34–46.

Robertson, Ian G. 2015 Investigating Teotihuacan through TMP Surface Collections and Observations. *Ancient Mesoamerica* 26 (1): 163–181.

Robin, Cynthia 2013 *Everyday Life Matters: Maya Farmers at Chan*. University Press of Florida, Gainesville.

Robinson, David M. 1929–1959 *Excavations at Olynthus*. 14 vols. Johns Hopkins University Press, Baltimore.

Rodrigo, Allen, Susan Alberts, Karen Cranston et al. 2013 Science Incubators: Synthesis Centers and Their Role in the Research Ecosystem. *PLoS Biology* 11 (1): e1001468.

Roesdahl, Else 1987 The Danish Geometrical Viking Fortresses and Their Context. *Anglo-Norman Studies* 9: 208–226.

Roesdahl, Else, Søren M. Sindbaek, Anne Pedersen, and David M. Wilson 2014 *Aggersborg: The Viking-Age Settlement and Fortress*. Jutland Archaeological Society and National Museum of Denmark, Moesgaard and Copenhagen.

Romanowska, Iza, Tom Brughmans, Philip Bes et al. 2022 A Study of the Centuries-Long Reliance on Local Ceramics in Jerash through Full Quantification and Simulation. *Journal of Archaeological Method and Theory* 29 (1): 31–49.

Romer, Paul M. 1986 Increasing Returns and Long-Run Growth. *Journal of Political Economy* 94 (5): 1002–1037.

Root, Margaret Cool 2015 Achaemenid Imperial Architecture: Performative Porticoes of Persepolis. In *Persian Kingship and Architecture: Strategies of Power in Iran from the Achaemenids to the Pahlavis*, edited by Sussan Babaie and Talinn Grigor, pp. 1–64. I. B. Taubris, London.

Roseberry, William 1988 Political Economy. *Annual Review of Anthropology* 17: 161–185.

Rosenswig, Robert M. 2015 A Mosaic of Adaptation: The Archaeological Record for Mesoamerica's Archaic Period. *Journal of Archaeological Research* 23 (2): 115–162.

Runge, Mads, and Mogens Bo Henriksen 2018 The Origins of Odense: New Aspects of Early Urbanisation in Southern Scandinavia. *Danish Journal of Archaeology* 7 (1): 2–68.

Rutter, Andrew F. 1971 Ashanti Vernacular Architecture. In *Shelter in Africa*, edited by Paul Oliver, pp. 153–171. Barrie and Jenkins, London.

Rykwert, Joseph 1988 *The Idea of a Town: The Anthropology of Urban Form in Rome, Italy, and the Ancient World*. MIT Press, Cambridge.

Sabloff, Jeremy A. (ed.) 2003 *Tikal: Dynasties, Foreigners, and Affairs of State: Advancing Maya Archaeology*. SAR Press, Santa Fe.

Sahlins, Marshall 1972 *Stone-Age Economics*. Aldine, Chicago.

Sampson, Robert J. 2009 Racial Stratification and the Durable Tangle of Neighborhood Inequality. *Annals of the American Academy of Political and Social Science* 621: 260–280.

2012 *Great American City: Chicago and the Enduring Neighborhood Effect*. University of Chicago Press, Chicago.

2017 Urban Sustainability in an Age of Enduring Inequalities: Advancing Theory and Ecometrics for the 21st-Century City. *Proceedings of the National Academy of Sciences* 114: 8957–8962.

Samuel, Delwen 1999 Bread Making and Social Interactions at the Amarna Workmen's Village, Egypt. *World Archaeology* 31: 121–144.

Sandeford, David S. 2021 A Quantitative Analysis of Intensification in the Ethnographic Record. *Nature Human Behaviour* 5: 1502–1509.

Sanders, William T., Jeffrey R. Parsons, and Robert S. Santley 1979 *The Basin of Mexico: Ecological Processes in the Evolution of a Civilization*. Academic Press, New York.

Sanders, William T., and Barbara J. Price 1968 *Mesoamerica: The Evolution of a Civilization*. Random House, New York.

Sanders, William T., and David Webster 1988 The Mesoamerican Urban Tradition. *American Anthropologist* 90: 521–546.

Sanmark, Alexandra 2017 *Viking Law and Order: Places and Rituals of Assembly in the Medieval North*. Edinburgh University Press, Edinburgh.

Satterthwaite, David 2016 Successful, Safe and Sustainable Cities: Towards a New Urban Agenda. *Commonwealth Journal of Local Governance* 19: 3–18.

Scheidel, Walter 2008 The Comparative Economics of Slavery in the Greco-Roman World. In *Slave Systems, Ancient and Modern*, edited by Enrico Del Lago and Constantina Katsari, pp. 105–126. Cambridge University Press, New York.

2009 In Search of Roman Economic Growth. *Journal of Roman Archaeology* 22: 46–70.

2015 Building for the State: A World-Historical Perspective. *Princeton-Stanford Working Papers in Classics*. www.academia .edu/12538322/Building_for_the_state_a_ world-historical_perspective.

Scheidel, Walter, Ian Morris, and Richard Saller 2007 *The Cambridge Economic History of the Greco-Roman World*. Cambridge University Press, New York.

Scheinkman, José A. 2008 Social Interactions. In *The New Palgrave Dictionary of Economics*, edited by Steven N. Durlauf and Lawrence Blume. 2nd ed. Palgrave Macmillan, Basingstoke, UK.

Schiffer, Michael B. 1987 *Formation Processes of the Archaeological Record*. University of New Mexico Press, Albuquerque.

Schmidt, Holger 1994 *Building Customs in Viking Age Denmark*. Poul Kristensen, Copenhagen.

Schnegg, Michael 2015 Reciprocity on Demand: Sharing and Exchanging Food in Northwestern Namibia. *Human Nature* 26 (3): 313–330.

Schug, Gwen Robbins, K. Elaine Blevins, Brett Cox, Kelsey Gray, and V. Mushrif-Tripathy 2013 Infection, Disease, and Biosocial Processes at the End of the Indus Civilization. *PLoS One* 8 (12): e84814.

Scott, James C. 1998 *Seeing Like a State: How Certain Schemes to Improve the Human Condition Have Failed*. Yale University Press, New Haven.

Scott, W. Richard 2001 *Institutions and Organizations*. 2nd ed. Sage, New York.

Searle, John R. 1995 *The Construction of Social Reality*. Free Press, New York.

Séjourné, Laurette 1959 *Un palacio en la ciudad de los dioses: Exploraciones en Teotihuacan, 1955–*

1958. Instituto Nacional de Antropología e Historia, Mexico City.

Semple, Sarah, and Alexandra Sanmark 2013 Assembly in North West Europe: Collective Concerns for Early Societies? *European Journal of Archaeology* 16 (3): 518–542.

Sen, Amartya K. 1959 The Choice of Agricultural Techniques in Underdeveloped Countries. *Economic Development and Cultural Change* 7: 279–285.

1999 *Development as Freedom.* Alfred Knopf, New York.

2013 The Ends and Means of Sustainability. *Journal of Human Development and Capabilities* 14 (1): 6–20.

Seo, Tatsuhiko 1986 The Urban Systems of Chang'an in the Sui and T'ang Dynasties. In *Historic Cities of Asia*, edited by Muhammad A. J. Beg, pp. 159–200. Percetakan Ban Huat Seng, Kuala Lumpur.

Service, Elman Rogers 1975 *Origins of the State and Civilization: The Process of Cultural Evolution.* Norton, New York.

Shaer, Matthew 2016 A Secret Tunnel Found in Mexico May Finally Solve the Mysteries of Teotihuacán. *Smithsonian Magazine* (online). www.smithsonianmag.com/history/discovery-secret-tunnel-mexico-solve-mysteries-teotihuacan-180959070/.

Shatzmiller, Maya 1994 *Labour in the Medieval Islamic World.* Brill, Leiden.

Shaw, Ian 2004 Identity and Occupation: How Did Individuals Define Themselves and Their Work in the Egyptian New Kingdom? In *Invention and Innovation: The Social Context of Technological Change 2: Egypt, the Aegean and the Near East, 1650–1150 BC*, edited by Janine Bourriau and Jacqueline Phillips, pp. 12–24. Oxbow Books, Oxford.

Sheehy, James J. 1996 Ethnographic Analogy and the Royal Household in 8th Century Copan. In *Arqueología Mesoamericana: Homenaje a William T. Sanders*, edited by Alba Guadalupe Mastache, Jeffrey R. Parsons, Robert S. Santley, and Mari Carmen Serra Puche, pp. 253–276, vol. 2.

Instituto Nacional de Antropología e Historia, Mexico City.

Shehata, A. M. A., and A. M. Z. Elzawahry 2016 Post-occupancy Evaluation of Pilgrims' Accommodation: A Case Study of Mina in Makkah City. *WIT Transactions on Ecology and the Environment* 204: 647–661.

Shipley, Graham 2005 Little Boxes on the Hillside: Greek Town Planning, Hippodamos and Polis Ideology. In *The Imaginary Polis*, edited by Mogens Herman Hansen, pp. 335–403. The Royal Danish Academy of Sciences and Letters, Copenhagen.

Short, William R. 2019 Families and Demographics in the Viking Age. *Hurstwic Blog.* www.hurstwic.org/history/articles/daily_living/text/Demographics.htm.

Shott, Michael J. 2004 Hunter-Gatherer Aggregation in Theory and Evidence: The North American Paleoindian Case. In *Hunter-Gatherers in Theory and Archaeology*, edited by George Crothers, pp. 68–102. Southern Illinois University Press, Carbondale.

Siders, A. R. 2019 Managed Retreat in the United States. *One Earth* 1 (2): 216–225.

Silberfein, Marilyn 1989 Settlement Form and Rural Development: Scattered Versus Clustered Settlement. *Tijdschrift voor Economische en Sociale Geografie* 80 (5): 258–268.

Silverman, Helaine 1994 Archaeological Identification of an Ancient Peruvian Pilgrimage Center. *World Archaeology* 26: 1–18.

Simmel, Georg 1898 The Persistence of Social Groups, II. *American Journal of Sociology* 3: 829–836.

Simmons, Alan H. 2007 *The Neolithic Revolution in the Near East: Transforming the Human Landscape.* University of Arizona, Tucson.

Simon, David 2008 Urban Environments: Periurban Issues. *Annual Review of Environment and Resources* 33: 167–185.

Simon, David, Corrie Griffith, and Harini Nagendra 2018 Rethinking Urban Sustainability and Resilience. In *Urban*

Planet: Knowledge towards Sustainable Cities, edited by Corrie Griffith, David Maddox, David Simon et al., pp. 149–162. Cambridge University Press, Cambridge.

Simpson, Deane 2007 RV Urbanism: Nomadic Network Settlements of the Senior Recreational Vehicle Community in the US. Paper presented at the Conference, Temporary Urbanism: Between the Permanent and the Transitory. www.holcim foundation.org/Portals/1/docs/F07/WK-Temp/F07-WK-Temp-simpson02.pdf.

Simpson, Ian 2008 Market Buildings at Jerash: Commercial Transformation at the Tetrakionion in the 6th to 9th Centuries C.E. In *Residences, Castles, Settlements. Transformation Processes from Late Antiquity to Early Islam in Bilad al-Sham*, edited by Karin Bartl and Abd al-Razzaq Moaz, pp. 115–124. Orient-Archäologie, vol. 24. Verlag Marie Leidorf, Rahden.

Sindbaek, Søren M. 2013 Broken Links and Black Boxes: Material Affiliations and Contextual Network Synthesis in the Viking Period. In *Network Analysis in Archaeology: New Approaches to Regional Interaction*, edited by Carl Knappett, pp. 71–84. Oxford University Press, New York.

2016 Northern Emporium: The Archaeology of Network Urbanism in Viking Age Ribe. *Carlsberg Foundation* (www.carlsbergfondet.dk/en/Forskningsaktiviteter/Research-Projects/Semper-Ardens-Research-Projects/Soren-Michael-Sindbaek_Northern-Emporium).

2018 Northern Emporium: The Archaeology of Urban Networks in Viking-Age Ribe. In *Urban Network Evolutions: Towards a High-Definition Archaeology*, edited by Rubina Raja and Søren M. Sindbaek, pp. 161–166. Centre for Urban Network Evolutions, Aarhus University, Aarhus.

Sinopoli, Carla M. 1994 Monumentality and Mobility in Mughal Capitals. *Asian Perspectives* 33: 293–308.

Sjoberg, Gideon 1960 *The Preindustrial City: Past and Present*. The Free Press, New York.

Skinner, G. William 1964 Marketing and Social Structure in Rural China, part 1. *Journal of Asian Studies* 24: 3–43.

Slach, Ondřej, Vojtěch Bosák, Luděk Krtička, Alexandr Nováček, and Petr Rumpel 2019 Urban Shrinkage and Sustainability: Assessing the Nexus between Population Density, Urban Structures and Urban Sustainability. *Sustainability* 11 (15): 4142.

Sluyter, Andrew 2005 Recentism in Environmental History on Latin America. *Environmental History* 10 (1). www.historycooperative.org/journals/eh/10.1/sluyter.html.

Smail, Daniel Lord 2000 *Imaginary Cartographies: Possession and Identity in Late Medieval Marseille*. Cornell University Press, Ithaca.

Smith, Adam 1979 *The Wealth of Nations, Books I–III*. First published, 1776. Penguin, Baltimore.

Smith, Adam T. 2003 *The Political Landscape: Constellations of Authority in Early Complex Polities*. University of California Press, Berkeley.

Smith, Carol A. 1974 Economics of Marketing Systems: Models from Economic Geography. *Annual Review of Anthropology* 3: 167–201.

1976a Analyzing Regional Social Systems. In *Regional Analysis, volume 2, Social Systems*, edited by Carol A. Smith, pp. 3–20. Academic Press, New York.

1976b Exchange Systems and the Spatial Distribution of Elites: The Organization of Stratification in Agrarian Societies. In *Regional Analysis, volume 2, Social Systems*, edited by Carol A. Smith, pp. 309–374. Academic Press, New York.

Smith, Michael E. 1977 State Systems of Settlement: Response to Crumley. *American Anthropologist* 79: 903–906.

1979 The Aztec Marketing System and Settlement Pattern in the Valley of Mexico: A Central Place Analysis. *American Antiquity* 44: 110–125.

1987 Household Possessions and Wealth in Agrarian States: Implications for Archaeology. *Journal of Anthropological Archaeology* 6: 297–335.

1989 Cities, Towns, and Urbanism: Comment on Sanders and Webster. *American Anthropologist* 91: 454–461.

1992 *Archaeological Research at Aztec-Period Rural Sites in Morelos*, Mexico. *Volume 1, Excavations and Architecture / Investigaciones arqueológicas en sitios rurales de la época Azteca en Morelos, Tomo 1, excavaciones y arquitectura.* Memoirs in Latin American Archaeology, vol. 4. University of Pittsburgh, Pittsburgh.

2002 Domestic Ritual at Aztec Provincial Sites in Morelos. In *Domestic Ritual in Ancient Mesoamerica*, edited by Patricia Plunket, pp. 93–114. Monograph, vol. 46. Cotsen Institute of Archaeology, UCLA, Los Angeles.

2003 Can We Read Cosmology in Ancient Maya City Plans? Comment on Ashmore and Sabloff. *Latin American Antiquity* 14: 221–228.

2004 The Archaeology of Ancient State Economies. *Annual Review of Anthropology* 33: 73–102.

2005a City Size in Late Postclassic Mesoamerica. *Journal of Urban History* 31: 403–434.

2005b Did the Maya Build Architectural Cosmograms? *Latin American Antiquity* 16: 217–224.

2006 *Reconocimiento superficial del Valle de Yautepec, Morelos: informe final.* Report submitted to the Instituto Nacional de Antropología e Historia. https://core.tdar.org/document/380993/reconocimiento-superficial-del-valle-de-yautepec-morelos-informe-final.

2007 Form and Meaning in the Earliest Cities: A New Approach to Ancient Urban Planning. *Journal of Planning History* 6 (1): 3–47.

2008 *Aztec City-State Capitals.* University Press of Florida, Gainesville.

2009 V. Gordon Childe and the Urban Revolution: An Historical Perspective on a Revolution in Urban Studies. *Town Planning Review* 80: 3–29.

2010a The Archaeological Study of Neighborhoods and Districts in Ancient Cities. *Journal of Anthropological Archaeology* 29 (2): 137–154.

2010b Sprawl, Squatters, and Sustainable Cities: Can Archaeological Data Shed Light on Modern Urban Issues? *Cambridge Archaeological Journal* 20: 229–253.

2011a Classic Maya Settlement Clusters as Urban Neighborhoods: A Comparative Perspective on Low-Density Urbanism. *Journal de la Société des Américanistes* 97 (1): 51–73.

2011b Empirical Urban Theory for Archaeologists. *Journal of Archaeological Method and Theory* 18: 167–192.

2011c Why Anthropology Is Too Narrow an Intellectual Context for Archaeology. *Anthropologies* 3: (online). www.anthropologiesproject.org/2011/05/why-anthropology-is-too-narrow.html.

2012a *The Aztecs.* 3rd ed. Blackwell Publishers, Oxford.

2012b *The Comparative Archaeology of Complex Societies.* Cambridge University Press, New York.

2012c El almacenamiento en la economía Azteca: una perspectiva comparativa. In *Almacenamiento prehispánico del Norte de México al Altiplano Central*, edited by Séverine Bortot, Dominique Michelet, and Véronique Darras, pp. 203–220. CEMCA (Centre d'études mexicaines et centroaméricaines), Mexico City.

2012d The Role of Ancient Cities in Research on Contemporary Urbanization. *UGEC Viewpoints (Urbanization and Global Environmental Change)* 8: 15–19.

2014 Housing in Premodern Cities: Patterns of Social and Spatial Variation. *International Journal of Architectural Research* 8 (3): 207–222.

2015 How Can Archaeologists Make Better Arguments? *The SAA Archaeological Record* 15 (4): 18–23.

2016a *At Home with the Aztecs: An Archaeologist Uncovers Their Domestic Life.* Routledge, New York.

2016b How Can Archaeologists Identify Early Cities: Definitions, Types, and Attributes. In *Eurasia at the Dawn of History: Urbanization and*

Social Change, edited by Manuel Fernández-Götz and Dirk Krausse, pp. 153–168. Cambridge University Press, New York.

2017a Cities in the Aztec Empire: The Interplay of Commerce, Imperialism and Urbanization. In *Rethinking the Aztec Economy*, edited by Deborah Nichols, Frances Berdan, and Michael E. Smith, pp. 44–67. University of Arizona Press, Tucson.

2017b Social Science and Archaeological Inquiry. *Antiquity* 91 (356): 520–528.

2017c The Teotihuacan Anomaly: The Historical Trajectory of Urban Planning in Central Mexico. *Open Archaeology* 3 (1): 175–193. www.degruyter.com/view/journals/opar/3/1/article-p175.xml.

2018 *The Importance of a Comparative Perspective in the Study of Ancient Economies*. Beiträge zur Wirtschaftsarchäologie. Habelt-Verlag, Bonn.

2019a Energized Crowding and the Generative Role of Settlement Aggregation and Urbanization. In *Coming Together: Comparative Approaches to Population Aggregation and Early Urbanization*, edited by Attila Gyucha, pp. 37–58. State University of New York Press, Albany.

2019b *Excavaciones de casas en la ciudad azteca de Yautepec, Morelos, México*. 2 vols. BAR International Series. Archaeopress, Oxford.

2019c Quality of Life and Prosperity in Ancient Households and Communities. In *The Oxford Handbook of Historical Ecology and Applied Archaeology*, edited by Christian Isendahl and Daryl Stump, pp. 486–505. Oxford University Press, New York.

2020a The Comparative Analysis of Early Cities and Urban Deposits. *Journal of Urban Archaeology* 2: 197–205. www.brepolsonline.net/doi/abs/10.1484/J.JUA.5.121537.

2020b Definitions and Comparisons in Urban Archaeology. *Journal of Urban Archaeology* 1: 15–30. www.brepolsonline.net/doi/abs/10.1484/J.JUA.5.120907.

2020c Mesoamerica's First World City: Teotihuacan in Comparative Context. In

Teotihuacan: The World Beyond the City, edited by Kenneth G. Hirth, David M. Carballo, and Barbara Arroyo, pp. 33–56. Dumbarton Oaks, Washington, DC.

2021a Durable Inequality in Aztec Society. *Journal of Anthropological Research* 77 (2): 162–186. www.journals.uchicago.edu/doi/10.1086/713639.

2021b Why Archaeology's Relevance to Global Challenges Has Not Been Recognized. *Antiquity* 95: 1061–1069.

n.d. Making Good Arguments in Archaeology. In *Discourse and Argumentation in Archaeology: Conceptual and Computational Approaches*, edited by Patricia M. Rodilla, César González-Pérez, and Martín Pereira-Fariña. Springer, New York. https://osf.io/preprints/socarxiv/ph3ys/.

Smith, Michael E., Abhishek Chatterjee, Sierra Stewart, Angela Huster, and Marion Forest 2019 Apartment Compounds, Households, and Population at Teotihuacan. *Ancient Mesoamerica* 30 (3): 399–418.

Smith, Michael E., Timothy Dennehy, April Kamp-Whittaker, Emily Colon, and Rebecca Harkness 2014a Quantitative Measures of Wealth Inequality in Ancient Central Mexican Communities. *Advances in Archaeological Practice* 2 (4): 311–323.

Smith, Michael E., Ashley Engquist, Cinthia Carvajal et al. 2015 Neighborhood Formation in Semi-Urban Settlements. *Journal of Urbanism* 8 (2): 173–198.

Smith, Michael E., Timothy S. Hare, Lisa Montiel, Anne Sherfield, and Angela C. Huster 2021a Settlement Patterns and Urbanization in the Yautepec Valley of Central Mexico. *Open Archaeology* 7 (1): 378–416. www.degruyter.com/document/doi/10.1515/opar-2020-0141/html.

Smith, Michael E., and Cynthia Heath-Smith 1994 Rural Economy in Late Postclassic Morelos: An Archaeological Study. In *Economies and Polities in the Aztec Realm*, edited by Mary G. Hodge and Michael E. Smith, pp. 349–376. Institute for Mesoamerican Studies, Albany.

Smith, Michael E., Cynthia Heath-Smith, Ronald Kohler, Joan Odess, Sharon Spanogle, and Timothy Sullivan 1994 The Size of the Aztec City of Yautepec: Urban Survey in Central Mexico. *Ancient Mesoamerica* 5: 1–11.

Smith, Michael E., Cynthia Heath-Smith, and Lisa Montiel 1999 Excavations of Aztec Urban Houses at Yautepec, Mexico. *Latin American Antiquity* 10: 133–150.

Smith, Michael E., and Carola Hein 2017 The Ancient Past in the Urban Present: The Use of Early Models in Urban Design. In *Routledge Handbook of Planning History*, edited by Carola Hein, pp. 109–120. Routledge, New York.

Smith, Michael E., and Frederic Hicks 2017 Inequality and Social Class. In *Oxford Handbook of the Aztecs*, edited by Deborah L. Nichols and Enrique Rodríguez-Alegría, pp. 425–436. Oxford University Press, New York.

Smith, Michael E., Timothy Kohler, and Gary M. Feinman 2018 Studying Inequality's Deep Past. In *Ten Thousand Years of Inequality: The Archaeology of Wealth Differences*, edited by Timothy Kohler and Michael E. Smith, pp. 3–38. University of Arizona Press, Tucson.

Smith, Michael E., and José Lobo 2019 Cities through the Ages: One Thing or Many? *Frontiers in Digital Humanities*, 6 (Special issue: *Where Do Cities Come From and Where Are They Going To? Modelling Past and Present Agglomerations to Understand Urban Ways of Life*): Article 12. www.frontiersin.org/articles/10.3389/fdigh.2019.00012/full.

Smith, Michael E., José Lobo, Matthew Peeples et al. 2021b The Persistence of Ancient Settlements and Urban Sustainability. *Proceedings of the National Academy of Sciences*. www.pnas.org/content/118/20/e2018155118.

Smith, Michael E., and Lisa Montiel 2001 The Archaeological Study of Empires and Imperialism in Prehispanic Central Mexico. *Journal of Anthropological Archaeology* 20: 245–284.

Smith, Michael E., and Juliana Novic 2012 Neighborhoods and Districts in Ancient Mesoamerica. In *The Neighborhood as a Social and Spatial Unit in Mesoamerican Cities*, edited by Marie Charlotte Arnauld, Linda R. Manzanilla, and Michael E. Smith, pp. 1–26. University of Arizona Press, Tucson.

Smith, Michael E., Scott G. Ortman, José Lobo et al. 2021c The Low-Density Urban Systems of the Classic-Period Maya and Izapa: Insights from Settlement Scaling Theory. *Latin American Antiquity* 32 (1): 120–137.

Smith, Michael E., and Peter Peregrine 2012 Approaches to Comparative Analysis in Archaeology. In *The Comparative Archaeology of Complex Societies*, edited by Michael E. Smith, pp. 4–20. Cambridge University Press, New York.

Smith, Michael E., Barbara L. Stark, Wen-Ching Chuang et al. 2016 Comparative Methods for Premodern Cities: Coding for Governance and Class Mobility. *Cross-Cultural Research* 50 (5): 415–451.

Smith, Michael E., Jason Ur, and Gary M. Feinman 2014b Jane Jacobs's "Cities-First" Model and Archaeological Reality. *International Journal of Urban and Regional Research* 38 (4): 1525–1535.

Smith, Monica L. 2003a Introduction: The Social Construction of Ancient Cities. In *The Social Construction of Ancient Cities*, edited by Monica L. Smith, pp. 1–36. Smithsonian Institution Press, Washington, DC.

2003b *The Social Construction of Ancient Cities*. Smithsonian Institution Press, Washington, DC.

2014 The Archaeology of Urban Landscapes. *Annual Review of Anthropology* 43: 307–323.

2018 Urbanism and the Middle Class: Co-Emergent Phenomena in the World's First

Cities. *Journal of Anthropological Research* 74: 299–326.

2019 *Cities: The First 6,000 Years.* Viking, New York.

Snow, C. P. 1959 *The Two Cultures and the Scientific Revolution.* Cambridge University Press, New York.

Soja, Edward W. 1996 *Thirdspace: Journeys to Los Angeles and Other Real-and-Imagined Places.* Blackwell, Oxford.

Sokal, Alan D. 2006 Pseudoscience and Postmodernism: Antagonists or Fellow Travelers? In *Archaeological Fantasies: How Pseudoarchaeology Mispresents the Past and Misleads the Public*, edited by Garrett G. Fagan, pp. 286–361. Routledge, New York.

Sørensen, Tim Flohr 2017 The Two Cultures and a World Apart: Archaeology and Science at a New Crossroads. *Norwegian Archaeological Review* 50 (2): 101–115.

Soskice, David, Robert H. Bates, and David Epstein 1992 Ambition and Constraint: The Stabilizing Role of Institutions. *Journal of Law, Economics, and Organization* 8: 547–560.

Southall, Aidan W. 1988 The Segmentary State in Africa and Asia. *Comparative Studies in Society and History* 30: 52–82.

Spicer, Edward H., Asael T. Hansen, Katherine Luomala, and Marvin K. Opler 1969 *Impounded People: Japanese Americans in the Relocation Centers.* University of Arizona Press, Tucson.

Spooner, Brian (ed.) 1972 *Population Growth: Anthropological Implications.* MIT Press, Cambridge.

Spruill, Tanya M. 2010 Chronic Psychosocial Stress and Hypertension. *Current Hypertension Reports* 12 (1): 10–16.

Stabel, Peter 2008 Public or Private, Collective or Individual? The Spaces of Late Medieval Trade in the Low Countries. In *Il mercante patrizio: palazzi e botteghe nell'Europa del Rinascimento*, edited by Donatella Calabi, pp. 37–54. Milan, Mondadori.

Stanley, Benjamin W. 2012 An Historical Perspective on the Viability of Urban Diversity: Lessons from Socio-Spatial Identity Construction in Nineteenth Century Algiers and Cape Town. *Journal of Urbanism* 5 (1): 67–86.

Stanley, Benjamin W., Timothy Dennehy, Michael E. Smith, Barbara L. Stark, Abigail York, George L. Cowgill, Juliana Novic, and Gerald Ek 2016 Service Access in Premodern Cities: An Exploratory Comparison of Spatial Equity. *Journal of Urban History* 42 (1): 121–144.

Stanley, Benjamin W., Barbara L. Stark, Katrina Johnston, and Michael E. Smith 2012 Urban Open Spaces in Historical Perspective: A Transdisciplinary Typology and Analysis. *Urban Geography* 33 (8): 1089–1117.

Stark, Barbara L. 2014 Urban Gardens and Parks in Pre-modern States and Empires. *Cambridge Archaeological Journal* 24 (1): 87–115.

2021 *The Archaeology of Political Organization: Urbanism in Classic Period Veracruz, Mexico.* Cotsen Institute of Archaeology, UCLA, Los Angeles.

Stark, Barbara L., Matthew A. Boxt, Janine Gasco et al. 2016 Economic Growth in Mesoamerica: Obsidian Consumption in the Coastal Lowlands. *Journal of Anthropological Archaeology* 41: 263–282.

Stark, Barbara L., and Christopher P. Garraty 2010 Detecting Market Exchange in Archaeology: A Review. In *Archaeological Approaches to Market Exchange in Pre-Capitalist Societies*, edited by Christopher P. Garraty and Barbara L. Stark, pp. 33–58. University Press of Colorado, Boulder.

Stark, Barbara, Michael E. Smith, Benjamin Stanley, and Abigail York n.d. Paper on urban service facilities (in preparation).

Stasavage, David 2020 *The Decline and Rise of Democracy: A Global History from Antiquity to Today.* Princeton University Press, Princeton, NJ.

Steinhardt, Nancy S. 1990 *Chinese Imperial City Planning.* University of Hawaii Press, Honolulu.

Steinkeller, Piotr 2015 Labor in the Early States: An Earl Mesopotamian Perspective. In *Labor in the Ancient World*, edited by Piotr Steinkeller and Michael Hudson, pp. 1–35. Islet Verlag, Dresden.

Stephens, John Lloyd, and Frederick Catherwood 1854 *Incidents of Travel in Central America, Chiapas, and Yucatan*. Arthur Hall, Virtue and Company, New York.

Stern, Eliahu, and Yehuca Gradus 1979 Cultural Considerations in Planning Towns for Nomads. *Ekistics* 46 (277): 224–230.

Stevens, Anna 2011 The Amarna Stone Village Survey and Life on the Urban Periphery in New Kingdom Egypt. *Journal of Field Archaeology* 36 (2): 100–118.

   2012 *Akhenaten's Workers: The Amarna Stone Village Survey, 2005–9*. 2 vols. Egypt Exploration Society, London.

Steward, Julian H. 1941 *Nevada Shoshone*. University of California Press, Berkeley.

Stiglitz, Joseph E., Amartya Sen, and Jean-Paul Fitoussi 2010 *Mismeasuring Our Lives: Why GDP Doesn't Add Up*. The New Press, New York.

Stinchcombe, Arthur L. 1965 Social Structure and Organizations. In *Handbook of Organizations*, edited by James G. March, pp. 142–193. Rand McNally, Chicago.

Stoddard, R. H., and A. Morinis (eds.) 1997 *Sacred Places, Sacred Spaces: The Geography of Pilgrimages*. Louisiana State University Press, Baton Rouge.

Stone, Elizabeth C. 2008 Patterns of Looting in Southern Iraq. *Antiquity* 82: 125–138.

Stone, Elizabeth C., and Paul Zimansky 2016 Archaeology Returns to Ur: A New Dialog with Old Houses. *Near Eastern Archaeology* 79 (4): 246–259.

Stone, Glenn Davis 1998 Settlement Concentration and Dispersal among the Kofyar. In *Rural Settlement Structure and African Development*, edited by Marilyn Silberfein, pp. 75–97. Westview, Boulder.

Storey, Glenn R. 2002 Regionaries-Type Insulae 2: Architectural/Residential Units at Rome. *American Journal of Archaeology* 106 (3): 411–434.

Storli, Inger 2010 Court Sites of Arctic Norway: The Remains of *Thing* Sites and Representations of Political Consolidation Processes in the Northern Germanic World during the First Millennium AD? *Norwegian Archaeological Review* 43 (2): 89–94.

Storper, Michael, and Anthony J. Venables 2004 Buzz: Face-to-Face Contact and the Urban Economy. *Journal of Economic Geography* 4 (4): 351–370.

Stott, David, Søren Munch Kristiansen, Achim Lichtenberger, and Rubina Raja 2018 Mapping an Ancient City with a Century of Remotely Sensed Data. *Proceedings of the National Academy of Sciences* 115 (24): E5450–E5458.

Stubbs, Steven H. 2005 *Mississippi's Giant Houseparty: The History of the Neshoba County Fair*. Dancing Rabbit Press, Philadelphia, MS.

Sugiyama, Saburo 2005 *Human Sacrifice, Militarism, and Rulership: The Symbolism of the Feathered Serpent Pyramid at Teotihuacan, Mexico*. Cambridge University Press, New York.

   2022 The Nature of Early Urbanism at Teotihuacan. In *Early Mesoamerican Cities: Urbanism and Urbanization in the Formative Period*, edited by Michael E. Love and Julia Guernsey, pp. 170–198. Cambridge University Press, New York.

Suzman, James 2017 *Affluence without Abundance: The Disappearing World of the Bushmen*. Bloomsbury, New York.

Swedberg, Richard, and Ola Agewall 2005 *The Max Weber Dictionary: Key Words and Central Concepts*. Stanford University Press, Stanford.

Tainter, Joseph A. 2019 Cahokia: Urbanization, Metabolism, and Collapse. *Frontiers in Sustainable Cities* 1 (article 6).

Tainter, Joseph A., and Temis G. Taylor 2014 Complexity, Problem-Solving, Sustainability and Resilience. *Building Research and Information* 42 (2): 168–181.

Talen, Emily 1999 Sense of Community and Neighbourhood Form: An Assessment of the Social Doctrine of New Urbanism. *Urban Studies* 36: 1361–1379.

2000 Measuring the Public Realm: A Preliminary Assessment of the Link between Public Space and Sense of Community. *Journal of Architectural and Planning Research* 17 (4): 344–360.

2005 *New Urbanism and American Planning: The Conflict of Cultures*. Routledge, New York.

Tambiah, Stanley J. 1977 The Galactic Polity: The Structure of Traditional Kingdoms in Southeast Asia. In *Anthropology and the Climate of Opinion*, edited by Stanley A. Freed, pp. 69–97. Annals, vol. 293. New York Academy of Science, New York.

Taylor, Michael 1982 *Community, Anarchy and Liberty*. Cambridge University Press, Cambridge.

Taylor, Peter J. 2012 Extraordinary Cities: Early "City-ness" and the Origins of Agriculture and States. *International Journal of Urban and Regional Research* 36 (3): 415–447.

Temin, Peter 1980 Modes of Behavior. *Journal of Economic Behavior and Organization* 1: 175–195.

Thing Project 2018 *Thing Sites: Discover the Viking Cradle of Democracy*. Website. www.thingsites.com.

Thirsk, Joan 1961 Industries in the Countryside. In *Essays in the Economic and Social History of Tudor and Stuart England, in Honor of R. H. Tawney*, edited by F. J. Fisher, pp. 70–88. Cambridge University Press, Cambridge.

Thomas, Elizabeth Marshall 1989 *The Harmless People*. Vintage, New York.

Thomas, Julian 2015 The Future of Archaeological Theory. *Antiquity* 89: 1287–1296.

Thomas, Reuben J., and Noah P. Mark 2013 Population Size, Network Density, and the Emergence of Inherited Inequality. *Social Forces* 92 (2): 521–544.

Thompson, J. Eric S. 1963 *Maya Archaeologist*. University of Oklahoma Press, Norman.

Tilley, Christopher, and Wayne Bennett 2004 *The Materiality of Stone: Explorations in Landscape Phenomenology, Volume 1*. Berg, Oxford.

Tilly, Charles 1985 War Making and State Making as Organized Crime. In *Bringing the State Back In*, edited by Peter Evans, Dietrich Rueschmeyer, and Theda Skocpol, pp. 169–186. Cambridge University Press, New York.

1992 *Coercion, Capital, and European States, AD 990–1990*. Blackwell, Oxford.

1998 *Durable Inequality*. University of California Press, Berkeley.

2000 Chain Migration and Opportunity Hoarding. In *Governance of Cultural Diversity*, edited by Janina W. Dacyl and Charles Westin, pp. 62–86. Centre for Research in International Migration and Ethnic Relations, Stockholm.

2001 Relational Origins of Inequality. *Anthropological Theory* 1 (3): 355–372.

2008 *Explaining Social Processes*. Paradigm Publishers, Boulder, CO.

Tipple, Graham, Bayo Amole, David Korboe, and Helen Onyeacholem 1994 House and Dwelling, Family and Household: Towards Defining Housing Units in West African Cities. *Third World Planning Review* 16 (4): 429–450.

Tracy, James D. (ed.) 2001 *City Walls: The Urban Enceinte in Global Perspective*. Cambridge University Press, New York.

Tremain, Cara Grace, and Donna Yates (eds.) 2019 *The Market for Mesoamerica: Reflections on the Sale of Pre-Columbian Antiquities*. University of Florida Press, Gainesville.

Trigger, Bruce G. 1972 Determinants of Urban Growth in Pre-Industrial Societies. In *Man, Settlement, and Urbanism*, edited by Peter J. Ucko, Ruth Tringham, and G. W. Dimbleby, pp. 575–599. Schenkman, Cambridge.

1990 Monumental Architecture: A Thermodynamic Explanation of Behavior. *World Archaeology* 22: 119–132.

2003 *Understanding Early Civilizations: A Comparative Study*. Cambridge University Press, New York.

Tucker, John T. 1949 Initiation Ceremonies for Luimbi Boys. *Africa* 19 (1): 53–60.

Turchin, Peter, and Sergey A. Nefedov 2009 *Secular Cycles*. Princeton University Press, Princeton.

Turner, B. L., II, and William E. Doolittle 1978 The Concept and Measure of Agricultural Intensity. *Professional Geographer* 30: 297–301.

Turner, Edith 2004 Rites of Communitas. In *Religion and Society: Encyclopedia of Religious Rites, Rituals, and Festivals*, edited by Frank Salamone, pp. 97–101. Routledge, New York.

   2012 *Communitas: The Anthropology of Collective Joy*. Palgrave, New York.

Turner, John F. C. 1991 *Housing by People: Towards Autonomy in Building Environments*. Marion Boyars, London.

Turner, Jonathan H. 1990 Emile Durkheim's Theory of Social Organization. *Social Forces* 68 (4): 1089–1103.

   2003 *Human Institutions: A Theory of Societal Evolution*. Rowman and Littlefield, New York.

Turner, Victor W. 1969 *The Ritual Process: Structure and Anti-Structure*. Aldine, Chicago.

Tuzin, Donald 2001 *Social Complexity in the Making: A Case Study among the Arapesh of New Guinea*. Routledge, New York.

Twain, Mark 2010 *Autobiography of Mark Twain, Volume 1*. University of California Press, Berkeley.

Twitchett, Denis, and Klaus-Peter Tietze 1994 The Liao. In *Cambridge History of China, Volume 6, Alien Regimes and Border States, 907–1368*, edited by Herbert Franke and Denis Twitchett, pp. 43–153. Cambridge University Press, New York.

UN-Habitat 1982 *Survey of Slum and Squatter Settlements*. United Nations Centre for Human Settlements, Development Studies Series, vol. 1. Tycooly International, Dublin.

Ur, Jason A. 2020 Space and Structure in Early Mesopotamian Cities. In *Landscapes of Preindustrial Urbanism*, edited by Georges Farhat, pp. 37–60. Dumbarton Oaks, Washington, DC.

Usman, Aribidesi A. 2003 Early Urbanism in Northern Yorubaland. In *Nigerian Cities*, edited by Toyin Falola and Steve Salm, pp. 47–78. African World Press, Trenton.

Van De Mieroop, Marc 1997 *The Ancient Mesopotamian City*. Oxford University Press, Oxford.

van der Graaff, Ivo 2018 *The Fortifications of Pompeii and Ancient Italy*. Routledge, New York.

van der Heijden, Manon, Elise van Nederveen Meerkerk, Griet Vermeesch, and Martijn van der Burg (eds.) 2010 *Serving the Urban Community: The Rise of Public Facilities in the Low Countries*. Aksant Press, Amsterdam.

van der Krogt, Peter 2008 Mapping the Towns of Europe: The European Towns in Braun and Hogenberg's Town Atlas, 1572–1617. *Belgeo: Revue Belge de Géographie* 3/4: 1–37.

van der Leeuw, Sander E. 2012 For Every Solution There Are Many Problems: The Role and Study of Technical Systems in Socio-Environmental Coevolution. *Geografisk Tidsskrift / Danish Journal of Geography* 112 (2): 105–116.

Van der Spek, Robartus J. 2011 The "Silverization" of the Economy of the Achaemenid and Seleukid Empires and Early Modern China. In *The Economies of Hellenistic Societies, Third to First Centuries BC*, edited by Zosia H. Archibald, John K. Davies, and Vincent Gabrielsen, pp. 402–420. Oxford University Press, New York.

van Gennep, Arnold 1960 (orig. 1908) *The Rites of Passage*. University of Chicago Press, Chicago.

Varinlioglu, Gunder 2012 Trades, Crafts, and Agricultural Production in Town and Countryside in Southeastern Isauria. In *Archaeology and the Cities of Asia Minor in Late Antiquity*, edited by Ortwin Dally and Christopher Ratté, pp. 173–187. Kelsey Museum Publications, vol. 6. Kelsey Museum of Anthropology, Ann Arbor.

Vésteinsson, Orri, Michelle Hegmon, Jette Arneborg, Glen Rice, and Will G. Russell 2019 Dimensions of Inequality. Comparing the North Atlantic and the US Southwest. *Journal of Anthropological Archaeology* 54: 172–191.

Vidale, Massimo 2010 Aspects of Palace Life at Mohenjo-Daro. *South Asian Studies* 26 (1): 59–76.

Vogel, Jefim, Julia K. Steinberger, Daniel W. O'Neill, William F. Lamb, and Jaya Krishnakumar 2021 Socio-Economic Conditions for Satisfying Human Needs at Low Energy Use: An International Analysis of Social Provisioning. *Global Environmental Change*: 102287.

Wallace, Anthony F. C. 1966 *Religion: An Anthropological View*. Random House, New York.

Walsh, Lorena S. 1988 Questions and Sources for Exploring the Standard of Living. *William and Mary Quarterly* 45 (1): 116–123.

Ward, Colin 1973 We House, You are Housed, They are Homeless (chapter 6). In *Anarchy in Action*, pp. 67–73. George Allen and Unwin, London.

——— 2000 Anarchy and Architecture. In *Non-Plan: Essays on Freedom, Participation, and Change in Modern Architecture and Urbanism*, edited by Jonathan Hughes and Simon Sadler, pp. 44–51. Architectural Press, Oxford.

Ward-Perkins, Bryan 2006 *The Fall of Rome and the End of Civilization*. Oxford University Press, New York.

Ware, John A. 2014 *A Pueblo Social History: Kinship, Sodality, and Community in the Northern Southwest*. SAR Press, Santa Fe.

Weber, Max 1950 *General Economic History*. The Free Press, Glencoe, IL.

——— 1958 *The City*. Translated by Don Martindale and Gertrud Neuwirth. Free Press, New York.

Wellman, Barry 2012 Commentary: Is Dunbar's Number Up? *British Journal of Psychology* 103 (2): 174–176.

Wengrow, David 2015 *Cities before the State in Early Eurasia: Goody Lecture, 2015*. Max Planck Institute for Social Anthropology, Halle.

Wengrow, David, and David Graeber 2015 Farewell to the "Childhood of Man": Ritual, Seasonality, and the Origins of Inequality. *Journal of the Royal Anthropological Institute* 21 (3): 597–619.

West, Geoffrey B. 2017 *Scale: The Universal Laws of Growth, Innovation, Sustainability, and the Pace of Life in Organisms, Cities, Economies, and Companies*. Penguin, New York.

West, Geoffrey B, James H Brown, and Brian J Enquist 1997 A General Model for the Origin of Allometric Scaling Laws in Biology. *Science* 276: 122–126.

Westenholz, Aage 2002 The Sumerian City-State. In *A Comparative Study of Six City-State Cultures*, edited by Mogens Herman Hansen, pp. 23–42. The Royal Danish Academy of Sciences and Letters, Copenhagen.

Wheatley, Paul 1971 *The Pivot of the Four Quarters: A Preliminary Enquiry into the Origins and the Character of the Ancient Chinese City*. Aldine, Chicago.

White, Leslie A. 1959 *The Evolution of Culture: The Development of Civilization to the Fall of Rome*. McGraw-Hill, New York.

Whitehouse, Harvey, and Jonathan A. Lanman 2014 The Ties That Bind Us: Ritual, Fusion, and Identification. *Current Anthropology* 55 (6): 674–695.

Whitelaw, Todd 2004 Estimating the Population of Neopalatial Knossos. In *Knossos: Palace, City, State*, edited by Gerald Cadogan, Eleni Hatzaki, and Adonis Asasilakis, pp. 147–158. British School at Athens, London.

——— 2017 The Development and Character of Urban Communities in Prehistoric Crete in their Regional Context. In *Minoan Architecture and Urbanism: New Perspectives on an Ancient Built Environment*, edited by Quentin Letesson and Carl Knappett, pp. 114–180. Oxford University Press, New York.

Widerquist, Karl, and Grant S. McCall 2017 *Prehistoric Myths in Modern Political Philosophy*. University of Edinburgh Press, Edinburgh.

Wiessner, Polly 1974 A Functional Estimator of Population from Floor Area. *American Antiquity* 39: 343–350.

——— 2014 Embers of Society: Firelight Talk among the Ju/'hoansi Bushmen. *Proceedings of the*

National Academy of Sciences 111: 14027–14035.

Wilk, Richard R., and Lisa C. Cliggett 2007 Economies and Cultures: Foundations of Economic Anthropology. 2nd ed. Westview Press, Boulder, CO.

Wilk, Richard R., and Robert McC. Netting 1984 Households: Changing Forms and Functions. In Households: Comparative and Historical Studies of the Domestic Group, edited by Robert McC. Netting, Richard R. Wilk, and Eric J. Arnould, pp. 1–28. University of California Press, Berkeley.

Wilk, Richard R., and William L. Rathje (eds.) 1982 Archaeology of the Household: Building a Prehistory of Domestic Life. Special Issue of American Behavioral Scientist, vol. 25 (6).

Wilkinson, Darryl 2019 Towards an Archaeological Theory of Infrastructure. Journal of Archaeological Method and Theory 26 (3): 1216–1241.

Wilkinson, T. J. 1994 The Structure and Dynamics of Dry-Farming States in Upper Mesopotamia. Current Anthropology 35: 483–520.

Willey, Gordon R. 1962 Mesoamerica. In Courses toward Urban Life: Archaeological Considerations of Some Cultural Alternates, edited by Robert J. Braidwood and Gordon R. Willey, pp. 84–105. Aldine, Chicago.

Williamson, Jeffrey G. 2010 Five Centuries of Latin American Income Inequality. Revista de Historia Económica 28 (Special Issue 02): 227–252.

Wilshusen, Richard H., and James M. Potter 2010 The Emergence of Early Villages in the American Southwest: Central Issues and Historical Perspectives. In Becoming Villagers: Comparing Early Village Societies, edited by Matthew S. Bandy and Jake R. Fox, pp. 167–183. University of Arizona Press, Tucson.

Wilson, Andrew, and Miko Flohr (eds.) 2016 Urban Craftsmen and Traders in the Roman World. Oxford University Press, New York.

Wilson, John A. 1960 Egypt through the New Kingdom: Civilization without Cities. In City Invincible, edited by Carl H. Kraeling and Robert M. Adams, pp. 124–136. University of Chicago Press, Chicago.

Wilson, Peter J. 1988 The Domestication of the Human Species. Yale University Press, New Haven.

Wirth, Louis 1938 Urbanism as a Way of Life. American Journal of Sociology 44: 1–24.

Wolf, Eric R. 1999 Envisioning Power: Ideologies of Dominance and Crisis. University of California Press, Berkeley.

Wolf, Kirsten 2004 Daily Life of the Vikings. Greenwood, New York.

Woods, Robert 2003a Urban-Rural Mortality Differentials: An Unresolved Debate. Population and Development Review 29 (1): 29–46.

2003b Urbanisation in Europe and China during the Second Millennium: A Review of Urbanism and Demography. International Journal of Population Geography 9 (3): 215–227.

Woolf, Greg 2020 The Life and Death of Ancient Cities: A Natural History. Oxford University Press, New York.

Woolley, Leonard (ed.) 1927–65 Ur Excavations. 9 vols. Publications of the Joint Expedition of the British Museum and the University Museum, University of Pennsylvania, Philadelphia, to Mesopotamia. British Museum and University Museum, University of Pennsylvania, London and Philadelphia.

1934 Ur Excavations, Volume II: The Royal Cemetery. 2 vols. British Museum, London.

Woolley, Leonard, and P. R. S. Moorey 1982 Ur "of the Chaldees": A Revised and Updated Edition of Sir Leonard Woolley's Excavations at Ur. Revised ed. Cornell University Press, Ithaca, NY.

Wootton, Will 2017 Mosaics from the North-West Quarter of Jerash. In Gerasa/Jerash: From the Urban Periphery, edited by Achim Lichtenberger and Rubina Raja, pp. 89–97. Centre for Urban Network Evolutions, Aarhus University, Aarhus.

Wouters, Barbora, Yannick Devos, Karen Milek et al. 2017 Medieval Markets: A Soil Micromorphological and Archaeobotanical Study of the Urban Stratigraphy of Lier (Belgium). *Quaternary International* 460 (Supplement C): 48–64.

Wrigley, E. A. 1990 Brake or Accelerator? Urban Growth and Population Growth before the Industrial Revolution. In *Urbanization in History: A Process of Dynamic Interactions*, edited by Ad van de Woude, Akira Hayami, and Jan de Vries, pp. 101–112. Clarendon Press, Oxford.

Wycherly, R. E. 1962 *How the Greeks Built Cities*. 2nd ed. Norton, New York.

Wylie, Alison 1985 The Reaction against Analogy. *Advances in Archaeological Method and Theory* 8: 63–111.

1996 Ethical Dilemmas in Archaeological Practice: Looting, Repatriation, Stewardship, and the (Trans)formation of Disciplinary Identity. *Perspectives on Science* 4: 154–194.

2000 Questions of Evidence, Legitimacy, and the (Dis)unity of Science. *American Antiquity* 65: 227–237.

2002 *Thinking from Things: Essays in the Philosophy of Archaeology*. University of California Press, Berkeley.

Wynne-Jones, Stephanie 2007 Creating Urban Communities at Kilwa Kisiwani, Tanzania, AD 800–1300. *Antiquity* 81: 368–380.

Xiong, Victor Cunrui 2000 *Sui-Tang Chang'an: A Study in the Urban History of Medieval China*. Center for Chinese Studies, University of Michigan, Ann Arbor.

Xu, Miao, and Zhen Yang 2009 Design History of China's Gated Cities and Neighbourhoods: Prototype and Evolution. *Urban Design International* 14: 99–117.

Yoffee, Norman 2005 *Myths of the Archaic State: The Evolution of the Earliest Cities, States, and Civilizations*. Cambridge University Press, New York.

2015 Conclusion: The Meanings of Early Cities. In *Early Cities in Comparative Perspective, 4000 BCE–1200 CE*, edited by Norman Yoffee, pp. 546–557. The Cambridge World History, volume 3. Cambridge University Press, New York.

2019 Introducing the Conference: There Are No Innocent Terms. In *The Evolution of Fragility: Setting the Terms*, edited by Norman Yoffee, pp. 1–7. McDonald Institute of Archaeology, Cambridge.

York, Abigail M., Michael E. Smith, Benjamin Stanley et al. 2011 Ethnic and Class Clustering through the Ages: A Transdisciplinary Approach to Urban Social Patterns. *Urban Studies* 48 (11): 2399–2415.

Young, Andrew T. 2017 *How the City Air Made Us Free: The Self-Governing Medieval City and the Bourgeoisie Revaluation*. Social Science Research Network, Working Paper.

Zangger, Eberhard 2018 James Mellaart's Fantasies. *Talanta: Proceedings of the Dutch Archaeological and Historical Society* 50: 125–182.

Zettler, Richard L., Lee Horne, and Donald P. Hansen (eds.) 1998 *Treasures from the Royal Tombs of Ur*. University Museum, University of Pennsylvania, Philadelphia.

Zhou, Weiqi, S. T. A. Pickett, and Timon McPhearson 2021 Conceptual Frameworks Facilitate Integration for Transdisciplinary Urban Science. *Urban Sustainability* 1 (1): 1.

Zimmermann, Andreas, Johanna Hilpert, and Karl Peter Wendt 2009 Estimations of Population Density for Selected Periods between the Neolithic and AD 1800. *Human Biology* 81 (3): 357–381.

INDEX

Milton Keynes UK
Ingram Content Group UK Ltd.
UKHW011809260824
447224UK00014B/51

9 781009 249003